AML/CFT in New Zealand

A Handbook for Lawyers and Accountants

2021 Edition

Disclaimer

AML/CFT in New Zealand

A Handbook for Lawyers and Accountants

Wolters Kluwer

2021 Edition

CCH New Zealand Limited
PO BOX 33-270, Takapuna
Auckland 0740
Telephone: 0800 500 224
www.wolterskluwer.co.nz

About Wolters Kluwer

Wolters Kluwer enables legal, tax, finance, and healthcare professionals to be more effective and efficient. We provide information, software, and services that deliver vital insights, intelligent tools, and the guidance of subject-matter experts.

We create value by combining information, deep expertise, and technology to provide customers with solutions that improve their quality and effectiveness. Professionals turn to us when they need actionable information to better serve their clients.

Wolters Kluwer. When you have to be right.

Enquiries are welcome on 0800 500 224.

A catalogue record for this book is available from the National Library of New Zealand.

ISBN 978-1-77547-399-2 (print)

Published by CCH New Zealand Limited

First published November 2021

Contents

Page

Preface

> *New Zealand faces money laundering threats from proceeds of crime generated both domestically and internationally. The country's large scale terrorist financing risks are mainly in relation to overseas-based groups. Using a comprehensive multi-tiered risk assessment process, the country has developed a robust understanding of these money laundering and terrorist financing risks. New Zealand has implemented an AML/CFT system that is effective in many respects. [Financial Action Task Force, Mutual Evaluation Report New Zealand – 2021* Documents - Financial Action Task Force (FATF) (fatf-gafi.org)*]*

> *DIA applies the same risk-based supervisory framework to DNFBPs as it does to FIs under its supervision. AML/CFT supervision for Phase 2 sectors is at an early stage. This has been conducted in an effective and well-managed way, but in the future DIA will need to progressively shift its emphasis from education towards supervision and enforcement. [*Mutual-Evaluation-Report-New-Zealand-2021.pdf (fatf-gafi.org)*]*

This handbook was written because New Zealand lawyers, and accountants, are special. Their professional relationships when acting for clients are not ordinary "customer" relationships, involving (as they do) high degrees of trust and confidence that must never be abused. Lawyers and accountants often know a great deal about their clients, and special legal and ethical rules (such as client confidentiality and privilege) exist to protect clients' interests.

Many things that lawyers and accountants do are completely irrelevant to the AML/CFT regime. Some lawyers, and some accountants, are not caught by the AML/CFT Act at all, or are exempted from the Act. A lawyer's, or accountant's, professional obligations have the potential to create problems when it comes to applying anti-money laundering and countering financing of terrorism (AML/CFT) rules. Indeed, some things that lawyers do (including representing clients in relation to criminal charges brought against them) are fundamental to the rule of law and may seem to run counter to the scheme and purpose of the AML/CFT regime.

When lawyers and accountants first became subject to the AML/CFT Act on 1 July 2018 (lawyers) and 1 October 2018 (accountants) as a result of the implementation of "Phase II" of the regime, many practitioners were afraid that they were being asked to act as detectives, or as unpaid informants for the government, or that, at the very least, they were being burdened with a great deal of compliance cost that was unnecessary, they and their clients could ill-afford, and it would ultimately harm their professional relationships. Some practitioners threatened to retire from practice. Many practitioners did not at first understand the risk-based approach required by the regime.

As things have turned out, by late 2021 both professions have (with a few hiccups) learned to live with the AML/CFT regime as it applies to them. The Department of Internal Affairs has established an Industry Advisory Group to listen to the sectors it supervises. The sky has not fallen.

The authors contend that New Zealand's AML/CFT legislation and associated regulations and administrative practice, as it applies to lawyers and accountants, must recognise that these 2 professions are special, and must strike a balance that recognises the fundamental differences for those 2 important sectors, while recognising and achieving the objectives of the AML/CFT Act. We consider that it is vital that the DIA, as the sector's supervisor, continues to develop its own understanding of these professions and their special aspects.

The authors also recognise, from their own experiences in New Zealand and in other jurisdictions, the importance and benefit of lawyers and accountants understanding their obligations, and of incorporating them into everyday practice and business processes. There is no doubt that the AML/CFT regime now places a significant burden on each of these professions. However, it is the authors' belief that, if well understood and implemented, the AML/CFT regime can be incorporated into daily professional practice in ways that enrich and improve client relationships, while minimising costs and being compliant with the law and supervisor guidance.

The authors are also well aware that, over time, increased scrutiny of law firms and accounting practices by the DIA as sector supervisor is inevitable, as the FATF Mutual Evaluation Report has concluded. Both professions need to be ready for that scrutiny.

The aim of this handbook is to help law firms and accounting practices to understand their obligations, and to act as a ready reference work for situations that they may come across in the course of a busy professional day. The law is stated as at 1 September 2021. We have had considerable help preparing this text from a number of people, especially Sarah Kelly and Alexandra Tunnicliffe, but all of the errors are our own.

Henry Brandts-Giesen

Neil Russ

About the Authors

Neil Russ, Director, Russ + Associates

Neil Russ heads up Russ + Associates, an Auckland-based law firm specialising in tax and AML/CFT matters. Neil is an expert in corporate and international income tax and GST issues, as well as M&A transactions. He has over 30 years' experience in England and New Zealand, including 25 years as a partner at a major New Zealand firm. Neil also has extensive experience in relation to banking, capital markets, derivatives, structured finance, venture capital and private equity transactions. He has been a member of the New Zealand Law Society's tax law committee since 2003, and convenor of that committee since 2013.

Henry Brandts-Giesen, Partner, Dentons Kensington Swan

Henry is the Head of Private Wealth at Dentons Kensington Swan. His advisory practice involves family office design, family business succession planning and governance, family trusts, foreign trusts, charitable trusts, residency by investment, estate planning, relationship property, superannuation trusts, private funds, energy trusts, employee share schemes, fiduciary risk management, captive insurance, FATCA/CRS, and AML/CFT. He is also frequently involved in applications to court and disputes concerning trusts, estates, and relationship property. Henry's private clients include family offices, athletes, performers, and captains of industry. He is often retained by law firms, regulators, banks, accountants, financial service providers, and professional trustees.

Authors' Acknowledgments

We would like to acknowledge Sarah Kelly (Associate, Dentons Kensington Swan) and Alexandra Tunnicliffe (Senior Associate, Russ and Associates) for their invaluable assistance with the drafting and review of this book.

Neil Russ

Henry Brandts-Giesen

September 2021

Chapter 1

Introduction to the AML/CFT regime

1-000 Introduction

This book is intended to assist lawyers and accountants, and others involved in advising on, and administering compliance with, the anti-money laundering (AML) and countering financing of terrorism (CFT) laws, regulations and guidance in New Zealand. The approach taken is to set out the history and international context of this new and evolving regime, and to analyse and comment on the specific legislative provisions and regulatory guidance and how they are implemented in New Zealand.

It sets out the basic concepts, giving a general overview of the problems created by money laundering (ML) and financing of terrorism (FT), the processes for addressing those issues, the various mechanisms for complying with the AML/CFT law in New Zealand, how the legislation applies to reporting entities (particularly lawyers, law firms, accountants and accounting practices), and other practical measures that reporting entities can take to manage risk.

The emphasis is on the AML/CFT regime as it applies to law firms, legal practitioners and accounting practices in New Zealand. Lawyers and accountants were the first of the so-called "Phase 2" entity types (law firms, accounting practices, real estate agents and high-value dealers) to become subject to the regime. "Phase 1" entities (financial institutions, casinos and virtual assets service providers) and their advisers seeking information and practical commentary about how the AML/CFT regime applies in this jurisdiction will also find this book useful.

The AML and CFT regime represent significant changes to the ordinary course of business for lawyers and accountants in New Zealand. Anti-money laundering and CFT compliance are similar to other compliance regimes that have been imposed on lawyers and accountants (such as United States' Foreign Account Tax Compliance Act (FACTA) and the Common Reporting Standard (CRS)) which require law firms, accounting practices and sole practitioners to gather much more information before accepting client engagements. The regimes also impose obligations to report information to law enforcement and government agencies, in certain circumstances. This is a paradigm shift from the traditional role of lawyers and accountants as trusted advisers. It is also likely to increase the cost of doing business — both for the professions and the clients.

These regimes are also a paradigm shift in the way that laws are enforced. Enforcement agencies and revenue authorities have shifted emphasis from the traditional approach of investigating offenders directly. Instead, they are imposing information-gathering and reporting obligations on the third parties and intermediaries with whom those offenders interact and have professional relationships. While this is likely to be effective, it is controversial and can have unintended consequences.

A number of public policy issues arise from this new approach to law and revenue enforcement. This book cannot possibly do justice to such a discussion. However, the reality is that these compliance regimes have been implemented in virtually every country around the world and are here to stay. The Rubicon has been crossed, and now law firms, sole practitioners and accounting practices must meet the challenge of compliance.

However, there is no need to reinvent the wheel. There is a great deal of experience and intellectual capital available, both within the profession and from external AML/CFT consultancy firms. With good advice and systems, the challenges can be met.

Glossary of terms and acronyms

This book uses the following terms and acronyms:

Amending Act: Anti-Money Laundering and Countering Financing of Terrorism Amendment Act 2017

AML: anti-money laundering

AML/CFT Act: Anti-Money Laundering and Countering Financing of Terrorism Act 2009

AML/CFT supervisors: Department of Internal Affairs, Financial Markets Authority and Reserve bank of New Zealand

CDD: customer due diligence

CFT: countering the financing of terrorism

DBG: designated business group

DIA: Te Tari Taiwhenua, Department of Internal Affairs
DNFBP: designated non-financial business or profession
FATF: Financial Action Task Force
FIU: Financial Intelligence Unit of the New Zealand Police
FMA: Te Mana Tātai Hokohoko, Financial Markets Authority
FT: financing of terrorism
IVCOP: Amended Identity Verification Code of Practice 2013
ML: money laundering
MOJ: Te Tāhū o te Ture, Ministry of Justice
NCC: National Co-ordination Committee
NZLS: Te Kāhui Ture o Aotearoa, New Zealand Law Society
OECD: Organisation for Economic Cooperation and Development
PEP: politically exposed person
PTR: prescribed transaction report
RBNZ: Te Pūtea Matua, Reserve Bank of New Zealand
SAR: suspicious activity report
SSF: Sector Supervisors' Forum.

Important note: Guidelines in the Appendices have been reproduced with the permission of the AML/CFT supervisors and belong to them. Readers should check the following websites to ensure they have the most recent version of the relevant document before relying on the information: Department of Internal Affairs (dia.govt.nz); Financial Markets Authority (fma.govt.nz); and Reserve Bank of New Zealand (rbnz.govt.nz). This also applies to content within the book itself where those guidelines and related materials are referenced.

1-001 What is money laundering?

Money laundering (ML) is the process by which criminals attempt to conceal the true origin of the proceeds of their criminal activities. This is typically achieved by placing the proceeds of crime into the financial system by creating complex layers of financial transactions to disguise the provenance of the funds, then integrating the laundered funds into the legitimate economy. The key elements of an ML offence are:

- dealing with any property with the purpose of concealing it, or assisting in dealing with property for this purpose, and
- knowing or believing that the property is the proceeds of a significant offence, or being reckless as to whether the property is the proceeds of such an offence (Financial Intelligence Unit of the New Zealand Police (FIU) *Quarterly Typology Report: First Quarter (Q1) 2014/2015* "Abuse of Trusts").

Historically, "money laundering" was synonymous with financial transactions related to organised crime. The term is now used to encompass a far wider range of activities and can be undertaken both by the culprits of the original crime as well as by third parties on their behalf. The scale of ML ranges from relatively minor crimes, such as regulatory breaches or tax evasion, through to global narcotics operations and financing acts of terror, such as those that occurred in the United States on 11 September 2001.

Terrorist financing relates to activities that provide capital to fuel individual terrorists or terrorist groups. These activities may involve drug trafficking, human trafficking, theft, graft (political corruption), robbery and fraud. These may even involve philanthropy or charitable giving. An offence of terrorist financing could involve:

- collecting funds intended to be used for a terrorist act or intended for a group known to perform terrorist acts
- knowingly dealing with any property owned or controlled by a designated terrorist entity
- providing financing to a designated terrorist entity.

See FIU Quarterly Typology Report.

Terrorist financing and ML involve similar processes and functionaries and are predicated on criminals moving funds across borders or within the financial sector to further their objectives.

Historically, anti-money laundering (AML) policies and legislation developed as a consequence of the global fight against the narcotics trade. Several decades ago, governments and law enforcement agencies realised that it was extremely difficult to combat narcotics themselves. An alternative approach was adopted, and governments and law enforcement agencies began to target the profits of the criminal organisations engaged in the production and distribution of drugs. The theory was that if the funding of the criminal organisation engaged in drug trafficking was stifled, the organisation would be adversely affected and eventually be unable to continue its activities.

It soon became clear that the same policies could be used to combat not only the trade in narcotics but all organised crime. Accordingly, AML policies were widened to include the proceeds of all criminal conduct.

A more recent trend has been to extend these same policies ever further to combat terrorist financing and fiscal crime, such as tax evasion.

1-002 The problem with money laundering

The proceeds of crime are virtually impossible to quantify on a global scale. There are various estimates, but it has been suggested that criminal profits in excess of US$1 trillion are laundered each year. It has been further suggested that money laundering is the world's third largest industry.

Money is the lifeblood of a professional criminal enterprise. The proceeds of crime can be applied to advance further criminal purposes and to facilitate an organisation's growth. Laundering the proceeds of crime reduces the risk that the offenders will be prosecuted and prolongs and enhances criminal activity.

Money laundering is thought to pervade, to some degree, all economic, political and social institutions. It affects financial markets as large amounts of money are moved across borders, thereby affecting exchange rates, interest rates, inflation, employment and economic stability. This has an especially material effect on developing countries, as capital (often in breach of exchange controls) is drained from their economies and development is constrained and poverty perpetuated. In some cases, a small group of oligarchs entrench themselves in positions of power, authority and prosperity directly or indirectly financed by the proceeds of crime.

Organised crime also often leads to the development of an alternative, underground economy, which is untaxed and unregulated and can contribute to societal problems. When all the assets and liabilities of every country in the world are added up, in theory, they should balance. However, economists have attempted to do this and invariably there is a significant "black hole" where assets are unaccounted for. This can lead to governmental fiscal deficits as public spending exceeds revenue receipts causing governments to borrow. Such borrowing may come with conditions which in turn inhibit social welfare programmes.

Furthermore, when criminal proceeds are laundered, they are often injected back into the economy by criminal organisations. This money may be used for bribes, thereby corrupting government, judicial and law enforcement officials. A consequence may be the deterioration of social structure, and increased injustice and human rights abuses, which can threaten stability and even the very existence of democracy.

Anti-money laundering and countering the financing of terrorism laws and regulations are aimed at detecting and preventing this type of activity.

1-003 The money laundering process

Typically, many functionaries may assist a criminal organisation to launder the proceeds of its crimes. These can include bankers, lawyers, trustees, accountants, real estate agents, wealth managers and stockbrokers. Some of these professionals provide their services in exchange for fees in the knowledge that they are assisting with criminal activity. Others will turn a blind eye. Most will assist inadvertently. This book is directed at the latter category of professional with the aim of raising awareness of what to look for in order to avoid being caught up in money laundering (ML) activities.

Money laundering generally involves a complex series of transactions. It typically involves 3 steps: placement, layering and integration.

Placement

The first stage in the ML process is to move funds from their criminal source to different parts of the financial system through banks, casinos, retail outlets or other financial institutions, or by purchasing assets. By doing so, the funds can be disguised and misrepresented as something other than criminal proceeds.

The most obvious way to place the proceeds of crime into the banking system is simply to deposit cash into a bank account. In times gone by criminals were known to take suitcases of cash openly into banks and other financial institutions. Often no questions were asked and the funds (and associated management fees) were gratefully received by bankers, who might charge a fee merely for counting the cash and then much more for investment management and related services.

Law enforcement agencies and law makers eventually began to regulate banks in this regard and introduced the concept of "customer due diligence" to enable ML to be recognised, and required financial institutions to notify the relevant authorities when ML was identified or suspected.

Another requirement imposed on banks was for cash transactions over a certain prescribed threshold, including deposits and withdrawals, to be reported by the financial institution in a prescribed transaction report. Accordingly, criminals had to resort to more sophisticated means to place the proceeds of crime into the financial system without attracting the attention of the relevant financial institution and activating reporting obligations. The following are just some of the techniques engaged:

- Purchasing financial instruments (such as bank drafts, travellers' cheques, money orders and postal orders) to convert the proceeds of crime into instruments of relatively low value which can then be deposited elsewhere and consolidated.
- Dividing a large deposit into a number of smaller transactions of amounts less than the prescribed threshold and making several deposits into single or multiple accounts on successive days. Often several different banks, accounts and even third parties (such as lawyers, brokers and real estate agents) will be used. In due course the moneys are then consolidated.
- Inter-mingling the proceeds of crime with money from legitimate sources, which is a time-honoured technique of money launderers. Usually moneys from a legitimate enterprise are augmented with the proceeds of a criminal enterprise before being deposited into the financial system disguised as profits of the legitimate business. Often businesses which handle large volumes of cash are used for this purpose, such as retail outlets, restaurants, currency exchanges and especially casinos.

- Using the proceeds of crime to buy assets rather than placing them directly into the financial system. Real estate, precious metals, art, classic cars, diamonds and antiques are popular and are often easily transferrable, transportable and saleable.

Layering

Once the proceeds of crime have been successfully placed into the financial system, the next stage is for a series of complex transactions to be conducted with the primary objective of disguising the audit trail. This can obstruct an investigation into the source of the illicit funds.

This may involve cross-border currency transfers using electronic (wire) transfers between accounts or between banks. This type of electronic money movement can be carried out quickly and globally. Funds moved in this manner, often in purported payment for goods sold or services rendered, ultimately become extremely difficult to trace.

An alternative form of layering is to use financial instruments such as letters of credit from one bank to another or shares in offshore companies.

Integration

- Integration is the final stage in the ML process whereby the proceeds of crime, having been subjected to a sufficient number of transactions, are returned to the legitimate economy.
- Common methods of integration include:
  - sale of property
  - redemption of financial assets, annuities or specified insurance contracts
  - loans between account holders and entities
  - bogus transactions fabricated by invoices for goods or services rendered at inflated prices
  - royalty payments for the use of intellectual property
  - a distribution from a trust fund, and
  - purported gifts, charitable donations, inheritances, distributions from trusts and dividends from companies.

A brief insight into traditional ML processes and activities is given above. However, there is a new frontier which is becoming increasingly relevant and difficult to regulate. The so-called "Dark Web" and "Deep Web" contain small peer-to-peer networks and can provide a haven for illegal activities. Similarly, the advent of cryptocurrencies and digital payment systems such as Bitcoin and the blockchain represent new challenges for governments and law enforcement agencies.

Actions that might give rise to an offence

Actions that might give rise to the offence of ML include:

- enabling the retention and control of the proceeds of crime for a client or customer, while knowing or suspecting that the client or customer has been engaged in criminal activity
- concealing, disguising, transferring, converting or removing property that is, or represents, the proceeds of crime, while knowing or suspecting that the property represents the proceeds of crime
- acquiring, using or having possession of property while knowing that the property is or represents the proceeds of crime.

After the laundering process has commenced, the nature of property may change from being the direct proceeds of crime to representing the proceeds of crime. For example, a bank may commit the offence of ML if it allows cash derived from illegal activity to be placed into an account. However, an offence may also be committed if, for example, the bank takes security over property which is derived from illegal activity and then provides credit to a criminal organisation.

1-004 Global AML and CFT initiatives

The prevention and detection of money laundering (ML) and terrorist financing is carried out by both the public and private sectors, and involves:

- legislation to criminalise ML, expedite prosecution and empower investigations and enforcement agencies, and
- due diligence and reporting obligations applying to financial institutions.

Because of the international nature and scale of the problem, these counter measures have to be consistent at both domestic and international levels. Without uniformity, there are jurisdictional arbitrage opportunities because money launderers are attracted to countries with less effective anti-money laundering (AML) and countering the financing of terrorism (CFT) mechanisms.

It has therefore been a major focus of supranational bodies such as the United Nations, Organisation for Economic Cooperation and Development, and Financial Action Task Force to raise awareness of the issues and devise a comprehensive global framework of laws and regulations which can then be enacted into domestic law.

The AML and CFT frameworks of most developed countries are very similar and comprise the following:

- legislation, which defines and criminalises ML
- regulations, which contain the procedural requirements that businesses must comply with to detect and prevent ML, and

- guidance notes, which are issued by the relevant supervisory and regulatory bodies and are intended to assist financial institutions to comply with the obligations contained in the primary legislation and regulations.

The following requirements for businesses are common to all AML and CFT legislation around the world:

- Conduct due diligence on clients and customers before undertaking any business activities with them. This is known as customer due diligence (CDD) and the objective of these procedures is to verify the identity of clients and customers and understand the nature of their business. The rationale is that this type of inquiry may expose a money launderer before the placement stage.
- Implement staff training, enforce compliance programmes and monitor transactions and activities which may, by nature, be connected to ML or are otherwise unusual in nature. The precise steps to be taken will depend on the sector and the business concerned.
- Report knowledge or suspicion that clients or customers are attempting to launder the proceeds of criminal conduct. Forming a suspicion is a conceptually challenging area of AML and CFT compliance and is discussed in more detail at 1-005.

1-005 The historical approach to money laundering in New Zealand

It might be tempting to dismiss money laundering as having no real relevance to New Zealand. As a nation, we take significant pride in the annual survey of Transparency International (predicated on World Bank and World Economic Forum data) which consistently ranks New Zealand as one of the least corrupt countries in the world. On the other hand, exotic Caribbean tax havens and pin-striped Swiss bankers may evoke images of shady dealings, gangsters and suitcases of cash. In many ways this perception is far from reality and the various offshore financial centres of the world generally have far more sophisticated anti-money laundering (AML) and countering the financing of terrorism (CFT) regimes than many of the Organisation for Economic Cooperation and Development countries, including New Zealand.

Nevertheless, in New Zealand there has for many years been a suite of legislation with direct relevance to money laundering and countering the financing of terrorism, including:

- Crimes Act 1961
- Criminal Proceeds (Recovery) Act 2009
- Mutual Assistance in Criminal Matters Act 1992
- Terrorism Suppression Act 2002

- Anti-Money Laundering and Countering Financing of Terrorism Act 2009 (AML/CFT Act), and
- Financial Transactions Reporting Act 1996 (repealed 1 August 2019).

Financial Transactions Reporting Act 1996

The Financial Transactions Reporting Act imposed obligations on financial institutions including:

- verification of customer identity, eg when new accounts are opened, certain transactions are conducted or where money laundering is suspected
- retention of transaction records and customer verification details, and
- reporting suspicious transactions.

The definition of "financial institution" in that Act included lawyers and accountants, but only to the extent that they received funds in the course of business for the purposes of deposit or investment or for (in the case of lawyers) settling real estate transactions.

Crimes Act 1961

Section 5 of the AML/CFT Act defines "money laundering offence" as:

> an offence against section 243 of the Crimes Act 1961 or section 12B of the Misuse of Drugs Act 1975 or any act committed overseas that, if committed in New Zealand, would be an offence under those sections of those Acts.

Under the Crimes Act, it is an offence to engage or assist another person in a transaction, or to be in possession of property derived from crime with intent to engage in money laundering, if the person knows or believes that the property involved is derived from crime or is reckless as to whether this is the case.

Section 243(2) of the Crimes Act provides:

> **243 Money laundering**
>
> ...
>
> (2) Subject to sections 244 and 245, everyone is liable to imprisonment for a term not exceeding 7 years who, in respect of any property that is the proceeds of an offence, engages in a money laundering transaction, knowing or believing that all or part of the property is the proceeds of an offence, or being reckless as to whether or not the property is the proceeds of an offence.

Section 243(3) further provides that:

> (3) Subject to sections 244 and 245, everyone is liable to imprisonment for a term not exceeding 5 years who obtains or has in his or her

possession any property (being property that is the proceeds of an offence committed by another person)—

(a) with intent to engage in a money laundering transaction in respect of that property; and

(b) knowing or believing that all or part of the property is the proceeds of an offence, or being reckless as to whether or not the property is the proceeds of an offence.

Criminal Proceeds (Recovery) Act 2009

The Criminal Proceeds (Recovery) Act provides for the restraining of property, proceeds or benefits derived directly or indirectly from significant criminal activity (such as money laundering) and their eventual forfeiture to the Crown. It repealed the Proceeds of Crimes Act 1992 on 1 December 2009.

Terrorism Suppression Act 2002

The Terrorism Suppression Act was an attempt to ratify a number of New Zealand's international obligations.

It is an offence under this Act to engage in a terrorist act, and a person who commits such an offence is liable on conviction to maximum penalty of imprisonment for life.

Section 8 of the Act directly targets terrorism financing. It provides that a person commits an offence who, directly or indirectly, wilfully and without lawful justification or reasonable excuse, provides or collects funds intending or knowing that they will be used in order to carry out a terrorist act.

Section 9 provides that it is an offence for a person to deal with any property without lawful justification or reasonable excuse and knowing that the property is owned or controlled by a designated or comes from a terrorist entity.

A major problem with the historical approach to AML and CFT in New Zealand was that this legislation, while helpful to law enforcement agencies in prosecutions, was unsatisfactory in the detection and prevention of money laundering.

Reference: Anti-Money Laundering and Countering Financing of Terrorism Act 2009, s 5.

1-006 The application of global AML standards in New Zealand

In 2009, the Anti-Money Laundering and Countering Financing of Terrorism Act 2009 (AML/CFT Act) became, and remains, the cornerstone of New Zealand's AML and CFT regime. It came into effect at the same time as the Financial Action Task Force (FATF) adopted its *Mutual Evaluation of New*

Zealand report (October 2013). The report found that there were "essential gaps" in New Zealand's regime against money laundering and terrorist financing. The AML/CFT Act was therefore an attempt to bring New Zealand into compliance with international AML and CFT standards.

The AML/CFT Act takes a risk-based, principled approach to AML and CFT, which means it is not as prescriptive as many other New Zealand laws. Consequently, it requires a broad and purposive approach to interpretation, and reference to a range of materials such as other legislations, regulations, codes of practice, guidelines and ministerial exemptions.

Financial Action Task Force

The FATF has published a general guidance document for legal professionals and one for accountants on the risk-based approach of the AML/CFT regime, which recognises the key elements of a risk-based approach as follows:

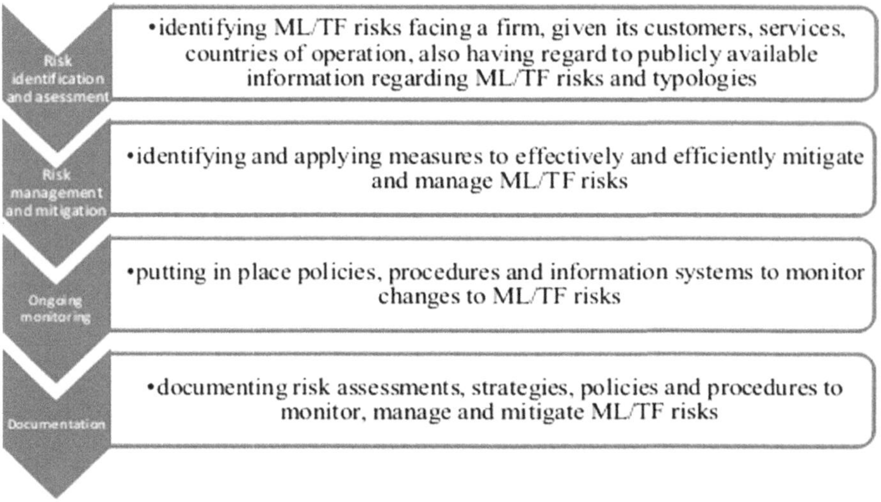

Source: FATF *Guidance for a Risk-Based Approach for Legal Professionals,* June 2019 at 19.

The FATF's general document of guidance for legal professionals expands on the FATF Recommendations for legal professionals who conduct specified activities for clients, such as asset planning or facilitating the sale and purchase of real estate. The FATF Recommendations provide further help for New Zealand's legal professionals in the discharging of their AML/CFT duties. However, the Recommendations only provide a broad understanding of AML/CFT obligations.

See also FATF *Guidance for a Risk-Based Approach for the Accounting Profession* (2019).

The AML/CFT Act

The purpose of AML/CFT Act is to create a framework for the:

- detection and deterrence of money laundering and financing of terrorism
- facilitation of co-operation between reporting entities, supervisors and government agencies
- maintenance of New Zealand's international reputation, and
- promotion of public confidence in New Zealand's financial system.

Territorial scope of the AML/CFT Act

The AML/CFT Act does not specify a territorial scope for the entities subject to its obligations. The High Court accepts that if enactments do not specify a territorial scope, there is a presumption that Parliament does not assert jurisdiction beyond its territorial limits (*Excelsior Markets Ltd v Financial Markets Authority* (2015) 11 NZCLC ¶98-038; [2015] NZHC 3334 at [112]).

The approach taken by the AML/CFT supervisors is that the AML/CFT Act only captures activities carried out in New Zealand in the ordinary course of business.

The AML/CFT supervisors (Department of Internal Affairs (DIA), Financial Markets Authority (FMA) and Reserve Bank of New Zealand (RBNZ)) state in their guidance (*Territorial Scope of the Anti-Money Laundering and Countering Financing of Terrorism Act 2009*, updated November 2019) in respect of territoriality that the following considerations apply when determining whether a person is a reporting entity for the purposes of the AML/CFT Act:

- A legal person incorporated or formed in New Zealand which, in the ordinary course of business, carries on one or more activities in New Zealand *will be* a reporting entity under the AML/CFT Act. This includes a natural person, eg a solicitor practising on their own account in sole practice who in the ordinary course of business carries on one or more activities in New Zealand.
- A legal person incorporated or formed in New Zealand (or a natural person) which in the ordinary course of business carries on activities wholly outside of New Zealand *will not be* a reporting entity under the AML/CFT Act. However, an activity is not provided wholly outside of New Zealand solely because the relevant service to which the activity relates is only provided to overseas persons. A person in this category is likely to be subject to AML/CFT requirements in the country where the activity is conducted.
- An overseas person carrying on business in New Zealand and engaging in one or more of the activities listed in the AML/CFT Act in New Zealand *will be* a reporting entity under the AML/CFT Act. This person is likely to be subject to AML/CFT requirements in their home country as well as in New Zealand with regard to their New Zealand activities.

- An overseas person not carrying on business in New Zealand *is unlikely to be* a reporting entity under the AML/CFT Act. A person in this category will only be subject to AML/CFT requirements in their home country.

AML/CFT supervisors

The AML/CFT regime in New Zealand is overseen by 3 supervisors. They are:

- RBNZ, in relation to registered banks, life insurers and non-bank deposit takers
- FMA, in relation to issuers of securities, trustee companies, futures dealers, collective investment schemes, brokers and financial advisers, and
- DIA, in relation to designated non-financial business or professions (eg law firms and accounting practices), casinos, non-deposit-taking lenders, money changers, and any other financial institutions not supervised by the RBNZ or the FMA.

In addition, the Ministry of Justice (MOJ) is responsible for drafting and administering the AML/CFT Act and regulations, while the Financial Intelligence Unit of the New Zealand Police performs the role of receiving and analysing suspicious transaction reports and providing related guidance.

The functions and powers of the AML/CFT supervisors are exercised in accordance with a core set of guiding principles to help achieve consistency and integrity in their approach. They allow reporting entities to identify and understand the common approach that is applied by all 3 AML/CFT supervisors as being:

- risk-based in approach
- accessible and relevant
- proportionate and responsive
- consistent and fair
- transparent and accountable, and
- co-operative.

See AML/CFT supervisors, *Supervisory framework* (updated November 2019).

National Co-ordination Committee

The AML/CFT Act also established the AML/CFT co-ordination committee, known as the National Co-ordination Committee (NCC). The NCC comprises of a representative from each of:

- Ministry of Justice
- New Zealand Customs

- AML/CFT supervisors
- New Zealand Police, and
- any other government agency employee as invited by the chief executive of the MOJ.

The role of the NCC is to ensure the consistent, effective and efficient operation of the regime by facilitating necessary connections between the AML/CFT supervisors, Police and other agencies.

The NCC is supported by the Sector Supervisors' Forum (SSF). The core membership of the SSF comprises representatives from the AML/CFT supervisors. Representatives from the Financial Intelligence Unit of the New Zealand Police (FIU) and MOJ may attend as observers. Other representatives from New Zealand government agencies may also attend by invitation from the SSF.

Sector Supervisors' Forum

The SSF supports the NCC by co-ordinating operational matters between the AML/CFT supervisors. The functions of the SSF include:

- facilitating consistent and co-ordinated approaches to developing and disseminating AML/CFT guidance and training
- facilitating good practice and consistent approaches to AML/CFT supervision
- providing a forum for sharing information on operational issues that have implications for the effectiveness of the AML/CFT regulatory system, and
- providing a forum to determine the reporting entity supervisor if there is a current or potential supervisory overlap.

1-007 Anti-Money Laundering and Countering Financing of Terrorism Act 2009 — Phase 1

Phase 1 of the Anti-Money Laundering and Countering Financing of Terrorism Act 2009 (AML/CFT Act) came into effect in 2013 and placed obligations on reporting entities to comply with AML obligations.

"Reporting entities" was then defined under s 5 of the AML/CFT Act to include only financial institutions and casinos and any person or class of person declared by or required under the regulations to be a reporting entity. Regulations declared certain financial advisers (authorised financial advisers (AFAs) and entities advising on category 1 products that arranged for a reporting entity to provide one of the financial activities to a customer) and trust and company service providers carrying out certain activities as the only or principal part of their business to be reporting entities.

A "financial institution" under s 5 of the AML/CFT Act is a person carrying out certain financial activities in the ordinary course of business and includes anyone declared by regulations to be a financial institution. The definition essentially captures banks, fund managers, money changers, life insurance companies and money lenders. The definition of financial institution is activity-based. The list of financial activities includes (s 5):

- accepting deposits or other repayable funds from the public
- lending to or for a customer, including consumer credit, mortgage credit, factoring (with or without recourse), and financing commercial transactions (including forfeiting)
- financial leasing
- transferring money
- issuing means of payment (eg credit or debit cards, cheques, travellers' cheques, money orders, bankers' drafts or electronic money)
- undertaking financial guarantees and commitments
- trading for the person's own account or for the accounts of customers in any of the following:
  - money market instruments (eg cheques, bills, certificates of deposit or derivatives)
  - foreign exchange
  - exchange, interest rate, or index instruments
  - transferable securities, and
  - commodity futures trading.
- participating in securities issues and the provision of financial services related to those issues
- managing individual or collective portfolios
- safe keeping or administering of cash or liquid securities on behalf of other persons
- investing, administering, or managing funds or money on behalf of other persons
- issuing, or undertaking liability under, life insurance policies as an insurer, and
- money or currency changing.

The definition has remained essentially unchanged since Phase 1.

Exclusions and exemptions

Regulations 16–24 of the Anti-Money Laundering and Countering Financing of Terrorism (Definitions) Regulations 2011 specifically include and exclude certain kinds of person from the definition of reporting entity. Excluded persons at the time of writing were (among others) the following:

- pawnbrokers
- providers of internet auctions
- certain registered auctioneers
- persons carrying out property management activities
- financial institutions that are in liquidation
- public service agencies, and
- the Reserve Bank of New Zealand.

In addition, the Anti-Money Laundering and Countering Financing of Terrorism (Exemptions) Regulations 2011 set out various activities that are exempt from the AML/CFT Act. Under s 157 of the Act the Minister of Justice also has the power to make exemptions. Ministerial exemptions may be granted for a maximum of 5 years before they are re-evaluated for appropriateness and necessity.

References: Anti-Money Laundering and Countering Financing of Terrorism Act 2009, ss 5, 157; Anti-Money Laundering and Countering Financing of Terrorism (Definitions) Regulations 2011, regs 16–24.

1-008 Anti-Money Laundering and Countering Financing of Terrorism Act 2009 — Phase 2

Section 6(2) of the Anti-Money Laundering and Countering Financing of Terrorism Act 2009 (AML/CFT Act) provided for the various sectors to be subject to a staged implementation:

- Lawyers and conveyancers have been bound by the provisions since 1 July 2018.
- Accountants have been bound by the provisions since 1 October 2018.
- Real estate agents have been bound by the provisions since 1 January 2019.
- The New Zealand Racing Board and high-value dealers have been bound by the provisions since 1 August 2019.

The legislation applied to trust and company service providers from 1 July 2018, if they were not already a reporting entity under reg 17 of the Anti-Money Laundering and Countering Financing of Terrorism (Definitions) Regulations 2011.

In June 2013, the Financial Action Task Force (FATF) had published a report, *Money Laundering and Terrorist Financing Vulnerabilities of Legal Professionals*. The report concluded that criminals seek out the involvement of lawyers in money laundering activities — sometimes because they are required to complete certain transactions, and sometimes to access specialised skills.

The report identified a number of common activities through which lawyers may become engaged in money laundering. These are:

- misuse of client accounts
- purchase of real estate
- creation of trusts and companies
- management of trusts and companies
- managing client affairs and making introductions
- undertaking certain litigation, and
- setting up and managing charities.

A particular challenge for legal and accounting professionals is that many services sought by criminals for the purposes of money laundering are also services used every day by clients for legitimate purposes.

In response to the release of the so-called Panama Papers (2016) (which exposed a network of more than 214,000 tax havens involving people and entities from 200 countries), and the potential reputational risk to New Zealand, the New Zealand Government commenced a formal inquiry into the foreign trust regime. The report that followed (*Government Inquiry into Foreign Trust Disclosure Rules*, June 2016) concluded that there was a risk that New Zealand could be perceived of as having inadequate controls to prevent and detect money laundering through foreign trusts. The report determined that there was a risk to New Zealand's reputation as a country that otherwise cooperates with other jurisdictions in anti-money laundering, counter terrorism and tax information exchange. While there was no direct evidence of tax abuse or illicit funds being hidden in New Zealand foreign trusts, the report considered it reasonable to conclude that they were being used in this way. Rightly or wrongly, it was perceived that the legal profession could be a weak link in the AML and CFT system. The report made a number of recommendations, one of which was to accelerate the extension of New Zealand's AML and CFT regime to lawyers and accountants.

The 2017 amendment Act

The Anti-Money Laundering and Countering Financing of Terrorism Amendment Act 2017 was enacted on 11 August 2017. It implemented Phase 2 of New Zealand's AML and CFT regime. It followed on from an exposure draft issued in December 2016 and an earlier consultation paper issued by the Ministry of Justice (MOJ) in August 2016. It extended the AML/CFT Act to more businesses that are at high risk of being misused by criminals. The amending Act designated the Department of Internal Affairs (DIA) as the relevant supervisor of the legal profession and accounting practices.

Captured activities for designated non-financial businesses or professions

The amending Act extended the AML/CFT Act to include a "designated non-financial business or profession (DNFBP) within the definition of reporting entity. A DNFBP is defined in the AML/CFT Act to mean a law firm, a conveyancing practitioner, an incorporated conveyancing firm, an accounting practice, a real estate agent, or a trust and company service provider that carries out specific activities during their *ordinary course of business* (referred to as "captured activities").

Section 5 of the AML/CFT Act defines the types of activities carried out by law firms and accounting practices and certain other types of business that are captured by the AML/CFT Act and which therefore require compliance with its rules:

(i) acting as a formation agent of legal persons or legal arrangements:

(ii) acting as, or arranging for a person to act as, a nominee director or nominee shareholder or trustee in relation to legal persons or legal arrangements:

(iii) providing a registered office or a business address, a correspondence address, or an administrative address for a company, or a partnership, or for any other legal person or arrangement, unless the office or address is provided solely as an ancillary service to the provision of other services (being services that do not constitute an activity listed in this subparagraph or subparagraphs (i), (ii), and (iv) to (vi)):

(iv) managing client funds (other than sums paid as fees for professional services), accounts, securities, or other assets:

(v) providing real estate agency work (within the meaning of section 4(1) of the Real Estate Agents Act 2008) to effect a transaction (within the meaning of section 4(1) of the Real Estate Agents Act 2008):

(vi) engaging in or giving instructions on behalf of a customer to another person for—

(A) any conveyancing (within the meaning of section 6 of the Lawyers and Conveyancers Act 2006) to effect a transaction (within the meaning of section 4(1) of the Real Estate Agents Act 2008), namely,—

- the sale, the purchase, or any other disposal or acquisition of a freehold estate or interest in land:
- the grant, sale, or purchase or any other disposal or acquisition of a leasehold estate or interest in land (other than a tenancy to which the Residential Tenancies Act 1986 applies):
- the grant, sale, or purchase or any other disposal or acquisition of a licence that is registrable under the Land Transfer Act 1952:

- the grant, sale, or purchase or any other disposal or acquisition of an occupation right agreement within the meaning of section 5 of the Retirement Villages Act 2003:

(B) a transaction (within the meaning of section 4(1) of the Real Estate Agents Act 2008); or

(C) the transfer of a beneficial interest in land or other real property; or

(D) a transaction on behalf of any person in relation to the buying, transferring, or selling of a business or legal person (for example, a company) and any other legal arrangement; or

(E) a transaction on behalf of a customer in relation to creating, operating, and managing a legal person (for example, a company) and any other legal arrangement . . .

Most medium-sized to large commercial law firms and accounting practices, and many smaller firms, carry out some if not all of the above captured activities. However, many smaller specialty law firms and barristers' chambers may not.

Lawyers and accountants conducting a captured activity in their personal capacity (as opposed to in their professional capacity) are not likely to be subject to the AML/CFT Act on the basis that they are not providing those activities in the ordinary course of business. A commonly used example is a lawyer acting as a trustee of a school or sports club or charity with which they have a personal connection.

More than ever before, terms of engagement will need to clearly set out the capacity in which the lawyer/accountant is acting, and indeed the capacity in which the client is acting, for the purposes of the engagement.

In particular, the AML/CFT Act defines "legal arrangement" to mean a trust, a partnership, a charitable entity, and any other prescribed arrangement that involves a risk of money laundering or the financing of terrorism (s 5). A "law firm" has been separately defined as a barrister or barrister and solicitor practising on their own account in sole practice; a partnership of barristers and solicitors; and an incorporated law firm. It is anticipated that most lawyers in private practice will be within the scope of the AML/CFT Act. An accounting practice is defined as an accountant in public practice on their own account in sole practice, a partnership of accountants and an incorporated accounting practice.

The DIA has prepared a flow chart in section 2 of its *Guideline: Lawyers and Conveyancers — Complying with the Anti-Money Laundering and Countering Financing of Terrorism Act 2009* (December 2017), which is intended to assist in determining when a law firm will be captured under the AML/CFT Act. A version of this flowchart is reproduced below. See also *Guideline: Accountants*

— *Complying with the Anti-Money Laundering and Countering Financing of Terrorism Act 2009* (March 2018) at 8.

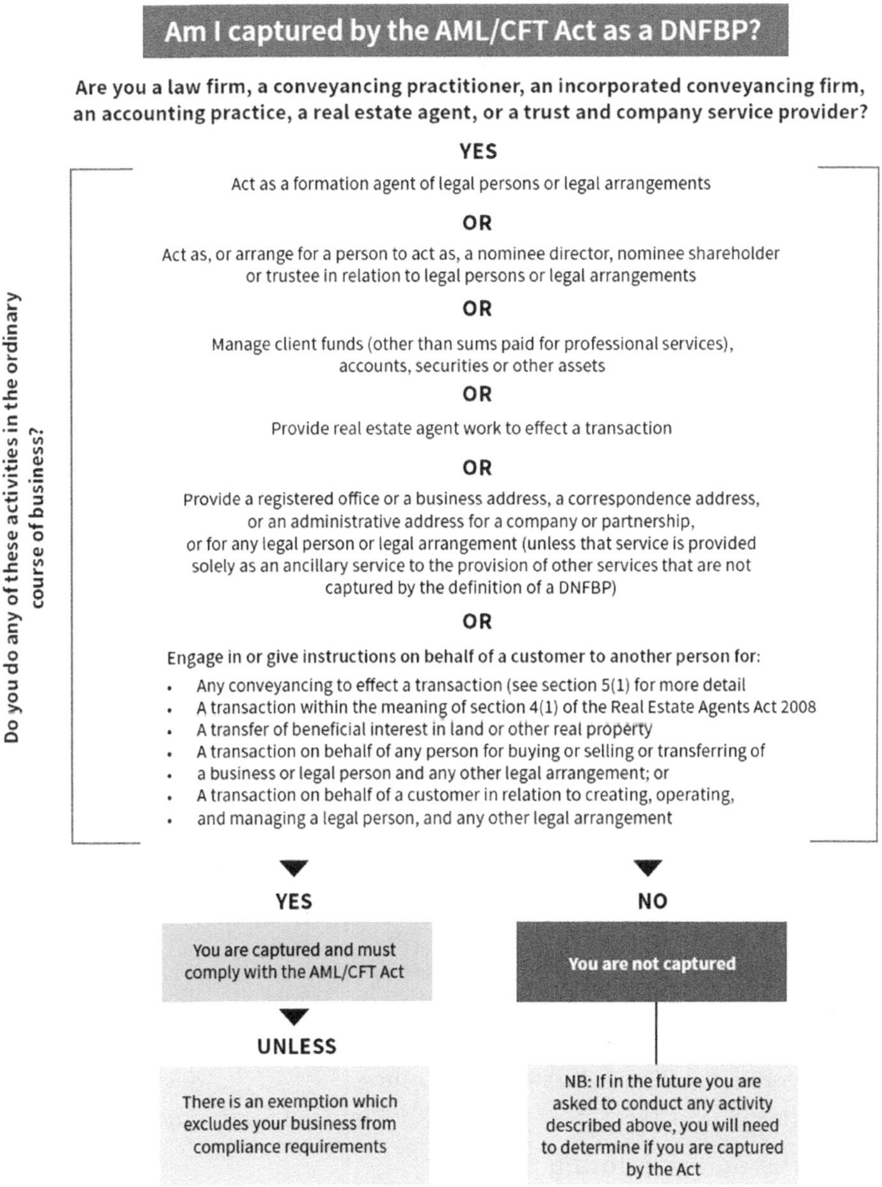

Exclusions and exemptions

Some entities, transactions or activities may be exempt from obligations under the AML/CFT Act. The Anti-Money Laundering and Countering Financing of Terrorism (Definitions) Regulations 2011 provide specific exclusions to the definition of "reporting entity" under the AML/CFT Act.

In addition, s 157 of the AML/CFT Act provides that the Minister may exempt a reporting entity or a class of reporting entities as well as a transaction or a class of transactions from any or all of the requirements under the AML/CFT Act. ("Minister" means the minister who is for the time being responsible for the administration of the AML/CFT Act.)

"Ordinary course of business"

The AML/CFT supervisors under the AML/CFT Act have jointly released a guideline on what is meant by "ordinary course of business" (*Interpreting "ordinary course of business" Guideline*, updated December 2017). The guideline sets out a number of factors to be considered when a reporting entity or a supervisor is determining whether an activity would occur in the ordinary course of business or not. For example, if the activity is frequent, regular and a significant source of income for the business, it is likely to be caught.

A law firm or accounting practice will only be captured by the AML/CFT Act if it carries out a captured activity "in the ordinary course of business". Where one or more captured activities are carried out in the ordinary course of a firm's business, the firm will be a reporting entity under the AML/CFT Act.

In most instances, it will be obvious whether an activity is within a law firm or accounting practice's ordinary course of business, but in some instances, a judgment call may be needed, taking into account the unique circumstances of the business (*Interpreting "ordinary course of business" Guideline* at 2).

When determining this, a firm or practice should consider whether the activity:

- is normal or otherwise unremarkable for its particular business (ie features in its systems, processes, advertising, staff training etc)
- is frequent
- is regular
- involves significant amounts of money
- is a source of income for its business
- involves significant allocation of resources
- is involved in a service or product that is offered to customers.

Law firms and accounting practices

The first question all law firms and accounting practices should address is whether they are or will be "reporting entities" under the AML/CFT Act.

Only reporting entities have customer due diligence (CDD) and reporting obligations under the AML/CFT Act. Where they are a reporting entity, they should register as such by notifying the DIA and Financial Intelligence Unit of the New Zealand Police (FIU). For more on determining whether a business is a reporting entity, see the definition in 1-006 and 1-007.

Registration with the DIA is completed by way of the DIA's online portal, "AML Online". In order to interact with AML Online, a "RealMe" identity is required.

AML Online allows compliance officers (or other delegated staff members) to undertake a range of activities, including managing business details, delegating access to others, submitting documents and sending queries.

Registration with FIU

Registering with the FIU is not a legal requirement. However, practitioners and reporting entities should be aware that in order to use the FIU's online reporting system, as an administrative matter there is a registration process which must be completed before reports can be filed.

Instructions on how to register with goAML, the FIU's reporting software, can be found on the New Zealand Police website (police.govt.nz).

NZLS Practice Briefing

The New Zealand Law Society has released a Practice briefing on AML/CFT compliance for legal practitioners entitled *Compliance with the AML/CFT Act*, which can be found on its website (lawsociety.org.nz).

The practice briefing emphasises that law firms should already have:

- appointed a compliance officer
- produced a written risk assessment, and
- established a written compliance programme.

Practitioners should familiarise themselves with the Practice Briefing, as well as the additional resources referred to in it.

References: Anti-Money Laundering and Countering Financing of Terrorism Act 2009, ss 5, 6(2), 157; Anti-Money Laundering and Countering Financing of Terrorism (Definitions) Regulations 2011, reg 17.

1-009 Department of Internal Affairs

The anti-money laundering (AML/CFT) regime, in respect of lawyers and accountants, is overseen by the Department of Internal Affairs (DIA).

Like the other AML/CFT supervisors, the DIA applies a risk-based and responsive regulatory approach. It aims to:

- make it easy for reporting entities that want to comply with the AML/CFT Act

- help reporting entities who are trying to comply with the AML/CFT Act
- use the full force of the law on reporting entities that refuse to comply with the AML/CFT Act.

The DIA monitors a reporting entity's compliance with AML/CFT obligations. This can be done by carrying out desk-based reviews of a reporting entity's AML/CFT documentation to test technical compliance, or through onsite inspections to test the effectiveness of the implementation of compliance programmes and to analyse annual reports and independent audits.

If a reporting entity fails to meet its obligations under the AML/CFT Act, a number of options exist. If the failure is not deliberate, and minor, the DIA may choose to implement a remediation plan with the reporting entity. Such a plan will include a set of expected outcomes that the reporting entity must complete within a set timeframe. In response to more serious or deliberate acts of non-compliance by a reporting entity, the DIA may:

- issue a formal warning
- accept an enforceable undertaking
- seek an injunction from the High Court, or
- seek a pecuniary penalty from the High Court.

If a reporting entity fails to comply with any of the AML/CFT requirements, and does so knowingly or recklessly, the reporting entity may be criminally liable.

Chapter 2

Compliance

2-000 Compliance officer

Section 56 of the Anti-Money Laundering and Countering Financing of Terrorism Act 2009 (AML/CFT Act) provides that a reporting entity must designate an employee as a compliance officer to administer and maintain its compliance programme. The legislation recognises that not every reporting entity has employees. In such a case, the reporting entity must appoint another person to act as its compliance officer (s 56(3)).

The Department of Internal Affairs (DIA) regards the compliance officer as a critical role for reporting entities. Section 56 of the AML/CFT Act provides that a reporting entity must establish, implement and maintain a compliance program that includes procedures, policies and controls to:

- detect money laundering (ML) and financing of terrorism (FT), and
- manage and mitigate the risk of ML and FT.

Section 56 further provides that the compliance officer must report to a senior manager of the reporting entity. It is generally accepted that medium to large law firms, accounting practices and other reporting entities will need to choose between appointing an existing, reasonably senior employee to the role (or expanding their job description to include the compliance officer role) and employing a new person for the purpose. Both approaches are being used in the market. A very large business may need a dedicated compliance officer. The compliance officer does not need to be legally trained.

Small firms

Some law firms and accounting practices may have very few employees. In theory it is possible for a business with one staff member to appoint that staff member as the compliance officer. In the case of a partnership one of the partners may be designated the compliance officer, irrespective of whether or not the partnership has employees. The partnership also needs to designate an additional partner (or partners) for the compliance officer to report to.

It appears to be possible for firms to "appoint" (rather than employ) a compliance officer, and in practice small firms will make use of specialist firms for this purpose. This may well be a good option for small firms that do not have sufficient internal resources to commit to the role. The DIA has commented (in its "Frequently Asked Questions for Reporting Entities") that sole practitioners may appoint an external person if there are no employees and the practitioner is unable to be the compliance officer.

The above comments are directed at small-to-medium firms with practice areas that carry a relatively high anti-money laundering (AML) and countering the financing of terrorism (CFT) compliance load, such as conveyancing. However, the administrative requirements of a small firm with a light AML/CFT footprint, such as an advisory or specialist litigation firm, could well be completed by a staff member with other duties (such as a senior lawyer in a law firm, senior accountant in an accounting practice, or, in other reporting entities, a senior administrative staff member).

Supervision of the compliance officer

The compliance officer must report directly to a senior manager of the reporting entity. It is the authors' opinion that, in the case of a reporting entity with a partnership structure, the compliance officer should report to a senior manager at partnership level rather than a senior administrative staff member (unless the business is sufficiently large to have an executive team separate from the partnership). If the compliance officer is a partner, they must report on AML/CFT matters to another partner designated for the purpose.

The compliance officer will, of course, need to have a good understanding of the AML/CFT Act, although they need not necessarily be a lawyer or accountant themselves. They will need to have, or to gain, a high degree of understanding of the activities undertaken by the reporting entity, and an appreciation of the risk assessment prepared by the reporting entity in relation to those activities.

Support from committee or reporting officer

The compliance officer should primarily be supported by the person (or people) to whom they report. However, all staff within the firm need to support the compliance officer by discharging their individual obligations adequately and working cooperatively with the compliance officer when necessary.

Firms with sufficient resources may support the establishment of an "AML/CFT committee", which could be constituted by a partnership subgroup or a group of senior employed lawyers or accountants or staff members (or both). The committee's purpose is to support the compliance officer and consider any issues that arise.

In smaller firms, the committee approach may not be possible or appropriate and so a single partner or director of the firm could be designated as the person to whom the compliance officer reports. This person might help fulfil a gatekeeper type role in relation to suspicious activity reports (SARs) to ensure that reporting obligations under the AML/CFT Act, and (where relevant) the rules of legal professional privilege, are reconciled.

Although the New Zealand regime does not prescribe a separate reporting role, in other jurisdictions this functionary is often referred to the "Money Laundering Reporting Officer" or "MLRO". While the terminology is not used in the AML/CFT Act, it is widely used throughout the world and could be useful in New Zealand in compliance programmes as well. Such a functionary could also operate as a gatekeeper for the purposes of balancing the business's potentially conflicting obligations to maintain legal professional privilege and file SARs.

Reference: Anti-Money Laundering and Countering Financing of Terrorism Act 2009, s 56.

2-001 Risk assessment

The Anti-Money Laundering and Countering Financing of Terrorism Act 2009 (AML/CFT Act) takes a risk-based, principled approach to anti-money laundering (AML) and countering the financing of terrorism (CFT), which means it is not as prescriptive as many other New Zealand laws. Consequently, it requires a broad and purposive approach to interpretation, and reference to a range of materials such as other legislation, regulations, codes of practice and ministerial exemptions. A reporting entity must assess the risks its business is exposed to, and apply suitable procedures, policies and controls to effectively manage these risks. Compliance resources can therefore be targeted primarily towards the high-risk areas of the reporting entity's business, reducing overall compliance costs.

The AML/CFT Act's risk-based approach can create challenges for legal professionals in relation to:

- culture of compliance and adequate resources
- significant variation in services and clients
- transparency of beneficial ownership of legal persons and arrangements
- risk of criminality, and
- the requirement to comply with AML/CFT obligations and the principle of legal professional privilege and secrecy.

Requirements

Before establishing a compliance programme, the first step a firm must undertake in complying with the AML/CFT regime is to complete an assessment of the risk of money laundering (ML) and financial terrorism that it may reasonably expect to face in the course of its business. The risk assessment must be particular to the reporting entity and take into account that firm's client base and usual activities. The risk assessment must be in writing and must:

- identify the risks faced by the firm in the course of its business
- describe how the firm will ensure that the assessment remains current, and
- enable the firm to determine the level of risk involved in relation to relevant obligations under the AML/CFT Act and regulations.

In assessing the risk, reporting entities must have regard to the following under s 58 of the AML/CFT Act:

- the nature, size, and complexity of the business
- the services it offers
- the methods by which it delivers its services
- the types of clients it deals with
- the countries it deals with
- the institutions it deals with
- any applicable guidance material produced by the AML/CFT supervisors (Department of Internal Affairs (DIA), Financial Markets Authority and Reserve Bank of New Zealand) or the Commissioner of Police relating to risk assessments, and
- any other factors that may be provided for in regulations.

The AML/CFT supervisors have provided guidance on how to conduct a risk assessment (*Risk Assessment Guideline*, May 2018). A working knowledge of this guidance is necessary for any compliance officer because the AML/CFT Act requires that law firms and accounting practices have regard to guidance produced by the AML/CFT supervisors when developing their risk assessments.

Reporting entities should review and update their risk assessment whenever there is a material change to the business, its service offerings, its customer base, or when deficiencies in the effectiveness of the risk assessment are identified, as well as at regular intervals unconnected to any of these "trigger events".

Red flags

As well as the mandated items for consideration under s 58, which are set out above, a good risk assessment should also consider the presence or otherwise of "red flags" in the entity's activities. These can then be addressed in the entity's compliance programme. The Financial Action Task Force (FATF) document *Guidance for a Risk-Based Approach for Legal Professionals* (June 2019) identifies the following activities or transactions as potential red flags for suspicious activity where they occur with no logical explanation or economic justification (at 92):

- The transaction is unusual, eg with regard to size, nature, frequency or manner of execution.
- The customer or third party is contributing a large cash sum as collateral provided by the borrower/debtor rather than using those funds directly.
- The source of the funds is unusual, eg funds from or to high-risk jurisdictions.
- The client is using multiple bank accounts.
- Private expenditure is funded by a company, business or government.
- Selecting the method of payment is deferred until very close to the scheduled date of notarisation, in a jurisdiction where the payment method is usually provided for in the contract, particularly if no guarantee securing the payment is established.
- An unusually short repayment period is set.
- Mortgages are repeatedly repaid significantly before the initially agreed maturity date.
- The asset is purchased with cash and quickly applied as collateral for a loan.
- There is a request to change the agreed payment procedures, especially when the suggested payment instruments are not appropriate for the common practice used for the transaction.

- Finance is provided by a lender — either a natural or legal person — other than a credit institution.
- The collateral provided for the transaction is located in a high-risk country.
- There has been a significant increase in capital for a recently incorporated company or successive contributions over a short period of time to the same company.
- There has been an increase in capital from a foreign country, which either has no relationship to the company or is high risk.
- The company receives an injection of capital or assets in kind that is excessively high in comparison with the business, its size or market value.
- There is an excessively high or low price attached to the securities transferred, with regard to any circumstances indicating such an excess (eg volume of revenue, trade or business, premises, size) or with regard to the sum declared in another operation.
- There are large financial transactions, especially if requested by recently created companies, that are not justified by the corporate purpose, the activity of the customer or the possible group of companies to which it belongs, or other justifiable reasons.

The FATF suggests that a simple template of risk assessment for legal professionals may look something like the following:

Geographic risk	Client-based risk	Service-based risk
Low/medium/high risk	Low/medium/high risk	Low/medium/high risk
Explanation	Explanation	Explanation
	Overall assessment: Low/Medium/High risk	
	Action plan	

Source: FATF *Guidance for a Risk-Based Approach for Legal Professionals*, June 2019 at 41.

This risk assessment template would work equally as well for accounting practices.

See also FATF *Guidance for a Risk-Based Approach for the Accounting Profession* (2019).

Inland Revenue released a factsheet in July 2019 to assist reporting entities with understanding the relationship between tax evasion, tax fraud and ML. See further at 4-004 Inland Revenue factsheet.

Shifting typologies

The methods and techniques of ML and terrorism financing are known as "typologies". As these typologies, or the activities of criminals adapt and change, the nature of the risks they pose to reporting entities will necessarily change.

The Financial Intelligence Unit of the New Zealand Police publishes Quarterly Typology Reports, which are available on its website. It is important that reporting entities keep up-to-date with changes in typologies to ensure that the practice's risk assessment remains relevant and effective. See further at 4-008.

Different reporting entities

Reporting entities have significant discretion in how they comply with many of the requirements under the AML/CFT Act. The system recognises that risks and vulnerabilities will be different between businesses and sectors. Not all businesses will adopt the same type and degree of counter measures for any given customer or transaction. It is simply about taking well-considered proactive steps based on a methodology appropriate to the business, to minimise and mitigate the risks as effectively as possible.

In practice, this means that a small firm providing services to long-standing local clients may have fewer AML/CFT obligations than a medium-sized real estate agency, which will have AML/CFT obligations arising from every client.

In addition, different practice areas within one law or accounting firm will have different risk profiles, as should be apparent when firms complete their risk assessments. For instance, higher risk areas may include transactional commercial and corporate work, secured lending transactions, trusts, and property/conveyancing work. Lower risk areas may include litigation (however, this isn't always the case so refer to the litigation-specific red flags listed above first), employment, and banking (provided that the banking team works predominantly with institutional banks).

Different work types

Even within a team that has a focused practice area, different work types may result in different risk assessments. A staff member in the property team who regularly advises on Overseas Investment Office procedures may be carrying on higher risk activities than their colleague who regularly assists with routine conveyancing transactions. Both activities present a high risk of ML, but the approach taken by the business to manage this risk will vary depending on how well known the client is and the value and regularity of the transactions (among other things).

In the same manner, a trusts and estates practice may have staff members who engage in trust formation, an activity that routinely separates legal and beneficial ownership and therefore disguises the true owner of property. Others in the same team may prepare wills and enduring powers of attorney. The former is higher risk than the latter (and in fact the latter is not caught by the AML/CFT Act).

The risk weighting process

Given that different levels of risk exist within a reporting entity, and in the teams and departments within it, it will not be appropriate for a risk assessment to consider a firm's activities as a whole without first considering the specific work carried out by staff and teams within the firm.

Whether one staff member's activities carry greater risk than another's is a matter for the judgement of the compliance officer and partner(s) of each law firm or accounting practice, with their knowledge of the firm's activities and client base. However, it should generally be expected that similar reporting entities will have similar ideas on which activities and clients are "riskier" than others. Failure to identify a risk is not a defence if the courts consider that a reporting entity should have identified the risk. See further at 3-002.

Lawyers in particular are advised to be cautious and detailed when considering the risks posed by different practice areas and for teams within their law firms. It is essential that lawyers not only do the right thing but are also seen to do the right thing. All reporting entities should be able to "show their working", document the steps taken and then carefully file the documentation in anticipation of the independent audit process and any potential review by the DIA.

Reference: Anti-Money Laundering and Countering Financing of Terrorism Act 2009, s 58.

2-002 Compliance programme

Once a reporting entity has completed its risk assessment, it must design and implement a compliance programme that contains procedures, policies and controls to directly manage the specific risks identified in the assessment. The Anti-Money Laundering and Countering Financing of Terrorism Act 2009 (AML/CFT Act) expressly states that this must be based on the risk assessment and cannot be based on a template or be otherwise generic in nature. This point is emphasised in guidance issued by the New Zealand Law Society ("How to use the New Zealand Law Society specimen compliance documents").

A compliance programme must include internal procedures, policies and controls to:

- detect money laundering (ML) and the financing of terrorism (FT), and
- manage and mitigate the risk of ML and FT.

The *AML/CFT Programme Guideline* (May 2018) produced by the the AML/CFT supervisors (Department of Internal Affairs, Financial Markets Authority and Reserve Bank of New Zealand) provides that a compliance programme should include (para 29 of the guide):

- **Policies** that set out expectations, standards and behaviours in the business.
- **Procedures** which are more detailed and set out day-to-day operations.
- **Controls** — tools that management use to ensure the business complies with the policies and procedures.

The minimum requirements for compliance programmes are set out under s 57 of the AML/CFT Act. A compliance programme must be based on the written risk assessment and include adequate and effective procedures, policies and controls for:

- vetting senior managers, the anti-money laundering (AML)/countering the financing of terrorism (CFT) compliance officer, and any other employee that is engaged in AML/CFT-related duties, and training those staff members
- complying with customer due diligence (CDD) requirements (including ongoing CDD and account monitoring)
- reporting suspicious activities
- reporting prescribed transactions
- record keeping
- setting out what the firm needs to do, or continue doing, to manage and mitigate the risks of ML and the FT
- examining, and keeping written findings relating to, complex or unusually large transactions; and unusual patterns of transactions that have no apparent economic or visible lawful purpose; and any other activity that the firm or practice regards as being particularly likely by its nature to be related to ML or the FT
- monitoring, examining, and keeping written findings relating to business relationships and transactions from or in countries that do not have, or have insufficient, AML or CFT systems in place and have additional measures for dealing with or restricting dealings with such countries
- preventing the use, for ML or the FT, of products and transactions that might favour anonymity
- determining when enhanced CDD is required and when simplified CDD might be permitted
- providing when a person who is not the reporting entity may conduct the relevant CDD on behalf of the firm and setting out procedures for this, and

- monitoring and managing compliance with, and the internal communication of and training in, those procedures, policies and controls.

The AML/CFT supervisors have confirmed that they will consider reporting entities who comply with the Amended Identity Verification Code of Practice 2013, as having met their AML/CFT obligations in that area. This means that while the codes are not mandatory, they are effectively a "safe harbour". Reporting entities can opt out of a code of practice if they comply with the relevant statutory obligation by some other equally effective means. See further on the Code of Practice at Appendices F and G..

Reference: Anti-Money Laundering and Countering Financing of Terrorism Act 2009, s 57.

2-003 Customer due diligence

Common to all Anti-money laundering (AML)/countering the financing of terrorism (CFT) legislation around the world are requirements for reporting entities to conduct customer due diligence (CDD) before undertaking any business activities with a customer. The term "customer" can be used interchangeably with "client", though "client" is the more commonly used term in the legal profession and has mainly been used as the term in this book.

It is very important for terms of engagement between a lawyer or accountant and the client to identify clearly who the client is for the purposes of the engagement and, by extension, AML/CFT purposes. For example, a law firm or accounting practice may take instructions from an individual, but the client may in fact be a trust or company associated with that individual.

The objective of CDD is to verify the identity of natural persons who are (or who own, control or otherwise benefit from) customers and to understand the nature of their business. The rationale is that this type of inquiry may expose a money launderer before the placement stage. For more discussion on placement, see 1-003. .

Guidance notes issued by the AML/CFT supervisors (Department of Internal Affairs, Financial Markets Authority and Reserve Bank of New Zealand) typically recommend that the identity of customers be established in a variety of ways. Generally, procuring a copy of a passport and evidence of residential address will be sufficient. Physical meetings with clients and customers are also strongly encouraged, to the extent possible.

Various software applications, such as World Check, Accuity and KYC 360, provide a front-end portal into which names can be entered. The powerful back-end capabilities of these applications can access data from the FBI, CIA, Mossad, MI5 and other intelligence agencies to verify the identity details of individuals and entities and to flag any adverse information about them that may be relevant to the AML/CFT process. These software applications can be subscribed to for a licence fee. Alternatively, Google and Bing searches can be a cost-effective and useful first line of defence for anyone conducting CDD.

Once sufficient information has been collated, reporting entities typically go through a process whereby the proposed new business engagement is considered and, if appropriate, authorised by the compliance officer and/or a principal.

2-004 Types of customer due diligence

Under s 11 of the Anti-Money Laundering and Countering Financing of Terrorism Act 2009 (AML/CFT Act) a law firm or accounting practice that is a reporting entity must conduct customer due diligence (CDD) on:

- its customers (ie clients)
- any beneficial owner of a customer, and
- any person acting on behalf of a customer.

The AML/CFT Act prescribes 3 types of CDD that must be conducted by reporting entities in different circumstances.

They are:

- standard CDD (s 14)
- simplified CDD (s 18), and
- enhanced CDD (s 21).

Reference: Anti-Money Laundering and Countering Financing of Terrorism Act 2009, ss 11, 14, 18, 21.

2-005 Standard customer due diligence

Standard customer due diligence (CDD) must be conducted in any of the following circumstances (unless enhanced CDD is conducted):

- If the reporting entity establishes a business relationship with a new customer.
- If a customer seeks to conduct an occasional transaction or activity through the reporting entity.
- If, in relation to an existing customer, and according to the level of risk involved, there has been a material change in the nature or purpose of the business relationship and the reporting entity considers that it has insufficient information about the customer.
- Any other circumstances specified in regulations.

Standard CDD must be carried out as soon as practicable after a reporting entity becomes aware that an existing account is anonymous.

Standard CDD requires the reporting entity to collect and verify specified identity information in relation to a customer, any beneficial owner of the customer, and any person acting on behalf of a customer. Sections 15 and 17 of the Anti-Money Laundering and Countering Financing of Terrorism Act 2009 (AML/CFT Act) prescribe the identity information required. This includes the person's full name and date of birth (in the case of an individual), confirmation of their relationship with the customer, their address or registered office, and their company identifier or registration number.

Section 17 of the AML/CFT Act also requires the reporting entity to obtain information on the nature and purpose of the proposed business relationship between the customer and the reporting entity, and sufficient information to determine if the customer should be subject to enhanced CDD.

Reference: Anti-Money Laundering and Countering Financing of Terrorism Act 2009, ss 14, 15, 16, 17.

2-006 Simplified customer due diligence

Simplified customer due diligence (CDD) may be conducted for specific "low-risk" customers under s 18(1) of the Anti-Money Laundering and Countering Financing of Terrorism Act 2009 (AML/CFT Act). A list of these low-risk customers is set out in s 18(2) of the AML/CFT Act and includes listed issuers, government departments, local authorities and the New Zealand Police. The list of low-risk entities was expanded by s 9 of the Anti-Money Laundering and Countering Financing of Terrorism Amendment Act 2017 to include more state-owned enterprises and other entities with a low risk of infringing.

A reporting entity may conduct simplified CDD if:

- it establishes a business relationship with one of the low-risk customers specified in s 18(2)
- one of the low-risk customers conducts an occasional transaction or activity through the reporting entity, or
- a customer conducts a transaction or obtains a product or service specified in regulations through the reporting entity.

A reporting entity may also conduct simplified CDD on a person who purports to act on behalf of a customer when the reporting entity:

- already has a business relationship with the customer at the time the person acts on behalf of the customer, and
- has conducted one of the specified types of CDD on the customer.

Where simplified CDD is available, the reporting entity is required to obtain the full name of the person acting on behalf of the customer, their date of birth and their relationship to the customer.

The reporting entity must also obtain information on the nature and purpose of the proposed business relationship between the customer and the reporting entity.

References: Anti-Money Laundering and Countering Financing of Terrorism Act 2009, ss 18, 19, 20, 21.

Anti-Money Laundering and Countering Financing of Terrorism Amendment Act 2017, s 9.

2-007 Enhanced customer due diligence

Enhanced customer due diligence (CDD) must be conducted if:

- the reporting entity establishes a business relationship with a customer that is, or if a customer seeks to conduct an occasional transaction or activity through the reporting entity and that customer is:
  - a trust or another vehicle for holding personal assets
  - a non-resident customer from a country that has insufficient anti-money laundering (AML) and countering the financing of terrorism (CFT) systems or measures in place
  - a company with nominee shareholders or shares in bearer form
  - seeking to conduct, through the reporting entity, a complex, unusually large transaction or unusual pattern of transactions that have no apparent or visible economic or lawful purpose
  - other situations when a reporting entity considers that the level of risk involved is such that enhanced due diligence should apply, and
  - any other circumstances specified in regulations
- the reporting entity establishes a business relationship with a customer who it determines is a "politically exposed person" (PEP). This is explained in more detail in 2-009.

Where enhanced CDD is required in the above circumstances, in addition to the requirements for standard CDD, a reporting entity must obtain information relating to the source of funds or the wealth of the customer. Note that information relating to the customer may need to be collected from a beneficial owner or a person acting on behalf of a customer (eg the shareholder of a company which is a customer may be asked to provide source of wealth information about the company).

If the customer is a trust, a reporting entity must also obtain the name and date of birth of each beneficiary of the trust, unless the trust is a discretionary trust or charitable trust or has more than10 beneficiaries. In that case, a description of each class or type of beneficiary must be obtained instead, and if the trust is a charitable trust, the objects of the trust. Overall, trusts are treated as persons under the Anti-Money Laundering and Countering Financing of Terrorism Act 2009 (AML/CFT Act).

The AML/CFT supervisors (Department of Internal Affairs, Financial Markets Authority and Reserve Bank of New Zealand) have issued *Enhanced Customer Due Diligence Guideline*, August 2020, which is a useful resource. It covers topics such as:

- identity requirements for enhanced CDD
- circumstances when enhanced CDD applies

- source of wealth and source of funds
- enhanced CDD and PEPs.

Existing customers

Section 10A of the Anti-Money Laundering and Countering Financing of Terrorism Amendment Act 2017 inserted a new s 22A (enhanced CDD required for certain activities requiring suspicious activities report) into the AML/CFT Act. The new section requires reporting entities to conduct enhanced CDD on an existing customer, or a customer engaging in an occasional transaction or activity, where a suspicious activity report is to be submitted for that customer.

Wire transfers and new or developing technologies or products that might favour anonymity

Enhanced CDD must also be conducted in the following circumstances:

- in accordance with ss 27–28 if the reporting entity is involved in a wire transfer that is equal to or above the applicable threshold, currently $1,000 (Anti-Money Laundering and Countering Financing of Terrorism (Definitions) Regulations 2011, reg 5A — discussed more fully in 2-019)
- in accordance with s 30 if:
  - the reporting entity establishes a business relationship with a customer that involves new or developing technologies, or new or developing products, that might favour anonymity, or
  - a customer seeks to conduct an occasional transaction or activity through the reporting entity that involves new or developing technologies, or new or developing products, that might favour anonymity.

Obtaining information about the source of funds or wealth of the customer is not a requirement for enhanced CDD under ss 27–28 or s 30.

Where enhanced CDD is required because a customer is involved in new or developing technologies, or new or developing products, that might favour anonymity, the reporting entity is required to carry out standard CDD and take any additional measures that may be needed to mitigate and manage the risk of such technologies or products from being used for money laundering (ML) or financing of terrorism (FT).

The additional measures that the reporting entity will take in each circumstance listed above should be set out in its compliance programme.

The AML/CFT Act also requires the compliance programme to set out adequate and effective procedures, policies and controls for preventing the use of products and transactions that might favour anonymity for ML or FT (s 57(1)(i)). It is the authors' view that this requirement may be satisfied by the CDD requirements in the Act. In some circumstances, further steps may need to be taken. Law firms and accounting practices should consider the circumstances, if any, in which the usual CDD requirements will not satisfy this obligation. The compliance programme should set out additional steps that may be taken if considered appropriate on a case-by-case basis. For example, this may include requiring a face-to-face meeting with a representative of a customer or requiring senior management approval to continue working with that customer.

Nominee director and shareholder relationships

On 9 July 2021, new AML/CFT amendment regulations became effective. The regulations include a new requirement for reporting entities dealing with companies, limited partnerships and overseas limited partnerships to establish and verify the existence of nominee directors, nominee shareholders and nominee general partners as part of their CDD requirements. If any of the above exist, the reporting entity must conduct enhanced CDD on the customer.

The supervisors jointly announced a transitional compliance period, from 9 July 2021 until 29 April 2022, in relation to these new requirements. Reporting entities are expected to comply with this obligation from 9 July 2021. However, supervisors will likely exercise discretion as to how to respond to non-compliance, and whether non-compliance will attract any adverse consequences during this transitional period.

References: Anti-Money Laundering and Countering Financing of Terrorism Act 2009, ss 22A, 27, 28, 30, 57(1)(i).

Anti-Money Laundering and Countering Financing of Terrorism (Definitions) Regulations 2011, reg 5A.

2-008 Verification of customer due diligence documents

As previously explained, s 11 of the Anti-Money Laundering and Countering Financing of Terrorism Act 2009 (AML/CFT Act) requires a reporting entity to conduct customer due diligence (CDD) on a customer, beneficial owner of a customer and any person acting on behalf of a customer before establishing a business relationship or conducting an occasional transaction or activity with the customer.

Sections 13, 16, 20 and 24 impose further obligations to verify that the CDD information and related documentation obtained are correct. It is therefore important to understand the distinction between 2 essential elements of CDD:

- **Identification**, which involves obtaining from the customer a range of information relating to that customer, as well as beneficial owners and persons acting on behalf of that customer where applicable.

- **Verification**, which involves confirming the above information against documents, data or information which has been issued by a reliable and independent source.

These sections anticipate verification being carried out by reference to "documents, data or information issued by a reliable and independent source". This gives reporting entities a wide scope to determine how they will verify different types of information, including by electronic means (discussed further below).

Identity Verification Code of Practice

In order to assist with verification, a code of practice (the Amended Identity Verification Code of Practice 2013, known as IVCOP) has been issued by all 3 of the AML/CFT supervisors in New Zealand (Department of Internal Affairs, Financial Markets Authority and Reserve Bank of New Zealand) and provides a suggested best practice guide for all reporting entities conducting name and date of birth identity verification on customers that are natural persons and that have been assessed to be low to medium. IVCOP does not apply to the identity verification of customers assessed by reporting entities to be high risk. Increased or more sophisticated measures must be applied for high-risk customers.

It is the authors' view that IVCOP is appropriate for verifying the identity of natural person beneficial owners of legal person owners, and persons acting on behalf of legal person customers.

The IVCOP provides for:

- 2 ways of conducting identity verification:
  - — documentary verification, and
  - — electronic verification, and
- certification of documents (to allow verification without a physical meeting with the customer).

Documentary identity verification

Documents

Part 1 of IVCOP provides that in order to verify a customer's name and date of birth, the following documentation is required:

- one form of photographic information, such as a passport, firearms licence or national identity card, or
- one form of non-photographic identification, such as a birth certificate in combination with a secondary or supporting form of photographic identification, such as a driver licence or 18+ card (now known as a KiwiAccess card).

See also "Expired passports" at 4-002.

A driver licence on its own is not sufficient to meet IVCOP's documentary identity verification requirements. Supporting documentation or confirmation of the licence on the National Register of Driver Licences is also required. This is not consistent with the acceptable forms of photographic identity for safe harbour set out in the Land Information New Zealand *Authority and Identity Guideline*, which is relied on by conveyancing practitioners in respect of e-dealings. A reporting entity may, taking a risk-based approach, choose to accept a licence on its own. However, in that case it will lose the benefit of the safe harbour of IVCOP. If a reporting entity is likely to accept a licence on its own, this should be set out in its compliance programme.

In order to comply with IVCOP, the reporting entity must have appropriate exception-handling procedures in place for circumstances when a customer demonstrates that they are unable to satisfy the requirements (eg an elderly person with no current passport or driver licence who is living in residential care).

The reporting entity must also have a process for checking that no other person with the same or similar name has presented to that reporting entity with the same identity information.

In all instances where documentary verification is being used, a reporting entity should verify the identity of the customer:

- in a face-to-face meeting, or
- by procuring copies of documents certified by a "trusted referee".

The Department of Internal Affairs (DIA) recommends that where identity is verified face-to-face, the reporting entity should take a copy of the document and note on the copy the date on which the original was sighted.

Certification of documents

Part 2 of IVCOP relates to the certification of documents used for verification and provides that in New Zealand a trustee referee must be at least 16 years of age and a member of one of the following classes of persons:

- Commonwealth representative
- member of New Zealand Police
- Justice of the Peace
- medical doctor
- *kaumatua*
- teacher
- minister of religion
- lawyer
- notary public
- honorary consul
- member of Parliament

- chartered accountant, and
- a person who has legal authority to take statutory declarations or the equivalent in New Zealand.

When certification occurs overseas, copies of international identification provided by a customer resident overseas must be certified by a person authorised by law in that country to take statutory declarations or equivalent in that country.

In addition, the trusted referee must:

- not be related to the customer
- sight the original documentary identification and make a statement to the effect that the documents provided are a true copy and represent the identity of the named individual
- include their name and signature and the date of certification and capacity to certify, and
- ensure that the certification is carried out in the 3 months preceding the presentation of the copied documents.

Electronic identity verification

IVCOP also provides for a customer's identity to be verified by electronic means. An electronic identity is a record kept in electronic form that contains authenticated core identity information about an individual. Electronic identity verification involves using that record to verify an individual's identity when a reporting entity is carrying out CDD.

IVCOP provides that "electronic verification" is *not* achieved by any of the following:

- an uploaded image of identity documents
- a selfie or video received from the person being dealt with online, including audio-visual or video conferencing technology
- the third-party provider that a reporting entity uses to conduct its online electronic verification, or
- an email, application or internet platform that the reporting entity uses to receive identity information or copies of identity documents.

Electronic verification has 2 components:

- confirming identity information via an electronic source or sources, and
- matching the person being dealt with to the identity they are claiming.

Both components must be satisfied (AML/CFT supervisors, *Explanatory Note: Electronic Identity Verification Guideline* updated in July 2021, at para 6).

To carry out electronic identity verification of a customer in accordance with IVCOP, a reporting entity must:

- verify the customer's name from either:
  - a single independent electronic source that is able to verify the individual's identity to a high level of confidence, or
  - at least 2 independent and reliable matching electronic sources, and
- verify the customer's date of birth from at least "one reliable and independent electronic source".

When determining what type of electronic sources will be considered reliable and independent, reporting entities must have regard to:

- accuracy
- security
- privacy
- method of information collection
- whether the electronic source has incorporated a mechanism to determine that the customer has been linked to the claimed identity (whether biometrically or otherwise)
- whether the information is maintained by a government body or pursuant to legislation, and
- whether the information has been additionally verified from another reliable and independent source (cl 17 of IVCOP).

If you are using 2 electronic sources with no mechanism to link the client to the claimed identity, you must implement additional methods to link the person you are dealing with online to the identity they are claiming to be (being the identity you are verifying) (cl 18 of IVCOP).

A reporting entity can satisfy electronic identity verification from a single independent electronic source if it can verify an individual's identity to a "high level of confidence". Only an electronic source that incorporates biometric information (or equivalent) enables an individual's identity to be verified to a "high level of confidence". When using an electronic source that is able to verify an individual's identity to a high level of confidence, there is no requirement to separately link the individual to the claimed identity. At the time of publication, only a verified RealMe identity can meet this requirement in New Zealand. By biometrically matching the person's photo and identity details against New Zealand Government records (the electronic source) it verifies the person's identity to a high level of confidence.

Where 2 reliable and independent sources are used, and they match each other, the "high level of confidence" requirements do not apply. Supervisors expect that the primary electronic source used to verify name and date of birth of an individual that is in New Zealand is:

- Confirmation Service (DIA)
- New Zealand driver licence (New Zealand Transport Agency).

Other common electronic sources in New Zealand that could be used as a second source to verify an individual's name include:

- credit bureaux
- Companies Office
- Land Registry (Land Information New Zealand)
- vehicle registration (New Zealand Transport Agency).

However, where 2 matching reliable and independent electronic sources are used, a reporting entity must still have regard to whether the electronic sources include a mechanism to determine if the customer can be linked to the claimed identity (whether biometrically or otherwise). None of the electronic sources listed above incorporate such a mechanism.

Reporting entities that use electronic verification must clearly describe in their compliance programmes how all the relevant criteria in IVCOP are satisfied. The following information should be described:

Include these	**Explanation**
When you will use electronic verification	Will you use it: • as the default method • as a back up • when you can't face-to-face on-board someone • in conjunction with face-to-face • for New Zealand residents only • for lower risk customers only, etc?
Electronic verification provider and product	If you rely on a third party to conduct electronic verification, detail the provider and the product that is being used. Also explain how you are using the product.
The electronic sources used to verify the person's name and date of birth	State the selected electronic sources that you are verifying your customer's name and date of birth against in New Zealand and elsewhere.
Record keeping processes	Describe how you will capture and record the information submitted by your customer and the evidence of the electronic verification. Many providers will not keep that information for longer than a few days.
How you checked your records that a prospective customer's details have not been previously used	—

Include these	Explanation
Exception and escalation processes	Unsuccessful electronic verification requires escalation and individual review.
If you are using a single independent source to a high level of confidence; or 2 (or more) reliable and independent matching sources	If using a single independent source to a high level of confidence you should document how this level of assurance is met. If using 2 matching reliable and independent electronic sources, you must follow and document the steps set out in cls 17 and 18 of the IVCOP (discussed above).

It is also important to note that the IVCOP is only applicable to customers that are assessed by a reporting entity as low-to-medium risk. It does not apply to clients assessed as high risk. The IVCOP states that increased or more sophisticated measures should be applied for high-risk clients.

A number of reporting entities in New Zealand use electronic verification as a means of reducing the administrative burden associated with documentary verification (eg procuring and handling certified "wet ink" copies of identification documents). In principle, this is sensible and there are a number of electronic verification software products with legitimate claims to being reliable and independent (eg Green ID and Cloudcheck) — at least as far as citizens of New Zealand and Australia are concerned.

However, the technology currently available does seem to have some limitations. The electronic verification software products available in New Zealand do not yet seem to have the functionality to verify identity documents for citizens of countries other than Australia and New Zealand.

Furthermore, it is not always possible or expedient for the electronic verification software products currently available in New Zealand to link the customer to the claimed identity. This is important because if a customer sends a copy of a passport to the reporting entity by email, there may not be a mechanism to prove that the customer sending the document is actually the person identified in the document.

Certain electronic verification software products have or will have functionality to verify foreign identity documents and there are biometric tools which enable linking between the customer and the identity document. However, the relevant technology is relatively new and still evolving.

As a consequence, the safe harbour of IVCOP does not appear to be currently available to reporting entities carrying out electronic verification. The *Explanatory Note: Electronic Identity Verification Guideline* confirms this when it states that, at the time of publication, only a verified RealMe identity can satisfactorily verify an individual's identity electronically from a single independent electronic source to a "high level of confidence". It then becomes a business decision for the reporting entity as to whether to take a risk-based approach and consciously operate outside the safe harbour or rather to insist upon documentary verification (and accept the concomitant administrative burden of procuring and handling original "wet ink" copies of documents certified by a trusted referee).

It is arguable that law firms and accounting practices carrying out low- to medium-risk activities could reasonably take the view that the requirement to link the customer to the claimed identity when using an electronic verification product is not essential and that other supplementary evidence should be available to contribute to a body of evidence which verifies the identity of the customer. Whether the statutory supervisors agree with this view remains to be seen.

Reference: Anti-Money Laundering and Countering Financing of Terrorism Act 2009, ss 11, 13, 16, 20, 24.

2-009 Politically exposed persons

As soon as practicable after establishing a business relationship or conducting an occasional transaction or activity with a customer, the reporting entity must take reasonable steps to determine whether the customer or any beneficial owner is a politically exposed person (PEP) (s 26).

A PEP is defined in s 5 as:

(a) an individual who holds, or has held at any time in the preceding 12 months, in any overseas country the prominent public function of—
  (i) Head of State or head of a country or government; or
  (ii) government minister or equivalent senior politician; or
  (iii) Supreme Court Judge or equivalent senior Judge; or
  (iv) governor of a central bank or any other position that has comparable influence to the Governor of the Reserve Bank of New Zealand; or
  (v) senior foreign representative, ambassador, or high commissioner; or
  (vi) high-ranking member of the armed forces; or
  (vii) board chair, chief executive, or chief financial officer of, or any other position that has comparable influence in, any State enterprise; and

(b) an immediate family member of a person referred to in paragraph (a), including—
  (i) a spouse; or
  (ii) a partner, being a person who is considered by the relevant national law as equivalent to a spouse; or
  (iii) a child and a child's spouse or partner; or
  (iv) a parent; and

(c) having regard to information that is public or readily available,—

(i) any individual who is known to have joint beneficial ownership of a legal entity or legal arrangement, or any other close relationship, with a person referred to in paragraph (a); or

(ii) any individual who has sole beneficial ownership of a legal entity or legal arrangement that is known to exist for the benefit of a person described in paragraph (a).

A common misconception about PEPs is that reporting entities are only required to determine whether customers who display indicia of having PEP status are PEPs, such as being resident in an overseas jurisdiction, or being well-known as politicians or political figures. In fact, s 26(1) of the Anti-Money Laundering and Countering Financing of Terrorism Act 2009 requires these checks to be performed routinely on *all* customers or beneficial owners of customers. There is no mandatory requirement to terminate a client relationship that arises solely from a customer or beneficial owner being a PEP. The additional steps are discussed below (under "If a customer or beneficial owner is a PEP").

The definition of PEP includes politicians, judges, diplomats, high ranking members of the armed forces and state-owned enterprises who currently hold that position *in any overseas country,* and their immediate family. The words in italics are crucial and exclude persons holding those positions in New Zealand, although a person who is resident in New Zealand but who held such a position in another country would be a PEP. For example, an overseas diplomat living in New Zealand would be a PEP. The definition also includes New Zealand citizens who hold one (or more) of the specified roles who are posted or deployed in a foreign country or jurisdiction.

It is also important to note that an individual holding joint or sole beneficial ownership of a legal entity or a legal arrangement with or for a person holding one of the specified roles is also a PEP. This can be very difficult to determine, so the definition provides that this category of PEP is to be determined "having regard to information that is publicly or readily available". At a minimum, this appears to require reporting entities to ask clients if they own legal entities or hold legal arrangements unconnected to them and, if necessary, for the identities of their co-owners or co-trustees.

This requirement could be satisfied by using common internet search engines to undertake checks. Additional checks (particularly if the circumstances indicate that a beneficial ownership arrangement could exist) with more specialist sources of such information, such as the Companies Office website, also appear to be required. Many online anti-money laundering/countering the financing of terrorism service providers include these searches as part of their offerings.

The reporting entity should set out in its compliance programme the steps it will take to determine if an individual is a PEP. The steps the reporting entity takes will depend on all the circumstances and the money laundering/financing of terrorism risks associated with the individual.

If a customer or beneficial owner is a PEP

If a reporting entity determines that a customer or beneficial owner with whom it has established a business relationship is a PEP, the reporting entity must (s 26(2)):

1. have senior management approval for continuing the business relationship, and
2. obtain information about the source of wealth or funds of the customer or beneficial owner and take reasonable steps to verify the source of that wealth or those funds.

The authors note that the second requirement above will already have been completed where enhanced customer due diligence has been conducted in respect of the customer.

If a reporting entity determines that a customer or beneficial owner with whom it has already conducted an occasional transaction or activity is a PEP, then the reporting entity must, as soon as practicable after conducting that transaction or activity, take reasonable steps to obtain information about the source of wealth or funds and verify the source of that wealth or those funds (ie step 2 above) (s 26(3)).

Reference: Anti-Money Laundering and Countering Financing of Terrorism Act 2009, ss 5, 26.

2-010 Source of wealth/funds

For most situations where enhanced customer due diligence (CDD) is required, the additional requirement imposed on reporting entities by s 23(1)(a) of the Anti-Money Laundering and Countering Financing of Terrorism Act 2009 is to procure and verify information about the source of the customer's wealth or funds. Neither of these terms or concepts is defined in the Act but the 3 AML/CFT supervisors in New Zealand (Department of Internal Affairs, Financial Markets Authority and Reserve Bank of New Zealand) have published an *Enhanced Customer Due Diligence Guideline*, August 2020 (ECDD Guideline) that attempts to clarify the requirements for reporting entities. See also 2-007 on enhanced CDD.

The ECDD Guideline provides that:

- source of wealth is the origin of the customer's entire body of assets, and
- source of funds is the origin of the specific funds used for the transactions or activities being carried out in relation to the customer's business relationship with the reporting entity (ie, the transaction or activity to which the instructions relate).

The wording of s 23(1)(a) requires the reporting entity to collect *either* source of wealth information *or* source of funds information. It is for the reporting entity to determine when to examine a customer's source of funds and when to focus on the customer's overall source of wealth, bearing in mind that the 2 may not exist in isolation of each other. The ECDD Guideline notes that where enhanced CDD is triggered by circumstances involving transactions or activities, it is likely to be more appropriate for the reporting entity to focus specifically on source of funds information. However, there will be occasions where both (source of wealth and source of funds) are appropriate.

Source of wealth or source of funds information must also be collected from beneficial owners and persons acting on behalf of the customer (s 23(1) (refer s 11(1)). However, it is important to note that the information required to be collected from these persons need only relate to the source of wealth or source of funds *of the customer* (s 23(1)(a)). In many cases the 2 will be linked (for instance a trustee and a trust), but it is not a requirement to obtain (for example) personal source of wealth information for the director of a client company, unless it is known that the company is funded personally by that director. Similarly, it is unlikely to be appropriate, or useful, to collect source of wealth information from a professional trustee.

A reporting entity with enhanced CDD obligations should request source of wealth or funds information from a customer and then record this information.

Verifying information

A reporting entity must take reasonable steps, according to the level of risk involved, to verify the information obtained using reliable and independent sources.

To help a reporting entity to verify information about the source of wealth and/or funds it may use publicly available information on the internet, or other commercially available databases. However, in many situations it will be necessary to procure documents issued by third parties that support the financial position.

If the reporting entity determines that collecting source of wealth information is appropriate in a particular circumstance, it must develop an understanding of the size and nature of the customer's overall wealth and, importantly, how it was acquired. This does not require verification of the entire financial history or every asset held.

It is not expected that every part of the source of wealth will be accounted for. However, the reporting entity must be satisfied that the nature and size of the customer's wealth matches what is known about them.

Verifying source of funds is a more granular process and the information, data or documents used should be specific to the business relationship or the relevant transactions or activities being conducted.

When a reporting entity is verifying its source of wealth and/or funds information, the "gold standard" is data or documents issued by a credible and reliable source such as a government department, regulated financial institution, tax authority, independent accountant and/or auditor.

Documentation

The ECDD Guideline lists the following as examples of acceptable documentation:

- Government-issued or registered documents or data
- full bank and other investment statements
- full payslip or wage slip or other documents confirming salary, GST number and Inland Revenue statement of earnings from the most recent year (for sole traders)
- inheritance (stamped grant of probate, stamped grant of letters of administration)
- audited financial accounts from a chartered accountant or Charities Services
- letter from an agent of the customer confirming they have knowledge of and established business relationships with the customer
- a copy of a will, and
- sales and purchase agreements.

However, practitioners are encouraged to think laterally about verification, especially in the case of customers who may not have relationships with large institutional banks or employ the services of a professional accountant. Other customers simply may not have this type of documentation at hand. The list of documentation types in the ECDD Guideline is not exhaustive, and provided there are good, risk-based reasons (which are recorded in sufficient detail) for varying from the recommendations, relying on other types of documentation should be sufficient.

Customers who conduct their business activities with a reporting entity should have a range of documents that could be used to verify how the funds have been acquired (ie contractual agreements, sale and purchase documents, or orders for probate).

Documentation accepted to verify the source of wealth and/or funds should depend on the level of risk presented by the customer. The higher the risk, the more comprehensive and reliable the documents procured must be.

Further research may also be carried out to supplement the information and documentation provided by the customer to evidence the source of wealth and/or funds. Many reporting entities incorporate searches and reports from the internet, media sources, databases and third-party professionals into their onboarding protocols.

Reference: Anti-Money Laundering and Countering Financing of Terrorism Act 2009, ss 11(1), 23(1).

2-011 Verification after establishing a business relationship

A reporting entity must collect the prescribed identity information about its customer (such as a person's name and date of birth) about before a business relationship with the customer is entered into or an occasional transaction or activity is conducted.

In contrast to this requirement, the *verification* of the information collected (such as by reference to a passport) may be completed after the business relationship has been established (although preferably this would be contemporaneous with the collection of the information) (s 24(3)). A delay in verification is permissible where:

- it is essential not to interrupt normal business practice
- money laundering and financing of terrorism risks are effectively managed through appropriate risk management procedures, and
- identity verification is completed as soon as practicable once the business relationship has been established.

The AML/CFT supervisors (Department of Internal Affairs, Financial Markets Authority and Reserve Bank of New Zealand) have commented that delayed verification procedure should be the exception rather than the rule of a reporting entity's regular business activity (*Enhanced Customer Due Diligence Guideline* August 2020, at para 47).

Reporting entities need to develop clear guidelines concerning when delaying verification is "essential not to interrupt normal business practice". The authors understand that a common view is that urgent instructions relating to a transaction that is settling imminently may be such a situation. In contrast, it may be that less leeway will be given to a real estate agency which, for example, does not complete verification before an auction that it has scheduled. As with many aspects of anti-money laundering (AML)/countering the financing of terrorism (CFT) compliance, what is normal in one sector will not be normal in another, and this can even vary between different reporting entities in the same sector. Regardless, it is clear that the AML/CFT supervisors will not accept delayed verification as a common occurrence in a reporting entity's business.

Reference: Anti-Money Laundering and Countering Financing of Terrorism Act 2009, s 24(3).

2-012 Customer due diligence required only for captured activities

It is important to reiterate that the Anti-Money Laundering and Countering Financing of Terrorism Act 2009 (AML/CFT Act), and the customer due diligence (CDD) obligations contained in it, only apply to reporting entities only to the extent they are carrying out activities which are captured by the Act (s 6(4)). For example, a law firm or an accounting practice, will only be a reporting entity if and to the extent that it carries out captured activities (see further at para 9 for captured activities). It follows that a law firm that is only providing legal advice or advocacy services for clients, or an accounting practice that is only carrying out bookkeeping or audit services, will not be subject to the AML/CFT Act at all. Similarly, the activities of a financial institution which are outside the definition of "financial institution" in s 5(1), including financial reporting, restructuring advice, budgeting and advisory activity, will not be subject to the AML/CFT Act. The difference of course is that a financial institution such as a bank will rarely have "non-captured" activities.

Section 11(6) of the AML/CFT Act confirms that due diligence is not required to be performed if a law firm or accounting practice is providing only services that are not captured activities. Accordingly, no due diligence should be necessary if captured activities are not being provided to the client in question.

For ethical as well as risk management reasons it is also important for legal practitioners to understand that the provision of advice only to a client is not a captured activity and therefore does not necessarily trigger compliance obligations. So, for example, carrying out due diligence on an item of real property and reporting to a client prior to any offer for purchase being made is not in itself a captured activity. If a law firm reporting entity then decided to file a suspicious activity report in relation to their client where the client was only seeking the due diligence report, there is a significant risk that the firm would not be obliged to file the report (because s 40 would not apply) and may be in breach of their ethical duty to protect and hold in strict confidence all information concerning a client, the retainer and the client's business and affairs acquired in the course of the professional relationship (Chapter 8 of the Lawyers and Conveyancers Act (Lawyers: Conduct and Client Care) Rules 2008.)

Some law firms might take the view that for operational and risk reasons they are better to carry out CDD before doing due diligence on the property. However, others may, quite reasonably, take the view that CDD is only required when the engagement with the client moves from an advisory phase to a transactional phase. Terms of engagement could be prepared to contemplate the various phases of a transaction (the first of which may be to provide advice only).

In other cases, a client will approach a law firm for assistance on a particular matter. The firm will in the ordinary course gather information about the client and provide some options. These options, if steps are taken, may or may not involve the firm performing captured activities (eg setting up a company). There is no requirement to carry out CDD until such time as those captured activities are to be performed. Until then, the firm is merely providing advice, which on its own is not a captured activity.

Reference: Anti-Money Laundering and Countering Financing of Terrorism Act 2009, ss 5(1)("financial institution"), 6(4), 11(6).

2-013 Ongoing customer due diligence and account monitoring

Under s 31 of the Anti-Money Laundering and Countering Financing of Terrorism Act 2009 (AML/CFT Act), reporting entities are obliged to conduct ongoing customer due diligence (CDD) and account monitoring on new and existing customers. This extends to regularly reviewing any information already held about an existing customer. When a customer changes their address or circumstances otherwise change, new information and documentation will from time-to-time need to be requested.

As a result of new information provided, it is possible that a reporting entity's assessment of the risk level of the customer may change. If the risk level of the customer is considered to have increased, additional due diligence at the appropriate level must be carried out on the customer.

The reporting entity's compliance programme should set out how the reporting entity proposes to meet this ongoing CDD and account monitoring requirement.

For law firms and accounting practices, an existing customer is a person who was in a business relationship with the firm immediately before the provisions of the AML/CFT Act began to apply to the law firm. In most cases, this was 1 July 2018 (for law firms) and 1 October 2018 (for accounting practices). Law firms and accounting practices were not required to update their CDD information for existing clients immediately upon the commencement of the AML/CFT regime. However, the compliance programme should set out how, over time and having regard to the risks involved, CDD will be updated and brought up to the level required by the AML/CFT Act. The provisions of the AML/CFT Act anticipate a staged, risk-based approach. In September 2020, the Department of Internal Affairs issued an explanatory note to assist law firms with this obligation: see "Customer due diligence obligations for 'existing customers' of law firms".

Reference: Anti-Money Laundering and Countering Financing of Terrorism Act 2009, s 31.

2-014 Look through to beneficial owners

The obligations of reporting entities to conduct customer due diligence (CDD) apply in relation to both individuals and entities (the term of which for anti-money laundering (AML)/countering the financing of terrorism (CFT) purposes typically encompasses legal arrangements such as trusts and partnerships).

Where a customer is an entity there are 2 lines of inquiry:

- The first line of inquiry requires verification that the entity actually exists. This can usually be achieved by searching any publicly available registers (eg the Companies' Office) or requesting copies of constitutional documents (eg the trust deed) and/or certificates of incumbency or good standing.
- The second line of inquiry relates to the beneficial owners and controllers. As a general rule, industry guidance notes typically prescribe that CDD should be undertaken on all beneficial owners with a share of more than 25% in the equity of the entity and all directors (in the case of companies), trustees (in the case of trusts) and partners (in the case of partnerships). In New Zealand, unlike some other countries (including, ironically, many so-called tax havens), there are no official registers of beneficial ownership. Therefore, it will not be sufficient to rely only on Companies Office search results when dealing with a New Zealand company.

2-015 Registers of beneficial ownership

On 19 June 2018, New Zealand's Ministry of Business, Innovation and Employment (MBIE) published a discussion document proposing the introduction of beneficial ownership registers for New Zealand companies and limited partnerships (termed corporate entities). See *Increasing the transparency of the beneficial ownership of New Zealand companies and limited partnerships*. This has the potential, at least in theory, to assist the customer due diligence (CDD) process. However, the practical realities and philosophical issues with this proposal require greater scrutiny.

The proposals are driven by high-profile cases of alleged criminal wrongdoing involving the use of New Zealand-registered corporate entities. (Whether the proposals would have stopped such wrongdoing is another matter.) They also implement the Financial Action Task Force Recommendation 24 into New Zealand law and are part of wider reforms to align New Zealand's anti-money laundering framework with international standards.

The discussion document sets out 3 potential options for reform:

- Option 1: the introduction of a specific requirement for corporate entities to hold up-to-date beneficial ownership information.

- Option 2: the introduction of a central beneficial ownership register, accessible to law enforcement agencies only.
- Option 3: option 2, but with the register being freely accessible by the public. MBIE states in the discussion document that this is their preferred option.

It is proposed that the definition of "beneficial owner" for the purposes of the register will align with the definition in the Anti-Money Laundering and Countering Financing of Terrorism Act 2009 (which follows the internationally accepted meaning).

The common situation where a corporate entity (perhaps a company operating a family business) is ultimately owned by the trustees of a discretionary family trust is a key area requiring further thought.

Family trusts are ubiquitous in New Zealand and are often used by families with only modest wealth. Successive governments have resisted calls for a register of trusts. However, under options 2 or 3 (and depending on the finer details of the proposals), a register of trusts would, in effect, be introduced for all trusts that hold an interest in a New Zealand corporate entity. This would increase compliance costs for many family trusts, which may prove politically contentious.

The discussion document (at 42) cites the European Union's 4th Anti-Money Laundering Directive (4AMLD) as an international example of beneficial ownership registration. Under the 4AMLD European Union member states must "ensure that their companies hold adequate, accurate and current information about their beneficial owners. States must have a central register that is available to law enforcement and tax authorities and AML reporting entities." On 9 July 2018, the European Union's 5th Anti-Money Laundering Directive (5AMLD) came into force. Among other matters, it required existing registers of beneficial ownership to be made freely available to the public by 10 January 2020. Although member countries were given 2 years to implement the changes, it seems many still do not have a centralised register of beneficial owners of companies that is available to the public.

The amendment met with significant opposition on the grounds that public access to what is (in many cases) private information infringes basic rights to privacy and data protection contained in the European Convention on Human Rights. The European Union's own data protection regulator issued an opinion on 2 February 2017 that was highly critical of these aspects of the amendments to 4AMLD.

There is no specific statutory right to privacy in New Zealand. However, the Privacy Act 2020 (which repealed the Privacy Act 1993 and came into force on 1 December 2020) provides a framework for protecting an individual's right to privacy of personal information.

Arguments that public registers infringe rights to privacy and data protection are particularly persuasive in New Zealand, which is a nation of small and often family-owned enterprises.

It is the authors' view that there is an appetite by government for increasing the transparency of the beneficial ownership of corporate entities and we wait with interest as discussions on the practical realities and philosophical issues unfold.

2-016 Suspicious activity reports

Information derived from a suspicious activity report (SAR) is used by the Financial Intelligence Unit of the New Zealand Police (FIU) to detect suspected offences.

Reports received by the FIU are analysed for activities and patterns that may indicate criminal offending. During the analysis, the FIU utilises various resources, including other information collected from reporting entities under the Anti-Money Laundering and Countering Financing of Terrorism Act 2009 (AML/CFT Act), intelligence received from New Zealand Police, partner agencies, international counterpart agencies, and information obtained from open-source databases. Where criminal activity appears to be occurring, cases may be referred to investigative agencies involved in law enforcement, asset recovery, taxation and national security.

By s 39A of the AML/CFT Act, a law firm or accounting practice must make an SAR if it has reasonable grounds to suspect that a transaction, proposed transaction, service or proposed service, or an inquiry, is or may be relevant to:

- the investigation or prosecution of any person for a money laundering offence
- the enforcement of the Misuse of Drugs Act 1975
- the enforcement of the Terrorism Suppression Act 2002
- the enforcement of the Proceeds of Crime Act 1991 or the Criminal Proceeds (Recovery) Act 2008, or
- the investigation or prosecution of an offence (within the meaning of s 243(1) of the Crimes Act 1961) — in this case an offence means an offence (or any offence described as a crime) that is punishable under New Zealand law, including any act, wherever committed, that would be an offence in New Zealand if committed in New Zealand.

Forming a suspicion

Forming a suspicion is a conceptually very challenging area of compliance and often gives rise to the question of what "knowledge" and "suspicion" actually mean. It is generally accepted that a person "knows" if they have no doubt about that thing. However, the position when someone is wilfully blind to red flags or recklessly fails to make inquiries that an honest and reasonable person would make is more nuanced. This issue was considered in *Baden v Société Générale pour Favoriser le Dévelopment du Commerce et de l'Industrie en France SA* [1992] 4 All ER 161 and the generally accepted position is that constructive knowledge is sufficient for anti-money laundering and countering the financing of terrorism purposes.

In the Privy Council case of *Hussein v Chong Fook Kam* [1970] AC 942 a defendant was charged with handling stolen goods, while knowing or suspecting that the goods were stolen. It was held that a suspicion is something less than knowledge but founded on a factual basis and predicated on more than mere speculation. In practice, a suspicion rarely arises instantly but evolves over time (possibly many years) and circumstance.

As a general rule, a suspicious activity will often be inconsistent with a client's known activities and profile, with the normal business expected for that type of client or the normal business expected through the reporting entity. An activity may have many factors that, when considered individually, do not raise suspicion, but when considered collectively suggest underlying criminal activity.

Reporting entities must submit SARs as soon as practicable but no later than 3 working days after forming a suspicion. This has been held to mean that a suspicious activity must be reported within 3 days of becoming aware of facts that would objectively justify a suspicion (or by reasonable diligence would have become aware of them). It is not a defence that a law firm or accounting practice did not actually consider an activity to be suspicious in circumstances where it objectively should have.

Service or proposed service

A reporting entity only has an obligation under the AML/CFT Act to make an SAR if it has reasonable grounds to suspect that a "transaction, proposed transaction, service or proposed service, or an inquiry" may be relevant to the investigation, prosecution or enforcement of a crime.

Section 39A of the AML/CFT Act applies a very narrow meaning to "service" and excludes activities that are not listed under s 6(4) (ie non-captured activities, such as advice).

"Service" is defined under s 39A of the AML/CFT Act to mean:

- an activity that is carried out by a reporting entity, but
- does not include an activity unless s 6(4) applies the AML/CFT Act to the reporting entity in relation to the activity (ie the activity must be a captured activity in order for it to be a service within the definition).

It is therefore relevant to consider whether the particular activity carried out by the law firm or accounting practice in relation to a client is an activity within the scope of the definition of "designated non-financial business or profession" (DNFBP) in s 5(1)). Where advice is given in relation to a potential captured activity without the activity being later carried out, the advice alone is not captured by the definition of DNFBP.

It could be argued that a purposive approach to interpreting the relevant provisions of the AML/CFT Act might lead to a different conclusion to that set out above. However, it is the authors' view that the narrow definition of "services" in s 39A is intentional and designed to ensure that clients of law firms and accounting practices continue to have open access to justice. There are obvious public policy benefits to protecting this fundamental human right.

What must be reported in a SAR?

An SAR submitted to the FIU must contain the information specified in sch 1 of the Anti-Money Laundering and Countering Financing of Terrorism (Requirements and Compliance) Regulations 2011. Such information includes:

- a statement of the reasonable grounds on which the reporting entity holds a suspicion
- an indication of any supporting documents that may help the FIU to analyse the SAR
- details that the reporting entity lawfully holds on the timing, parties and accounts for transactions or services that are sought or provided, and
- customer or other party details — names and addresses, business names and addresses — and other supporting identity information (if collected as part of CDD).

All SARs must explain why the transaction or activity (or proposed transaction or activity) is suspicious. For example, it might state that a personal or business transaction is suspicious because the transaction is large without any supporting information or the explanation is not sufficient and does not satisfy the "reasonable grounds" element.

How to submit an SAR

Like prescribed transaction reports (PTRs), SARs are submitted electronically via goAML. In urgent situations an SAR may be made orally. Circumstances in which suspicious transactions and activities can be reported orally include:

- where a reporting entity thinks that a situation requires urgent attention, and
- when a reporting entity has more than a reasonable suspicion, knowledge or belief that the transaction is related to serious criminal offending.

Where a suspicious transaction or activity has been reported orally, the reporting entity must submit an electronic version of the report to the FIU as soon as practicable, but no later than 3 working days after forming its suspicion.

Tipping off

Reporting entities must not disclose SAR information, or the existence of an SAR, to their clients. This is for 2 reasons:

- the identity of staff and reporting entities who make SARs need to be protected for their safety, and
- the subject of an SAR may be part of a criminal investigation and clients should not be advised of this.

Under s 46 of the AML/CFT Act, a reporting entity may only disclose SAR information, or the existence of an SAR, to the following persons:

- a Police employee who is authorised by the Commissioner of the Police to receive the information
- the reporting entity's AML/CFT supervisor
- an officer or employee of the reporting entity, for any purpose connected with the performance of that person's duties
- a lawyer, for the purpose of obtaining legal advice or representation in relation to the matter, or
- another member of a designated business group of which the reporting entity is a member, to the extent necessary for the reporting entity to decide whether to make an SAR.

Auditors may report suspicious activities. This does not just include auditors who are undertaking an audit of a law firm or accounting practice's compliance with the AML/CFT Act — it includes any person acting in their occupation as an auditor.

Under s 143 of the AML/CFT Act the Commissioner of Police has vast information-gathering powers. The Commissioner may:

- order production of or access to all records, documents, or information from any reporting entity that is relevant to analysing information received by the Commissioner under the AML/CFT Act, with or without a court order, and
- share SARs, PTRs, cash reports, suspicious property reports, and other financial information and intelligence with regulators and domestic and international authorities.

It is important to be reiterate that the obligations under the AML/CFT Act only apply to reporting entities. A law firm or accounting practice will only be a reporting entity to the extent that it is carrying out a captured activity. If in relation to a particular matter the firm or practice is not carrying out a captured activity, then it has no obligations under the AML/CFT Act. This means that there is no obligation (or even any lawful authority) for a law firm or accounting practice to make an SAR in relation to a matter which does not involve a captured activity — even if it would otherwise be suspicious and reportable. Were a SAR to be made in such circumstances, it could be in breach of client confidentially and legal professional privilege obligations.

Confidentiality

Lawyers will be aware of their obligations under the Rules of Conduct and Client Care for Lawyers (RCCC), made in accordance with the Lawyers and Conveyancers Act 2006. Chapter 8 of the RCCC is dedicated to the duty a lawyer has to protect, and hold in strict confidence, all information concerning a client and their business and affairs.

Lawyers may find it challenging to reconcile duties under the AML/CFT Act and the RCCC. An obvious area of difficulty is likely to arise when a lawyer is obliged to consider making an SAR. However, another example might be when the Department of Internal Affairs (DIA) conducts an audit of a law firm and, in the process, it may be required to review information and documentation relating to clients that is held on the lawyer's CDD files. This type of audit and review of client information may be routine and not necessarily predicated on any knowledge or suspicion of money laundering (ML).

Exceptions

There are of course exceptions to the duty not to disclose confidential information. For example, under r 8.4 of the RCCC a lawyer may disclose confidential information relating to the business or affairs of a client to a third party (eg the DIA or FIU) where (among other things):

- the client authorises the disclosure
- the information relates to the anticipated commission of a crime or fraud
- the lawyer reasonably believes that the lawyer's services have been used by the client to perpetrate or conceal a crime or fraud and disclosure is required to prevent, mitigate or rectify substantial injury to the interests, property or reputation of another person that is reasonably likely to result or has resulted from the client's commission, or
- disclosure is necessary for the effective operation of the lawyer's practice.

There is likely to be sufficient scope within r 8.4 to allow disclosure of confidential information in the manner contemplated by the AML/CFT Act. Even if there is no evidence of the anticipated commission or concealment of a crime or fraud, disclosure in some circumstances is likely to be necessary for the effective operation of the lawyer's practice. Nevertheless, lawyers should consider their standard terms of engagement and whether new wording should be included to allow disclosure of confidential information in circumstances contemplated by the AML/CFT Act. By agreeing to those terms, clients would authorise disclosure under r 8.4 and provide lawyers with an additional layer of comfort. Terms of engagement are discussed further below.

Legal professional privilege

Common law legal professional privilege provides the necessary conditions for a client to fully discuss matters with a lawyer. The client is free to disclose all relevant matters to their lawyer, safe in the knowledge that these communications cannot be disclosed or compelled. Legal professional privilege precludes communications between a lawyer and client made for the purposes of obtaining or receiving legal assistance from being disclosed without the permission of the client.

Crucially, lawyers do not have to disclose "privileged communications", which are defined in s 42 to include confidential communication between lawyers and between lawyers and clients. Practitioners should note that the Terrorism Suppression Act 2002 also protects privileged communications.

The provisions of the AML/CFT Act reflect the fundamental importance of legal professional privilege. Under the AML/CFT Act, a lawyer is not required to disclose any information that the lawyer believes on reasonable grounds to be a privileged communication. Additionally, the AML/CFT Act does not require disclosure of privileged information to the DIA (as the AML/CFT supervisor). However, if it is possible to file an SAR without disclosing a privileged communication, the law firm must do so. In some cases, however, this will not be possible.

Section 42 of the AML/CFT Act defines "privileged communication":

42 Privileged communication defined

(1) A communication is a **privileged communication** if—

(a) it is a confidential communication (oral or written) (including any information or opinion)—

(i) that passes between—

(A) a lawyer and another lawyer in their professional capacity; or

(B) a lawyer in his or her professional capacity and his or her client; or

(C) any person described in subparagraph (A) or (B) and the agent of the other person described in that subparagraph (or between the agents of both the persons described) either directly or indirectly; and

(ii) that is made or brought into existence for the purpose of obtaining or giving legal advice or assistance; or

(b) it is a communication (including any information or opinion) that—

(i) is subject to the general law governing legal professional privilege; or

(ii) is specified in section 53, 54, 55, 56, or 57 of the Evidence Act 2006.

This definition is consistent with the definition of "legal professional privilege" in the Evidence Act 2006 and covers the concepts of legal advice privilege and litigation privilege.

Legal advice privilege

Legal advice privilege is covered under s 42(1)(a) of the AML/CFT Act. This relates to confidential communications between lawyer and client made in the course of, and for the purpose of, obtaining or giving legal assistance or advice.

The conditions for legal advice privilege are essentially that:

- the lawyer holds a current practising certificate
- the document for which privilege is claimed must have come into being in the course of and for the purposes of obtaining professional legal services, and
- the communicated is intended to be confidential.

Litigation privilege

Litigation privilege is covered under s 42(1)(b) of the AML/CFT Act. This relates to communications between a lawyer and their client. Unlike legal advice privilege it also extends to communications with third parties relating to the preparation of court proceedings. It enables lawyers and their clients to freely gather evidence and prepare their case without fear of disclosure to their opponents.

The conditions for litigation privilege are essentially that:

- the communication or information came into existence when litigation was either already underway or was "reasonably apprehended", and
- the "dominant purpose" for creating the document must have been to enable the client's legal adviser to prepare for the case, conduct the case or advise the client on that litigation.

When privilege does not apply

Section 42(2) of the AML/CFT Act provides that a communication is not a privileged communication if:

- there is a prima facie case that it is made, received, compiled or prepared for a dishonest purpose or to enable or aid the commission of an offence, or
- the information consists wholly or partly of (or relates to) receipts, payments, income, expenditure or financial transactions of any person

and is contained in (or comprises the whole or part of) any book, account, statement or other record kept by the lawyer in connection with the lawyer's trust account.

In determining what a "prima facie case" is, lawyers may consider whether there is some credible evidence that a communication is made for a dishonest purpose or to enable the commission of a crime. When making such assessment, detailed records should be kept.

Section 42(2)(a) of the AML/CFT Act recognises the long-accepted common law standing that it is not in the interests of justice to protect documents that are made for a dishonest purpose. This applies to both legal advice privilege and litigation privilege. An objective test applies when determining what a "dishonest purpose" is.

Protection under the AML/CFT Act

It is a defence to a prosecution for failing to report suspicious activity if a reporting entity believes on reasonable grounds that the documents or information relating to the activity were privileged communications.

However, there is no defence to civil, criminal or disciplinary action against a lawyer for disclosing privileged information if the information was disclosed or supplied in bad faith. There is also no defence if a lawyer disclosing or supplying information did so despite there being reasonable grounds to believe that the information was a privileged communication.

Legal privilege provided by the AML/CFT Act is consistent with the more generic immunity from civil or criminal liability available under s 77 of the AML/CFT Act, which applies to all reporting entities that act reasonably and in good faith.

Continuing to act after filing an SAR

The fact that a law firm or accounting practice has grounds to suspect its client may be involved in ML or financing of terrorism does not mean that the duty to complete the retainer no longer exists. It will depend on the individual circumstances, such as the nature of the suspicion, the stage a particular transaction is at, any risk of "tipping off" and the firm's professional obligations in the particular case.

A law firm and accounting practice may seek to be discharged from an engagement by a client or seek an agreement with the client that the law firm or accounting practice no longer acts on the matter. However, before doing so, the firm needs to consider the "tipping off" provisions in the AML/CFT Act because there is risk that, in advising a client that they are no longer prepared to act, may effectively "tip off" the client to the fact that the firm is suspicious and is filing an SAR. Section 46 of the AML/CFT Act prohibits disclosure of SARs and s 94 makes it an offence for a reporting entity to unlawfully disclose an SAR.

A law firm, without "tipping off" concerns, may consider ending the relationship with a client. However, before doing so, consideration must be given to whether there is "good cause" to terminate, as required under r 4.2 of the Lawyers and Conveyancers Act (Lawyers: Conduct and Client Care) Rules 2008. Three of the grounds for "good cause" in r 4.2.1 may be relevant in the circumstances of a client whose conduct or instructions raise suspicion. These are:

- instructions that require a lawyer to breach any professional obligations
- the client misleading or deceiving the lawyer in a material respect, or
- except in litigation matters, the adoption by the client, against the advice of the lawyer, of a course of action that the lawyer believes is highly imprudent and may be inconsistent with the lawyer's fundamental obligations.

There will be occasions when the requirement to file an SAR coincides with a client providing the law firm with good reason to terminate the retainer. For example, if the client begins to shape the retainer in a way that involves concealing an illegal activity, the law firm would have "good cause" under r 4.2 to terminate.

Terms of engagement

There is merit in a law firm or accounting practice amending its standard terms of engagement to expressly reference that, where it is carrying out a captured activity, it may be required to disclose information to FIU relating to:

- suspicious activities (if any), and
- certain transactions prescribed by the AML/CFT Act.

The following wording is an example of wording that might be used:

> We are obliged to comply with all laws applicable to us in all jurisdictions, including (but not limited to):
>
> - anti-money laundering and countering financing of terrorism laws, and
> - laws relating to tax and client reporting and withholdings.
>
> We may be required to undertake customer due diligence on you, persons acting on your behalf and other relevant persons such as beneficial owners and controlling persons. We may not be able to begin acting, or to continue acting, for you until that is completed.
>
> To ensure our compliance and yours, we may be required to provide information about you, persons acting on your behalf or other relevant persons to government agencies. There may be circumstances where we are not able to tell you or such persons if we do provide information.
>
> Please ensure that you and/or any of the persons described previously are aware of and consent to this. It is important to ensure that all

information provided to us is accurate. If the information required is not provided, or considered by us to be potentially inaccurate, misleading, or in contravention of any law, we may terminate or refuse to enter into an engagement.

The DIA has prepared the following flowchart, which can be used to assist lawyers (and accountants) when they are considering whether to file an SAR (see DIA *Guideline: Lawyers and Conveyancers*, December 2015 at 15):

Lawyers may find it helpful to ask the following questions when considering whether to file an SAR:

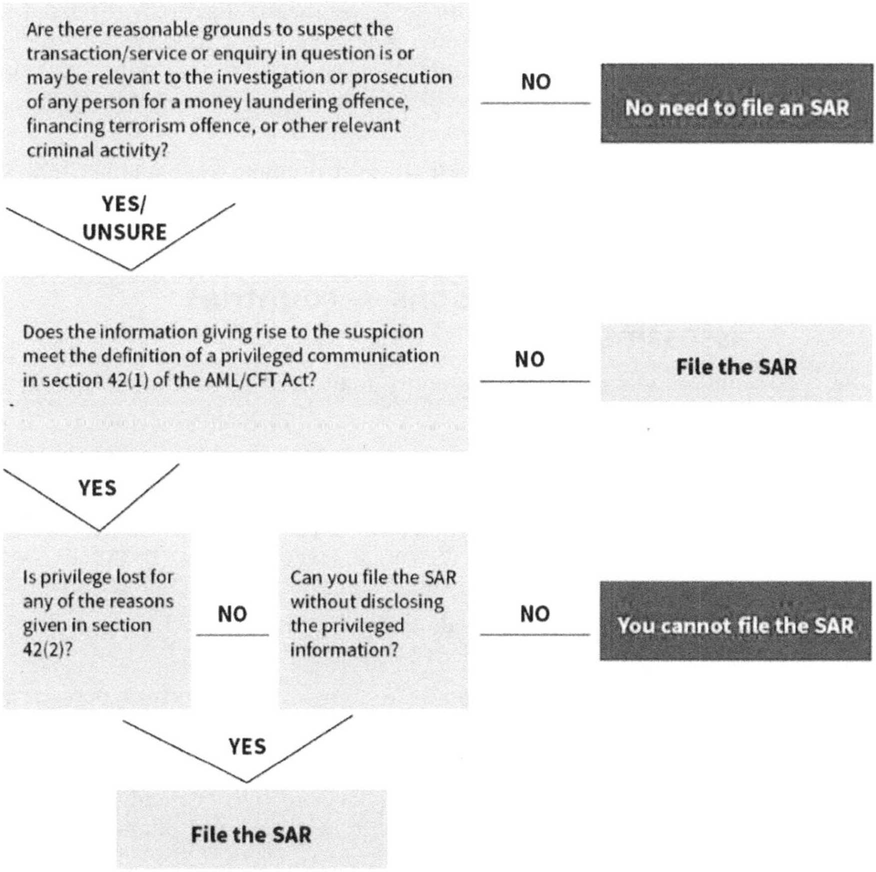

References: Anti-Money Laundering and Countering Financing of Terrorism Act 2009, ss 5(1), 6(4), 39A, 42, 46, 77, 143.

Anti-Money Laundering and Countering Financing of Terrorism (Requirements and Compliance) Regulations 2011, sch 1.

2-017 Suspicious property reports

Although hopefully much less relevant to lawyers and accountants than suspicious activity reports and prescribed transaction report s, the Anti-Money Laundering and Countering Financing of Terrorism Act 2009 also imposes an obligation on reporting entities to submit "suspicious property reports" under the Terrorism Suppression Act 2002.

This obligation arises when a law firm or accounting practice is in control of property that a practitioner suspects (on reasonable grounds) is owned or controlled, directly or indirectly, by a "designated terrorist entity" (or property derived or generated from that type of property). In these circumstances, a lawyer or accountant must report that suspicion in accordance with ss 43 and 44 of the Terrorism Suppression Act as soon as practicable after forming the suspicion.

Designated terrorist entities are identified on a publicly available list that is updated by the New Zealand Police, which is available on the New Zealand Police website (police/govt.nz).

2-018 High-risk jurisdictions — countries assessment

The circumstances when a reporting entity may need to conduct a countries assessment include:

- when undertaking a risk assessment and establishing a compliance programme
- when establishing a business relationship with, or conducting an occasional transaction or activity for, a customer who is not a New Zealand resident
- when the reporting entity intends to form a designated business group and one of the members is resident overseas
- when the reporting entity intends to rely on an overseas person to conduct customer due diligence on its behalf.

The countries assessment required in each particular case will depend on the relevant circumstances. The AML/CFT supervisors (Department of Internal Affairs (DIA), Financial Markets Authority and Reserve Bank of New Zealand) have produced a *Countries Assessment Guideline* (2012) designed to help reporting entities undertake a countries assessment. See also *Guideline: Assessing Country Risk*, June 2021, which sits adjacent to it and has been produced by the DIA with application to its reporting entities.

The DIA has also published other material on its website relating to countries assessments, including information about the requirement in s 57(1)(h) for the compliance programme to have adequate and effective procedures, policies and controls for "monitoring, examining and keeping written findings relating to business relationships and transactions from or in countries that do not have or have insufficient AML/CFT systems in place, and have additional measures for dealing with or restricting dealings with such countries" (see "Legal Sector Regulatory Findings", 21 July 2020).

In its Legal Sector Regulatory Findings item, the DIA commented that "in practice, the Financial Action Task Force (FATF) list of high-risk and monitored jurisdictions (FATF website) should assist your AML/CFT programme relating to countries with insufficient AML/CFT systems".

The list of high-risk and monitored jurisdictions on the FATF website as at June 2021 is:

- The Democratic People's Republic of Korea
- Iran
- Albania
- Barbados
- Botswana
- Burkina Faso
- Cambodia
- Cayman Islands
- Haiti
- Jamaica
- Malta
- Mauritius
- Morocco
- Myanmar
- Nicaragua
- Pakistan
- Panama
- Philippines
- Senegal
- South Sudan
- Syria
- Uganda
- Yemen
- Zimbabwe

FATF and equivalent regional bodies have called upon these jurisdictions to implement anti-money laundering/countering the financing of terrorism regimes or action plans and will continue to work with these jurisdictions to achieve this.

To meet the requirements under s 57(1)(h), a law firm or accounting practice's compliance programme should also set out how it will deal with any clients from these countries.

Reference: Anti-Money Laundering and Countering Financing of Terrorism Act 2009, s 57(1).

2-019 Wire transfers

The obligations under the Anti-Money Laundering and Countering Financing of Terrorism Act 2009 (AML/CFT Act) in relation to wire transfers are complicated. They are potentially very confusing for lawyers and accountants because the rules are designed for financial institutions rather than professional services firms.

Under s 5 of the AML/CFT Act:

> **wire transfer** —
>
> (a) means a transaction carried out on behalf of a person (the **originator**) through a reporting entity by electronic means with a view to making an amount of money available to a beneficiary (who may also be the originator) at another reporting entity; and
>
> (b) includes a transfer or transaction, or class of transfers or transactions, declared by regulations to be a wire transfer for the purposes of this Act; but
>
> (c) excludes—
>
> (i) transfers and settlements between financial institutions or other reporting entities if both the originator and the beneficiary are financial institutions or other reporting entities acting on their own behalf; and
>
> (ii) credit and debit card transactions if the credit or debit card number accompanies the transaction; and
>
> (iii) any other transfer or transaction or class of transfers or transactions declared by regulations not to be a wire transfer for the purposes of this Act.

There are 2 primary obligations in relation to wire transfers that pass through a law firm or accounting practice's trust account:

- to report prescribed transactions, and
- to gather certain information about the parties to a wire transfer.

These obligations are distinct and independent of each other, but easily confused. The following rules of thumb may aid understanding:

- The obligations to report prescribed transactions apply to international wire transfers and cash receipts.
- The obligations to gather information about the parties to a wire transfer:
  - apply to both domestic and international wire transfers
  - refer to enhanced customer due diligence (CDD) being required, but apply a different standard to the enhanced CDD required for CDD.

Prescribed transaction reports

Section 48A of the AML/CFT Act requires reporting entities to report "prescribed transactions" to the Financial Intelligence Unit of the New Zealand Police (FIU). Such a report has become known as a "prescribed transaction report" or "PTR" (although this is not a defined term in the AML/CFT Act).

By s 5 of the AML/CFT Act:

> **prescribed transaction,** in relation to a reporting entity, means a transaction conducted through the reporting entity in respect of:
>
> (a) an international wire transfer of a value equal to or above the applicable threshold value; or
>
> (b) a domestic physical cash transaction of a value equal to or above the applicable threshold value.

Under reg 6 of the Anti-Money Laundering and Countering Financing of Terrorism (Prescribed Transactions Reporting) Regulations 2016, the applicable threshold values for a prescribed transaction are as follows:

- a wire transfer — $1,000
- a domestic cash transaction — $10,000.

Law firms and accounting practices are required to report on prescribed transactions by providing a PTR in electronic form to the FIU. PTRs need to be submitted as soon as practicable but within 10 working days from the date the transaction took place.

PTRs help to build an intelligence picture across the entire financial system and add further transparency to the financial system by making particular money laundering and financing of terrorism typologies even more difficult to hide, as well as improving the detection, and thus disruption, of organised crimes, fraud and tax evasion.

Under s 48C and ss 43–48 of the AML/CFT Act a law firm or accounting practice must also report to the FIU any suspicious activities related to any prescribed transactions. This contemplates that, in some circumstances, a PTR and a suspicious activity report may both need to be filed.

How to submit a PTR

Having some knowledge of how many large cash transactions (LCTs) and international funds transfers (IFTs) a law firm or accounting practice will need to submit, and how often, will help identify the best way to submit PTRs. Generally, law firms and accounting practices do not deal in physical cash so the number of LCTs should be minimal (if any).

There are 3 methods that can be used to submit PTRs to the FIU:

- manual entry using the goAML Web forms
- bulk XML document upload via goAML Web, and
- business-to-business (B2B) full automated upload.

GoAML is a software system developed by the United Nations Office on Drugs and Crime for Financial Intelligence Units worldwide to counter FT and ML. GoAML Web is the prescribed method by which reporting entities must submit SARs and PTRs to the FIU. Reporting entities need to register in goAML. Instructions on how to register can be found on the New Zealand Police website (GoAML — Financial Intelligence Unit Reporting Tool).

In the ordinary course, law firms and accounting practices should not have many LCTs and IFTs that require a PTR so the best approach will be to manually submit PTRs via the goAML web form. This requires a user to login to the goAML web form and an online form to be completed for an LCT and an IFT. The FIU strongly suggest that reporting entities submitting PTRs via goAML use the test environment before submitting real PTRs into the live (production) environment. The test environment is set up in the same way as the production environment and allows reporting entities to familiarise themselves with the structure and requirements of the online forms. To access the test environment, and for further information, email goAMLconsult@police.govt.nz.

Details to be contained in a PTR are set out in sch 2 of the Anti-Money Laundering and Countering Financing of Terrorism (Prescribed Transactions Reporting) Regulations 2016 and include:

- the name and business address of the law firm or accounting practice and the name of their AML/CFT supervisor
- transaction details for each transaction
- transaction details in relation to the originator or beneficiary (who in most cases is likely to be a client of the law firm or accounting practice)
- the client's details, and
- additional details for facilities involved in the transaction.

The form is prescribed and does not involve the law firm or accounting practice making any difficult decisions.

Law firms and accounting practices should set out in their compliance programme procedures, policies and controls for meeting the AML/CFT Act's requirements relating to PTRs.

Enhanced CDD

A law firm or accounting practice's trust account is of course frequently used by one person to conduct transactions by electronic means (eg internet banking), to make money available to another person. Accordingly, in the ordinary course of business, a law firm or accounting practice that operates a trust account will be involved in numerous wire transfers.

Section 22(3) of the AML/CFT Act provides that enhanced CDD diligence must be conducted in accordance with ss 27 and 28 of the AML/CFT Act if the firm is an "ordering institution", an "intermediary institution" or a "beneficiary institution" in relation to a wire transfer.

The parties to a wire transfer are as follows.

- The person who authorises the wire transfer by giving the instruction as the account holder. This could be the client of a law firm or accounting practice. This person is known as the payer or originator.
- An **ordering institution** is a person who has been instructed by the payer to electronically transfer funds controlled by the payer to another person (known as the payee). In a transaction involving a law firm or accounting practice, the ordering institution could be:
  - — the bank used by a client where the trust account is not being used, or
  - — a law firm or accounting practice where the trust account is being used.
- An **intermediary institution** is a person who participates in an electronic transfer of funds but is not an ordering institution or a beneficiary institution. A law firm or accounting practice could, in theory, be an intermediary institution in situations where funds electronically pass through its trust account as part of a transaction not directly involving a client. However, this would be unlikely in the ordinary course of business.
- A **beneficiary institution** is a person who receives an electronic transfer of funds from an ordering institution or an intermediary institution and then makes those funds available to a payee by crediting it to an account held by the payee or paying it to the payee. In a transaction involving a law firm or accounting practice, the beneficiary institution could be:
  - — the bank used by a client where the trust account is not being used, or
  - — a law firm or accounting practice where the trust account is being used.

Under s 27(1) of the AML/CFT Act, where a law firm or accounting practice is an ordering institution (eg it is transferring the funds), it must identify the originator of a wire transfer that is equal to or above the applicable threshold value (ie $1,000) by obtaining the following information:

- the originator's full name
- the originator's account number or other identifying information that enables the transaction to be identified and traced to the originator, and
- any one of the originator's address, national identity number, customer identity number, or place and date of birth.

This information should accompany the wire transfer.

In the ordinary course, if the originator is the client of the law firm or accounting practice, the firm or practice would have already obtained some or all of this information during the CDD process. If it is not possible to procure this information, at least in relation to domestic wire transfers, s 27(2) provides a mechanism for compliance by allowing a lower standard, provided there is some way of tracing the transaction back to the originator. While this is helpful in theory, ordinarily it should not be necessary.

It is the authors' (and the DIA's) view that the "originator's account number" refers to the unique identifier that the law firm or accounting practice has allocated to its client such as a client matter number.

Under s 27(5) of the AML/CFT Act, if a law firm or accounting practice is a beneficiary institution (eg it is receiving the funds) it must take a risk-based approach and consider whether a wire transfer received without the relevant information specified above constitutes a suspicious activity. This could happen quite frequently given that many law firms and accounting practices publish their trust account details.

The practical approach that many law firms and accounting practices are taking is to set up systems to collect and hold the relevant information in relation to any funds received and sent from the trust account.

It may not be helpful for law firms and accounting practices to try and determine whether they are an ordering, intermediary or beneficiary institution in this context.

If a law firm or accounting practice is a party to a wire transfer by:

- receiving funds into its trust account
- transferring funds between client ledgers within its trust account, and/or
- paying funds out of its trust account

then the firm is almost certainly going to have wire transfer enhanced CDD obligations (and may have PTR obligations — see further below).

It is important for law firms to note the following in respect of these enhanced CDD requirements:

- They apply to both domestic and international wire transfers but do not of themselves trigger any external reporting obligations (eg PTRs). The obligations require internal information gathering and record keeping, which is why these obligations are distinct from PTRs.
- They apply to funds that are transferred between solicitors' trust accounts and funds that are transferred to a law firm or accounting practice from parties who are not clients of the firm.
- They involve a different standard of enhanced CDD to the usual standard that must be applied in relation to trusts or clients from high-risk countries. Enhanced CDD under ss 27 and 28 of the AML/CFT Act is prescribed and quantitative, whereas enhanced CDD in the ordinary course is qualitative. Enhanced CDD in relation to wire transfers, at least in theory, should be relatively easy for law firms and accounting practices to deal with because it is prescribed and does not involve the firm or practice making any difficult decisions.

The relationship between PTRs and wire transfers

The obligation to file PTRs only applies to international wire transfers — so it does not apply to electronic funds transfers made between parties who are all residents within New Zealand.

Under s 5(1) of the AML/CFT Act, an "international wire transfer" means a wire transfer where at least one of the relevant parties to the transaction (usually a financial institution) is in New Zealand and at least one of the relevant parties to the transaction (usually a financial institution) is outside of New Zealand.

Furthermore, the obligation applies only to transfers equal to or above the "applicable threshold value", which is $1,000 for wire transfers (under reg 6 of the Anti-Money Laundering and Countering Financing of Terrorism (Prescribed Transactions Reporting) Regulations).

Therefore, the PTR obligations apply only to international wire transfers equal to or above $1,000 received or paid by a law firm or accounting practice as trustee of its trust account.

On the other hand, the enhanced CDD obligations apply to all wire transfers (ie both domestic and international) equal to or above $1,000 received or paid by a law firm or accounting practice as trustee of its trust account.

If the law firm or accounting practice has a trust account, its compliance programme should set out how it proposes to meet the obligations under the AML/CFT Act in relation to wire transfers.

References: Anti-Money Laundering and Countering Financing of Terrorism Act 2009, ss 5(1)("international wire transfer"), 22(3), 27, 28, 43–48, 48A, 48C,.

Anti-Money Laundering and Countering Financing of Terrorism (Prescribed Transactions Reporting) Regulations 2016, reg 6, sch 2.

2-020 Record keeping

Section 49 of the Anti-Money Laundering and Countering Financing of Terrorism Act 2009 (AML/CFT Act) provides that for every "transaction" that is conducted through a reporting entity the reporting entity must keep records sufficient to enable that transaction to be readily reconstructed at any time. The records must contain the following information:

- the nature of the transaction
- the amount of the transaction and the currency in which it was denominated
- the date on which the transaction was conducted
- the parties to the transaction
- the facility through which the transaction was conducted, and any other facilities directly involved in the transaction (if applicable)
- the name of the officer, employee or agent of the reporting entity who handled the transaction, if that officer, employee or agent:
  - — has face-to-face dealings in respect of the transaction with any of the parties to the transaction, and
  - — has formed a suspicion (of the kind referred to in s 40(1)(b)) about the transaction
- any other information prescribed by regulations.

Under s 5(1) of the AML/CFT Act:

> **transaction —**
>
> (a) means any deposit, withdrawal, exchange, or transfer of funds (or any denominated currency), whether —
>
> (i) in cash; or
>
> (ii) by cheque, payment order, or other instrument; or
>
> (iii) by electronic or other non-physical means; and
>
> (b) without limiting paragraph (a), includes —
>
> (i) any payment made in satisfaction, in whole or in part, of any contractual or other legal obligation; and
>
> (ii) a transaction or class of transactions declared by regulations to be a transaction for the purposes of this Act; but
>
> (c) excludes the following:
>
> (i) the placing of any bet unless authorised under the Racing Act 2003:

(ii) participation in gambling (as defined in section 4(1) of the Gambling Act 2003) unless authorised under the Racing Act 2020:

(iii) a transaction or class of transactions declared by regulations not to be a transaction for the purposes of this Act.

Such records must be retained for at least 5 years after the completion of the transaction or, if applicable, any longer period that **the** Department of Internal Affairs specifies to the reporting entity.

Under s 50 of the AML/CFT Act, customer identity and verification records must be retained for at least 5 years after the business relationship ends, the occasional transaction or activity is completed, or the wire transfer is completed, as the case may be (s 50).

Section 51 also requires the retention of other types of records, such as those relevant to the establishment of the business relationship and relevant to risk assessments, compliance programmes and audits.

Reference: Anti-Money Laundering and Countering Financing of Terrorism Act 2009 ss 5(1) ("transaction"), 49, 50, 51.

2-021 Audit of risk assessment and compliance programme

A law firm or accounting practice's risk assessment and compliance programme must be reviewed regularly and audited every 3 years or at any other time at the request of the relevant AML/CFT supervisor (Department of Internal Affairs (DIA), Financial Markets Authority or Reserve Bank of New Zealand). This requirement was increased from 2 years to 3 years by the AML/CFT amendment regulations which came into force on 9 July 2021. The purpose of this is to ensure its risk assessment and compliance programme remains current and effective and to enable changes to be made if necessary.

The Anti-Money Laundering and Countering Financing of Terrorism Act 2009 (AML/CFT Act) does not specify how an audit is to be conducted. However, the AML/CFT supervisors have released *Audit Guideline for Risk Assessment and AML/CFT Programme*, October 2019, which provides an overview of matters to consider when arranging an audit.

The Act does not specify that the AML/CFT risk assessment audit and the compliance programme audit should be conducted by the same person.

It is important to note that the auditor may provide options regarding the level of assurance they will seek to obtain when conducting the audit. The AML/CFT Act does not require an auditor to provide a specific level of assurance. Therefore, the entity can choose whether to receive a limited assurance audit or a reasonable assurance audit.

The DIA and independent auditors will have overarching criteria as to the adequacy of any particular risk assessment or compliance programme. This involves verification of how compliant they are with various obligations under the AML/CFT Act and their practical application in meeting these legislative requirements.

Under s 43 of the AML/CFT Act, an auditor may submit suspicious transaction reports to the New Zealand Police if the auditor comes across information that causes them to have grounds for suspicion.

A copy of the audit does not have to be submitted to the AML/CFT supervisor unless requested by the supervisor. Each law firm or accounting practice is required by s 60 to submit an annual report on its risk assessment and compliance programme to the DIA, at a time specified by the DIA. The annual report must:

- be in the prescribed form
- take into account the results and implications of the audit required by s 59(2) of the AML/CFT Act, and
- contain any information prescribed by regulations.

AML/CFT supervisors are granted "all the powers necessary" under the AML/CFT Act to carry out their functions in the supervision of reporting entities.

The functions of the DIA are supported by a broad range of powers. For example, the DIA can, on notice, require the production of or access to all documents relevant to its supervision and monitoring of reporting entities for compliance with the AML/CFT Act. The DIA may therefore request a reporting entity's risk assessment, compliance programme, audit reports and any associated documents as it sees fit.

As a result, the reviews and internal audits of the risk assessment and compliance programme are extremely important. Both the risk assessment and compliance programme must be reviewed sufficiently regularly to ensure that:

- both documents remain up to date
- any deficiencies in their effectiveness are identified, and
- any necessary updates or amendments are made.

There are some important differences between an audit of the risk assessment and the compliance programme.

Audits of risk assessments are limited to assessing whether the document complies with all of the obligations in s 58(3) of the AML/CFT Act. Accordingly, the auditors will assess the nature and extent of the risk assessment and the application; however, the auditor is not required to audit the judgment calls made in the risk assessment.

The audit of a risk assessment focuses on the fulfilment of the following requirements:

- it must be presented formally in writing
- it must identify the risks faced by the entity in the course of is business
- it must provide a description of how the reporting entity will ensure that the risk assessment remains up to date, and
- it must enable the reporting entity to ascertain the risks involved in relation to the relevant obligations under the AML/CFT Act and its regulations.

In contrast, audit of the **compliance programme** includes an assessment of whether:

- it complies with all obligations in s 57 of the AML/CFT Act
- the procedures, policies and controls are based on the risk assessment
- the procedures, policies and controls are adequate, and
- the procedures, policies and controls have operated effectively throughout the time period.

It would be prudent to conduct a review or internal audit at regular periodic intervals. Ideally, these would be in addition to any specific triggers that have been formalised in the compliance programme.

These reviews and internal audits should gather information in relation to the administration of the reporting entity's current compliance regime. It may include the following, although these examples are in no way exhaustive:

- reviewing the effectiveness of the compliance programme across its various areas
- assessing whether the money laundering/financing of terrorism risks facing New Zealand, the industry of the reporting entity, or the reporting entity itself have changed
- identifying any non-compliance with any of its procedures and policies
- noting the learning opportunities that have arisen as a result of the non-compliance, or from other suspicious activities that occurred during the reporting period
- compiling a register of training sessions that have been delivered, and who may require further training and development, and
- providing evidence or proposals as to how the reporting entity has incorporated or will incorporate improvements to the regime.

External audits — independent person

The person appointed to conduct the external audit must be an "independent person." Any member of staff involved in developing and maintaining the reporting entity's risk assessment or compliance programme will not be an independent person. However, the *Risk Assessment Guideline* (May 2018) and *Audit Guideline* (October 2019) produced by the AML/CFT supervisors both state that it would be suitable for an external audit to be carried out by a member of staff who is sufficiently separated from the parts of the business that deal with risk assessment and the compliance programme.

The external auditor must be someone "appropriately qualified to conduct the audit." This broadens the options beyond chartered accountants and those specifically qualified to undertake financial audits. The DIA has confirmed that, in principle, a law firm or accounting practice could audit another law firm or accounting practice.

Reciprocal audits

The authors are aware of law firms and accounting practices performing audits on each other. These are known as "reciprocal audits" and they carry a number of risks that should be carefully considered by a firm before deciding to take that approach. For example, it can be "harder to illustrate the independence of the person conducting your audit in the context of reciprocal audits . . . because in a reciprocal audit context you may know the person who conducts your audit, they may be familiar with your business, and/or you may have relationships with the same third parties". See *What is a reciprocal AML/CFT audit and when is it appropriate? Guidelines for undertaking reciprocal audits for reporting entities supervised by the DIA* at 5, which are guidelines the DIA has produced for undertaking reciprocal audits. These are available by emailing the DIA at amlcft@dia.govt.nz. The DIA also recommends discussing this approach with the DIA before starting the process.

Reference: Anti-Money Laundering and Countering Financing of Terrorism Act 2009, ss 43, 57, 58(3), 59(2), 60.

2-022 Annual reports

Each reporting entity is required by s 60 of the Anti-Money Laundering and Countering Financing of Terrorism Act 2009 (AML/CFT Act) to submit to its AML/CFT supervisor (Department of Internal Affairs (DIA), Financial Markets Authority or Reserve Bank of New Zealand), at a time specified by the supervisor, an annual report on its risk assessment and compliance programme. This should be submitted to the DIA between 1 July and 31 August of each year, in the prescribed format as set out by the Anti- Money Laundering and Countering Financing of Terrorism (Requirements and Compliance) Regulations 2011. The DIA has information on its website regarding annual reporting obligations — see *Annual Reports for Designated Non-Financial Businesses or Professions (DNFBPs)* — updated June 2021.

Under the guidelines the annual report must:

- be in the prescribed form
- take into account the results and implications of the audit required by s 59(2), and
- contain any information prescribed by regulations.

The annual report should cover the following 5 broad topics:

- business contact details and organisation structure (Part 1)
- risk assessment and compliance programmes (Part 2)
- products and services, customers and channels (Part 3)
- captured activities (Part 4)
- ministerial exemption (Part 5), and
- declaration and signature (Part 6).

The annual report also requires declarations in respect of:

- whether a procedure is in place for independent audits
- when the last audit was undertaken
- if any deficiencies have been highlighted, and
- whether the changes previously identified have been implemented to address deficiencies.

Failure to file an annual report may attract fines of up to $200,000 for an individual or $2 million for a body corporate or partnership. Knowingly or recklessly failing to file an annual report may be considered an offence under s 91 of the AML/CFT Act. For further information on this, see the Enforcement section of this book.

The annual reporting process provides an opportunity to identify and remedy any areas of the risk assessments that may need revising due to changes in circumstances.

Reference: Anti-Money Laundering and Countering Financing of Terrorism Act 2009, s 60.

Chapter 3
Enforcement

3-000 Enforcement overview

The enforcement regime of the Anti-Money Laundering and Countering Financing of Terrorism Act 2009 (AML/CFT Act) is divided into civil and criminal liability provisions.

Civil proceedings

For civil penalty proceedings, an application for a civil penalty under Pt 3 of the AML/CFT Act must be made no later than 6 years after the act causing the breach occurred. The standard of proof is the same as that applied to civil proceedings generally. If a civil liability act is alleged to have occurred, the relevant supervisor may do one or more of the following (see "Enforcement options for supervisors" below):

- issue a formal warning
- accept an enforceable undertaking and seek a court order for breach of that undertaking
- seek an injunction, and
- apply to the court for a pecuniary penalty.

A civil liability act can further predicate an offence if the reporting entity engages in that conduct knowingly or recklessly. Other statutes such as the Crimes Act 1961 also prescribe a series of offences for money laundering and terrorism financing.

Under s 78 of the AML/CFT Act, a civil liability act occurs when a reporting entity fails to comply with any of the AML/CFT requirements, including (but not limited to) the following:

- it fails to conduct customer due diligence (CDD)
- it fails to adequately monitor accounts and transactions
- it enters into or continues a business relationship with a person who does not produce satisfactory evidence of identity
- it enters into or continues a correspondent banking relationship with a shell bank

- it fails to report prescribed transactions in accordance with subpart 2A of Pt 2 of the AML/CFT Act
- it fails to keep records in accordance with subpart 3A of Pt 2 the AML/CFT Act
- it fails to establish, implement or maintain an AML/CFT programme, or
- it fails to ensure its branches and subsidiaries comply with AML/CFT requirements.

The failure to report a suspicious activity is regarded as an omission of civil liability, as with any other acts or omissions of non-compliance with requirements under Pt 2 of the AML/CFT Act.

Approaches taken by the AML/CFT supervisors

The Financial Markets Authority

The Financial Markets Authority (FMA) has issued a number of formal warnings to reporting entities under s 80 of the AML/CFT Act. The FMA supervises financial institutions rather than law firms and accounting practices, but the approach taken is instructive.

In February 2019, the FMA carried out a risk-based assessment of independent audit reports for reporting entities it supervises, targeting 69 reporting entities. (The FMA supervises around 800 reporting entities, of whom roughly two-thirds define themselves as financial advisers.)

Following this review, the FMA issued:

- 5 formal warnings to reporting entities for failing to have their risk assessment and AML/CFT programme audited every 2 years, and
- 5 formal warnings to reporting entities that had their risk assessment and AML/CFT programme audited, but the audit was not done in a timely manner, occurring months after its due date.

Fourteen further desk-based reviews and 4 monitoring visits were to be carried out in response to this work.

The FMA also issued a compliance letter to one additional reporting entity requesting follow-up action by the entity.

The FMA has previously said it expects to see more robust AML/CFT policies and procedures in place, given that AML/CFT laws have been in force for more than 5 years. It highlighted that in future there would be an increased focus on reviewing independent audit reports on AML/CFT processes.

The Department of Internal Affairs

On 30 April 2019, the Department of Internal Affairs (DIA) issued a formal warning to Auckland-based trust and company service provider Denton Morrell for failing to meet AML/CFT Act requirements over the period from 17 November 2015 to 2 May 2018, which included:

- failing to conduct CDD
- failing to adequately monitor accounts and transactions, and
- failing to establish, implement or maintain a compliance programme.

The following extracts from the DIA press release relating to Denton Morrell Limited are instructive:

- "We are committed to helping businesses understand and fulfil their AML/CFT obligations as we know how important brand and reputation are to businesses in New Zealand. We also know how disruptive and harmful it can be to a business who is unwittingly taken advantage of by money launderers or those involved in financing terrorism" (Mike Stone, Director of the Department's AML Group).
- "It is imperative registered entities keep tabs on who they're doing business with and constantly review potential customers and transactions. In the case of Denton Morrell Limited, many of its customers are from countries considered high risk jurisdictions by international AML/CFT standards. It failed in its AML/CFT obligations to conduct enhanced customer due diligence and there were inconsistencies with source of funds/wealth verification."

The DIA required Denton Morrell Limited to take immediate action to rectify all areas where it was non-compliant with its AML/CFT obligations. The DIA was to continue to monitor the company and consider further enforcement action if it engaged in conduct that did not comply with the AML/CFT Act.

Solicitors Regulation Authority (UK)

Similarly, the Solicitors Regulation Authority (SRA) launched disciplinary action against 26 law firms in the United Kingdom in 2019. This action followed a 2018 review of trust and company service providers (*A thematic review of trust and company service providers*), which found many breaches of the anti-money laundering regulations. The review found that a significant minority of law firms carrying out trust and company service provider work were not meeting their obligations to tackle money laundering, with some falling seriously short. Risk assessments and appropriate customer due diligence were the weakest points.

The SRA announced it would judge each of the 26 disciplinary cases on their facts and be looking for evidence that firms were "moving swiftly to comply with their obligations." The SRA warned that they would "take strong action against firms where we have serious concerns that they could be enabling money laundering, and/or those who fail to address our concerns promptly". Disciplinary action would be seriously considered if firms did not cooperate or the breaches were significant.

The failure of many reporting entities, both in New Zealand and abroad, to comply with their AML/CFT obligations is an indication of the stringent and potentially intimidating requirements of the AML/CFT Act. However, as can be seen from the investigation action of the FMA and the SRA, this does not excuse non-compliance. The financial burden imposed by these obligations should be passed on to customers, provided that, as always, a fair and transparent approach is adopted. It is the view of the New Zealand Law Society (NZLS) that the regulatory framework under the Lawyers and Conveyancers Act 2006 does not prevent lawyers from passing on a genuine compliance cost associated with the provision of regulated services to clients.

It is important to note that if the AML/CFT requirements require a breach in a contractual arrangement that the reporting entity may be subject to, the AML/CFT requirements will have greater weight. In a situation of conflict between contractual obligations and AML/CFT obligations, the possibility of contractual breach will not be considered a justification for non-compliance.

Enforcement options for supervisors

The following table provides details of the enforcement options at the disposal of the DIA and other supervisors, as discussed above.

Source or AML/CFT Section	**Enforcement Measure**	**Grounds**
DIA *Guideline: Lawyers and Conveyancers* DIA *Guideline: Accountants*	Remediation plans	If it becomes apparent to the DIA that a reporting entity is failing to meet its obligations, a remediation plan will outline a set of expected targets that must be achieved within a certain time frame. Progress towards meeting the obligations should be measurable.
80	Formal warning	The DIA may issue a formal warning if it has reasonable grounds to believe the reporting entity has engaged in a civil liability act.
81	Enforceable undertaking	The DIA can enforce an undertaking by the reporting entity in relation to its compliance with the AML/CFT obligations.
85	Injunction (performance)	The DIA must apply for a performance injunction to the High Court. This will be relevant if the reporting entity refuses or fails to act in such a way that the refusal will mean it is civilly liable.

Source or AML/CFT Section	Enforcement Measure	Grounds
87	Injunction (restraining)	The DIA must apply for a restraining injunction to the High Court. This will be relevant if the reporting entity needs to be restrained from acting in such a way that would constitute a contravention of the AML/CFT Act.
90	Pecuniary penalty	If, on application to the High Court by the DIA, the court is satisfied that a reporting entity has engaged in an act or omission that would mean it is civilly liable.

The maximum pecuniary penalty is $200,000 for individuals, and $2 million for body corporates.

Criminal proceedings

Criminal proceedings may be commenced regardless of whether civil penalty proceedings have been commenced in connection with the same conduct. However, the "one penalty only rule" applies under the AML/CFT Act — a court shall not impose a civil or criminal penalty on a reporting entity if a penalty, either civil or criminal, has already been imposed for substantially the same conduct.

The following table summarises the offences provided for in the AML/CFT Act.

AML/CFT Act Section	Description of Offence	Maximum Penalty (ss 100 & 112 of the AML/CFT Act)
91	Engaging in a civil liability act knowingly or recklessly	Individual: 2 years' imprisonment and/or $300,00 fine Body corporate: $5m fine
92	Failure to report suspicious activity	Individual: 2 years' imprisonment and/or $300,00 fine Body corporate: $5m fine
93	Providing false or misleading information in relation to suspicious activity reports or prescribed transaction reports	Individual: 2 years' imprisonment and/or $300,00 fine Body corporate: $5m fine

AML/CFT Act Section	Description of Offence	Maximum Penalty (ss 100 & 112 of the AML/CFT Act)
94	Unlawful disclosure of suspicious activity reports or prescribed transaction reports	Individual: 2 years' imprisonment and/or $300,00 fine Body corporate: $5m fine
95	Failure to retain adequate records in relation to suspicious activities or prescribed transactions	Individual: 2 years' imprisonment and/or $300,00 fine Body corporate: $5m fine
96	Obstruction of investigations in relation to suspicious activity reports or prescribed transaction reports	Individual: 2 years' imprisonment and/or $300,00 fine Body corporate: $5m fine
97	Contravention of s 47(1) or s 48(1)	Individual: 2 years' imprisonment and/or $300,00 fine Body corporate: $5m fine
101	Structuring a transaction to avoid an AML/CFT Act obligation	Individual: 2 years' imprisonment and/or $300,00 fine Body corporate: $5m fine
102	Obstructing a supervisor	Individual: 3 months' imprisonment and/or $10,000 fine Body corporate: $50,000 fine
103	Providing false or misleading information to a supervisor	Individual: 3 months' imprisonment and/or $10,000 fine Body corporate: $50,000 fine
106	Failure to report cash $10,000 or more moved into or out of New Zealand	Individual: 3 months' imprisonment and/or $10,000 fine Body corporate: $50,000 fine
107	Failure to report cash $10,000 or more received by a person in New Zealand from overseas	Individual: 3 months' imprisonment and/or $10,000 fine Body corporate: $50,000 fine
108	Structuring cross-border transportation of cash to avoid AML/CFT obligations	Individual: 3 months' imprisonment and/or $10,000 fine Body corporate: $50,000 fine
110	Providing false or misleading information in connection with a cash report	Individual: 3 months' imprisonment and/or $10,000 fine Body corporate: $50,000 fine
111	Obstructing or not answering questions from Customs officers	Individual: 3 months' imprisonment and/or $10,000 fine Body corporate: $50,000 fine

Reference: Anti-Money Laundering and Countering Financing of Terrorism Act 2009, ss 78, 80, Pt 3, subparts 2A, 3A.

3-001 Supervisor enforcement activity

During the first 2 years of the inclusion of Phase 2 entities in the regime, the Department of Internal Affairs (DIA) appeared to limit its enforcement activities to mostly carrying out desktop reviews and issuing guidance for the professions that were new to the regime.

Since early 2021, there has been an observable increase in the DIA's public enforcement activity, with formal warnings being issued to a law firm, a real estate agency and financial institutions in 2021.

Kidd Legal

- On 17 March 2021, the DIA announced that on 27 January 2021 it had issued a formal warning under the Anti-Money Laundering and Countering Financing of Terrorism Act 2009 (AML/CFT Act) to the law firm Kidd Legal. The DIA stated that this was the first formal warning issued to the legal sector under the Act.
- The press release from the DIA stated that Kidd Legal had failed to meet several of its AML/CFT obligations relating to the establishment, implementation and maintenance of its AML/CFT compliance programme, and was unable to demonstrate how it would ensure compliance from staff. It had also failed to adequately assess the risk of ML or TF within the business
- The DIA required Kidd Legal to take immediate action to rectify all areas of non-compliance. In addition, the DIA noted that the issue of the warning would be referred to the New Zealand Law Society.

Property Brokers Limited

- On 1 March 2021, the DIA announced that on 14 January 2021 it had issued a formal warning to Property Brokers Limited, a real estate agency. The DIA stated that this was the first formal warning issued to a real estate agent under the Act.
- The press release from the DIA stated that Property Brokers Limited had failed to meet several of its AML/CFT obligations relating to the establishment, implementation and maintenance of its AML/CFT programme and the hiring and training of compliance staff. It also failed to establish adequate policies, procedures and controls for monitoring compliance, and failed to follow guidance material from the AML/CFT supervisors.

- The DIA required Property Brokers Limited to take immediate action to rectify all areas of non-compliance. The DIA noted that it would continue to closely monitor Property Brokers Limited.

Comment

The press releases issued by the DIA in relation to each of the formal warnings were very similar and provided little or no detail about how the reporting entities had specifically breached their duties under the AML/CFT Act. However, the use of a warning rather than prosecution action indicates that the DIA did not consider the breaches to be at the most serious end of the spectrum. It is not expected that a press release will accompany every formal warning issued by the DIA.

The authors expect that the next formal warning (accompanied by a press release) issued by DIA will be in respect of an accountant or accounting firm.

Warnings in relation to financial institutions

The other supervisors — the FMA and the RBNZ — have been much more active due entering the regime in 2009. Prosecution action can take months or years to complete. In June 2020, CLSA Premium New Zealand Limited, a derivatives issuer, was accused by the FMA of breaches of the AML/CFT Act. The breaches related to activity that occurred between April 2015 and November 2018. In May 2021, the reporting entity admitted the breaches, which included failures to conduct customer due diligence (CDD), to report suspicious transactions and activity, and in record keeping. At the time of writing, penalties were yet to be imposed; however, the company has provisioned $1 million in relation to the claims.

Westpac Banking Corporation

On 11 August 2021, the RBNZ issued a formal warning to the New Zealand branch of Westpac Banking Corporation (Westpac) for failing to report prescribed transactions as required by the Act. RBNZ found that Westpac designed and configured its prescribed transaction report (PTR) systems in a way that failed to detect and report all eligible international wire transfers, resulting in it failing to report almost 8,000 corporate transactions to overseas recipients between July 2018 and February 2019. It was stated that the "formal warning reflects the importance of the PTR regime in building an intelligence picture across New Zealand's financial system, and reiterates the seriousness with which we view non-compliance with the Act" (Police Financial Intelligence Unit, Deputy Governor and General Manager of Financial Stability, Geoff Bascand).

Sharesies Limited

On 13 August 2021, the FMA issued a formal warning to Sharesies Limited (Sharesies) for failing to comply with ss 16 and 17 of the Anti-Money Laundering and Countering Financing of Terrorism Act 2009.

In relation to the s 16 breach, the FMA found that Sharesies had not completed CDD verification for up to 7,815 of its customers (with an account balance of more than $1,000) before establishing a business relationship in accordance with the Amended Identity Verification Code of Practice 2013.

In relation to the s 17 breach, the FMA found that Sharesies failed to obtain information on the nature and purpose of its proposed business relationship from most of its customers and that it failed to obtain sufficient information to determine whether certain customers had opened an account on behalf of a trust and should be subject to enhanced CDD.

The issues were highlighted in a review of Sharesies processes by the FMA. There was no suggestion that the company had engaged in money laundering/financing of terrorism activity.

FMA director of supervision, James Greig, stated, "We have made this warning public because Sharesies' contraventions appeared to be symptomatic of a business that has grown quickly without ensuring fully effective processes and controls were in place from AML/CFT". He did not consider Sharesies' breaches to be deliberate.

The FMA has stated that the following actions must be taken by Sharesies to ensure compliance with the Act and to rectify its current breaches:

- Develop and implement an effective process to complete identity verification at the time of onboarding customers and provide training to staff on the process.
- Complete adequate customer identity verification on all customers and either:
  - — restrict withdrawals or transfers of financial products from those customers' accounts for which Sharesies has not completed adequate identity verification until such time as it has been completed, or
  - — comply with s 37 of the Act (prohibitions if CDD is not completed).
- Obtain sufficient information from all customers that have used the word "trust" in the account application process to determine if the individuals have opened an account as trustee of a trust or otherwise on behalf of a trust.
- Include a question in the account application process asking prospective customers for information on the nature and purpose of the proposed business relationship.
- Completed enhanced CDD on all customer accounts that are trusts.

Reference: Anti-Money Laundering and Countering Financing of Terrorism Act 2009, ss 16, 17.

3-002 Reported judgments

Below are judgments which have been issued in the High Court for conduct by reporting entities constituting civil liability acts under the Anti-Money Laundering and Countering Financing of Terrorism Act 2009 (AML/CFT Act).

Ping An Finance

A judgment (*DIA v Ping An Finance (Group) New Zealand Co Ltd & Xiaolan Xiao* [2017] NZHC 2363; (2017) 10 NZBLC 99-733) was issued in the Auckland High Court in September 2017 making orders requiring Ping An Finance (Group) New Zealand Company Limited (Ping An Finance) to pay a total of $5.29 million in pecuniary penalties. It also granted injunctions restraining the company and its sole director, Mr Xiaolan Xiao, from providing financial services that would cause either of them to be a reporting entity under the AML/CFT Act.

Following an investigation, the Department of Internal Affairs (DIA) brought an application for pecuniary penalties against Ping An Finance for multiple breaches of the AML/CFT Act. The DIA also sought injunctions restraining Ping An Finance and its sole director and shareholder, Mr Xiaolan Xiao (the second respondent), from carrying out financial activities.

Ping An Finance is a New Zealand incorporated company in the business of providing money remittance and foreign currency services. As it provides a financial service, it is a "reporting entity" and is subject to the customer due diligence (CDD), monitoring, reporting and record keeping obligations under the AML/CFT Act.

The Court was satisfied on a balance of probabilities that Ping An Finance had breached 5 different obligations under the AML/CFT Act and that each breach justified the imposition of pecuniary penalties payable to the Crown. The Court also granted the injunctions preventing Ping An Finance from carrying out financial activities until further order of the Court.

Comment

While this case is at the higher end of non-compliance, in that Mr Xiao was found to have demonstrated a "complete disregard for the AML/CFT Act's requirements", the penalties imposed reflect the serious consequences that will be imposed by the court for breaches of the AML/CFT Act.

This case demonstrates that reporting entities must not just comply with the AML/CFT Act but also be able to demonstrate their compliance via their records. Directors and boards of reporting entities must ensure that there are processes and procedures so that employees have sufficient guidance to fulfil the AML/CFT Act's requirements, and that these processes and procedures are sufficiently robust to effectively fulfil their AML/CFT Act obligations. Directors and boards of reporting entities must also be alive to the obligation to monitor and report suspicious transactions promptly.

Qian DuoDuo Ltd

A decision on 27 July 2018 against Qian DuoDuo Ltd (QDD) resulted in an order to pay $356,000 in pecuniary penalties (*DIA v Qian DuoDuo Ltd* [2018] NZHC 1887).

The DIA commenced an investigation into QDD's conduct in 2015. The investigation disclosed 4 civil liability acts which related to QDD's failure to:

- adequately identify and record the nature of several money remittance relationships with other businesses in risk assessments that were required under the AML/CFT Act
- carry out extended CDD in respect of a number of large or complex transactions and wire transfers
- conduct adequate ongoing CDD and account monitoring, and
- keep adequate records for most of its transactions during the relevant period.

Comment

It is notable that QDD was heavily reliant on advice provided by external consultants with regard to its compliance with the AML/CFT Act. In submissions, QDD argued that at all times it intended to comply with the regime and that it placed reliance on the consultant and the DIA in order to comply. QDD argued that its culpability in committing the civil liability acts should be reduced accordingly.

The High Court's decision is noteworthy for its discussion of the extent to which those performing captured activities can rely on the expertise of independent consultants to meet their obligations under the AML/CFT Act. On this occasion, the facts clearly illustrated that QDD had placed considerable reliance on advice provided by the consultant.

The Court acknowledged that the technical and complicated nature of the compliance regime under the AML/CFT Act, and the need for QDD to develop tailored solutions to achieve compliance, meant that QDD was essentially entirely reliant on the consultant. Despite the apparent shortcomings in QDD's compliance programme, the Court noted that on several occasions there were indications that the consultant believed QDD was largely compliant or on track to achieve compliance.

It was accepted that QDD was genuine in its desire to comply with the AML/CFT Act. Given its reliance on the consultant, and, in light of representations made by the consultant, the Court considered it difficult to identify what additional steps QDD could have been expected to have taken to ensure it was meeting its obligations. The consultant's approach was criticised as being process-driven and lacking necessary insight into how QDD actually operated its business.

The Court considered that this provided critical context to the shortcomings of QDD's actions. QDD's culpability in failing to comply with the AML/CFT Act was reduced considerably, and its liability assessed as being at the lowest end of the scale.

Despite the reduction in culpability of QDD, the judgment should not be seen as a decision which transfers the responsibility of compliance from service providers to external consultants. Ultimately, those performing captured activities are still responsible for their compliance with the AML/CFT Act, irrespective of whether they engage the services of independent consultants or not.

While the penalties imposed were much less than those in the previous decision of *Ping An Finance*, a penalty of $356,000 for conduct considered to be at the lowest end of the culpability scale serves as a reminder of the significant cost consequences of falling foul of the DIA in relation to these matters (Jack Stringer, Wynn Williams, "The cost of non-compliance: falling foul of AML/CFT obligations", 9 November 2018).

Jin Yuan Finance

Jin Yuan Finance was charged for repeated non-compliance with the AML/CFT regime. The DIA sought pecuniary penalties and restraining orders against the company and Rex Young, a shareholder and director.

The High Court found that Jin Yuan Finance committed high-end non-compliance breaches against the AML/CFT Act (*DIA v Jin Yuan Finance Ltd and Rex Young* [2019] NZHC 2510). These breaches included:

- failing to conduct CDD
- failing to adequately monitor accounts and transactions
- entering into or continuing a business relationship with an individual who did not provide satisfactory evidence of their identity
- failing to report suspicious transactions, and
- failing to keep records of suspicious transactions.

The Court was further influenced by the fact that it believed Jin Yuan Finance to have engaged in misleading conduct. This was inferred from evidence that Jin Yuan Finance deliberately concealed its use of non-disclosed bank accounts and made artificial representations to the DIA.

Jin Yuan Finance admitted to civil liability acts without specification. The Court charged Jin Yuan Finance with a pecuniary penalty to the sum of $4,007,750. The penalty reflected the company's persistent failure to comply with the AML/CFT regime.

OTT Trading Group Ltd (Auckland) and MSI Group Ltd (Christchurch)

The DIA commenced proceedings against these 2 New Zealand-based money remitters seeking injunctions against the companies and 3 individuals associated with the companies that would prevent them from providing regulated services in the future.

The individuals agreed to settle the proceeding (*DIA v OTT Trading Group Ltd* [2020] NZHC 1005). Under the settlement, the individuals agreed that injunctive relief was appropriate. In respect of 2 of the individuals, Lang J made various orders restraining each of them from acting as the compliance officer of any reporting entity, engaging in any activity that would make them a "senior manager" of any reporting entity, and engaging in any activity that would make them a reporting entity. The third individual, OTT's compliance officer, was restrained from acting as the compliance officer of any reporting entity.

The DIA then sought judgment against the companies. In particular, it sought both a civil pecuniary penalty and injunctions restraining each company from carrying out any financial activity in the future that would cause it to be a reporting entity under the AML/CFT Act (*DIA v OTT Trading Group Ltd* [2020] NZHC 1663).

The DIA alleged that both companies failed to meet their AML/CFT obligations to:

- establish, implement or maintain a compliance programme — maximum penalty $2 million
- conduct CDD — maximum penalty $2 million
- adequately monitor accounts and transactions — maximum penalty $1 million, and
- keep records — maximum penalty $2 million.

In respect of OTT, the High Court found that it consistently failed to meet the requirements of the AML/CFT Act. There were deficiencies in the compliance programme "in part caused by deficient risk assessments". The compliance officer did not know which of OTT's risk assessments was the current version. The compliance programme was not appropriately implemented. The company regularly failed to conduct CDD. Enhanced CDD had not been carried out in circumstances required by the AML/CFT Act. In fact, the compliance officer was unaware of the circumstances in which OTT would be required to undertake enhanced CDD. OTT had no policies, procedures or controls to ensure that transactions were in line with OTT's knowledge of customers and their risk profiles. On multiple occasions, OTT was unable to provide the DIA with records requested.

MSI had no written policies or procedures to enable compliant CDD, transaction monitoring or record keeping. It undertook no account monitoring. It never submitted an annual report. It had poor record keeping systems. Although MSI attempted to obtain basic identity information and evidence, it completely ignored its obligation to carry out enhanced CDD. Lang J commented at [69]:

> "Ms Duan's admission that MSI did not seek information required for enhanced due diligence out of fear of losing customers is particularly concerning. It suggests a conscious decision not to comply with the regulatory regime for fear of the financial consequences that would follow. Such conduct requires the imposition of a stern penalty."

OTT was ordered to pay a pecuniary penalty of $3.1 million and MSI a pecuniary penalty of $4.485 million. When deciding the amount of the penalties, the Judge considered that the conduct of each of the companies (which included misleading the DIA) was an aggravating factor that increased the amount of the penalties. There were no mitigating factors.

Injunctive relief restraining OTT from carrying out any financial activities that would cause it to be deemed a "financial institution" as defined in s 5 of the AML/CFT Act was also granted. MSI had been struck off the Companies Register. It was reinstated for the purpose of the proceeding, but the Judge decided there was no practical purpose of issuing injunctive relief against it.

Jiaxin Finance

In November 2019, the High Court ruled on the first criminal prosecution since the AML/CFT regime came into force. This case marked the first time that the suspicious transactions test arose in criminal prosecution (*R v QF, FC and JFL* [2019] NZHC 3058).

The case involved charges in relation to 311 transactions that had a sum total of approximately $53 million. The transactions were carried out on behalf of an overseas client.

The company and 2 individuals (Ms Che and Mr Fu) were charged for failing to:

- conduct CDD (specifically for wire transfers)
- report a suspicious transaction, and
- keep adequate records relating to a suspicious transaction.

Ms Che was additionally charged with structuring a transaction to avoid requirements of the AML/CFT regime.

The individuals unsuccessfully argued that the overseas client was a customer of one of the individuals, rather than a customer of the company. The Court found that the client was a customer of the company "in substance".

The Court found the parties guilty on all charges. The judgment qualified that the offence of failing to report or keep adequate records about a suspicious transaction requires the defendant to have considered all known circumstances and have reasonable grounds to suspect that the transaction is, or may be, suspicious. The Court applied an objective test of limited *mens rea,* rather than imposing strict liability. (This position aligns with current legal precedent in the United Kingdom, which is also an objective test.)

This case established criminal precedent for the crime of artificially structuring operations to escape liability under the AML/CFT regime. Accordingly, it is the first criminal prosecution since the introduction of the AML/CFT regime in 2013. The judgment also provides detail of the legal standard for suspicious transaction obligations.

A sentencing hearing was held on 3 March 2020.

Jiaxin Finance — sentencing

Jiaxin Finance Ltd, a money-remitting and currency exchange business, assisted by its owner Qiang Fu and his mother, Fuqin Che, were sentenced for offences under the AML/CFT Act.

Jiaxin Finance Ltd was sentenced to pay a fine of \$2.55 million for breaches of ss 91, 92 and 95 of the Act. Mr. Fu was sentenced to pay a fine of \$180,000 for breaches of ss 91, 92 and 95, and Ms Che was sentenced to pay a fine of \$202,000 for breaches of ss 91, 92, 95 and 101. See *R v Jiaxin Finance Ltd, Qiang Fu and Fuquin Che* [2020] NZHC 366.

Starting point

The defendants faced 3 separate representative charges: failure to conduct CDD, failure to keep records and failure to report a suspicious transaction. Ms Che was subject to a fourth charge: structuring a transaction to avoid the application of the AML/CFT Act. She did this by making 14 separate cash deposits totalling \$710,772 into his New Zealand bank account. These payments were spread over a period of 4 days and made at different branches of the bank.

Justice Walker applied a 2-stage approach to sentencing. Section 13 of the Sentencing Act 2002 requires that a fine is regarded as the presumptively appropriate sentence, unless the presumption is displaced when:

- the purpose for which the sentence is being imposed cannot be achieved by imposing a fine, or
- the application of any of the principles in s 8 [of the Sentencing Act] make a fine inappropriate, or

- any provision applicable to the particular offence in [the Sentencing Act] or any other enactment provides a presumption in favour of imposing any other sentence or requires the court to impose any other sentence, or
- a fine on its own or in addition to a sentence of reparation, would otherwise be clearly inadequate in the circumstances.

Justice Walker said 3 cases have been taken in New Zealand by the DIA against money remittance businesses under the civil regime. In each, significant civil pecuniary penalties had been ordered. In her sentencing notes she stated at [17]:

> "While the risk of reoffending by those found guilty of these sorts of offences may be low, the community still requires a sentence which acts as a deterrent to others."

Walker J at [60]–[63] noted:

> "[60] . . . I propose to set a global starting point of 60 per cent of the maximum fine available for a single charge. I do so on the basis that the offending, although serious, falls below the most serious of its kind in the context of an industry coming to grips with the regulatory scheme. I therefore adopt the following starting points:
>
> (a) Jiaxin — a fine of $3 million;
>
> (b) Mr Fu — a fine of $180,000;
>
> (c) Ms Che — a fine of $180,000.
>
> [61] Ms Che is also convicted of a further charge of structuring a transaction to avoid the application of the AML/CFT Act. The maximum penalty for this offence is also two year's imprisonment and a fine of up to $300,000.
>
> [62] The Crown, relying on two Australian decisions under the equivalent legislation, suggests a starting point of 50 per cent in the first instance. However, when considering totality, the Crown submits that the appropriate sentence is the imposition of a further fine of $50,000 and an increase of six months' imprisonment.
>
> [63] The Australian cases have limited utility. However, I accept that a further fine is warranted. The starting point for this offence is a fine of $45,000."

Aggravating and mitigating factors

- Mr Fu
  - The starting point for Mr Fu was unchanged.
  - The Crown's assertion of prior convictions was put to one side. While Mr. Fu had a prior conviction in China, the documentary evidence of the conviction could not be reliably proved to the

requisite standard. The exact nature of the regulatory non-compliance was also unclear from the translation of the Chinese language facsimile. Further, Walker J determined that there was no evidence to suggest that Mr Fu lacked the means to pay a fine.

- — Walker J was satisfied that the fines imposed were substantial, they punished the behaviour, and they were high enough to deter others from offending. She did not consider a term of imprisonment.

- Jiaxin
  - — The starting point for Jiaxin was reduced by 15%, bringing the fine to $2.55 million.
  - — Walker J gave credit for Jiaxin's prior record, and she also took into account the impact on Mr Fu as sole shareholder and director.
- Ms Che
  - — A discount of 10% was awarded, reducing the fine imposed to $202,000.
  - — Ms Che had no previous convictions; she was 65 years old and had suffered ill health since 2013. Counsel argued that these factors bore witness to a reduced probability of reoffending.
  - — Walker J noted her concern that the Provisional Advice to Court report suggested that Ms Che did not have any real insight into her offending and lacked remorse.
  - — Walker J was not persuaded that an additional sentence of home detention or term of imprisonment was needed.

Westpac Australia

In September 2020, the Australian Transaction Reports and Analysis Centre (AUSTRAC) and Westpac Banking Corporation Australia (Westpac Australia) agreed that Westpac Australia would pay an A$1.3 billion penalty, relating to millions of breaches of Australia's Anti-Money Laundering and Counter-Terrorism Financing Act 2006 (the Australian AML/CFT Act). The penalty was confirmed by the Federal Court of Australia (FCA) in October 2020.

The Statement of Agreed Facts and Admissions which was lodged in the FCA on 24 September 2020 set out the basis for the orders, which were founded upon the agreed facts regarding Westpac's repeated non-compliance with the Australian AML/CFT Act. Westpac Australia agreed with AUSTRAC's contention that this non-compliance was established by contravention of the AML/CFT Act on over 23 million occasions.

The Statement of Agreed Facts and Admissions stated that Westpac Australia failed to:

- appropriately monitor and assess money laundering (ML) and terrorism financing (TF) risks in correspondent banking relationship

- report over 19.5 million international funds transfer instructions to AUSTRAC for transfers in and out of Australia, for almost 5 years
- supply other banks in the transfer chain with information about the source of funds
- record the origin of some international fund transfers, and
- conduct adequate CDD on transactions to countries with financial risk, such as South East Asia and the Philippines.

In addition to AUSTRAC's original allegations, which were agreed, Westpac Australia also admitted to approximately 76,000 additional contraventions which expanded the original statement of claim. These new contraventions related to additional reporting failures, failures to reasonably monitor customers for transactions related to possible child exploitation, and failures to assess the ML and TF risks associated with correspondent banking relationships.

The Reserve Bank of New Zealand has said that it will monitor the findings against Westpac Australia for potential relevance to Westpac's New Zealand operations.

Andrew Simpson

A 41-year-old Auckland lawyer, Andrew Simpson, pleaded guilty in November 2019 to ML transactions that aided the Comancheros Motorcycle Club. This case relates to substantive money-laundering, as well as resultant breaches of the AML/CFT Act. Mr Simpson also used his knowledge of the anti-money laundering (AML)/countering the financing of terrorism (CFT) regime to assist the Comancheros to evade detection by AML/CFT processes that were in place at the financial institutions the gang used to launder money.

Mr Simpson was arrested following a series of police raids across Auckland in April 2019, which saw more than $3.7 million in assets seized, along with luxury cars, motorcycles, luxury luggage and jewellery.

Mr Simpson pleaded guilty on 13 counts of ML totalling more than $2.4 million.

Sentencing of Andrew Simpson

Mr Simpson was sentenced to 2 years and 9 months' imprisonment after pleading guilty to 13 charges of money laundering under s 243(2) of the Crimes Act 1961 (*R v Daniels* [2020] NZHC 275). He surrendered his practising certificate upon his guilty plea.

In his 25 February 2020 sentencing notes, van Bohemen J said Mr Simpson was the solicitor employed by members of and people affiliated with the New Zealand chapter of the Comanchero motorcycle gang.

A Police investigation, which began in 2018, uncovered a sophisticated operation for the import and supply of controlled drugs and associated ML. Mr Simpson and Comancheros vice president Tyson Daniels were arrested.

Justice van Bohemen noted at [6]:

> "The money was deposited into structured trust accounts, usually in amounts of less than $10,000 at a time at various bank branches in an effort to disguise their origin and to avoid raising suspicion. To further avoid detection, the money was also channelled through associated companies such as Heavy Heavy Ltd, which provided an apparently legitimate source of income for Mr Daniels and others in the group and was also used to launder funds derived from criminal activity."

He said that, as the gang's solicitor, Mr Simpson was the facilitator of the ML operation.

Knowledge

Justice van Bohemen stated at [9]:

> "You used your specialist knowledge as a lawyer to advise on structuring the laundering scheme across the multiple trust accounts you set up. You also channelled money through your solicitor's trust account and made deposits into the accounts yourself. You knew what you were doing was dodgy. Intercepted phone calls reveal that you told one of the others involved in the scheme that if he deposited 'nine' at each 'drop' it would not get 'flagged' by which you clearly meant avoiding the banks' reporting thresholds."

Approximately $1.2 million was deposited or transferred into accounts that Mr Simpson established for the scheme. He retained a little over $18,000 as remuneration for his work as a lawyer. The balance was transferred into trust accounts Mr Simpson set up for gang members. Using cash laundered through his trust account, he authorised payments on behalf of the trusts and made payments directly to luxury motor dealers for vehicles purchased by gang members — including 2 Rolls Royces, a Bentley, a Lamborghini and 2 top-end Mercedes Benz. He also assisted in the purchase of a $1.38 million property using several different trust accounts and creating another purpose-built trust account for the transaction to avoid detection.

Mr Simpson contested the quantum in the charges to which he had pleaded guilty, which came to a total of just over $2.2 million. His counsel argued that he should be sentenced on the basis that he dealt culpably with just over $1.4 million.

However, Justice van Bohemen noted at [15]:

> "Having regard to section 24(2) of the [Sentencing] Act [2002], I have indicated that I do not regard the difference between $1.4 million and $2.2 million as materially different in the context of offending by a man

> in Mr Simpson's position and the difference in amounts has not affected the starting point I set for your sentence or the overall length of the sentence."

Starting point

In setting the starting point of Mr Simpson's sentence, van Bohemen J had regard to the following circumstances:

- Mr Simpson was a key facilitator of the ML scheme and made it work. He set up the trusts through which the funds flowed.
- He made it work because of his position as a lawyer and as a member of a professional body. He used his professional skill and knowledge, and solicitor's trust fund, both to make it happen and to lend respectability.
- He did not just set up the legal and administrative arrangements to enable the operation, but took part in it personally and advised others on how to avoid triggering the banks' reporting thresholds.
- Mr Simpson said he was duped and he did not appreciate the nature of the transactions in which he had become involved. However, he acknowledged that he had suspicions that some of the transactions may have involved tax avoidance. He said he turned a blind eye to the source of the funds.
- It was only very late in the offending, in November 2018, that Mr Simpson undertook his own investigations and appreciated that his clients had been deported from Australia for gang-related offending.

Justice van Bohemen commented at [44]:

> "There can be little doubt that you were at least naive and incredibly foolish to get involved in this scheme. I accept that you did not know directly, as Mr Daniels knew, that you were involved in laundering funds from serious drug offending. I also accept that the fee charged for your time would not have been unreasonable had your advice been for setting up trusts to enable lawful transactions, and that in comparison to the benefits enjoyed by Mr Daniels, the benefits of your participation in the operation were modest."

In addition, Mr Simpson was acting in his professional capacity, and when he chose to continue his involvement, even when his suspicions were raised, he not only placed his personal gain above his duties as a lawyer risked bringing his profession into disrepute. That was a significant distinguishing factor (at [47]).

There was a significant difference between Mr Simpson's situation of largely reckless involvement in a scheme devised by others with only modest personal gain, and that of Mr Daniels, who knew exactly what was going on and gained a substantial personal benefit.

A starting point of 4 years and 6 months' imprisonment was appropriate for Mr Simpson.

Mitigating factors

Mr Simpson's pre-sentencer stated that he felt huge regret; that he had found the experience humiliating; and that his offending stemmed from naivety, although he acknowledged that things "ramped up". The report writer had noted he had strong family and community connections.

Justice van Bohemen said he was satisfied that Mr Simpson's remorse was genuine as was his commitment to rehabilitation. These factors, combined with the lack of a previous criminal record, the strong community support he continued to enjoy, and the support of his family, warranted a substantial discount of 15%.

That reduced his sentence to 3 years and 9 months' imprisonment, to which was added a further reduction of 12 months for an early guilty plea. That produced an end sentence of 2 years and 9 months' imprisonment.

Duress?

There is no mention of pressure or duress in the judgment of van Bohemen J. It begs the question: did the Comancheros make it difficult for Mr Simpson to refuse to become involved? If so, was Mr Simpson reluctant to reveal this information to the court?

Reference: Anti-Money Laundering and Countering Financing of Terrorism Act 2009, ss 5, 91, 92, 95, 101.

Chapter 4

Current issues and recent developments

4-000 Current issues affecting lawyers

The New Zealand Law Society (NZLS) has been engaging regularly and constructively with the Department of Internal Affairs (DIA) and the Ministry of Justice (MOJ) in relation to anti-money laundering (AML)/countering the financing of terrorism (CFT) matters since 2016, when it was recommended that lawyers be subject to the regulation in this area.

There is concern within the legal community that the compliance burden is placing significant additional pressure on resources and staff wellbeing in an already highly regulated profession. The following is a summary of some of the areas causing concern.

AML/CFT audits

Lawyers are required to complete an audit under s 59 of the Anti-Money Laundering and Countering Financing of Terrorism Act 2009 (AML/CFT Act). Two potential barriers to compliance with this section are as follows:

- There is a shortage of AML/CFT auditors appropriately qualified to audit law firms in New Zealand. Although an increasing number of organisations are offering AML/CFT audits, many do not understand law firms, the specific AML/CFT issues facing them or a lawyer's obligation of client confidentiality.
- There are compliance costs associated with engaging an independent auditor.

The default time for AML/CFT independent audits has recently increased from 2 years to 3 years, with some businesses potentially being eligible to be audited every 4 years. This will go a little way to alleviating concerns relating to the compliance costs associated with independent audits.

Other relevant issues regarding audits are as follows:

- Auditors should not be provided with suspicious activity report (SAR) records. Under s 46 of the AML/CFT Act a reporting entity may only disclose information relating to suspicious activities to certain specified persons, and auditors are not included.
- The quality of audits and the requirement to report any deficiencies to the DIA in the annual report is an issue. A thorough audit by an appropriately qualified auditor is likely to reveal certain deficiencies in the law firm's risk assessment or compliance programme, especially if it is the law firm's first audit. The law firm will be required to disclose these to the DIA in its annual report. The same deficiencies may not have been picked up by a less experienced or qualified auditor or by an auditor carrying out a less thorough audit.

Designated business groups

Creating a designated business group (DBG) is potentially a way for law firms to alleviate some of the compliance burden. In theory, reporting entities that are part of the same group of companies can design and implement a compliance programme for the group, rather than each entity having its own compliance obligations. However, NZLS is aware that the current definition of a DBG in the AML/CFT Act effectively prevents lawyers from utilising a DBG to expedite compliance.

This is because law firms in New Zealand are typically structured as partnerships, but the DBG provisions in the AML/CFT Act contemplate corporate structures.

Under the Lawyers and Conveyancers Act 2006, a law firm cannot technically "own" or be a subsidiary of another law firm. Therefore, law firm arrangements cannot fall under the definition of DBGs.

The definition of DBG includes a group of 2 or more law firms where each member is "a related law firm . . . that is a reporting entity in New Zealand". The DIA released guidance on the "meaning of 'related' for DBGs by DNFBPs" in August 2020. This states that "related" in this context should be interpreted to mean "connected" or "associated":

> "That means that a commercial agreement or alliance between a group or [sic] law firms, or group of accounting practices . . . may cause those firms to be related.
>
> . . .

> Relevant considerations are likely to include the type of commercial agreement . . . and the extent of the connection or association between the potential DBG members."

The DIA determines the eligibility to form a DBG on a case-by-case basis. However, this interpretation of "related" by the DIA may assist those law firms who are parties to commercial alliance arrangements to form DBGs.

The obligations of client confidentiality and legal professional privilege applicable to lawyers present additional complications for the use of DBGs by law firms.

Disbursements received in advance being treated as "managing client funds"

Regulation 24AB of the AML/CFT (Exemptions) Regulations 2011 states that if a law firm or accounting practice receives a payment from a customer for the purpose of making a payment to one of the below parties, the transaction is not captured by the AML/CFT Act:

- a New Zealand Government department, the New Zealand Police, or a local authority
- a barrister, or
- any other third party carrying out business in New Zealand, where the payment relates to the provision of that business, and where the value of the transaction (or series of transactions) is less than $1,000.

Customer due diligence on existing trust clients and clients from AML/CFT deficient jursidictions

Different law firms have been taking different approaches as to whether customer due diligence (CDD) is necessary for existing trust clients and clients from AML/CFT deficient jurisdictions if there has been no material change in the nature or purpose of the business relationship.

On 9 September 2020, the DIA released new guidance in "Customer due diligence obligations for 'existing customers' of law firms". This states that, at 1 July 2018, a law firm was not required to immediately conduct or update its CDD for its existing clients. Rather, a staged approach is anticipated in which CDD for existing clients is gradually brought up to the required level over time as new instructions from these clients are received.

Where there has been no material change in the nature or purpose of the business relationship for existing trust clients and clients from AML/CFT deficient jurisdictions, the AML/CFT Act contains other inter-related provisions in which CDD must be undertaken, including in the following circumstances:

- If the client seeks to conduct a complex, unusually large transaction or unusual pattern of transactions with no apparent or visible economic or lawful purpose, enhanced CDD is required.
- If the client is the originator of a wire transfer, enhanced CDD in accordance with ss 27–28 is required.
- As part of ongoing CDD and account monitoring, a law firm must regularly review any information it holds about the client. Given that the AML/CFT Act is risk-based, existing clients who are higher risk (such as trusts and clients from AML/CFT deficient jurisdictions) should be prioritised for CDD review or update.

For a full list of circumstances, refer to the DIA's guidance in "Customer due diligence obligations for 'existing customers' of law firms".

Simplified CDD and registered banks

The "existing customer" provisions in the AML/CFT Act are considered sufficient to cover a lawyer's relationship in existence on 1 July 2018 with a registered bank.

Any new business relationships with registered banks will only warrant simplified CDD in accordance with ss 18–20 of the AML/CFT Act.

Advising in advance of a transaction taking place

In principle, in urgent circumstances advice can be provided before completing CDD. However, it may be difficult to file a SAR if red flags arise when providing initial advice and no CDD has been completed.

Lawyers should make a file note if they believe they are required to provide urgent advice for a transaction. The DIA has suggested that this would help prevent a negative ruling during subsequent audits.

Real estate agents, and lawyers advising real estate agents, should take particular note of ss 14(3) (standard CDD), 18(3A) (simplified CDD) and 22(6) (enhanced CDD) of the Act, which prescribe different and more onerous rules for real estate agents completing client due diligence. These sections, in concert with reg 24A of the Anti-Money Laundering and Countering Financing of Terrorism (Definitions) Regulations 2011, provide that a real estate agent must, in relation to commercial lease transactions, conduct CDD before the real estate agent presents an offer of lease to the landlord of the commercial property, and, in relation to all other real estate transactions, conduct CDD before entering into an agency agreement (within the meaning of s 4(1) of the Real Estate Agents Act 2008) with a customer.

Domestic wire transfers — proposed exemption

The DIA has advised that further guidance is coming in relation to domestic wire transfers.

There is potential for the exemption of wire transfers in the future, based on the position that the obligation to report on wire transfers is essentially a duplication of the trust account requirements. However, at the time of writing this exemption was considered low on the priority list.

Administration of estates — exemption

An exemption exists where a reporting entity carries out the role of executor or administrator of an estate (reg 24AD of the Anti-Money Laundering and Countering Financing of Terrorism (Exemptions) Regulations 2011) and a limited exemption exists for services provided to an executor or administrator of an estate (reg 24AE).

When a law firm is carrying out the role of executor or administrator of an estate, it does not have to conduct CDD in respect of captured activities provided to the estate and will be exempt from all AML/CFT obligations in relation to those captured activities, except those relating to SAR and associated record keeping.

When a law firm performs a captured activity for an executor or administration (but is not the executor or administrator itself), the law firm is exempt from the requirements to verify the source of wealth/funds when conducting enhanced CDD on the executor/administrator and does not need to terminate the business relationship where CDD cannot be completed. In all other respects, when providing services to the executor/administrator, the law firm must comply with the AML/CFT Act obligations. The only exception to this is where the law firm is providing services to an executor/administrator that is also a reporting entity. In these circumstances, the law firm will not need to conduct CDD on the executor/administrator and is only required to comply with SAR and associated record keeping obligations.

Exemptions in relation to barristers

There is a class exemption for barristers sole from certain provisions of the AML/CFT Act, valid from 15 March 2021 until 15 March 2026. There are 2 circumstances where the exemption may apply:

- barristers who receive instructions from a solicitor (who is not an in-house lawyer, other than an in-house lawyer employed by the Crown) in respect of the customer, or
- barristers who receive instructions from the Crown.

The exemptions from each of these situations are slightly different from each other. See Anti-Money Laundering and Countering Financing of Terrorism (Class Exemptions) Amendment Notice (No 2) 2021, which inserts a new Pt 15 into the 2018 principal Exemption Notice.

Barristers who receive instructions from a solicitor (who is not an in-house lawyer, other than an in-house lawyer employed by the Crown) in respect of the customer are exempt from the following provisions of the Act in relation to the customer:

- ss 11 (CDD) and 12 (reliance on risk assessment when establishing level of risk)
- ss 14–21 (standard and simplified CDD)
- s 22(1), (2), and (5) (circumstances in which enhanced CDD applies)
- ss 11A–25 (enhanced CDD)
- s 26 (politically exposed persons (PEPs))
- s 30 (new or developing technologies, or products, that might favour anonymity)
- s 31 (ongoing CDD and account monitoring)
- ss 37–39 (prohibitions)
- ss 56 (reporting entity must have AML/CFT programme and AML/CFT compliance officer) and 57 (minimum requirements for AML/CFT programme)
- ss 58 (risk assessment) and 59 (review and audit of risk assessment and AML/CFT programmes)
- s 59B (who carries out audit)
- s 60 (annual AML/CFT report).

Barristers who receive instructions from the Crown are exempt from the following provisions of the Act:

- s 11 (CDD)
- s 12 (reliance on risk assessment when establishing level of risk)
- ss 14–17 (standard and simplified CDD)
- s 22(2) and (5) (circumstances in which enhanced CDD applies)
- s 26 (PEPs)
- s 30 (new or developing technologies, or products, that might favour anonymity)
- ss 56 (reporting entity must have AML/CFT programme and AML/CFT compliance officer) and 57 (minimum requirements for AML/CFT programme)
- ss 58 (risk assessment) and 59 (review and audit of risk assessment and AML/CFT programmes)
- s 59B (who carries out audit)
- s 60 (annual AML/CFT report).

Exemption in relation to corporate trustee companies

The MOJ is also currently considering an exemption for situations where a law firm or accounting practice's trustee company is a reporting entity under the AML/CFT Act. As an interim measure, a limited exemption was put in place in respect of annual reporting. The MOJ is considering the options in respect of either an alternate approach or an exemption. See DIA "Extension on interim solution for corporate trustee annual report obligations", 17 May 2021.

The waiver of the annual report obligation included terms that the parent reporting entity include information about the corporate trustee company's activities in its own annual report. The exemption also extended to corporate trustee companies wholly owned by:

- an accountant in public practice, and practising in partnership, who is a partner
- a solicitor in public practice, and practising in partnership, who is a partner
- a solicitor in sole practice, and
- an accountant in sole practice.

(See DIA *Corporate Trustee Annual Reporting Requirements 2019.*)

Corporate trustee companies are, for the time being, treated as being in a DBG with their parent reporting entity.

Application of SAR provisions

There has been concern regarding the level of uncertainty in the application of the SAR provisions to law firms.

More specifically, an issue arises if a reporting entity is carrying out work for a client that would warrant a SAR, except in the instance such work is not a captured activity.

Additionally, the AML/CFT Act currently provides auditors with a greater ability to report SARs than the reporting entity itself. It is assumed that this was not the intention. The view taken by NZLS is that an external auditor should not have access to privileged material.

Clarity is required on these points.

Late filing of annual reports

In April 2020, the DIA advised that no adverse compliance action would be taken against any DNFBP that was not able to complete its first independent audit by the relevant deadline, providing they had acted in good faith. However, this relief did not apply to the filing of the 2020 annual report.

Failure to file an annual report may attract fines. Knowingly or recklessly failing to file an annual report may be considered an offence. For further information, see the Enforcement section of this book.

References: Anti-Money Laundering and Countering Financing of Terrorism Act 2009, ss 11, 12, 14, 15, 16, 17, 18, 19, 20, 21, 22(1), (2), (5), (6), 23, 24, 25, 26, 27, 28, 30, 31, 37, 38, 39, 46, 56, 57, 58, 59, 59B, 60.

Anti-Money Laundering and Countering Financing of Terrorism (Exemptions) Regulations 2011, reg 24AB.

Anti-Money Laundering and Countering Financing of Terrorism (Definitions) Regulations 2011, reg 24A.

Anti-Money Laundering and Countering Financing of Terrorism (Exemptions) Regulations 2011, regs 24AD, 24AE.

Anti-Money Laundering and Countering Financing of Terrorism (Class Exemptions) Amendment Notice (No 2) 2021.

4-001 The high value dealers' regime

High value dealers (HVDs) were included in the anti-money laundering (AML)/countering the financing of terrorism (CFT) regime with effect from 1 August 2019. The Department of Internal Affairs (DIA) is the relevant supervisor of HVDs.

The HVD sector is particularly vulnerable to money laundering and terrorism financing. Criminals target HVDs to launder the proceeds of their crimes to avoid detection. Some criminals may buy expensive goods with cash, and then simply re-sell these goods in a bid to obtain "clean money". This may be for personal use or to fund more criminal activity. Others may retain the expensive goods to use personally, trade with other criminals, or take them to markets overseas to avoid detection in New Zealand.

Summary of Anti-Money Laundering and Countering Financing of Terrorism Act 2009 obligations not applicable to HVDs

The obligations of HVDs under the Anti-Money Laundering and Countering Financing of Terrorism Act 2009 (AML/CFT Act) are less onerous than those of other reporting entities.

HVDs do not need to:

- appoint a compliance officer
- undertake a risk assessment
- develop an AML/CFT compliance programme
- submit suspicious activity reports (SARs) (although they may do so), and
- conduct enhanced customer due diligence (CDD).

High-value dealer

Section 5(1) of the AML/CFT Act defines a "high-value dealer" as follows:

- a person who is in trade and, in the ordinary course of business, buys or sells all or any of the following articles by way of a cash transaction or a series of related cash transactions, if the total value of the transactions is equal to or above the applicable threshold value:

- — jewellery
- — watches
- — gold, silver, or other precious metals
- — diamonds, sapphires, or other precious stones
- — paintings
- — prints
- — protected foreign objects (within the meaning of s 2(1) of the Protected Objects Act 1975)
- — protected New Zealand objects (within the meaning of s 2(1) of the Protected Objects Act 1975)
- — sculptures
- — photographs
- — carvings in any medium
- — other artistic or cultural artefacts
- — motor vehicles (within the meaning of s 6(1) of the Motor Vehicle Sales Act 2003)
- — ships (within the meaning of s 2(1) of the Maritime Transport Act 1994), and

- includes any person who carries out the activities referred to above as a registered auctioneer (within the meaning of s 4(1) of the Auctioneers Act 2013), but,
- does not include any person, to the extent that they are engaged in providing services other than the buying or selling of articles referred to above, including the following services:
  - — mining precious metals or precious stones
  - — manufacturing jewellery
  - — crafting or polishing precious stones, and
- does not include any person to the extent that they are engaged in the buying or selling of precious metals or precious stones for industrial purposes.

Regulation 5AB of the Anti-Money Laundering and Countering Financing of Terrorism (Definitions) Amendment Regulations 2019 (the 2019 Regulations) provides:

> "For the purposes of the definition of high value dealer in section 5(1) of the Act, the applicable threshold is $10,000."

Regulation 21AB of the 2019 Regulations clarifies and restricts the manner in which registered auctioneers are within the scope of the AML/CFT Act by declaring that such a person is not a reporting entity unless they:

- provide real estate agency work
- carry out trading activity in any of the items specified in the definition of HVD, or
- are otherwise a reporting entity for any other reason.

If somebody is an HVD, they will be captured by the AML/CFT Act if all 3 of the following conditions are met:

- they buy or sell goods of the type listed in the definition above in the ordinary course of business, and
- cash is the means of payment for the transaction, and
- the cash transaction (or related cash transaction) is $10,000 or more.

Exclusions

Below are some examples of where the HVD would not be captured under the AML/CFT Act:

- buying, selling, or trading goods of the type listed in the definition otherwise than in the ordinary course of business
- buying, selling, or trading goods of the type listed in the definition using a means of payment other than cash
- trading in cash below $10,000 (although related cash transactions of $10,000 or more are captured by the AML/CFT Act), and
- buying or selling goods that are not listed in the definition.

See DIA guideline *High value dealers: Complying with the Anti-Money Laundering and Countering Financing of Terrorism Act 2009* (updated March 2021) at 12.

High value goods

If somebody is providing services in relation to high-value goods they, are not captured. Examples of services performed in relation to high-value goods include:

- mining of precious metals or stones
- manufacturing or maintenance of jewellery
- crafting, maintaining or polishing precious stones.

Buying or selling precious metals or stones for industrial purposes is not captured, and private sales of high-value goods are similarly not captured.

It therefore follows that if an HVD is involved in a cash transaction (or a series of related cash transactions) equal to or above the prescribed threshold of $10,000, they will be captured by the AML/CFT Act. It is important to note that if the transaction is not completed with cash, the activity will not be captured and there will be no corresponding AML/CFT obligations. The definition of cash is therefore very important.

Cash

Cash is defined in s 5(1) of the AML/CFT Act as meaning physical currency (either New Zealand dollars or any other foreign currency), or bearer-negotiable instruments. Bearer-negotiable instruments are defined as including the following:

- a bill of exchange
- a cheque
- a promissory note
- a bearer bond
- a traveller's cheque
- a money order, postal order, or similar order
- any other instrument prescribed by regulations.

It is important to note that all cheques, including bank drafts, are considered bearer-negotiable instruments for the purposes of the AML/CFT Act.

The distinction between transactions involving physical currency and those involving bearer-negotiable instruments is mainly concerned with prescribed transaction reports (PTRs): PTRs are required where the transaction is being facilitated with physical currency, but are not necessary for transactions involving bearer-negotiable instruments.

Because cheques are considered bearer-negotiable instruments, HVDs cannot avoid their AML/CFT obligations by telling customers to use bank cheques rather than cash in the form of notes and coins in these transactions. However, if customers deposit cash directly into the bank account of the HVD, this will not be captured.

Compliance obligations applicable to HVDs

HVDs have fewer obligations under the AML/CFT Act than certain other reporting entities. The following obligations apply to HVDs if they are captured by the AML/CFT Act:

- CDD
- reporting to the Financial Intelligence Unit of the New Zealand Police (FIU)
- record keeping, and
- audit.

Customer due diligence

Crucially, s 6(4)(d) of the AML/CFT Act provides that the obligations outlined in that section only apply to an HVD to the extent that the HVD carries out activities described in the definition in s 5(1).

Section 6(4) therefore significantly reduces the compliance obligations of HVDs compared to other types of reporting entities. One of the practical consequences is that there are no circumstances in which it is necessary for an HVD to carry out enhanced CDD.

Prescribed transaction reporting

The Anti-Money Laundering and Countering Financing of Terrorism (Prescribed Transactions Reporting) Regulations 2016 (PTR Regulations) set the following applicable threshold values for a prescribed transaction for most reporting entities:

- a wire transfer — $1,000
- a domestic cash transaction — $10,000.

Crucially, these threshold values were modified for HVDs by the 2019 Regulations, which provide that the applicable threshold for HVDs is $10,000.

HVDs must submit PTRs for a domestic physical cash transaction (this includes physical currency, but not bearer-negotiable instruments) that meets or exceeds $10,000. This must be done within 10 working days from the date the transaction took place.

Record keeping

HVDs must keep records of identity and verification documentation, SARs filed, and audits. These obligations are much more circumscribed than those applicable to other reporting entities under the AML/CFT Act.

Suspicious activity reports

Under s 6(4) of the AML/CFT Act the obligation to report suspicious activities to the FIU which ordinarily applies to reporting entities is not extended to HVDs. Instead, the section provides that a HVD *may* report suspicious activities to the Commissioner of Police. This concession, although perhaps a surprising one, may be a pragmatic approach to something that would otherwise present enforcement issues.

Nevertheless, the legislation expressly preserves the possibility that such reports may be made by a HVD from time to time.

Audit

An HVD is required to undergo an independent audit of its AML/CFT compliance obligations under s 59A only if requested by an AML/CFT supervisor (Department of Internal Affairs, Financial Markets Authority or Reserve Bank of New Zealand).

References: Anti-Money Laundering and Countering Financing of Terrorism Act 2009, ss 5(1), 6(4), 59A.

Anti-Money Laundering and Countering Financing of Terrorism (Definitions) Amendment Regulations 2019, regs 5AB, 21AB.

Anti-Money Laundering and Countering Financing of Terrorism (Prescribed Transactions Reporting) Regulations 2016.

4-002 Expired passports

The AML/CFT supervisors (Te Tari Taiwhenua, Department of Internal Affairs, Financial Markets Authority and Reserve Bank of New Zealand) have released guidance about the use of expired passports to meet customer due diligence obligations and how this is relevant to the Amended Identity Verification Code of Practice 2013 (IVCOP): see *Guidance on Expired Passports for Identification in Customer Due Diligence.*

Part 1, section 1 of IVCOP provides that a passport is an example of primary photographic identification. The AML/CFT supervisors have stated that this means a valid passport at the time a business relationship was established; therefore, an expired passport would not meet the necessary standard and could not be used in the ordinary course of business. However, Part 1, section 4 of IVCOP provides that a reporting entity must have an exception-handling procedure where a customer demonstrates that they are unable to comply with the prescribed information requirements in IVCOP. An expired passport may be acceptable for the purposes of such an exception.

4-003 National Risk Assessment 2019

The Financial Intelligence Unit of the New Zealand Police (FIU) published its *National Risk Assessment of Money Laundering and Terrorism Financing Assessment* in November 2019. The National Risk Assessment is the primary element of the anti-money laundering (AML)/countering the financing of terrorism (CFT) risk assessment system. It provides information on the crime of money laundering (ML) and the development of the AML/CFT regime.

The National Risk Assessment has identified the main current ML vulnerabilities in New Zealand as being:

- international wire transfers
- alternative payment methods and remittance systems
- new technologies
- gatekeeper professional services
- cash use
- businesses used as fronts (eg cash intensive businesses), and
- high-value goods and real estate assets.

The National Risk Assessment also identified that risks and ongoing issues were expected to arise around:

- correspondent relationships
- the displacement of transactions from regulated to less controlled sectors
- de-risking by deciding not to conduct business with classes of customers, rather than managing risks posed by individual customers, and
- technological development.

The FIU has estimated that $1.35 billion of domestic proceeds are created for laundering in New Zealand per annum. This money is generated from drug offending ($750 million), fraud ($500 million) and other offences such as burglary ($100 million). The estimated total does not include tax offending and overseas predicate offences. The National Risk Assessment has identified that the 3 major predicate offence types in New Zealand are:

- drug offending
- fraud, and
- tax offending.

The FIU has identified significant external transnational ML threats to New Zealand including:

- organised crime connected to New Zealand networks
- illicit funds associated with overseas criminals with no connection to New Zealand, and
- international criminal networks specialising in ML services.

4-004 Inland Revenue factsheet

Inland Revenue released a factsheet — *Tax evasion, tax fraud and money laundering factsheet* (IR1061) in July 2019 to assist reporting entities with understanding the relationship between tax evasion, tax fraud and money laundering (ML).

Tax evasion, tax fraud and ML are usually intertwined, given criminals need to launder their proceeds in order to benefit from their crime. As New Zealand's tax system encompasses a number of different tax types and different rules, the relationship has been described by Inland Revenue as complex. It can therefore be difficult for reporting entities such as lawyers to form a suspicion that tax evasion or tax fraud may have occurred, considering the reporting entity usually has limited visibility or understanding of a customer's tax affairs.

To assist reporting entities with detecting and deterring tax evasion and tax fraud and ML, Inland Revenue released a list of general red flags:

- no payments are made to Inland Revenue as part of the customer's ordinary course of business

- activities that are outside the norms of an industry or the habits of the client
- no cash sales when some would be expected, or cash sales when they would not be expected
- use of a personal bank account for business transactions
- cash sales out of proportion with the business/industry (eg deposits of $40,000 per week for a person who says they operate a food truck)
- transactions involving known low- or no-tax jurisdictions
- use of shell companies or other opaque entities
- complex, unusual patterns of transactions or uncharacteristic transactions
- back-to-back transactions (including loans) and multiple transfers through conduit entities or trusts
- payment of large transaction fees to professional service providers of dubious reputation
- a lack of supporting documentation or a lack of willingness to provide supporting documentation
- someone living beyond their apparent means without an obvious income stream
- income or means that appear insufficient for the apparent lifestyle
- secrecy about the type of work a customer does, and unwillingness to explain sources of money
- statements such as "I'm doing this for tax purposes" or "will Inland Revenue find out?"
- claiming that the money came from non-taxable transactions (large casino winnings, lottery prizes, inheritances, etc)
- all of the funds in the specified bank account come from the Inland Revenue – there are no other sources eg employment income
- use of a child's or relative's bank account to either hold money or transfer money rapidly
- purchases of property or mortgages being paid off quickly outside of the customer's regular financial profile
- financial statements that are noticeably different from those of similar businesses, have not been prepared professionally or where there are 2 sets of financial statements.

4-005 Virtual asset service providers

Virtual assets are digital values that can be digitally traded or transferred and which can be used for payment or investment purposes. See "Virtual Asset Service Providers" (November 2019) on the Department of Internal Affairs

(DIA) website. Virtual assets provide greater opportunities for cross-border payments and permit greater levels of anonymity. As a result, virtual assets can be particularly vulnerable to money laundering (ML). A virtual asset service provider (VASP) is considered a "financial institution" under s 5(1) of the Anti-Money Laundering and Countering Financing of Terrorism Act 2009 (AML/CFT Act).

The DIA in the above document has laid out 5 relevant categories of VASP for the New Zealand context:

VASP		*Types of virtual asset activities*
Virtual Asset Exchanges	> >	Providing a digital online platform facilitating virtual asset transforms and exchanges. Exchanges may occur between one or more forms of virtual assets or between virtual assets and currency Issuing own virtual assets in order to facilitate virtual asset transfers and exchanges
Virtual Asset Wallet Providers	>	Providing storage for virtual assets or flat currency on behalf of others and them facilitating exchanges or transfers between one or more virtual assets, or between virtual assets and flat currency.
Virtual Asset Broking	>	Arranging transactions involving virtual assets, or involving virtual asset and flat currency.
Initial Coin Offering (ICO) Providers	> >	Issuing and selling virtual assets to the public. May involve participating in and providing financial services relating to the ICO.
Providing investment opportunities in virtual assets	>	Providing an investment vehicle enabling investment in/ purchase of virtual assets (i.e. via a managed investment scheme or a derivatives issuer providing virtual asset options, or via a private equity vehicle that invests in virtual assets).

The Financial Action Task Force (FATF) has released a document setting out international expectations and definitions of virtual assets called *Guidance for a Risk-Based Approach to Virtual Assets and Virtual Asset Service Providers*. The document contains the FATF's updated definition of VASP, which is much broader than before. The new definition covers transfers, exchanges and administration of virtual assets, and the provision of virtual asset-related financial services.

VASPs are subject to anti-money laundering (AML)/countering the financing of terrorism (CFT) obligations, such as:

- reporting suspicious activities and certain transactions

- verifying the identity of customers in some circumstances, and
- assessing and mitigating ML and FT risks.

The DIA is the designated AML/CFT supervisor for most VASPs. However, depending on the services provided, the FMA may act as the supervisor in some instances.

Reference: Anti-Money Laundering and Countering Financing of Terrorism Act 2009, s 5(1)("financial institution").

4-006 Sector risk assessments

The Department of Internal Affairs (DIA) released 2 sector risk assessments on 13 February 2020:

- *Financial Institutions Sector Risk Assessment*
- *Designated Non-Financial Businesses and Professions (DNFBPs) and Casinos Sector Risk Assessment.*

These sector risk assessments replace the Phase 1 and Phase 2 sector risk assessment documents published in 2017 and 2018. The naming of the documents reflects that the implementation of Phase 2 of New Zealand's anti-money laundering (AML)/countering the financing of terrorism (CFT) regime is now complete.

In addition to the name changes, there have been some updates to the risk assessment content. Reporting entities should consider whether they need to review and update their own risk assessments and compliance programmes.

Financial institutions previously covered in the 2018 Phase 1 sector risk assessment should now refer to the *Financial Institutions Sector Risk Assessment.*

This sector risk assessment covers:

- money remitters
- currency exchangers
- payment providers
- non-bank non-deposit taking lenders (NBNDTLs)
- non-bank credit cards
- stored value cards
- tax pooling
- cash transport
- debt collection
- factoring
- financial leasing
- payroll remittance
- safe deposit boxes
- virtual asset service providers (VASPs).

All other types of reporting entity (including trust and company service providers and casinos) should now refer to the *Designated Non-Financial Businesses and Professions (DNFBPs) and Casinos Sector Risk Assessment*. This sector risk assessment covers:

- lawyers
- accountants
- conveyancers
- real estate agents
- trust and company service providers (TCSPs)
- casinos
- high value dealers (HVDs)
- the Racing Industry Transition Agency (RITA), formerly known as the New Zealand Racing Board (NZRB).

Updates relating to financing of terrorism risks

Updates to the content on terrorism financing issues are in Part 21 of the *Financial Institutions* document and Part 14 of the *DNFBPs and Casinos* document.

These reflect the updates to the National Risk Assessment 2019 relating to financing of terrorism (FT) risk in New Zealand.

All reporting entities should consider whether they should update their own risk assessments and compliance programmes relating to FT risks.

Addition of VASP sector

The VASP sector has been included in the *Financial Institutions Sector Risk Assessment*.

This sector has an inherent money laundering (ML)/FT risk rating of High.

This content is relevant for VASPs, as well as other reporting entities that interact with them.

Conveyancing sector inherent ML/FT risk rating

The inherent ML/FT risk rating for the conveyancing sector has changed from Low to Medium.

This change follows a review of DIA's methodology and an increased understanding of the ML/FT typologies that the conveyancing sector faces.

4-007 Department of Internal Affairs Regulatory Findings Report 2019–2020

The Department of Internal Affairs (DIA) has released its regulatory findings report for 2019–2020. The report identified areas of good practice and also areas for improvement.

Areas of good practice identified included the following:

- Risk assessment and anti-money laundering (AML)/countering the financing of terrorism (CFT) programme: Almost all reporting entities, including the new designated non-financial business or profession (DNFBP) sectors, have undertaken written risk assessments and established an AML/CFT programme. In many cases, these AML/CFT programmes are aligned with and operate alongside other business processes.
- Compliance officers: Reporting entities have appointed an AML/CFT compliance officer to administer and maintain their AML/CFT programme.
- Identifying risks and understanding AML/CFT obligations: The identification and understanding of the money laundering (ML)/financing terrorism (FT) risks, AML/CFT obligations and the requirements of a risk-based approach is improving across the sectors supervised by the DIA.
- Reviewing/updated AML/CFT programme: As understanding of ML/FT risks and AML/CFT obligations develops, many reporting entities are reviewing and updating risk assessments and AML/CFT programmes to ensure they are effective.
- Suspicious activity reporting: More than one-third of all suspicious activity reports (SARs) to the Financial Intelligence Unit of the New Zealand Police (FIU) are submitted by reporting entities supervised by the DIA. This includes some high-quality SARs submitted by reporting entities in the DNFBP sectors.
- Prescribed transaction reporting: Many reporting entities are submitting prescribed transaction reports (PTRs) for large cash transactions of NZ$10,000 and over, and for international wire transfers of NZ$1,000 and over (when an ordering or beneficiary institution).

Areas for improvement included:

- Inconsistent implementation of AML/CFT programmes: Written AML/CFT policies, procedures and controls are not always implemented consistently or effectively. This means that some reporting entities are more compliant on paper (technical compliance) than they are at implementation in practice (effectiveness).
- Generic templates: Generic content is useful as a starting point, but risk assessments and the AML/CFT programmes must be specific to each reporting entity and the ML/FT risks.
- Registration with goAML: While many reporting entities are registered for goAML with the FIU, there are many reporting entities that are not. Those reporting entities that have not registered primarily comprise law

firms, accountants and real estate agents. All reporting entities should register for goAML so that they are able to submit SARs and PTRs within the required timeframe.

- Unidentified/risks not understood: While improving, ML/TF risks that are not fully identified or understood remains an issue for some reporting entities. The DIA is also concerned that the risks that had been identified (in the risk assessment), are not evident in training material and that staff involved in implementing the AML/CFT programme have low knowledge of the reporting entity's ML/FT risks.
- Unidentified/unverified source of funds or wealth: Higher-risk customers, activities and transactions are not consistently being identified, verified and monitored. Undertaking enhanced customer due diligence to verify wealth and source of funds is key to distinguishing between a high-risk but legitimate customer, and one that is potentially suspicious should be reported and/or have business refused.

4-008 Financial Intelligence Unit of the New Zealand Police quarterly typology reports

The Financial Intelligence Unit of the New Zealand Police (FIU) has produced several reports on typologies used in AML/CFT. An overview of the substance of the reports is given below.

Money Laundering Typology — Wire Transfers (2013–2014, Q1)

The report considered the emerging factors impacting on the anti-money laundering (AML)/countering the financing of terrorism (CFT) environment. It discussed the role of the New Zealand Police asset recovery units under the Criminal Proceeds (Recovery) Act (CPRA) 2009, which had investigated assets worth an estimated $293 million at the time of reporting. The report also examined the fact that the National Risk Assessment 2010 classified wire transfers as the highest risk typology for New Zealand. The FIU outlined possible indicators of wire transfer abuse as including:

- significant and/or frequent cash payments for transfers
- transfers to or from locations that have poor AML/CFT regimes or high exposure to corruption
- transfers to high-risk countries or known tax havens
- transfers to numerous offshore jurisdictions with no business rationale
- multiple transfers sent to the same person overseas by different people
- the same home address being provided by multiple remitters
- departure from New Zealand shortly after transferring funds, and
- reluctance to provide a retailer with identification details.

In particular, the report considered the relationship between terrorism financing and wire transfers. The FIU highlighted potential terrorist financing indicators as:

- individuals undertaking international funds transfers under false names
- individuals transferring funds offshore from their personal bank accounts to provide support for overseas terrorist groups or activities
- frequent and/or significant cash payments for transfers
- numerous transactions to offshore jurisdictions with no business rationale
- multiple transfers to the same overseas individual by different people
- the same contact details appearing in multiple transfers, and
- the use of false identification details or reluctance to provide identification.

Key terms outlined in the report included:

- *Investigated assets*: assets investigated since the implementation of the CPRA 2009.
- *Restrained assets*: assets transferred from the control of alleged offenders to the Official Assignee while further investigations take place.
- *Forfeited assets*: restrained assets that have been forfeited to the Crown.
- *Smurfing*: utilising third parties or groups of people to carry out structuring.

Money Laundering through Third Party Intermediaries and Terrorism Financing through Intermediaries (2013–2014, Q2)

The report examined the practice of money laundering and terrorist financing through the use of third-party intermediaries. The FIU identified that the process may be as simple as a criminal transferring funds to a third party and instructing them to make a transaction on their behalf. There are generally 2 categories of intermediaries used for this process:

- those who perform non-specialised services, and
- those who offer specialised services.

Those who perform non-specialised services range from unwitting "mules" obtained through internet scams, to complicit family members. Those who offer specialised services are often professionals and so can facilitate money laundering through more complex schemes. Professional intermediaries can also provide access to financial services or products.

The FIU indicated some red flags that may indicate that intermediaries are being used to obscure criminal activity. These include:

- unexplained activity that does not fit the profile of the customer
- customers who do not know the origin of the funds

- customers who do not know the receiver of funds
- an individual accompanying and instructing the person making the transaction
- valuable asset purchases made in the name of a third party
- unusual transactions involving a professional or company account
- involvement of a company with off-shore directors, and
- unusually complex transaction arrangements involving multiple jurisdictions.

The report also highlighted that intermediaries may be used to aid in fundraising for terrorist financing.

Money Laundering and Terrorist Financing through Professionals Client Accounts (2013–2014, Q3)

The report was based on the Financial Action Task Force (FATF) document relating to the vulnerabilities of lawyers and accountants to money laundering and the financing of terrorism. The FIU acknowledged that client accounts are attractive to criminals at all stages of money laundering as they can:

- be used in the process of converting the proceeds of crime into less suspicious assets
- permit criminal access to the financial system where the individual would otherwise be considered undesirable or suspicious
- facilitate in hiding the ownership information of criminally derived funds or other assets, and
- be used as an essential link between different money laundering techniques, including setting up trusts and purchasing real estates.

The FIU discussed that the 3 main ways criminals exploit client accounts for money laundering (ML) and financing of terrorism (FT), as identified by FATF, were:

- using a client account for a transaction without an underlying legal service
- clients seeking services or advice as to how to structure payments to avoid AML/CFT obligations, and
- aborted transactions, which are used to avoid the restriction on transacting without an underlying professional service.

Co-Mingling with Business Revenue (2013–2014, Q4)

The report discussed the role of businesses in money laundering. The FIU considered businesses to be attractive to criminals because of:

- their ability to act as a front for ML — the regularity of business transactions can provide effective cover for illegitimate transactions
- their ability to fund transactions connected to laundering rings

- the potential to conceal criminal wealth through legitimate business and earnings.

The FIU also acknowledged that businesses are attractive to terrorist financiers as:

- a front for layered funding, or
- a source of funds to be diverted to terrorism.

Abuse of Trusts (2014–2015, Q1)

The report considered the use of trusts as a vehicle for ML and/or terrorist financing. The FIU concluded that the abuse of trusts is a significant issue for New Zealand due to the high density of trusts per capita. Trusts as attractive to criminals due to the ability for users to hide their involvement in illegal transactions or their beneficial ownership of criminal proceeds. Money launderers and terrorist financiers can exploit tax privacy afforded to trusts in New Zealand. New Zealand's settlor-based tax regime and foreign trust rules make it an attractive jurisdiction for criminals. The criminal abuse of trusts is a major issue for the legal professions due the role of lawyers in the creation and managing of trusts.

Abuse of Shell Companies (2014–2015, Q2)

The report considered the use of shell companies for large scale ML, tax avoidance and fraud. The FIU defined a shell company as a company used to conduct specific transactions, but without significant assets or operations. Shell companies are attractive for criminal activities as they:

- permit criminals to conceal individual involvement — the company can conduct necessary transactions while beneficial ownership is concealed using nominee shareholders and/or directors
- provide the appearance of legitimate business transactions.

The FIU recognised that New Zealand's company landscape may be particularly attractive for this purpose as:

- New Zealand has a reputation as a well-regulated jurisdiction
- it is simple and cost-effective to register companies in New Zealand as compared to other jurisdictions, and
- historically, it was not necessary for the company to have significant links to New Zealand.

The report concluded that shell companies may be an especially attractive option for international and transnational launderers. The FIU found that New Zealand shell companies were most often used as a vehicle for foreign offenders to legitimise the proceeds of crime by funnelling the proceeds into New Zealand.

The FIU highlighted a number of possible indicators of shell company abuse, including that:

- the company's office address is the same as that for several other companies
- the supplied address is a residential office or a "virtual office"
- company formation agents operate accounts and facilities
- there is a lack of information about overseas beneficiaries/directors
- there are complex ownership structures
- there are structures with no visible economic or other rationale
- a natural person is the director of a large number of single director companies
- a natural or legal person is the shareholder of numerous single-shareholder companies, and
- the use of a small number of "agents" who conduct transactions with the Companies Register.

High Value Assets (2014–2015, Q3)

The report discussed how the buying and selling of high value assets can aid criminals in the placement and layering stages of ML and/or terrorist financing. Such transactions are attractive as they can allow criminals to avoid direct interaction with the regulated financial sector. High value assets are also and attractive option because:

- criminals do not require any specialised skills, knowledge or resources to handle them
- they do not generally receive the same regulatory attention as money to the same value
- they present many resale opportunities, and
- they can be easily concealed and distributed.

The FIU recognised that, historically, New Zealand has not experienced a significant degree of exposure to high value assets. However, the FIU also acknowledged that this would likely change with the growth of e-commerce.

Real Estate (2014–2015, Q4)

The use of real estate in the crimes of ML and terrorist financing was discussed in the report. The FIU identified that property may be attractive for this purpose for a number of reasons, including that:

- property can be used to explain the source of funds
- real estate transactions are substantial, thus allowing large sums to be laundered
- values may be difficult to access as real estate is a speculative market — this could facilitate ML as it could enable under/over valuing
- real estate transactions can link to other financial vehicles, such as mortgages, which can also be used for ML, and

- real estate or real estate investment may be a less conspicuous option for foreign investment.

The report also considered a 2007 FATF typology study on real estate, which identified areas vulnerable to money launderers, including:

- use of complex credit finance or loans
- use of professionals to access financial services or act as intermediaries
- use of corporate vehicles, such as trusts and shell companies
- manipulation of the valuation or appraisal of property
- use of monetary instruments, such as cash for lease/rent arrangements
- use of mortgages to mingle criminal proceeds with money lent by financial institutions, and
- co-mingling income from property with criminal proceeds.

The FIU concluded that, while real estate is a significant area of concern with regard to ML and FT, it does not occur on the same scale in New Zealand as in other overseas jurisdictions, such as the United Kingdom.

Capital Markets (2015–2016, Q1)

The report examined the relationship between capital markets, ML and FT. Capital markets can be useful for these offences as they allow fast transactions, including transnational transactions, and provide for relative anonymity. ML through capital markets generally involves the buying, selling and exchanging of securities, or value manipulation through trades between parties. Capital markets are useful to criminals for this purpose because they are considered legitimate and so may be subject to less regulatory scrutiny than other areas. Capital market investments may also be the final intention for the proceeds of crime.

The Financial Markets Authority regulates New Zealand's capital markets. Owing to the comparatively small scale of the New Zealand market, the FIU has assessed New Zealand's capital market to have a low level of vulnerability concerning ML and FT.

Terrorist Financing (2015–2016, Q2)

The report focused on the offence and regulation of FT in New Zealand. It discussed the traditional techniques of FT, as outlined by FATF, which include:

- income generation via donations, non-profit organisations, financial activity through high-risk jurisdictions, fraud, kidnapping, scams, and legitimate commercial enterprise, and
- movement of funds through banks, money value transfer systems or cash.

The FIU concluded that New Zealand's level of threat in relation to FT is low in comparison to partner countries. However, the FIU acknowledged that New Zealand is vulnerable to terrorist financing in relation to:

- financiers of overseas groups within New Zealand, and
- overseas-based groups who may use New Zealand as a conduit for funds.

In particular, the FIU concluded that FT in New Zealand would most likely take the form of international illicit capital flows. The report found that international AML/CFT regimes will likely compensate for the lack of specific counter measures for FT, so long as these regimes are flexible enough to address both offences.

Predicate Offence (2015–2016, Q3)

The report examined "predicate offences", which are offences that could be the subject of any of the ML offences listed under the UN Convention. Generally, the terms are used in relation to offences that underlie ML and/or FT activity. However, the treatment of predicate offences varies under the law of different jurisdictions. Section 243 of the Crimes Act 1961 defines the ML offence, and so defines what constitutes a predicate offence in New Zealand.

The FIU concluded that the most prevalent predicate offences for ML in New Zealand are fraud, tax evasion and drug offences. The FIU estimated that, at the time, $1.35 billion of domestic proceeds were laundered into New Zealand per annum.

Alternative Banking Platforms (2015–2016, Q4)

The report discussed the use of alternative banking platforms for ML and FT offences. The FIU defined "alternative banking platforms" as systems which provide the services of a bank but operate external to the traditional global banking space. Due to their separation from the rest of the banking sector, alternative banking platforms can allow criminals to circumvent the AML/CFT obligations of banks and thus evade law enforcement attention. The FIU recognised that alternative banking platforms generally operate in tax havens.

The FIU found that, in a number of instances, New Zealand offshore finance companies had facilitated the transfer of illegal proceeds. The FIU also found that criminal alternative banking platforms had been established by New Zealand trust and company service providers on behalf of overseas clients for a criminal purpose.

Cryptocurrency (2016–2017, Q1)

The report considered a 2014 FATF report on virtual currencies (*Virtual Currencies: Key Definitions and Potential AML/CFT Risks*), which defined a cryptocurrency as "a math-based, decentralised convertible virtual currency that is protected by cryptography." Cryptocurrencies are attractive to criminals because they provide for anonymous peer-to-peer transactions that can occur independently from traditional intermediaries such as banks. The transactions occur using blockchain technology, which records, among other things, cryptocurrency transactions.

The FIU discussed the features of cryptocurrencies/new payment technologies that make them attractive to ML and terrorist financing, such as:

- they allow criminals to exploit communication and regulatory gaps between international borders
- they can circumvent and defeat AML/CFT controls
- they allow for the fast and remote reintegration of proceeds of crime into the financial system.

FIU identified anonymity as the most valuable feature of cryptocurrencies for criminals. Transactions are conducted using strings of letter and numbers as identifiers, removing the need to input any personal information. The FIU found that a small number of domestic exchangers of digital currencies were in New Zealand and identified links between the use of cryptocurrencies and the importing of illegal goods into New Zealand. The FIU recognised that cryptocurrencies such as Bitcoin were not regulated in New Zealand at the time of the report, but blockchain regulation was beginning to be developed.

Human Trafficking and People Smuggling (2016–2017, Q2)

The report considered the link between ML and the crimes of human trafficking and people smuggling. Human trafficking is the use or transportation of people by threat, force or other coercion, for the purpose of exploitation. Like ML, it involves a 3-stage process: the recruitment or abduction of individuals, their transfer to a point of exploitation and exploiting these individuals for gain. Human trafficking is desirable for criminals as it is hard to detect and prosecute. People smuggling involves illegal border-crossing. Unlike human trafficking, participation is voluntary.

Both offences generate large profits for the criminals who implement them. Human trafficking creates returns from the exploitation of non-consenting individuals, while people smuggling involves voluntary participants paying cash for a service. Criminals behind these activities often turn to ML to process their profits. The FIU outlined number of ways in which ML may occur in relation to these offences, including:

- couriers transporting cash across borders
- investment in high-value commodities
- investment in legal businesses and real estate.

Historically, AML regulations did not sufficiently address the detection and prevention of human trafficking activities. At the time of the report, the FIU acknowledged that reliable money laundering and human trafficking typologies were in place, despite the fact that the FATF found there to be a low number of SARs relation to people smuggling and human trafficking. The FIU concluded that more effective regulation of these offences could be found in the space between traditional detection systems; for example, low-dollar purchases may be a sign that victims are accessing necessities.

4-009 The Financial Action Task Force Mutual Evaluation Report

Between February and March 2020, officials from Financial Action Task Force (FATF) visited New Zealand in order to analyse New Zealand's level of compliance with the FATF 40 Recommendations and the level of effectiveness of New Zealand's anti-money laundering (AML)/countering the financing of terrorism (CFT) system. In April 2021, the conclusions from this review were summarised in the *Mutual Evaluation Report*, which also provided recommendations for how New Zealand's AML/CFT system could be strengthened.

The full report is highly detailed and runs to over 200 pages. It contains a number of recommendations that are likely to significantly impact designated non-financial businesses and professions (DNFBPs) and the related professions — particularly law, accounting, trust and company service providers, and real estate.

Findings

The most significant findings are summarised below.

- A low number of suspicious transaction reports (STRs) and suspicious activity reports (SARs) are reported by DNFBPs (as opposed to financial institutions). FATF noted that the registration and filing process with the Financial Intelligence Unit of the New Zealand Police (FIU) presents a barrier to effective reporting.
- The New Zealand legal profession provides a full suite of legal services. Lawyers and accountants are assessed by the DIA as having a medium-high money laundering (ML)/FT risk owing to their easy access and the wide geographic spread of legal services, coupled with their use in every phase of ML/FT and in many different typologies. FATF noted that in New Zealand, lawyers also carry out trust and company service provider services.
- A lawyer was a key participant in a large and sophisticated ML operation by the Comanchero Outlaw Motorcycle Gang (the Andrew Simpson case is discussed at 3-002). The police investigation, Operation Nova, reconstructed financial activities across 131 separate bank accounts and approximately 100,000 individual transactions. The operation included the Australian Federal Police, the Australian Criminal Intelligence Commission, the New South Wales Police, the US Drug Enforcement

Agency, the Department of Homeland Security, the Fiji Police, Interpol, the Canadian Border Services Agency, and AUSTRAC. Investigative techniques involved physical and electronic surveillance. Ultimately $3.7 million worth of assets were seized and 8 people were arrested.

- Law firms and accounting practices are relatively new to the AML/CFT Act and consequently the level of understanding varies across the sector. Larger law firms and accounting practices have developed robust internal processes and a higher level of understanding in their staff. Smaller and medium-sized firms have a more variable level of understanding and compliance, with risk assessments and programmes ranging from generic templates to documents of a high standard. Smaller law firms and accounting practices are disproportionately burdened by compliance costs and administrative requirements.
- Larger law firms and accounting practices have AML/CFT policies in place and have implemented ongoing reviews in order to keep their customer due diligence information up to date. Identification of source funds is a challenge, as is understanding beneficial ownership and source of wealth/source of funds requirements.
- FATF noted that some lawyers do not agree with the sector risk rating of medium-high and see ML and TF as being carried out by a few complicit individuals rather than there being a sector-wide vulnerability.
- Other DNFBPs have a low reporting rate, particularly in relation to suspicious activity. The quality of the reports that are filed is high. Interestingly, despite not being required to do so, high value dealers are voluntarily submitting SARs (13 over the years 2016–2019).
- Multiple reporting entities raised the concern about insufficient independent auditors being available to conduct the required audits every 2 years. FATF noted that there are no standards applicable to independent auditors that would ensure the consistency and quality of audits. (The authors note that since the FATF visit, the audit cycle has been extended to every 3 years, or 4 years in some cases.)
- Reporting entities in the legal sector require further guidance in relation to how legal professional privilege intersects with their AML/CFT obligations (particularly SAR filing and independent audits). The Department of Internal Affairs (DIA) also considers that this area remains unclear.
- FATF noted that the DIA does not have the power in relation to DNFBPs to suspend, restrict or withdraw licencing or registration as a sanction for serious non-compliance with AML/CFT obligations. This remains the obligation of the pre-existing regulators and professional bodies of those professions (eg New Zealand Law Society, Chartered Accountants Australia and New Zealand, Real Estate Institute of New Zealand).

Most of the findings in the FATF report are complimentary of New Zealand's AML/CFT regime, and the administration of and compliance with that regime.

FATF's recommendations are likely to have a significant influence on any future changes to the regime, including those already signalled by the Ministry of Justice (MOJ).

Recommendations

FATF's key recommendations are listed below:

- That the AML/CFT Act as it relates to DNFBPs requires "consolidation".
- Beneficial ownership information should be more readily available, accurate and up to date, and steps should be taken to mitigate the risks posed by nominee shareholders and directors. (The authors note that the MOJ has already signalled further changes that are likely in this area.)
- Improvements should be made to the FIU's ability to identify new trends in criminal financial activity.
- The AML/CFT supervisors (Department of Internal Affairs, Financial Markets Authority, Reserve Bank of New Zealand) should have sufficient enforcement options available to them, including, particularly, adequate financial resources.
- Improvements should be made in relation to the supervision and enforcement of targeted financial sanctions obligations.
- Licencing and registration of reporting entities should be a greater feature of the regime.
- Measures should be taken to increase the number of ML prosecutions.

Appendices
Guidance and legislation

Guidelines in the Appendices have been reproduced with the permission of the AML/CFT supervisors (Department of Internal Affairs, Financial Markets Authority and Reserve Bank of New Zealand), and belong to them. Readers should check the websites noted in Appendix 1 to ensure they have the most recent version of the relevant document before relying on the information.

Appendix 1 Key resources

Department of Internal Affairs: www.dia.govt.nz (AML/CFT pages)

New Zealand Police Financial Intelligence Unit: www.police.govt.nz (FIU)

Financial Action Task Force: www.fatf-gafi.org

Ministry of Justice: www.justice.govt.nz (AML/CFT pages)

Reserve Bank of New Zealand: www.rbnz.govt.nz (AML pages)

Financial Markets Authority: www.fma.govt.nz (AML/CFT pages)

New Zealand Law Society: www.lawsociety.org.nz — "Anti money laundering and countering the financing of terrorism legislation AMLCFT and New Zealand law firms" (Practice briefing)

Legislation (Acts and Regulations): www.legislation.govt.nz

Appendix 2 Captured activities flowchart

AML / CFT Compliance for Law Firms

A matter will be a "Captured Activity" if it involves:

Acting as a formation agent of legal persons or legal arrangements

OR

Acting or arranging for a person to act as, a nominee director, nominee shareholder or trustee in relation to legal persons or legal arrangements

OR

Managing client funds (other than sums paid for professional services), accounts, securities or other assets

OR

Providing a registered office or a business address, a correspondence address, or an administrative address for a company or partnership, or for any legal person or legal arrangement (unless that service is provided solely as an ancillary service to the provision of other services that are not captured)

OR

Engaging in, or giving instructions on behalf of, a customer to another person for:

- Any conveyancing to effect a transaction
- A transaction within the meaning of s 4(1) of the Real Estate Agents Act 2008
- A transfer of beneficial interest in land or other real estate property
- A transaction on behalf of any person for buying or selling or transferring of a business or legal person and any other legal arrangement , or
- A transaction on behalf of a customer in relation to creating, operating, and managing a legal person, or any other legal arrangement.

YES

The matter is captured and must comply with the AML/CFT Act

NO

The matter is not captured but should be kept under review

Appendix 3A Customer Due Diligence for Trusts

Trusts

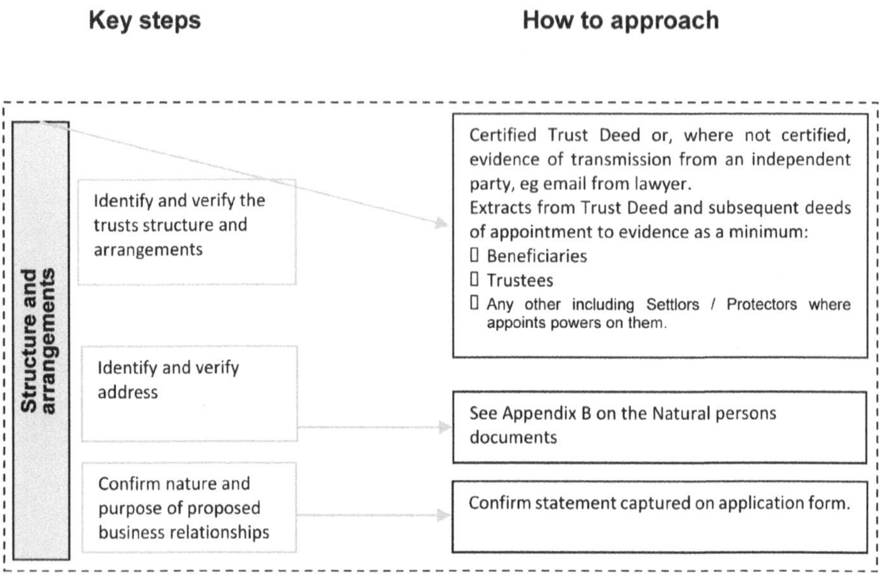

Trusts *cont*

Beneficiaries

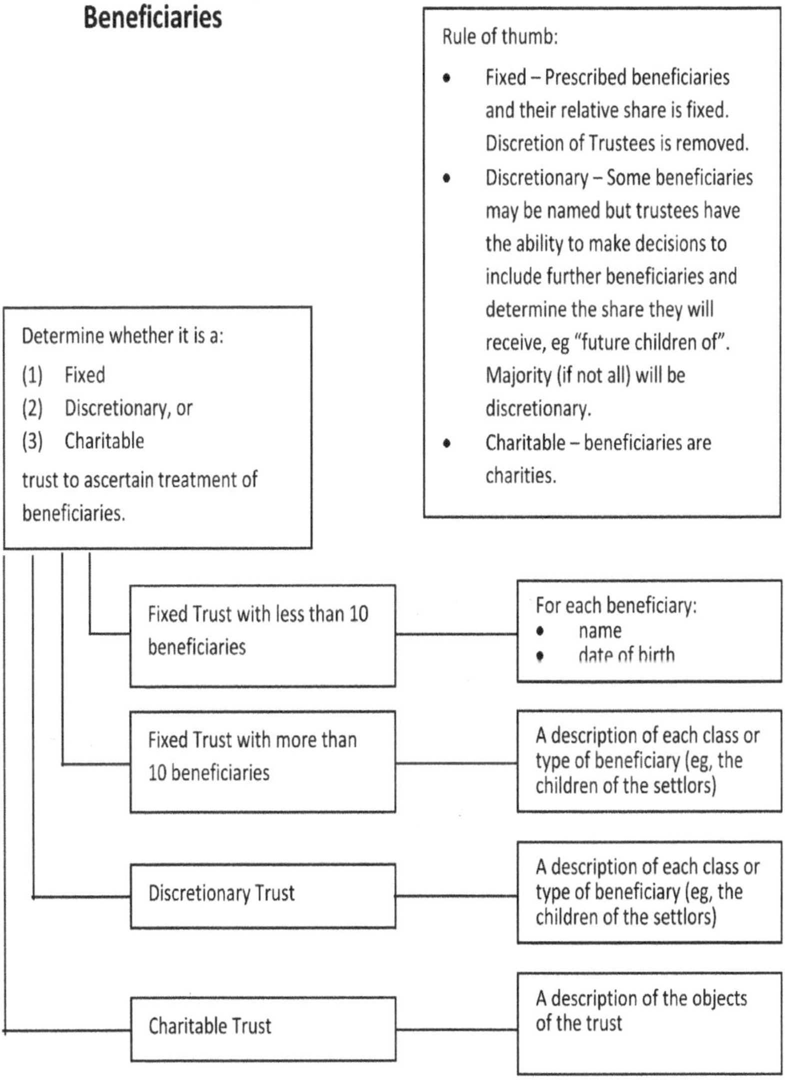

Trusts *cont.*

	Key steps		How to approach
Control (as subset of beneficial owners)	Establish the entities and individuals that exercise control over the Trust	Individual Trustees	Identify and verify name, date of birth and address for <u>all trustees</u>, eg through passport, Drivers licence+ other, utility bill
	Where present	Professional Trustee Companies	1. Identify and verify trustee company existence, eg search companies register and obtain a copy of the Certificate of Incorporation and Shareholder/ Director list, AND 2. Identify and verify individual (name, date of birth and address) of individuals in the Trustee Company that have effective control over the Trust Customer (eg directors and shareholders unless client has been able to demonstrate a smaller list of persons with effective control)
	Where present	Trustee Corporation (unlikely)	Complete identity verification on the person or persons that have the authority to operate.
	Where present	Other individuals that are considered beneficial owners	Are there any individuals not covered above that can carry out transactions, give instructions on trust customer assets? If so, identify and verify them in accordance with individual standards.
			Through reviewing the Trust Deed are there any individuals not covered above, e.g. settlors, protectors, that have the ability to: • amend the trust deed • remove or appoint Trustees If so need identify and verify the name, date of birth and address of each person (Passport, drivers licence + one other and, utility)
SoW or SoF	Obtain information on source of wealth or funds of the Trust customer and take reasonable steps to verify it		Option 1 — funds attributable to the Settlor (the individual who settles assets into the Trust), [may have inherited family wealth, accumulated business earnings, or funds from the sale of property etc], and/or Option 2 — identify the source of any income that the trust is receiving. , eg income from an underlying company or simply a monthly deposit from a family bank account. Achieved through financial due diligence not an audit and extent aligned to risk. Requires explanation and something independent to corroborate explanation.

Trust *cont.*

IMPORTANT NOTES

- PEP screening should be on file for all beneficial owners.
- Corroboration of certifier status should be on file for each person acting as a certifier, eg confirmation they are a teacher, lawyer.
- Watch if there's anything to indicate certifier is not independent (eg from same firm, wife).
- Trustee Corporation: eg Guardian Trust, Te Tuma Paeroa, Trustees Executors Limited, Perpetual Trust Limited, New Zealand Permanent Trustees Limited, The New Zealand Guardian Trust Company Limited.

Appendix 3B Customer Due Diligence for Companies

Companies

Structure and arrangements

Key steps	How to approach
Identify and verify the Company's identity (existence)	Extract from Companies Office website matching company name. If not a NZ Company will need to be an equivalent extract, eg Certificate of Incorporation, Memorandum/ Articles of Association.
Identify and verify registered address of Company	Extract from Companies Office website containing Company registered address. If not a NZ Company will need to be an equivalent extract, eg Certificate of Incorporation, Memorandum/ Articles of Association.
Confirm nature and purpose of proposed business relationships	Confirm statement captured on application form.

Companies *cont.*

Beneficial owner/acting on behalf

Key steps		How to approach
Establish the entities and individuals that exercise control/ own the company.		Documentation (Companies Office register) should show the beneficial owners (shareholders (25%) and Directors (effective controllers). Assuming these are individuals, (client) will need to identify and verify the name, DOB and address for each unless there is a basis for excluding verification.
Where present	Company as a shareholder	Need to trace through intermediary layers to identify the individuals whom are the ultimate beneficial owner ('warm blood' principle). This theoretically could be through several layers. The ultimate beneficial owners ('people') are the individuals that need their identity verified considering the concept of aggregation and dilution. When going through these layers of ownership (client) will need to consider any additional holders (>25% in aggregate) (at intermediary level) that will require their identity verified. Bring to Compliance attention where any company has 'Nominee' in the title or appears to be a Trust and Company Service Provider or is a 'Look Through Company'. These will need the Source of Wealth identified and verified. What is required at each layer is to be determined
Where present	Trust as a shareholder	Obtain certified copy of the Trust Deed and verify identity of Trustees behind it unless advised otherwise. This scenario can be identified as company house records for share ownership which will list trustees, importantly without detailing shareholding. This is an indicator the owner is a Trust.
Identify those who are able to act on the 'customer's' behalf, ie make decisions.		Likely be the controllers above, but if different, will need to identify and verify the name, date of birth and address for each. This should be noted on the application form.

Companies *cont.*

Notes:

- Source of wealth/funds information will not generally be required. Where a company has nominee shareholders or shares in bearer form, or is in a high-risk country, or is a vehicle for holding personal assets, then source of wealth/funds information may be required.
- PEP screening should be on file for all beneficial owners, sense check matches and clearance.
- Watch if there's anything to indicate certifier is not independent (eg from same firm, wife).
- Corroboration of certifier status should be on file for each person acting as a certifier, eg confirmation they are a teacher, lawyer.

Appendix 3C Customer Due Diligence for Natural persons

Natural persons	Key steps	How to approach
Identify and verify	Name and date of birth of the person(s) where joint	See identity verification Appendix A (overleaf).
	Address of the person(s) where joint	See identity verification Appendix B (overleaf).
Acting on behalf	Identify whether there are any persons who are able to act on the 'customers' behalf, i.e. make decisions.	eg Accountant, Power of Attorney. Will be marked on the application form. Where this exists will need to identify and verify their name, date of birth and address. Will also require the Power of Attorney agreement giving the authority to Act.
Nature and purpose	Confirm nature and purpose of proposed business relationships	Confirm statement captured on application form.
PEP Screen	Ensure reasonable steps have been taken to determine whether client is a politically exposed person.	Confirm each person has been screened adequately in accordance with compliance programme (for example, this may be done via a specific PEP screening provider.)

Natural persons *cont.*

Appendix A

Acceptable ID type combinations

There are three different options you can use as identification.
The simplest option is to pick ONE form of ID from Option 1 below; Options 2 and 3 require at least two forms (photo and non-photo).

OPTION 1
Choose ONE of the following as personal identification:
- New Zealand passport
- New Zealand certificate of identity
- New Zealand firearms licence
- Emergency travel document
- Overseas passport
- Foreign-issued national identity document
- New Zealand refugee travel document

OPTION 2
ONE of the following photo identification:
- New Zealand driver licence
- 18+ card (Hospitality Association)
- A valid and current international driving permit

Plus ONE of the following non-photo identification:
- New Zealand full birth certificate
- Certificate of New Zealand citizenship
- Citizenship certificate offered by a foreign government
- Full birth certificate issued by a foreign government

OPTION 3
Photo identification:
- New Zealand driver licence

Plus ONE of the following non-photo identification:
- An embossed credit card, debit card or an EFTPOS card issued by a registered NZ bank
- An original bank statement issued by a registered NZ bank within 12 months of your application
- An original document issued by a NZ Government agency with your name and signature (eg Super Gold card)
- A statement issued by a NZ Government agency within 12 months of your application (eg IRD statement)

Natural persons *cont.*

Certification

Each copied form of identification must be certified by an independent trusted person (including other documentation, eg Trust Deed, Power of Attorney Instrument). A trusted person must not be your spouse or partner, related to you, someone who lives at the same address as you or someone with an interest or ownership in your investment. A trusted person must be any one of the following:

- Police Officer
- Justice of the Peace
- Registered Medical Doctor
- Registered Teacher
- Minister of Religion
- Lawyer
- Notary Public
- NZ Honorary Consul
- Member of Parliament
- Chartered Accountant
- Kaumatua
- Commonwealth Representative

The trusted person must sign the document and provide a written statement to the effect that the copy provided is a true and correct copy and represents your identity. Certification must include the name, occupation and signature of the trusted person, the date of confirmation and must have been carried out in the 3 months preceding the presentation of the copied documents.

Appendix B

Identity Verification (address)

As well as providing a form of identification from page 1, we are also required to verify your address.
In order to verify your address, please provide an original OR certified copy of one of the following:

- utility or rates bill
- telephone bill
- bank statement (as delivered by mail, not via internet banking)
- IRD tax notice or statement

Each form needs to be dated in the last 12 months and addressed to you at your residential address.
Where original bank statements, utility bills etc are provided they do not require certification as the certification is to confirm their authenticity.

Appendix 4 A day in the life of an AML reporting entity

A Day in the Life of an AML Reporting Entity in NZ

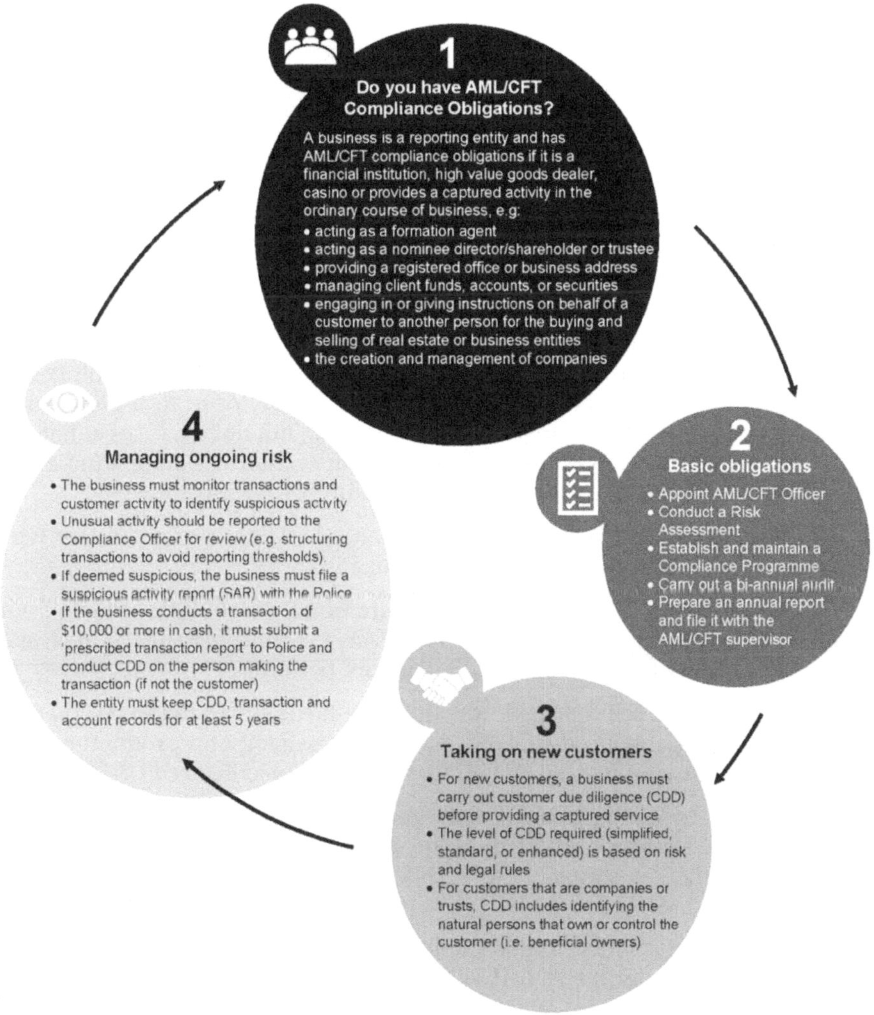

Appendix 5 Enhanced Customer Due Diligence Guideline (September 2020)

Reproduced from the Department of Internal Affairs website, with permission.

Introduction

1. This guideline assists you to conduct **enhanced customer due diligence (enhanced CDD)** on your customers under the **Anti-Money Laundering and Countering Financing of Terrorism (AML/CFT) Act 2009 (the Act).**

2. The Act sets out a number of specific situations in which enhanced CDD is required. In addition, enhanced CDD is required when you consider, based on your **money laundering and terrorism financing (ML/TF) risk assessment (risk assessment),** that the level of risk involved means that enhanced CDD should apply.

3. Enhanced CDD requires the collection and verification of the same identity information that is required for standard customer due diligence. However, when undertaking enhanced CDD, you may need to use increased or more sophisticated measures to do this. In most, but not all, cases enhanced CDD also requires the collection and verification of information relating to the **source of wealth (SoW)** or **source of funds (SoF)** of your customer.

4. This guideline does not address enhanced CDD requirements for wire transfers and correspondent banking relationships.

5. Your **AML/CFT programme (programme)** must outline how your business will determine when enhanced CDD is required for a customer and when other types of customer due diligence are permitted.

6. A risk-based approach allows you some flexibility in the steps you take when conducting enhanced CDD. Your risk assessment and programme will determine the amount of time and effort you spend on enhanced CDD.

7. A risk-based approach does not stop you from engaging in transactions/activities or establishing business relationships with higher risk customers. Rather, it should help you to effectively manage and prioritise your response to ML/TF risks.

8. Examples provided in this guideline are suggestions to help you meet your obligations under the Act. They are not exhaustive and are illustrative in nature.

9. This guideline has been produced by the AML/CFT supervisors under section 132(2) of the Act. It cannot be relied on as evidence of complying with the requirements of the Act. This guideline does not constitute legal advice.

10. Section 57(2) of the Act requires you to have regard to this guideline, it is important that you have read and taken this guidance into account when developing your AML/CFT programme. After reading this guideline, if you still do not understand any of your obligations you should contact your AML/CFT supervisor or seek legal advice.

11. Where AML/CFT guidance material is referenced, it can be accessed at the following websites:

Department of Internal Affairs:	http://bit.ly/2gQ3Iev
New Zealand Police Financial Intelligence Unit:	http://bit.ly/2zpmWPJ
Reserve Bank of New Zealand:	http://bit.ly/2n6RYdp
Financial Markets Authority:	http://bit.ly/2hV45oJ

Terms used in this enhanced CDD guideline

12. The Act does not define the terms set out below. For the purposes of this guideline, the following definitions apply.

"Reasonable steps": Refers to an objective view of what actions would be proportionate and suitable given the risks involved and the obligations of the Act. For instance, the level of identity verification you undertake on your customer.

"Material change": ML/TF risk is not static and a customer's ML/TF risk profile can change quickly. A material change is an event, activity, or situation that you identify during interactions with your customer (or via ongoing customer due diligence and account monitoring) that could change their level of ML/TF risk. This may result in the need for enhanced CDD.

"Risk-based approach": Refers to the proportionate AML/CFT measures that you implement in response to identified risks. An effective risk-based approach (sometimes called RBA) allows you to exercise informed judgement when conducting enhanced CDD on your customers. Under a risk-based approach, there is no such thing as "zero risk".

"According to the level of risk": Consistent with a risk-based approach, this refers to your assessment of ML/TF risk associated with your customer.

"Inherent risk": This is the assessed ML/TF risk before any AML/CFT controls and measures are in place.

"Residual risk": This is the assessed ML/TF risk after AML/CFT controls and measures have been put in place.

13. All footnote references refer to the AML/CFT Act 2009 unless stated otherwise.

14. On 1 July 2018, **suspicious transaction reports (STRs)** were replaced by **suspicious activity reports (SARs)**. We use the acronym SAR to denote both types of reporting for the purposes of this guideline.

Part 1: Enhanced customer due diligence

What is enhanced CDD?

15. Customer due diligence (CDD) is a cornerstone of your programme. CDD is the process through which you develop an understanding of your customers and the ML/TF risks they pose to your business.

16. In some higher ML/TF risk circumstances an increased level of CDD is required. This is known as **enhanced CDD, "ECDD"** or **"EDD".** As part of standard CDD, you **must** obtain sufficient information to determine whether you require enhanced CDD on your customer.[1]

17. Enhanced CDD has two core requirements over and above standard CDD:

- You may need to use increased or more sophisticated measures to obtain and verify your customer's details, their beneficial ownership structure, and the details of representatives and other key persons. You **must** take reasonable steps to do this according to the level of risk involved.[2] (This is covered in Part 2 of this guideline.)
- You should usually obtain and verify information relating to the **source of wealth (SoW)** or **source of funds (SoF)** of your customer.[3] The circumstances in which you need to do this are detailed within the Act.[4] You **must** take reasonable steps to do this according to the level of risk involved.[5] (This is covered in Part 4 of this guideline.)

18. You **must** base your programme on your risk assessment. Your programme **must** contain your enhanced CDD procedures, policies and controls that manage and mitigate the ML/TF risks presented by your customers.[6]

Why is enhanced CDD required?

19. Enhanced CDD is required for certain types of customers and some transactions or activities. This includes situations where you consider (based on your risk assessment) that the level of risk involved is such that enhanced CDD should apply.[7]

1 Section 17(b)
2 Sections 16(1) and 24(1)(b)
3 Sections 23(1)(a), 26(2)(b) and 26(3)
4 Section 22
5 Sections 23(1)(a), 24(1)(b), 26(2)(b) and 26(3)
6 Sections 57(1)(c) and 57(1)(j)
7 Section 22(1)(d)

20. For instance, enhanced CDD helps you:

- Determine whether complex beneficial ownership structures are legitimate and intended to facilitate business or if they are deliberately complicated to hinder investigation and conceal the identity of the beneficial owners.[8]
- Determine whether a customer's SoW or SoF are legitimately derived, or intended for legitimate use, or whether there are reasonable grounds to suspect it may be the proceeds of crime.
- Distinguish between a customer that has a higher risk profile but is not involved in ML/TF, as opposed to a customer whose transactions or activities may be linked to ML/TF.
- Comply with the requirement that SARs are reported to the **New Zealand Police Financial Intelligence Unit (FIU).**

When is enhanced CDD required?

21. There are various circumstances set out in the Act where enhanced CDD is required. These circumstances may apply to a customer that is seeking to conduct an occasional transaction or activity with you, or a new customer you are establishing a business relationship with. You should usually conduct enhanced CDD on your customer before any activities or transactions have commenced. Exceptions can apply – see paragraphs 47-49.

22. Enhanced CDD may also be required at subsequent points during a business relationship as part of your ongoing CDD and account monitoring procedures.[9]

When must enhanced CDD be conducted for new customers?

23. You **must** conduct enhanced CDD when taking on certain types of new customer. This includes establishing a business relationship with a customer or if a customer seeks to conduct an occasional transaction or activity.

24. Customers that **must** have enhanced CDD are:[10]

- A trust or another vehicle for holding personal assets
- A non-resident customer from a country that has insufficient AML/CFT systems or measures in place
- A company with nominee shareholders or shares in bearer form
- A politically exposed person (PEP)

---

8 Section 5

9 Section 31

10 Section 22

- A customer seeking to conduct a complex, unusually large transaction or unusual pattern of transactions that have no apparent or visible economic or lawful purpose
- Any other customer or circumstances that you assess (based on your risk assessment and standard CDD) to be of high ML/TF risk[11]
- A business relationship with a customer that involves new or developing technologies, or new or developing products, that might favour anonymity
- A customer seeking to conduct an occasional transaction or activity through the reporting entity that involves new or developing technologies, or new or developing products, that might favour anonymity.

25. Unless you have doubts about the adequacy or veracity of the information, data and documents that you have obtained and verified relating to your customer, you are not required to conduct enhanced CDD again.[12] However, enhanced CDD could be required again as a result of any material changes in your business relationship with your customer or due to ongoing CDD and account monitoring.

When must enhanced CDD be conducted again?

26. As part of your ongoing CDD and account monitoring processes you **must** regularly review your customer's details, account activity and transaction behaviour.[13] This is to ensure that it is consistent with your knowledge and understanding of their business and risk profile, as well as their business relationship with you. You should be more frequent and thorough in your scrutiny of a higher risk customer's transactions and activities than those of a lower risk customer.

27. You **must** have regard to your customer's ongoing level of ML/TF risk,[14] which will determine if enhanced CDD is required. If, as part of your ongoing CDD, you identify any of the following situations you should conduct enhanced CDD:

- A review of a high-risk customer's account activity and transaction behaviour shows that their level of ML/TF risk remains high
- A review of a low- or medium-risk customer's account activity and transaction behaviour shows that their level of ML/TF risk has increased since your previous assessment

---

11 Section 22(1)(d)

12 Section 11(4)

13 Section 31

14 Section 31(3)(b)

- When you consider, based on your risk assessment and programme that the level of risk involved is such that enhanced CDD should apply to a particular situation.[15]

28. You **must** conduct enhanced CDD where your customer seeks to conduct a complex, unusually large transaction or unusual pattern of transactions that have no apparent or visible economic or lawful purpose.[16]

29. As a general principle, you should review CDD (including enhanced CDD) for higher risk customers more regularly than for lower risk customers. For example, you may wish to review higher risk customers CDD on a regular basis. For low- to medium-risk customers you may want to design review processes based on longer periods of time or where there are opportunities to update CDD information – for example, during face-to-face interactions with your customer. The final decision will be yours to make based on your risk assessment and programme.

When must enhanced CDD be conducted for existing customers?

30. An existing customer is a customer that you have a business relationship with at the time your obligations under the Act come into effect.[17]

31. Customers **must** be subject to ongoing CDD and account monitoring.[18] Where there has been a material change in the nature and purpose of an existing customer's business relationship with you, and you consider that you have insufficient information about them, then CDD **must** be undertaken. This includes enhanced CDD where required by the Act or specified in your risk assessment or your programme.

When must SoW or SoF information be obtained?

32. SoW or SoF information is required when you conduct enhanced CDD in accordance with sections 22(1) and 22(2) of the Act. This includes most cases of enhanced CDD, such as when you are dealing with a Trust, a Politically Exposed Person (PEP), or higher risk circumstances.

33. SoW or SoF information is not required when you conduct enhanced CDD in accordance with sections 22(3)-(5) of the Act. This includes circumstances such as for wire transfers, correspondent banking relationships and those involving new or developing technologies, or new or developing products that might favour anonymity.

15 Section 22(1)(d)

16 Section 22(1)(c)

17 Section 5

18 Section 31

What does "according to the level of risk" mean?

34. When conducting enhanced CDD, you **must** verify the information provided to you by the customer using documents, data or information issued by a reliable and independent source. You **must** take reasonable steps to verify the information provided to you by the customer according to the level of risk involved.

35. "Reasonable steps" does not mean "no steps". The Act is founded on a risk-based approach where there is no such thing as zero risk. For instance, verification **must** be carried out on the SoW or SoF of trusts even if you assess them as presenting lower ML/TF risk (family trusts for example). Your risk assessment and programme will direct the degree of your verification measures.

36. This means that you have some flexibility in the level of validation and corroboration that you undertake. You can use your judgement on the level of verification you use depending on the situation, customer, activity, or transaction. However, the steps that you take should be objective, appropriate for your business and proportionate with the level of ML/TF risk.

How important is "nature and purpose" for enhanced CDD?

37. When on-boarding a customer, you **must** obtain information on the nature and purpose of the proposed business relationship.[19] The information you obtain on the nature and purpose of the proposed business relationship will help you determine whether your customer requires enhanced CDD, and it will help you with your ongoing CDD and account monitoring.

38. Information on the nature and purpose of the business relationship could include the reason the customer would like a particular product or service, the estimated total dollar value that may be received per annum, or the expected outgoings. It could also include information on the expected pattern, level, and type of activity (i.e. transaction volumes and frequency).

39. Your procedures, policies and controls should set out how you define and collect the nature and purpose of the proposed business relationship. For instance, you could include specific nature and purpose questions in your customer on-boarding form requesting this mandatory information or you could have nature and purpose as part of your scheduled ongoing CDD requirements.

What does "material change" mean for enhanced CDD purposes?

40. Your ongoing CDD and account monitoring should identify if there is material change in the nature and purpose of your customer's business relationship with you. A material change could present an increase in ML/TF risk.

19 Section 17(a)

41. Such material change could include circumstances where your customer asks for new and higher risk products or services, or if they are creating new corporate or trust structures. On the other hand, it could be if your customer starts undertaking unexpected and unexplained activity in overseas locations. Alternatively, the volume or size of your customer's transactions or activities may increase beyond what is reasonably expected.

42. For example, you may have a local customer who requested straightforward transactional services from you at on-boarding, so you assessed them as low-risk and conducted standard CDD. However, ongoing CDD and account monitoring identifies that this customer has moved to a higher risk jurisdiction and there has been an unexpected increase in transaction volume and/or value. In these circumstances, you may now require enhanced CDD as part of your ongoing CDD.

What if you cannot complete enhanced CDD?

43. If you are not able to complete enhanced CDD for a customer, you must not carry out any occasional transaction or activity for them, nor establish a business relationship with them.[20] If you already have a business relationship with the customer, this **must** be terminated.[21]

44. This prohibition applies to circumstances where a customer fails or refuses to provide the relevant information, data, or documents that you have requested. This also applies if the information, data, or documents that the customer provides are inadequate, or if you have reasonable grounds to believe they are fraudulent.

45. As part of your programme, you should include your procedures, policies and controls for situations when enhanced CDD, or any other type of CDD, cannot be conducted.[22] This should cover the following situations:

- When enhanced CDD is unable to be conducted at on-boarding
- When the business relationship has been established and enhanced CDD was incorrectly conducted during on-boarding
- When enhanced CDD could not be conducted following a review during ongoing CDD and account monitoring
- When enhanced CDD cannot be conducted after a material change in the business relationship.

46. If you are unable to conduct enhanced CDD, you **must** consider whether to submit a **suspicious activity report (SAR).**[23] It will be useful to

20 There are limited circumstances where the verification aspects of enhanced CDD can be completed after forming a business relationship.

21 Section 37

22 Your programme could also describe how you request, receive, and follow up on enhanced CDD requirements that are not met.

23 Section 37(1)(d)

record your enhanced CDD efforts during this time and include those in your SAR.[24]

Can you delay identity verification during enhanced CDD?

47. You can complete verification of customer identity for both standard CDD and enhanced CDD after you form a business relationship.[25] However, this should be the exception rather than part of your regular business activity. You can use delayed verification when it is essential not to interrupt normal business practice **and** verification is completed **as soon as practicable** once the business relationship has been established.

48. In addition to the above, you **must** effectively manage the ML/TF risks through transaction limitations and account monitoring or through other appropriate risk management procedures. For instance, limiting or stopping your customer's ability to withdraw funds until enhanced CDD has been conducted. Your programme should provide detail on your procedures, policies, and controls in relation to delayed verification.

49. You should not use delayed verification or exception policies to circumvent enhanced CDD procedures. This is particularly important if you have a suspicion of ML/TF or you become aware of anything that causes you to doubt the identity or intentions of your customer or their beneficial owner.

What enhanced CDD record keeping do you need to do?

50. Your programme **must** have procedures, policies and controls for record keeping.[26] In relation to enhanced CDD, you **must** keep copies of all the information, data or documents you have used to verify your customer's identity and details, their beneficial ownership (if applicable) and their SoW or SoF (if applicable).[27]

51. You should keep written notes or findings that justify the level of verification you undertook and the reasons behind your AML/CFT decisions. For example, you should record the reasons why you delayed your enhanced CDD verification of a customer, or why you escalated a transaction monitoring alert to an SAR after conducting enhanced CDD. This could be part of a formal decision log or contained in your SAR procedures.

24 To reduce ML/TF risk when you terminate a relationship where funds or other assets have been received, you should return the funds or assets to the source from which they were received. In general, this means that the funds or assets should be returned to your customer, but this may not always be possible. Where your customer requests that money or other assets be transferred to third parties, you should assess whether this provides grounds for suspicion of ML/TF and submission of a SAR.

25 Sections 16(3) and 24(3)

26 Section 57(1)(e)

27 Section 50 (3)(a)

52. Your record keeping should be clear and logical so that another party reading the notes can understand the risk-based decision that you made. This is important for supervisory and audit purposes.

53. Record keeping is an essential part of the audit trail for the detection, investigation, and confiscation of criminal or terrorism property/funds. Record keeping helps investigating authorities to establish a financial profile of persons of interest and to trace criminal or terrorism property/funds. It also helps the Court to examine past transactions to assess whether property/funds are connected to criminal or terrorism-related offences.

Do you need enhanced CDD as part of your training?

54. Training is an important part of your AML/CFT system and **must** be part of your programme.[28] Well-designed enhanced CDD procedures, policies and controls may be compromised if you (or your staff) are not adequately trained.

55. Your training should incorporate when and how enhanced CDD will be undertaken, including on-boarding customers, conducting ongoing CDD and submitting SARs. In addition, your enhanced CDD training should also look at what reliable and independent sources of information you can use to verify customer identity, beneficial ownership, and SoW or SoF. Your training should also cover recognised methods and trends in ML/TF that could be deterred or detected by enhanced CDD, as well as any new and emerging techniques.

Can you conduct enhanced CDD via a third party?

56. The Act allows for CDD, including enhanced CDD, to be undertaken for you by a third party. This may be a member of your designated business group, your agent or other reporting entities or persons in another country when certain conditions are met. The Act requires that the third-party consents to conducting the CDD for you and to providing you all relevant information.[29]

57. If a third party is undertaking CDD (including enhanced CDD) for you this **must** be considered in your risk assessment and the procedures, policies and controls included in your programme. Liability for carrying out CDD (including enhanced CDD) remains with you unless certain conditions are met.[30]

28 Section 57(1)(b)

29 Section 32-34

30 Section 33(3)(a)

Part 2: Enhanced CDD and identity requirements

Obtaining and verifying identity information

58. When conducting enhanced CDD on a customer, you **must**[31] obtain the same identity information that is required for standard CDD. This includes the customer's full name, date of birth and address (if an individual) or company identifier or registration number and registered office (if not an individual) and any other information prescribed by the Act or regulations.

59. You **must** take reasonable steps to verify that information, data, or documents are from reliable and independent sources.[32] As you are conducting enhanced CDD, you may need to use increased or more sophisticated measures to do this than you would for standard CDD.

60. To help you determine the level of enhanced CDD verification required for customers that are individuals, you should refer to the **Amended Identity Verification Code of Practice 2013 (IVCOP)** guidance material, and its **explanatory note**. The IVCOP provides suggested best practice to verify the identity of individuals that are low- or medium-risk customers.

Persons acting on behalf of a customer and beneficial owners

61. You **must** identify and verify the identity of any person acting on behalf of the customer and any beneficial owner(s) of the customer. In relation to a person acting on behalf of the customer, and according to the level of risk involved, reasonable steps **must**[33] be taken to verify the information collected so that you are satisfied who the person is *and* that they have the authority to act.

62. In relation to the beneficial owner(s) of the customer, and according to the level of risk involved, reasonable steps **must**[34] be taken to verify the information collected so that you are satisfied that you know the identity of the beneficial owner(s).

Exception handling procedures

63. To comply with the IVCOP, you **must** have appropriate exception handling procedures in place, for circumstances when a customer demonstrates they are unable to satisfy the requirements of the IVCOP.[35] **However, this does not apply to enhanced CDD due to the higher risk of ML/TF.**

31 Section 23

32 Section 13

33 Section 16(1)(c)

34 Section 16(1)(b)

35 Point 4 IVCOP

Enhanced CDD and beneficial owner

64. A core requirement of enhanced CDD is to identify and verify your customers' beneficial ownership arrangements to ensure that you fully understand them. It is crucial to know who the beneficial owner(s) are so that you can make appropriate decisions about the level of ML/TF risk presented by your customer.

65. If you want to do business with a customer, you **must** identify and verify the identity of the beneficial owner(s).[36] You should establish and understand the customer's ownership structure at each layer. The beneficial owner is not necessarily one individual; there may be several beneficial owners in a structure. Where there are complex ownership layers with no reasonable explanation, you should consider the possibility that the structure is used to hide the beneficial owner(s). If so, enhanced CDD may be required.

66. Refer to **Beneficial Ownership Guideline** material for further information on beneficial ownership.

Part 3: Circumstances when enhanced CDD applies

67. This section provides information on the different types of circumstances and customers for whom enhanced CDD is required. This applies equally to business relationships with a customer and occasional transactions and activities.

Trusts

68. You **must** conduct enhanced CDD on a trust or another vehicle for holding personal assets.[37] The requirement for enhanced CDD on trusts recognises the potential use of trusts to disguise the criminal origin of funds or the true ownership and effective control of the trust. This is particularly the case where ownership and control arrangements are sophisticated or complex. Your risk assessment and programme will determine the level of enhanced CDD you conduct on these entities and the assessed ML/TF risk associated with them.

69. For instance, your risk assessment may assess the level of inherent ML/TF risk presented by a domestic 'family' trust as lower than the risk presented by an overseas trust from a jurisdiction with weak AML/CFT measures or high levels corruption. You will still need to conduct enhanced CDD, including verification of SoW or SoF, on the family trust but it will not need to be as in-depth as with the overseas trust. The level of enhanced CDD you decide to undertake should be proportionate to the risks involved.

36 Section11 – Except in circumstances where simplified CDD applies.

37 Sections 22(1)(a)(i) and 22(1)(b)(i)

70. You **must** take reasonable steps, according to the level of risk involved, to verify the identity of any beneficial owners of your customer.[38] This includes instances where the beneficial owner of your customer may be an individual behind another legal arrangement[39] or a company.

71. For a customer that is a trust, you **must** obtain the name and date of birth of each beneficiary of the trust.[40] There is no requirement to verify this information. However, if the customer is a discretionary trust or a trust with more than 10 beneficiaries, you **must** instead obtain a description of each class or type of beneficiary.[41] If the trust is a charitable trust, you **must** also obtain the objects of that trust.[42]

72. To identify the SoW or SoF of a trust you will need to identify the individual(s) who are the settlor(s), and the origin of the settlor's wealth. For example, the settlor may have inherited family wealth, accumulated business earnings, or received funds from the sale of property. You will also need (if relevant) to identify the source of any income that the trust is receiving. For example, it may be income from an underlying company or simply a monthly deposit from a family bank account. See Part 4 for more information.

73. Further information can be found in the **Beneficial Ownership Guideline,** the **CDD fact sheet on trusts** and the associated **"Clarification of the position"** document.

Countries with insufficient AML/CFT measures

74. If your customer is non-resident and from a country with insufficient AML/CFT measures and/or higher ML/TF risks you **must** undertake enhanced CDD.[43] To help you to determine which countries have insufficient AML/CFT measures in place, you should refer to the **Countries Assessment Guideline** published by the AML/CFT supervisors, as well as other guidance material such as those published by FIU, Ministry of Justice, and the Financial Action Task Force (FATF).

Companies with nominee shareholders

75. You **must** conduct enhanced CDD on a customer that is a company with nominee shareholders.[44] The use of nominee shareholders makes it more difficult to identify the beneficial owners of a company, increases the complexity of the company structure and adds another level of obfuscation. This increases the ML/TF risk and enhanced CDD measures are necessary.

38 Section 16(1)(b) and 24(1)(a)

39 Section 5

40 Section 23(2)(a)

41 Section 23(2)(b)(i)

42 Section 23(2)(b)(ii)

43 Sections 22(1)(a)(ii) and 22(1)(b)(ii)

44 Section 22(1)(a)(iii)

Companies with shares in bearer form

76. Shares in bearer form present a high risk of ML/TF. You **must** conduct enhanced CDD on a customer that is a company with some or all of its shares in bearer form.[45] A higher risk of ML/TF exists when a company has some, or all, of its capital in the form of bearer shares. It is often difficult to identify the beneficial owners of a company with bearer shares because they are not registered with any authority. Instead, ownership is based on the customer who physically holds the share document. This means that any transfer of ownership is not registered or regulated. Companies that issue bearer shares are often in higher risk jurisdictions.

Complex or unusual transactions

77. You **must** conduct enhanced CDD on a customer if they conduct:

- A transaction that is complex
- A transaction that is unusually large
- An unusual pattern of transactions that have no apparent or visible economic or lawful purpose.[46]

78. Adequate and effective CDD provides context and helps you understand the types of transactions that your customer should be conducting. It also helps you identify complex and unusual transactions or patterns of transactions, and the situations when you need to conduct enhanced CDD.

79. Your account monitoring is also a vital element in identifying these types of transactions. Whether an automated or manual system is used, this should generate ML/TF alerts for review and examination. You should base your thresholds and scenarios for these alerts on your risk assessment and you should detail your procedures, policies, and controls in your programme.

Assessed risk for a particular situation

80. You **must** conduct enhanced CDD when you consider the level of risk in a particular situation is such that enhanced CDD should apply.[47]

81. This requirement applies to any other situation where there is ML/TF risk not otherwise or specifically identified in the Act. The situations where these ML/TF risks arise should be based on the findings of your risk assessment and they will be particular to your business. The situations may arise from a combination of vulnerabilities associated with the size, nature and complexity of your business, your types of customers, your products and

45 Section 22(1)(a)(iii)

46 Section 22(1)(c)

47 Section 22(1)(d)

services and your methods of delivery, as well as the types of institutions and countries that you deal with.

82. In relation to the countries you deal with, it is important to understand that the risks associated with a country are wider than having insufficient AML/CFT measures in place. Country risk can result from:

- Ineffective AML/CFT measures
- High levels of organised crime
- Perceived levels of bribery and corruption
- Association with TF
- Conflict zones and their bordering countries
- Production and/or transnational shipment of illicit drugs.

83. The **Countries Assessment Guideline** will assist you in determining when enhanced CDD may be required due to country risk. The guideline refers to information sources that can help you in assessing country risk, including, but not limited to:

- FATF identification of jurisdictions with strategic AML/CFT deficiencies
- FATF mutual evaluation reports
- Basel AML Index
- United Nations Office on Drugs and Crime reports
- Transparency International Corruption Perceptions Index
- Reliable and independent media sources.

84. While your risk assessment is the starting point to identify situations where there is ML/TF risk, other indicators may only be identifiable as you administer your programme. This will include your customer's behaviour, the CDD or enhanced CDD you have conducted, your account monitoring and the wider AML/CFT environment. Your risk assessment and programme **must** also have regard to supervisory AML/CFT guidance.[48]

Suspicious activity reports (SARs)

85. As soon as practicable after you become aware that you must report an SAR, you **must** conduct enhanced CDD.[49] You will need to ensure that in conducting the enhanced CDD you do not tip off the customer that you will be submitting an SAR. Unlawful disclosure of SARs (and prescribed transaction reports) is an offence.[50]

86. Conducting enhanced CDD in these circumstances could include asking your customer further questions about their activity or transactions

48 Sections 58(2)(g) and 57(2)

49 Section 22A(2)

50 Section 94

and confirming the nature and purposes of the business relationship. Such enquiries, when conducted properly and in good faith, do not constitute tipping off. It may be the case that after conducting enhanced CDD you determine that your customer's activity is no longer suspicious, and a SAR will not be required.

87. Maintaining clear and logical records of decisions made, by whom, and the reasons for them will help you demonstrate your appropriate handling of unusual or suspicious activities.

New and developing technologies and products

88. New and developing technologies and products can present unknown ML/TF risks and vulnerabilities, and new methods of delivery may be able to bypass existing AML/CFT measures to allow anonymity.

89. Where you have a customer who wants to establish a business relationship, or conduct an occasional transaction/activity, involving new and developing technology and products that might favour anonymity, you **must** take additional enhanced CDD measures to mitigate and manage these ML/TF risks.[51] It is for you to determine what measures are required according to the level of risk involved.

90. Your risk assessment should consider whether your business is, or may be, exposed to customers involved in new and developing technologies and products. Your programme should then detail the procedures, policies, and controls that you will implement for this type of customer and technology.[52]

Part 4: Enhanced CDD and SoW and SoF

91. In many cases, SoW or SoF information and documents required for enhanced CDD will be readily available and quickly provided by your customer. In other cases, you may need to inquire further into complex ownership or control structures, or you may need to examine the origins of your customer's wealth in detail.

92. There are several different forms of enhanced CDD established by the Act,[53] and establishing your customer's SoW or SoF is not always a requirement of enhanced CDD. Reporting entities should determine the requirements of enhanced CDD as it applies to their customer's circumstances.[54] In the circumstances where it applies, you **must** collect information relating to the SoW or SoF of your customer[55] and you **must**,

51 Section 22(5)

52 Section 30

53 Sections 23-30

54 Section 22

55 Section 23(a)

according to the level of risk involved, take reasonable steps to verify[56] that information. Your programme should set out how you will do this.

93. For instance, a high-risk, overseas customer will require greater effort and more comprehensive investigation to verifiy SoW or SoF information than a low-risk, domestic customer. **Even for low-risk customers you must conduct some verification measures.**

What is the difference between SoW and SoF?

94. Your customer's SoW is the origin of their entire body of assets. This information gives an indication of the amount of wealth your customer would be expected to have and a picture of how they acquired it.

95. Your customer's SoF is more narrowly focused. It is the origin of the funds used for the transactions or activities that occur within the business relationship with you. This also applies for an occasional transaction or activity.

96. In circumstances where you are establishing or updating your customer's risk profile you may need to collect and verify information regarding their SoW. However, when enhanced CDD is triggered by circumstances involving transactions or activities, you may need to focus more specifically on the SoF.

97. It is important to remember that your customer's SoW and SoF do not exist in isolation of each other. In a situation where an individual transaction is disproportionately large compared to your knowledge of a customer's wealth, this should trigger a more detailed examination of that transaction or activity. It is for you to determine when to examine your customer's SoW, when to examine their SoF, or when to examine both.

How do you obtain and verify information about SoW or SoF?

98. You should ask your customer to provide you information about their SoW or SoF and record this information.[57] You **must** take reasonable steps, according to the level of risk involved, to verify this information using reliable and independent sources.

99. Where you identify that the origin of your customer's funds or wealth has come from their beneficial owner(s), it may be necessary, according to the level of risk involved, for you to extend your level of verification to include the SoW or SoF of these persons. However, you should not obtain and verify SoW or SoF for every beneficial owner where they have nothing to do with the "customer's" SoW or SoF.

100. To help you verify information about SoW and SoF, you may be able to use publicly available information on the internet, or other commercially available databases. However, in many situations, it will be necessary for your

56 Section 24(1)(b)

57 Section 23

customer to provide you with documents issued by third parties that support their financial position. In higher risk circumstances, it may be necessary to seek further information, either from your customer or directly from the relevant third party.

101. You **must**[58] develop an understanding of the size and nature of your customer's overall wealth and, importantly, how it was acquired. This does not require you to verify their entire financial history or identify every asset that they hold. They may have multiple income streams and assets making this extremely difficult.

102. It may be useful to establish the different categories of income or assets that make up their total wealth. Examples could include their various investments, salary, family income or different types of commercial activity. Where there are multiple categories or income streams, you should focus your verification on the larger of them, as well as those that are the most complex or obfuscated. Once categorised and examined, it should be easier to understand your customer's overall level of wealth.

103. It is not expected that every part of the SoW will be accounted for. However, you **must** be satisfied that the nature and size of your customer's wealth matches what you know about them.

How do you determine SoF?

104. Verifying your customer's funds should be a more granular process. The information, data, or documents that you use should be specific to the business relationship or to their activities and transaction behaviour. This is important when your verification relates to a specific transaction, or sequence of transactions, that your customer is involved in. This also applies to any occasional transaction or activity that you conduct for a customer.

What documents can verify SoW or SoF?

105. When you verify SoW or SoF information, you should use data or documents issued by a credible and reliable source such as a multi-national company, a reputable third-party commercial provider, or a government department from a low-risk country with sufficient AML/CFT measures.

106. The types of data and documents that you use for verification will vary depending on the circumstances and the information that the customer provides to you. The following documents, data, or information could be considered reliable and independent:

- Government-issued or registered documents or data
- Full bank and other investment statements
- Full payslip or wage slip or other documents confirming salary
- GST number and IRD statement of earnings from the most recent year (for sole traders)

58 Sections 23(1)(a) and 24(1)(b)

- Inheritance (stamped grant of probate, stamped grant of letters of administration)
- Audited financial accounts from a chartered accountant or Charities Services
- Letter from an agent of the customer confirming they have knowledge of and established business relationships with the customer
- A copy of a will
- Sales and purchase agreements.

107. For customers who conduct their business activities with you there should be a range of documents you can use to verify how funds have been acquired. Depending on the type of business, this could include contractual agreements, sales and purchase records or import and export related documents for the shipment of goods.

108. Documentation accepted to verify SoW or SoF should depend on the level of ML/TF risk presented by the customer. The higher the risk, the more comprehensive and reliable documents you obtain should be. For instance, we would expect certified copies or originals to be sighted, or verification via other reliable measures such as disclosure registers, for higher risk customers. However, in other circumstances such as in low risk situations or if the original document was only ever signed electronically, you may be able to rely on a copy received by email. You may also need to exercise caution with documents signed by relationship managers that have a vested interest in on-boarding or retaining a customer. In addition, you should be wary of documents that appear fraudulent or altered.

Additional notes regarding SoW or SoF

109. You are, of course, able to conduct your own research to supplement the information and documents that your customer provides you regarding their SoW or SoF. This could be at on-boarding, during ongoing CDD or prior to submitting an SAR. Sources could include:

- Internet
- Trusted intermediaries
- Reliable media
- Publicly available databases
- Professional third-party providers.

110. An accurate understanding of a customer's SoW or SoF is best achieved when it occurs in conjunction with the identification of beneficial owners, and with comprehensive information obtained on the nature and purpose of a business relationship.

Part 5: Enhanced CDD and Politically Exposed Persons (PEPs)

111. A PEP is a person who in the last 12 months has held a prominent overseas position. The term PEP includes their relatives and close associates, which are sometimes called RCAs. It also includes people who have beneficial ownership of legal entities or arrangements existing to benefit PEPs.

112. You **must** as soon as practicable after establishing a business relationship (or occasional activity or transactions) take reasonable steps to determine if your customer, or their beneficial owner, is a PEP.[59]

113. You **must** ensure that you have adequate and effective procedures, policies, and controls to identify customers that are PEPs. This will depend on the size, nature and complexity of your business and the likelihood of having a PEP as a customer.

114. You **must** conduct enhanced CDD on a customer who is a PEP.[60] In addition, your senior management (if applicable) **must** approve continuing the business relationship with a PEP.[61] You **must** obtain and take reasonable steps to verify the PEP's SoW or SoF.[62]

115. According to the level of risk involved, it may be appropriate, as part of your enhanced CDD, to use internet/media searches and publicly available reports to check if your customer is a PEP, especially when they are from a country with high levels of bribery, corruption, and organised crime. With larger or more complex businesses, you may want to consider using the services of a third-party provider and commercially available databases to screen for PEPs.

116. For ongoing CDD and account monitoring of a higher risk PEP, you may need to undertake ongoing media monitoring or increase transaction monitoring activity. You may wish to conduct more frequent enhanced CDD reviews and submit quicker, more thorough SARs.

117. Key enhanced CDD questions to consider are:

- Is the PEP's transaction/activity in line with expectations?
- Is the PEP's identity data, address, employment, SoW or SoF and relatives and close associates' status up to date?
- Are there any unexplained changes to the PEP's details?
- If the PEP's net worth has grown substantially in a short amount of time, do you have a clear explanation for the sudden growth?
- Have you sought clarification from the PEP where necessary and updated their details?

59 Section 26
60 Section 22(2)
61 Section 26(2)(a)
62 Section 26(2)(b)

Part 6: Table of Abbreviations and Acronyms

AML/CFT	Anti-money laundering and countering financing of terrorism
AML/CFT supervisors	The Department of Internal Affairs, the Financial Markets Authority, and the Reserve Bank of New Zealand
The Act	AML/CFT Act 2009
CDD	Customer due diligence
FATF	Financial Action Task Force
FIU	New Zealand Police Financial Intelligence Unit
IVCOP	Amended Identity Verification Code of Practice 2013
ML	Money laundering
PEP	Politically exposed person
Programme	AML/CFT programme
RBA	Risk-based approach
RCA	Relative and close associate
Risk assessment	AML/CFT risk assessment
SAR	Suspicious activity report
SoF	Source of funds
SoW	Source of wealth
STR	Suspicious transaction report
TF	Terrorism financing

Revision History

Dec 2017	Original Version
Mar 2019	Updated Version
Sep 2020	• Structure table moved to front of document. • Updated wording in paragraphs 9 & 10 – there is no substantial meaning change. • Addition of section 'When must SoW or SoF information be obtained?' (paragraphs 32 & 33) – following paragraphs renumbered accordingly. • Update to paragraphs 17 & 21 – replacement of 'must' with 'should usually'. • Addition of bullet point on 'new or developing technologies' to paragraph 24. • Deletion of bullet point on 'material change' from paragraph 27. • Replaced 'should' with 'must' in paragraph 50 (previously 48) in relation to keeping copies of documentation. • Rewording of paragraphs 70 & 71 (previously paragraphs 68 & 69). There is no substantial meaning change. • Addition of sentence to paragraph 108 (previously paragraph 106) relating to electronic copies of documents.

Appendix 6 Amended Identity Verification Code of Practice 2013

Reproduced from the Department of Internal Affairs website, with permission.

(Anti-Money Laundering and Countering Financing of Terrorism Act 2009 sections 16, 20, 24 and 28 for all reporting entities)

The Identity Verification Code of Practice (the code) was approved by notice in the New Zealand Gazette on the 1st day of September 2011 by the Ministers of Finance, Commerce and Internal Affairs under section 64 of the Anti-Money Laundering and Countering Financing of Terrorism Act 2009 (AML/CFT Act). This amended code of practice was approved by notice in the New Zealand Gazette on the 10th day of October 2013.

Introduction

The Identity Verification Code of Practice 2013 Explanatory Note provides background information and resources and should be read in conjunction with this code.

What is this code of practice for?

This code of practice provides a suggested best practice for all reporting entities conducting name and date of birth identity verification on customers (that are natural persons) that have been assessed to be low to medium risk. Identification involves obtaining from the customer a range of information about him or her ("identity information"). Verification involves confirming some of that information against documents, data or information obtained from a reliable and independent source.

Under section 11 of the AML/CFT Act a reporting entity must conduct customer due diligence on a customer; a beneficial owner of a customer; and any person acting on behalf of a customer. In this code of practice, *customer* refers to all natural persons that fall within these categories assessed by reporting entities as low to medium risk (that is falling within sections 11(1)(a) – (c)).

This code of practice provides for two ways of conducting identity verification, via documentary verification and electronic verification (Parts 1 and 3 of the code). Part 2 of the code provides for the certification of documents. This allows for non face-to-face documentary verification.

The AML/CFT Act also requires that reporting entities conduct verification of a customer's address using documents, data or information issued by a reliable and independent source.[1] This code of practice does not prescribe the way in which reporting entities can fulfil this obligation.

1 Sections 13, 16 and 24 of the Act

This code of practice does not apply to the identity verification of customers (that are natural persons) assessed by reporting entities to be high risk. Increased or more sophisticated measures should be applied for high risk customers.

Legal obligations relating to identity verification

Subpart 1 of Part 2 of the AML/CFT Act outlines customer due diligence requirements. A reporting entity's AML/CFT programme, established under sections 56 – 57 of the Act, must include adequate and effective policies, procedures and controls for complying with customer due diligence requirements.

A reporting entity must base its AML/CFT programme, including its assessment of risk for the purpose of customer due diligence, on the AML/CFT risk assessment undertaken in accordance with section 58.

This code of practice applies to customers (that are natural persons) assessed by reporting entities as low to medium risk, for the verification of name and date of birth as required by:

i. Section 16 – standard customer due diligence: verification of identity requirements
ii. Section 20 – simplified customer due diligence: verification of identity requirements
iii. Section 24 – enhanced customer due diligence: verification of identity requirements[2]
iv. Section 28 – wire transfers: verification of identity requirements.

The Financial Markets Authority, Reserve Bank of New Zealand and the Department of Internal Affairs will consider reporting entities who comply with this code of practice to have met their obligations to verify name and date of birth under sections 16, 20, 24 and 28 of the AML/CFT Act for low to medium risk customers (that are natural persons).

> Note: A word or expression used in this code of practice has the same meaning as in the AML/CFT Act (see section 34 of the Interpretation Act 1999).

What will you find in this code of practice?

This code of practice covers all reporting entities in all AML/CFT sectors.

This code of practice is in three parts

PART1: DOCUMENTARY IDENTITY VERIFICATION

PART2: DOCUMENT CERTIFICATION

PART3: ELECTRONIC IDENTITY VERIFICATION

2 The Act requires enhanced due diligence in certain circumstances, however the Act does not predetermine that customers for whom enhanced due diligence is required be assessed as high risk. For example a politically exposed person might be assessed as a low to medium risk customer, but will always be subject to enhanced due diligence as required by section 24.

PART 1: DOCUMENTARY IDENTITY VERIFICATION

In order to conduct documentary verification of a customer's name and date of birth, the following is required:

1. One form of the following primary photographic identification:

a) New Zealand passport

b) New Zealand certificate of identity issued under the Passports Act 1992

c) New Zealand certificate of identity issued under the Immigration New Zealand Operational Manual that is published under section 25 of the Immigration Act 2009

d) New Zealand refugee travel document issued under the Passports Act 1992

e) emergency travel document issued under the Passports Act 1992

f) New Zealand firearms licence

g) overseas passport or a similar document issued for the purpose of international travel which:

  i. contains the name, date of birth, a photograph and the signature of the person in whose name the document is issued; and

  ii. is issued by a foreign government, the United Nations or an agency of the United Nations.

h) a national identity card issued for the purpose of identification, that:

  i. contains the name, date of birth and a photograph of the person in whose name the document is issued and their signature or other biometric measure included where relevant; and

  ii. is issued by a foreign government, the United Nations or an agency of the United Nations.

OR

2. One form of the following primary non-photographic identification:

a) New Zealand full birth certificate

b) certificate of New Zealand citizenship issued under the Citizenship Act 1977

c) a citizenship certificate issued by a foreign government

d) a birth certificate issued by a foreign government, the United Nations or an agency of the United Nations

in combination with a secondary or supporting form of photographic identification, for example:

e) New Zealand driver licence

f) 18+ Card

g) valid and current international driving permit as defined in rule 88(1)(b) of the Land Transport (Driver Licensing) Rule 1999 and a licence from another country with a translation.

Points 2 (e) – (g) above are not an exhaustive list of secondary or supporting forms of photographic identification that may be acceptable. Reporting entities must ensure they are satisfied that any secondary or supporting photographic identification they accept is independent and reliable.

Confirmation that the identity information presented in the secondary or supporting form of photographic identification is consistent with the records held by a reliable and independent source (for example the information that is recorded for the purposes of the Births, Deaths, Marriages, and Relationships Registration Act 1995 or the Citizenship Act 1977 by the Department of Internal Affairs can be substituted for the primary non-photographic identification required in points 2(a)-(d).

OR

3. The New Zealand driver licence and, in addition, one of the following:

a) confirmation that the information presented on the driver licence is consistent with records held in the National Register of driver licences

b) confirmation that the identity information presented on the New Zealand driver licence is consistent with the records held by a reliable and independent source (for example the information that is recorded for the purposes of the Births, Deaths, Marriages, and Relationships Registration Act 1995, the Citizenship Act 1977, or the Passports Act 1992 by the Department of Internal Affairs)

c) a document issued by a registered bank that contains the person's name and signature, for example a credit card, debit card or eftpos card

d) a bank statement issued by a registered bank to the person in the 12 months immediately preceding the date of the application

e) a document issued by a government agency that contains the person's name and signature, for example a SuperGold Card as defined in the Social Security (SuperGold Card) Regulations 2007

f) a statement issued by a government agency to the person in the 12 months immediately preceding the date of the application, for example a statement from the Inland Revenue Department.

> Note: Regulation 13(3) of the Health Entitlement Cards Regulations 1993 places strict restrictions on those who can legally demand or request a community services card as a form of identification. Reporting entities may accept a community services card under point 3(e) if the customer offers it; however they cannot request it.

Appendix 6

4. In order to comply with this code, the reporting entity must have appropriate exception handling procedures in place, for circumstances when a customer demonstrates that they are unable to satisfy the requirements in 1 to 3 above.

5. Reporting entities must have a process in place to check that no other person with the same or similar names has presented the same identity information or documents.

6. Where documents are provided in a language that is not understood by the person carrying out the verification, an English translation must be provided.

7. In all instances where documentary verification is being used a reporting entity should verify the identity of the customer:

a) face to face; or by
b) copies of documents provided that are certified by a trusted referee (see below for certification requirements).

PART 2: DOCUMENT CERTIFICATION

8. In New Zealand a trusted referee must be at least 16 years of age and one of the following:

a) Commonwealth representative (as defined in the Oaths and Declarations Act 1957)
b) Member of the police
c) Justice of the peace
d) Registered medical doctor
e) Kaumātua (as verified through a reputable source)
f) Registered teacher
g) Minister of religion
h) Lawyer (as defined in the Lawyers and Conveyancers Act 2006)
i) Notary public
j) New Zealand Honorary consul
k) Member of Parliament
l) Chartered accountant (within the meaning of section 19 of the New Zealand Institute of Chartered Accountants Act 1996)
m) A person who has the legal authority to take statutory declarations or the equivalent in New Zealand

Certification when overseas

9. When certification occurs overseas, copies of international identification provided by a customer resident overseas must be certified by a person authorised by law in that country to take statutory declarations or equivalent in the customer's country.

10. In addition, the trusted referee must not be:

a) related to the customer; for example, a trusted referee cannot be their parent, child, brother, sister, aunt, uncle or cousin
b) the spouse or partner of the customer
c) a person who lives at the same address as the customer
d) a person involved in the transaction or business requiring the certification.

11. The trusted referee must sight the original documentary identification, and make a statement to the effect that the documents provided are a true copy and represent the identity of the named individual (link to the presenter).

12. Certification must include the name, signature, and the date of certification. The trusted referee must specify their capacity to act as a trusted referee from sections 8(a)-(m) above.

13. Certification must have been carried out in the three months preceding the presentation of the copied documents.

PART 3: ELECTRONIC IDENTITY VERIFICATION

14. An electronic identity is a record kept in electronic form that contains authenticated core identity information about an individual. Electronic identity verification is using that record to verify an individual's identity when a reporting entity is conducting customer due diligence.

15. In order to conduct electronic identity verification of a customer's name and date of birth a reporting entity must;

a) verify the customer's name from either:
   a. a single independent electronic source that is able to verify an individual's identity to a high level of confidence; or
   b. at least two independent and reliable matching electronic sources.
b) verify the customer's date of birth from at least one reliable and independent electronic source.

16. Reporting entities must check the person's details against their customer records, to ensure that no other person has presented the same identity information or documents.

17. When determining what type of electronic sources will be considered reliable and independent, reporting entities must have regard to:

a) accuracy (how up-to-date is the information and what are the error rates and matching parameters);

b) security;

c) privacy (including whether the management and provision of the information is consistent with the Information Privacy Principles 5 to 11 in section 6 of the Privacy Act 1993);

d) method of information collection;

e) whether the electronic source has incorporated a mechanism to determine the customer can be linked to the claimed identity (whether biometrically or otherwise);

f) whether the information is maintained by a government body or pursuant to legislation; and

g) whether the information has been additionally verified from another reliable and independent source.

18. Reporting entities that use electronic identity verification methods must include information in their AML/CFT compliance programme that describes:

a) the forms of electronic identity verification methods that are considered reliable and independent and in what circumstances they will be used for the purposes of identity verification;

b) how the methods have regard to the matters described in clause 17; and

c) any additional methods that will be used to supplement electronic identity verification or otherwise mitigate any deficiencies in the verification process.

> Note: Nothing in this code of practice prevents a reporting entity from obtaining multi-source verification from a single provider, so long as they are satisfied that the requirements in Part 3 are complied with.

Appendix 7 Explanatory Note: Electronic Identity Verification Guideline: For Part 3 – Amended Identity Verification Code of Practice 2013 (July 2021)

Reproduced from the Department of Internal Affairs website, with permission.

Introduction

1. This Explanatory Note and guideline should be read in conjunction with the Amended Identity Verification Code of Practice 2013 (**the code**).

2. The code was approved in October 2013. This followed implementation of the Electronic Identity Verification Act 2012 and the Identity Information Confirmation Act 2012.

3. This Explanatory Note and guideline replaces the previous Explanatory Note that was published by the Supervisors in December 2017. It includes additional content identifying commonly used electronic sources in New Zealand. It also sets out the supervisors' expectations when they review or inspect a reporting entity's Electronic Identity Verification (**EIV**) procedures, policies and controls. Various examples of EIV practices are included at the end of this guideline.

4. This guideline has been produced by the supervisors under s132(2) of the Anti-Money Laundering and Countering Financing of Terrorism Act 2009 (the AML/CFT Act). It cannot be relied on as evidence of complying with the requirements of the AML/CFT Act. This guideline does not constitute legal advice.

What is electronic identity verification under the code

5. EIV is where a customer's identity is verified remotely or non-face-to-face.

6. EIV has two key components, both of which must be satisfied:

- Confirmation of identity information via an electronic source(s); and
- Matching the person you are dealing with remotely to the identity that they are claiming (*i.e. are they the same person*)?

7. An electronic source is the underlying database where authenticated core identity information is held, and against which the individual's identity is verified. In most circumstances, this is going to be information that is maintained by a government body or pursuant to legislation.

8. For electronic identity verification, it is important to remember that an electronic source is not any of the following:

- The person that the reporting entity is dealing with online who provides their biographical information.
- A selfie photo or video received from the person being dealt with online, including audio-visual link or video conferencing technology.
- An uploaded image of the person's identity document(s).
- An email, app or internet platform through which the reporting entity receives information or copies of identity documents.
- The third-party provider (EIV Provider) that a reporting entity uses to conduct its EIV.

Using a single independent source

9. Under the code, a reporting entity can satisfy EIV requirements from a single independent electronic source that is able to verify an individual's identity to a high level of confidence.

10. Only an electronic source that incorporates biometric information or information which provides a level of confidence equal to biometric information enables an individual's identity to be verified to a high level of confidence.[1]

11. When using an electronic source that is able to verify an individual's identity to a high level of confidence, you are not required to separately link the individual to the claimed identity.

12. Biometric information includes measurements of an individual's physical characteristics that can be recorded and used for comparison and automated recognition of that individual *e.g. photographs. Other biometric possibilities in the future could include iris structure or fingerprint information.*

Using two reliable and independent matching sources

13. The code also allows a reporting entity to verify an individual's identity from at least two electronic sources. The individual's name and date of birth must be verified from one source, whereas only the name must be verified from another source. The two electronic sources must be:

- Reliable, and
- Independent, and
- Match each other.[2]

---

1 At the time of publication, only a verified RealMe® identity can meet this requirement in New Zealand. By biometrically matching the person's photo and identity details against New Zealand government records (the electronic source) it verifies the person's identity to a high level of confidence.

2 A reporting entity may verify an individual's identity from two or more "reliable and independent" sources via a single third-party EIV provider.

14. Where two "reliable and independent" sources are used and they match each other, the "high level of confidence" required of a single independent source is not required.

15. Supervisors expect that the primary electronic source used to verify name and date of birth of an individual that is in New Zealand is:

- Confirmation Service (DIA) — Government source - name and date of birth verification from passport, birth, deaths and citizenship database.
- NZ Driver Licence (NZTA) — Government source - name and date of birth verification from NZTA driving licence records.

16. Other common electronic sources in New Zealand that could be used as the second source to verify an individual's name include:

- Credit Bureaus
- Companies Office
- Land Registry (LINZ)
- Vehicle registration (NZTA)

17. Where two matching reliable and independent electronic sources are used, a reporting entity must still have regard to whether the electronic sources include a mechanism to determine if the customer can be linked to the claimed identity (whether biometrically or otherwise). None of the electronic sources listed in paragraphs 15 and 16 above incorporate such a mechanism.

Additional methods required to link the customer to their claimed identity

18. Clause 17(e) of the code requires a reporting entity to consider whether the electronic source(s) has incorporated a mechanism to determine whether the customer can be linked to their claimed identity (whether biometrically or otherwise). If the electronic source(s) does not have such a mechanism, or it is not robust enough, then clause 18 of the code requires that a reporting entity must adopt **additional methods** that will be used to supplement it, or to otherwise mitigate any deficiencies in the process. The additional methods must ensure that the person that the reporting entity is dealing with is the genuine holder of the identity they are claiming.

19. Some examples of additional methods are noted below.[3] At the end of this guideline are further examples of how a person being dealt with online may be linked to the identity that is being verified. How this can be achieved depends, to some extent, on the type of reporting entity, its products and

3 Note: supervisors do not consider the use of video conferencing technology to engage with a customer as a method to link the customer to the identity they are claiming under the code (see example 5 below).

services and how these are delivered to customers. Other considerations include whether an occasional transaction is being conducted, or whether a business relationship is being established (which may enable alignment with the AML/CFT Act's delayed verification provisions).

- Require the first credit into the customer's account or facility to be received from an account/facility held at a New Zealand registered bank in the customer's name that cannot be altered or changed. The list of New Zealand registered banks that do not allow the customer to alter or change the payer name is provided in the appendix.

  If you are utilising this as an additional method, it is important that you have controls in place to ensure the name matches your customer's identity. This is because there are no industry standards relating to naming conventions and character restrictions in banking systems can impede the completeness of a person's name received. If the payment arrives and the name does not match, there must be an escalation process.

- Issue a letter that contains a unique reference/identifier to the customer's address that has been verified by a reliable and independent source. The letter/unique reference number must be returned (either physically or via an electronic channel) to the reporting entity before the customer's account or facility is fully operational e.g. before any withdrawals/debits can be conducted.

- Robust steps to ensure the authenticity of any identification document electronically provided by the customer. This will require the use of an EIV provider able to confirm the identity document is authentic and that it was issued to the person being dealt with online. This process must ensure the document has not been forged, altered or tampered with in any way, including the photo on the document (see example 2 below).

  If you are using an EIV provider in this way, you should assess and document the level of assurance provided. We expect your EIV provider to be able to assist you with this. Considerations should include how the images are obtained, for example incorporating liveness test, the steps taken to confirm the authenticity of the image on the identity document and the reliability of facial recognition software used.

- Phone the customer on a number that has been verified by a reliable and independent source before the customer's account or facility is fully operational e.g. before any withdrawals/debits can be conducted. For example, phoning a customer on a fixed line through an employer.

- Robust security type questions based on reliable and independent information obtained about a person's financial footprint. This information should not be publicly available or easily obtained.

This is not an exhaustive list and there may be other adequate additional measures. Please contact your AML/CFT Supervisor to discuss further.

Document your EIV procedures

20. Under clause 18 of the code, reporting entities that utilise EIV must clearly document as part of their AML/CFT Programme how all the relevant criteria within the code are satisfied. The key principle is that your EIV procedures are documented. The following information should be described:

Include	Explanation
When you will use EIV.	Will you use it: • As the default method • As a backup • When you can't face-to-face on-board someone • In conjunction with face-to-face • For NZ residents only • For lower risk customers only, etc.
EIV provider and product.	If you rely on a third party to conduct EIV (EIV Provider), detail your EIV provider and the EIV product that you are using. If you are using multiple providers or different providers for NZ resident customers and those abroad, explain this. You should also explain how you are using the product. Do you log into your provider's product and enter your customers' details directly or is there an integrated feed? Are you using a combination of different offerings from your provider?
The electronic source(s) used to verify the person's name and date of birth.	What selected electronic sources are you verifying your customer's name and date of birth against in NZ and elsewhere? EIV providers often allow you to choose a range of electronic sources to verify customer details against.[4] You must explain which sources your EIV providers are using. You must ensure the sources you choose meet all relevant requirements or provide the necessary level of assurance. It is harder to fake identity information across multiple data sources. The more sources used to verify identity information, the increased assurance this provides.

4 Note: In our experience, all EIV providers offer multi source verification for customers resident in NZ and Australia. This broadly uses the same databases. For access to EIV sources outside of NZ and Australia, there are different EIV providers depending on the country. We are aware of some offshore based providers promoting EIV solutions that do not verify customer identity information against an underlying source (such as a government database). If you have customers outside of NZ and Australia, you should discuss this with your EIV provider to ensure the EIV sources they offer, meet your requirements.

Include	Explanation
Record keeping processes.	You should describe how you will capture and record the information submitted by your customer and the evidence of the EIV (the result). Many EIV providers will not keep that information for longer than a few days.
How you check your records that a prospective customer's details have not previously been used.	These are not unique requirements because you use EIV. These are requirements for all customer due diligence (CDD) activity (refer to clauses 5 and 16 of the code).
Exception and escalation processes	Unsuccessful EIV requires escalation and individual review. In some circumstances, a person's identity may not be verifiable to the required level. Rather than accepting a lower standard, it may be necessary to adopt face-to-face or certified copy verification under Part 1 or 2 of the code.

21. Your documented EIV procedures should make it clear if you are using a single independent source to high level of confidence; or two (or more) reliable and independent matching sources.

Single independent source

22. If using a single **independent electronic source** able to verify an individual's identity to a high level of confidence, you should document how this level of assurance is met.

Two reliable and independent sources

23. If using two matching **reliable and independent** electronic sources, you must follow and document the steps set out in clauses 17 and 18 of the code. This should include your consideration of:

Include	Explanation
Clause 17 of the code requires you to assess and document their reliability and independence. This should include your consideration of: a) Accuracy b) Security c) Privacy	If you rely on an EIV Provider, we would generally expect your EIV provider to assist you to assess and document the reliability and independence of the electronic sources they use. You should keep evidence of your analysis.

Include	Explanation
d) Method of information collection e) If the source can link a customer to their claimed identity f) Whether the information is maintained by a government body or pursuant to legislation g) Whether the information has been additionally verified from another reliable and independent source	We also expect that you treat an outsourced EIV provider as you would all key outsourced relationships. We may ask you to explain the due diligence (DD) performed on engaging your EIV provider and any ongoing DD performed to ensure the EIV provider continues to meet your expectations. How you continue to assess independence and reliability of your electronic sources should be part of your regular DD review and should be documented as well.
Clause 18 of the code requires that if you are using two electronic sources with no mechanism to link customer to claimed identity, you implement additional methods to link the person you are dealing with online to the identity they are claiming to be (being the identity you are verifying).	You must document what additional methods are used and explain how this supplements your EIV or mitigates any deficiencies in the verification process (see clause 18(c) of the code).

Customers who established a business relationship before 30 June 2013

24. Electronic sources could also be used to verify or 'top up' identity information for existing customers who established a business relationship with a reporting entity before 30 June 2013. Requirements in the code will still apply. In some situations, the linking mechanism may not be required for the existing customers if the reporting entity has evidence that the customer was 'linked' via face-to-face when they first established a business relationship.

Examples

Example 1. NZ based reporting entity accepting domestic and overseas customers (Additional method – initial deposit requirements)

ABC Limited, a reporting entity based in New Zealand, has customers in New Zealand and two other countries. To verify a new customer's name and date of birth, ABC Limited:

a) Utilises an EIV provider and two electronic sources in all three countries and always checks the verification result is positive.

b) The electronic sources used by ABC Limited have mechanisms that check that the identity is genuine but do not have mechanisms that link the person being dealt with online to that identity.

c) Requires the customer's first deposit of funds to the reporting entity from a bank account in the customer's name. There are controls in place to ensure this occurs, that the name matches when the bank transfer is received and there is an escalation process if it does not.

Supervisor view:

ABC Limited's EIV process provides a pathway to comply with the code. To ensure compliance, ABC Limited must follow the steps set out in clauses 17 and 18 of the code. This includes assessing whether the electronic sources in the respective countries are maintained by a government database or pursuant to legislation. In practice, the supervisor's view is that the primary electronic source used for name and date of birth verification should be a government database.

As none of their EIV Provider's electronic sources link the person being dealt with to the identity being verified, it is necessary to adopt an additional method. ABC Limited's process for checking the transfer is received from a bank account in customer's name is a way of meeting this requirement. They should also confirm the transfer is from a bank registered in New Zealand and listed in the Appendix to this guideline. If the transfer is from a bank registered in New Zealand but **not** listed in the Appendix to this guideline, they should adopt a separate method for linking the customer to their identity. For overseas customers, a credit from an account at a bank registered in a country with sufficient AML/CFT systems is likely sufficient to link the customer to their identity.

Example 2. Identity document authentication, then verification from two reliable and independent reliable and independent electronic sources (Additional method – robust electronic tamper checks and facial recognition software)

DEF Limited uses an EIV provider with access to electronic sources, including the DIA Confirmation Service. However, neither the DIA Confirmation Service nor any of the other electronic sources that the EIV provider uses incorporate a mechanism to determine whether the customer can be linked to the claimed identity (whether biometrically or otherwise).

Therefore, additional methods are required under clause 18 of the code. The EIV provider offers a solution that can validate the authenticity of an identity document, as well as use facial recognition software to match the image of the person on that document with an image of the person being dealt with online.

DEF Limited wants to electronically verify the identity of a new customer, who is a New Zealand citizen. To verify the new customer's name and date of birth, the EIV provider:

a) Collects the full name and date of birth of the customer, along with their New Zealand passport number and its expiry date.

b) Captures an image of that passport.

c) Captures an image of the person being dealt with online using a robust liveness detection system.

d) Uses facial recognition software to match the image of the person being dealt with online to the image of that person on the New Zealand passport.

e) Checks are undertaken to assure there has been no tampering with the passport, including validating machine-readable zone data and other passport security features.

f) Verification of the full name and date of birth of the customer, and their NZ passport, is then undertaken using the DIA Confirmation Service.

g) The customer's name is also verified from another electronic source.

Supervisor view:

DEF Limited's EIV process provides a pathway to comply with the code. This combines verification of the name and date of birth of the customer from two reliable and independent sources, together with additional methods to link the person being dealt with online to the identity being verified.

In this example, the additional method occurs at steps (c), (d) and (e) of the process. It occurs when the image of the person being dealt with online is captured and then matched using facial recognition software to the image on the passport, with tampering checks also performed on the passport. The matched identity is then verified from two reliable and independent sources. One of these is the DIA Confirmation Service that verifies the person's identity and passport from the DIA passport database.

Example 3. Facial recognition software technology as a standalone solution without electronic sources

GHI Limited uses an EIV provider with a facial recognition technology solution. Similarly to example 2) above, the EIV provider's product requires a customer to take a photo of their passport, together with an image captured from a live video feed of themselves. Using the EIV provider's facial recognition technology, an image of the customer captured from the live video feed is then matched to the image on the passport. Checks are also undertaken to validate security features on the image of the passport, including for the machine-readable zone. However, there is no verification undertaken to authenticate that the identity on the passport is genuine.

Supervisor view:

This does not comply with the code. Even though a facial recognition software solution is being used, there is no verification from any reliable and independent electronic source.

Example 4. Delayed verification (Additional method – delayed verification in person)

MNOP Limited is often instructed by a new customer by phone or email to establish a business relationship relating to a captured activity. At a later point the customer must attend the office of MNOP Limited in person to sign a contract and other paperwork related to the captured activity. MNOP Limited's EIV process is as follows:

a) Collect identity information from the new customer and ask them to email a scanned (uncertified) copy of their passport information page.

b) Undertake verification of the customer's name and date of birth from two reliable and independent electronic sources, one of which verifies the passport using the DIA Confirmation Service.

c) Commence providing the captured activity to the customer, but not conclude it.

d) When the customer attends the MNOP Limited office, the original passport must be sighted.

Supervisor view:

MNOP Limited's EIV process provides a pathway to comply with the code when establishing a business relationship with a client. The customer's identity is being verified from two reliable and independent electronic sources, but neither source incorporates a method to link the customer to the identity they claim to be. This required additional method is achieved later when the customer attends the office with their original passport. This relies on the delayed verification provisions of s16(3) and s24(3) of the AML/CFT Act but is conditional on:

a) Remote onboarding being essential not to interrupt normal business practice; and

b) Money laundering/terrorism financing risks are effectively managed through procedures of transaction limitations and account monitoring or (if the reporting entity is not a financial institution) through other appropriate risk management procedures; and

c) Verification of identity is completed as soon as practicable once the business relationship has been established.

Note that the delayed verification provisions are only applicable when establishing a business relationship. (i.e. they may not be relied on for a customer that is undertaking an occasional transaction or occasional activity through a reporting entity).

Example 5. Video conferencing technology

QRST Limited onboards all customers remotely. It uses an EIV provider with access to electronic sources, including the DIA Confirmation Service to confirm the identity information. To then link the customers to the identity they claim, QRST Limited will arrange a video conference call with the customer. During the call, they request the customer to hold up the identity document on the photo page.

Supervisor view

QRST Limited's method for remotely matching their customer to the identity that they are claiming **does not meet the requirements of the Code.** A purely visual human eye inspection on a video conference call is insufficient to link the customer to their claimed identity to satisfy the requirements of the code.

Example 6. RealMe

When WXY Limited onboards a new customer, it verifies the customer's name and date of birth from a single independent electronic source using RealMe. This is only for customers that have a verified RealMe identity.

Supervisor view:

This complies with the code. RealMe is enabled by the Electronic Identity Verification Act 2012, the purpose of which is to provide "a high degree of confidence in an individual's identity". There is a biometric matching process in that the person must have their photo taken, which is then matched to the photo in the DIA passport database (or in some circumstances, the Immigration NZ database). This provides "a high degree of confidence in an individual's identity".

High-risk customers

25. The code is only applicable for customers that are assessed by the reporting entity as low to medium risk. It does not apply to customers assessed as high-risk. The code states that increased or more sophisticated measures should be applied for high-risk customers.

26. While the code is not applicable for high-risk customers, the supervisors' view is that it can still be used as a basis for a reporting entity to develop its name and date of birth verification procedures for high-risk persons.

27. However, the supervisors consider that the code should be the minimum level of verification that is applied to a high-risk customer. The types of further verification steps that are required for high-risk customers (beyond those outlined in the code) will depend on the customer and the reason they are assessed as high-risk.

28. If the reporting entity is satisfied that the high-risk customer's name and date of birth are correct, it may not be necessary to adopt any additional verification steps beyond those in the code. Instead, the reporting entity should place increased focus on other components of CDD. This may include obtaining further information on the nature and purpose of the business relationship and/or verifying the customer's source of funds or wealth (as part of enhanced CDD).

29. However, if the reporting entity is not satisfied that the high-risk customer's name and date of birth are correct, then additional verification steps (beyond those in the code) should be adopted. For customers being verified by EIV, these could include:

- Using three or more electronic sources to verify name and date of birth;
- Adopting further additional methods, including in combination with each other;
- Requiring the customer to visit the reporting entity in person with their original identity documents.

New and emerging risks and threats

30. Reporting entities should consider new and emerging risks or threats to the EIV tools and processes that they utilise, including associated mitigation.

About codes of practice

31. Codes of practice are intended to provide a statement of practice to assist reporting entities to comply with certain AML/CFT Act obligations. Codes of practice are dealt with in subpart 5 of the AML/CFT Act. Codes of practice set out the suggested best practice for meeting obligations. Some codes will cover all sectors, while others will be applicable to specific sectors or sub-sectors.

32. Complying with a code of practice is not mandatory. The AML/CFT regime allows for flexibility and scope for innovation because reporting entities can opt out of a code of practice. However, if fully complied with, codes of practice operate as a 'safe harbour'. The legal effect of a code of practice is described in section 67 of the AML/CFT Act. Note: This guideline does not operate as a 'safe harbour'.

33. If a reporting entity opts out of the code of practice it does not receive the benefit of the safe harbour. In these circumstances, the reporting entity must comply with the relevant statutory obligation by some other equally effective means. In order for this to be a defence to any act or omission by the reporting entity, the reporting entity must have provided written notification to its AML/CFT supervisor that it has opted out of compliance with the code and intends to satisfy its obligations by some other equally effective means.

Resources for the Amended Identification Verification Code of Practice 2013:

- Identification Management Standards available on the Department of Internal Affairs' website
- Te Kāhui Māngai, a directory of Iwi and Māori organisations available on Te Puni Kokiri website.

Appendix

First credits that can be relied upon to determine whether the customer can be linked to their claimed identity can come from any of the following registered banks:

ANZ Bank New Zealand Ltd

ASB Bank Limited

Australia and New Zealand Banking Group Limited

Bank of Baroda (New Zealand) Limited

Bank of China Limited

Bank of China (New Zealand) Limited

Bank of India (New Zealand) Limited

China Construction Bank Corporation

China Construction Bank (New Zealand) Limited

Citibank N A

Commonwealth Bank of Australia

Heartland Bank Limited

Industrial and Commercial Bank of China (New Zealand) Limited

JPMorgan Chase Bank NA

Kiwibank Limited

Kookmin Bank

MUFG Bank, Ltd

Coöperatieve Rabobank U.A. trading as Rabobank Nederland

Rabobank New Zealand Limited

Southland Building Society

The Co-operative Bank Limited

The Hongkong and Shanghai Banking Corporation Limited

TSB Bank Limited

Westpac Banking Corporation

Westpac New Zealand Limited

Version History

2013	Amended Identity Verification Code of Practice - Explanatory Note 2013
December 2017	Amended Identity Verification Code of Practice - Explanatory Note 2017 - Replaced Explanatory Note 2013 - Updated to include clarification regarding requirement to link person to claimed identity through additional methods.
July 2021	Explanatory Note: Electronic Identity Verification Guideline – 2021 - Replaced Explanatory Note 2017 - Includes additional content regarding documenting EIV procedures, supervisor expectations and examples of EIV solutions.

Appendix 7

Appendix 8 Interpreting "ordinary course of business" Guideline (Updated December 2017)

Reproduced from the Department of Internal Affairs website, with permission.

What is this guideline for?

1. This guideline is designed to help clarify the meaning of the phrase "in the ordinary course of business". The meaning of this phrase is important if your business conducts one (or more) of the activities listed under the definitions of financial institution", "designated non-financial business or profession", and "high-value dealer" in the Anti-Money Laundering and Countering Financing of Terrorism Act 2009 (AML/CFT Act).

2. If you conduct the activity "in the ordinary course of business", your business will be a reporting entity under the AML/CFT Act. (This is the case unless any regulation or notice has declared your business not to be a reporting entity for the purposes of the AML/CFT Act.)

3. If you are unsure whether an activity you conduct is considered to be "in the ordinary course of business", this guideline may help you. It explains how your AML/CFT supervisor is likely to approach the interpretation of this phrase.

4. This guideline sets out a number of factors which, when considered together, may indicate whether an activity is in your ordinary course of business. However, it cannot take into account the unique circumstances of your business. Further, it does not constitute legal advice from any of the AML/CFT supervisors and cannot be relied on as such.

The meaning of "ordinary course of business" in the AML/CFT Act

5. Whether an activity is in your "ordinary course of business" will depend on your particular business. It is ultimately a question of judgement, which takes into account certain factors.

6. For most businesses, it will be obvious whether an activity they conduct is in their "ordinary course of business". For example, it is in the ordinary course of business for most retail banks to accept deposits from the public.

7. Some businesses may, however, find it difficult to interpret this phrase. For example, a business that conducts an activity rarely, or in a very limited capacity, or only on certain occasions, may be unsure whether that activity is in its ordinary course of business.

8. If you are unsure whether an activity your business conducts is in your "ordinary course of business", you should consider whether the activity:

- Is normal or otherwise unremarkable for your particular business (ie, features in your systems, processes, advertising, staff training etc.)
- Is frequent
- Is regular
- Involves significant amounts of money
- Is a source of income for your business
- Involves significant allocation of resources
- Is involved in a service or product that is offered to customers

9. You should consider the extent to which each factor accurately describes the activity in your business. Each factor is not definitive by itself; instead, all factors should be taken into consideration. Together, they will indicate whether the activity is in your ordinary course of business.

10. For example, you may conduct an activity that is insignificant in scale or extent but it still may be in your ordinary course of business if you conduct it frequently and it features prominently in your advertising and staff manuals.

11. If, after considering these factors, you are still unsure whether you are a reporting entity, you should seek professional legal advice, or contact your AML/CFT supervisor. If you have not established a relationship with a supervisor, contact your AML/CFT supervisor and they will advise you on what you need to do. If you are unsure of who your AML/CFT supervisor is, contact any of the AML/CFT supervisors for further assistance.

Activity considered normal or otherwise unremarkable

12. Activities that are very unusual for a business, given its history and normal operations, are less likely to be considered "ordinary". Various aspects of a business or operation may help you with this analysis. For example, if an activity features in your company's staff manual and training, or if you have a prescribed procedure for it, it is more likely to be in your ordinary course of business. Likewise, if you advertise the activity, it is more likely to be in your ordinary course of business.

Frequency of the activity

13. As with all factors set out in this guideline, whether an activity occurs frequently will require an assessment of the activity in the context of your business. The more frequent the activity over a period of time, the more likely it is to be an ordinary part of your business.

Regularity of the activity

14. How regularly you conduct the activity is also a relevant factor. "Regular" in this sense means predictable, uniformly occurring and consistent. The more "regular" an activity, the more likely it is to be in your ordinary course of business.

15. For the avoidance of doubt, regularity in this context is closely related to frequency. However, they are distinct considerations: an activity that is conducted on the 4th of April each year is regular but not frequent.

Financial scale of the activity

16. The amount of money involved in an activity, proportional to the rest of your business, is also relevant. The more money it involves, the more likely it is to be in the ordinary course of your business.

17. To assess this factor, we suggest you take a period of time and consider the money involved in the activity. Please consider both transaction values and the revenue your business derives from it. This averaging will give a more accurate indication of the nature of the activity in your business. For the avoidance of doubt, low-value activities may still be an ordinary part of your business, depending on the other factors outlined in this guideline.

Activity generates revenue

18. A related, although separate, factor is whether the activity is involved in the generation of revenue. Naturally, an activity is more likely to be in the ordinary course of business if it is conducted with the intention of generating revenue.

Resources committed to the activity

19. The more resources an activity consumes, the more likely it is to be in the ordinary course of business. Resources could mean staff time, capital expenditure and/or any other input. Once again, we suggest you take a period of time and consider the resources you commit to the activity in question.

20. For example, if you have a staff member who is permanently involved in a particular activity, it is very likely this activity is an ordinary part of your business.

Activity involved in offering to customers

21. Most of the activities listed under the definitions of "financial institution" and "designated non-financial business or profession" in the AML/CFT Act explicitly involve a customer or third party. If an activity is involved in the offering of a product or service to customers or third parties, it is much more likely to be considered in the ordinary course of business.

AML/CFT supervisors' contact details:

Reserve Bank of New Zealand	Department of Internal Affairs	Financial Markets Authority
Phone: 64 4 472 2029	Phone 64 4 495 7200	Phone 64 4 472 9830
Email: amlcft@rbnz.govt.nz	Email: amlcft@dia.govt.nz	Email: aml@fma.govt.nz

Appendix 9 Guideline: Lawyers and Conveyancers Complying with the Anti-Money Laundering and Countering Financing of Terrorism Act 2009 (December 2017)

Reproduced from the Department of Internal Affairs website, with permission.

Executive summary

It is likely that money laundering is currently going undetected in New Zealand. Money laundering is the method by which people disguise the illegal origins of the proceeds of crime and protect and enjoy their assets. Some people in New Zealand may also be financing the activities of terrorists and known terrorist organisations. Financers of terrorism use similar techniques to money launderers to avoid detection by authorities and to protect the identity of those providing and receiving the funds.

People with criminal intentions value anonymity and are looking for ways to distance themselves from their activities while still enjoying the proceeds of their crime. Both domestic and international evidence suggests that using gatekeepers, such as lawyers and conveyancers, is a way for criminals to create a false perception of legitimately acquired wealth. The recent changes to the Anti-Money Laundering and Countering Financing of Terrorism Act 2009 (the AML/CFT Act or the Act) included lawyers and conveyancers in the AML/CFT system.[1]

The AML/CFT Act is activities-based. Only lawyers and conveyancers who undertake specified activities will need to develop a programme to ensure they comply with the requirements in the Act. The flow chart on page 8 of this guideline can help you determine if you are captured by the AML/CFT Act.

You must comply with the AML/CFT Act by ensuring you identify, understand and can assess the risks of money laundering and terrorist financing (ML/ TF) to your business, and by implementing an AML/ CFT programme to manage those risks. AML/CFT programmes will vary from business to business according to each management's judgement about how to best manage the specific risks they have assessed. This guideline provides a summary of what businesses must include in their AML/CFT programme to ensure they comply with the Act.

Lawyers and conveyancers need to know their customers. Before conducting captured activities, they need to conduct customer due diligence (CDD) according to the level of risk posed by their customers. CDD is not optional.

1 The recent changes were made by the Anti-Money Laundering and Countering Financing of Terrorism Amendment Act 2017 (the AML/CFT Amendment Act).

When lawyers or conveyancers are not able to complete CDD, they must not undertake a captured activity or transaction for that customer. To do so would be a breach of the AML/CFT Act.

The Department of Internal Affairs (DIA) is the supervisor charged with monitoring lawyers' and conveyancers' compliance with the AML/CFT Act. We recognise that adjusting to the new AML/CFT system will take time and effort. Lawyers will have the additional task of ensuring they uphold legal professional privilege. This guideline, and other existing guidelines, can help law firms, conveyancing practitioners and incorporated conveyancing firms to develop robust awareness of the risks posed by ML/TF and provide prompts on what to think about when developing programmes to manage these risks. We are available to respond to queries, and we are working with professional bodies in the legal and conveyancing sectors to ensure that the sectors are well supported to meet their obligations under the AML/CFT Act.

Disclaimer

This guideline is provided for information only and cannot be relied on as evidence of complying with the requirements of the AML/CFT Act. It does not constitute legal advice and cannot be relied on as such. After reading this guideline, if you do not fully understand your obligations you should seek legal advice or contact your AML/CFT supervisor. DIA can be contacted at amlphase2@dia.govt.nz.

Glossary

AML/CFT Act	Anti-Money Laundering and Countering Financing of Terrorism Act 2009
AML/CFT Amendment Act	Anti-Money Laundering and Countering Financing of Terrorism Amendment Act 2017
Captured activities	Activities that are specified under the definition of "designated non-financial business or profession" in the AML/CFT Act
CDD	Customer due diligence
Compliance officer	An individual (usually an employee) appointed to administer and maintain the AML/CFT compliance programme
Customers/Clients	While the term "clients" is more commonly used in both the legal and conveyancing sectors, the term "customers" is used throughout the AML/CFT Act. In this guideline please read the term "customers" as referring to your "clients"
DBG	Designated business group
DIA	Department of Internal Affairs
DNFBP	Designated non-financial business or profession
FATF	Financial Action Task Force
FIU	New Zealand Police Financial Intelligence Unit

Financing terrorism offence	As defined in section 8(1) of the Terrorism Suppression Act 2002
goAML	FIU reporting portal
Law firm	A barrister or a barrister and solicitor who is practising on the barrister's or a barrister and solicitor's own account in sole practice; or, two or more barrister and solicitors practising law in partnership, (ie, a partnership); or, an incorporated law firm
ML/TF	Money laundering or terrorist financing
Money laundering offence	As defined in section 243 of the Crimes Act 1961
PEP	Politically exposed person
PTR	Prescribed transaction report
Reporting entities	Casinos; designated non-financial businesses or professions; financial institutions; high-value dealers; and the New Zealand Racing Board
SAR	Suspicious activity report
SPR	Suspicious property report
Supervisors	Supervisors have responsibility for monitoring compliance with the AML/CFT Act. DIA is the supervisor for reporting entities in the legal and conveyancing professions among other sectors. The Reserve Bank of New Zealand and the Financial Markets Authority supervise other sectors

Introduction

This guideline is for law firms, conveyancing practitioners and incorporated conveyancing firms who have compliance obligations under the Anti-Money Laundering and Countering Financing of Terrorism Act 2009 (the AML/CFT Act or the Act) from 1 July 2018.[2] Those that do are "reporting entities" for the purposes of the Act. The Department of Internal Affairs (DIA) is the supervisor for the legal and conveyancing professions.[3]

2 "Law firms", "conveyancing practitioners" and "incorporated conveyancing firms" are defined in section 5(1) of the AML/CFT Act: http://bit.ly/2xHGfmy

3 Section 130(c), AML/CFT Act (http://bit.ly/2A2AKj7). There are two other supervisors for other reporting entities: the Reserve Bank of New Zealand and the Financial Markets Authority. References to "the supervisors" in this document refer to all three agencies collectively.

As your supervisor, DIA expects lawyers[4] and conveyancers to:

1. Know your money laundering and terrorist financing (ML/TF) risks
2. Know if the AML/CFT Act applies to your business
3. Know how legal professional privilege applies
4. Know your compliance requirements
5. Know your customer
6. Know the red flags of ML/TF
7. Know your AML/CFT supervisor
8. Know where to get support

This guideline will help reporting entities in the legal and conveyancing professions to meet each of the expectations identified above. The AML/CFT Act requires that reporting entities have regard to any guidance produced by the AML/CFT supervisor and the Commissioner of Police when developing their risk assessment and AML/CFT programme.[5]

This guideline does not provide a "how to" guide or additional prescription to complement the AML/CFT Act. A one-size-fits-all approach will not work well for most reporting entities. Instead, this guideline will help lawyers and conveyancers increase their awareness of ML/TF risks, and provides prompts for how to manage your compliance.

Over time new case law may become available, new regulations may be made, or existing regulations amended, and this guideline will be updated. The DIA website provides a reference page to find the relevant regulations.[6] DIA will inform reporting entities of any new regulations or updates to existing guidance. The AML/CFT supervisors have already produced a wide range of guidance, much of which lawyers and conveyancers are likely to find useful. The guidelines are all available on the DIA website and are referred to throughout this guideline where relevant.[7] Other guidelines may be produced in the future as needed.

You can contact us at amlphase2@dia.govt.nz if you have further questions.

1. Know your ML/TF risks

Undetected financial crime reduces the integrity of national and international financial systems, distorts the economy and diminishes opportunities for

4 While the AML/CFT Act refers to "law firms, conveyancing practitioners, and incorporated conveyancing firms", this guide refers to "lawyers and conveyancers" for ease of reference. You should read these terms to have the same meaning – as defined in section 5(1) of the AML/CFT Act: http://bit.ly/2xHGfmy

5 Sections 58(2)(g) (http://bit.ly/2ly11Dz) and 57(2) (http://bit.ly/2h2nN59) of the AML/CFT Act.

6 AML/CFT Act and Regulations: http://bit.ly/2hpGU5V

7 Codes of Practice and Guidelines: http://bit.ly/2gQ3Iev

legitimate economic activities. The Government loses tax revenue, while people are rewarded for criminal behaviour. New Zealand is at risk of being targeted by international criminal networks to inject the proceeds of crime into the international financial system. Money laundering and financing of terrorism are not solely international crimes. Domestic criminals use a variety of methods to conceal the proceeds of their criminal activities from authorities in New Zealand.

The Financial Action Task Force (FATF) is an intergovernmental body that sets standards for combating ML/TF and other related threats to the integrity of the international financial system. New Zealand has included legal and conveyancing professionals in the AML/CFT system in response to recommendations made by the FATF.[8] The FATF has provided the following diagram to describe the two potential trajectories of legal professionals' involvement in ML/ TF.[9]

Using legal professionals is attractive to some people because these professionals are required for the completion of certain kinds of transactions and because their specialist legal or notarial skills can be misused to assist the laundering of criminal proceeds or funding terrorism. Both legal and conveyancing professionals add respectability to transactions.

When these professionals lack ML/TF awareness, they are more at risk of inadvertently helping criminals.

Given these risks, and the FATF recommendations, the Government has chosen to engage gatekeeper professions in the collective efforts to deter and detect these crimes. The more eyes and ears attuned to the indicators (or red flags) of these crime types, the more likely people will struggle to benefit financially from criminal activities. By expanding the AML/CFT system to include the gatekeeper professions, the Government intends that gatekeepers will be better able to protect themselves from customers who launder money and finance terrorism. The AML/CFT system has been designed to help businesses achieve the level of compliance required to assist authorities to identify criminal customers.

Compliance also has a value for business risk management. Professionals closely guard their reputations. It is in their interest to avoid relationships with customers who will cause them disrepute in the legal community or censure by their professional bodies or government authorities. Businesses that fail to comply and are misused by criminals risk negative media coverage

8 FATF evaluations of New Zealand: http://bit.ly/2nY08F1

9 Financial Action Task Force, (June 2013), Money Laundering and Terrorist Financing Vulnerabilities of Legal Professionals, FATF, Paris, p. 35. Please note, where it refers to STR in the diagram, it means "suspicious transaction report". We now refer to these as "suspicious activity reports" (SARs).

both in New Zealand and internationally. This also diminishes New Zealand's international reputation as a safe place to do business.

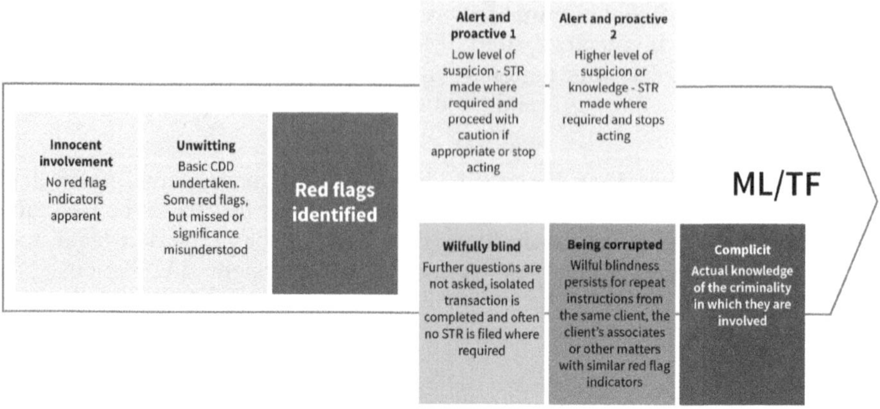

2. Know if the AML/CFT Act applies to your business

Law firms, conveyancing practitioners and incorporated conveyancing firms will have obligations under the AML/ CFT Act when they conduct certain activities (referred to throughout this guidance as "captured activities"). This section provides more detail about these captured activities and why they are included in the Act. The following flow chart provides a quick way to check if you are captured under the AML/CFT Act.

Am I captured by the AML/CFT Act as a DNFBP?

Are you a law firm, a conveyancing practitioner, an incorporated conveyancing firm, an accounting practice, a real estate agent, or a trust and company service provider?

YES

Do you do any of these activities in the ordinary course of business?

Act as a formation agent of legal persons or legal arrangements

OR

Act as, or arrange for a person to act as, a nominee director, nominee shareholder or trustee in relation to legal persons or legal arrangements

OR

Manage client funds (other than sums paid for professional services), accounts, securities or other assets

OR

Provide real estate agent work to effect a transaction

OR

Provide a registered office or a business address, a correspondence address, or an administrative address for a company or partnership, or for any legal person or legal arrangement (unless that service is provided solely as an ancillary service to the provision of other services that are not captured by the definition of a DNFBP)

OR

Engage in or give instructions on behalf of a customer to another person for:

- Any conveyancing to effect a transaction (see section 5(1) for more detail)
- A transaction within the meaning of section 4(1) of the Real Estate Agents Act 2008
- A transfer of beneficial interest in land or other real property
- A transaction on behalf of any person for buying or selling or transferring of a business or legal person and any other legal arrangement; or
- A transaction on behalf of a customer in relation to creating, operating, and managing a legal person, and any other legal arrangement

YES

You are captured and must comply with the AML/CFT Act

UNLESS

There is an exemption which excludes your business from compliance requirements

NO

You are not captured

NB: If in the future you are asked to conduct any activity described above, you will need to determine if you are captured by the Act

How to know if you are captured by the AML/CFT Act

The AML/CFT Act is activities-based. Lawyers and conveyancers need to develop a thorough understanding of:

- Exclusions to and exemptions from the AML/ CFT Act
- What conducting captured activities "in the ordinary course of business" means
- What obligations are related to the captured activities
- How to determine whether advice to a customer is a captured activity
- The nature of each of the activities that are captured by the AML/CFT Act

This section elaborates on the captured activities that lawyers and conveyancers may conduct. The AML/CFT Act imposes obligations only for these captured activities.[10] The obligations of the AML/CFT Act do not apply to any other activities that a lawyer or conveyancer carries out in the ordinary course of business.

Exclusions to and exemptions from the AML/CFT Act

There are a number of ways in which entities, transactions or activities can be exempt from the Act's requirements. For instance, the AML/CFT (Definitions) Regulations 2011[11] provide a number of specific exclusions to the definition of "reporting entity", and the AML/CFT (Exemptions) Regulations 2011[12] provide a range of exemptions for specific classes of transactions and services. There are also Ministerial exemptions, which can exempt (from any or all of the provisions of the Act) either specific reporting entities, or classes of reporting entities, as well as transactions or classes of transactions.[13] The AML/CFT (Class Exemptions) Notice 2014[14] provides further detail about class exemptions.

The Ministry of Justice handles Ministerial exemption applications and provides advice to the appropriate Minister who makes the final decisions. Exemptions may be granted by the Minister subject to sections 157 to 159 of the AML/CFT Act.[15] Please review these sections if you are considering making an application.

---

10 For the full text of the activities please see section 5(1) of the AML/CFT Act under the definition of "designated non-financial business or profession": http://bit.ly/2xHGfmy

11 AML/CFT (Definitions) Regulations 2011: http://bit.ly/2hrFYy3

12 AML/CFT (Exemptions) Regulations 2011: http://bit.ly/2lAImH6

13 AML/CFT ministerial exemptions: http://bit.ly/2xCmQU6

14 AML/CFT (Class Exemptions) Notice 2014: http://bit.ly/2zly18h

15 Sections 157–159 AML/CFT Act: http://bit.ly/2zuN9wq

Interpreting "ordinary course of business"

Activities must be done in the ordinary course of business to be captured by the Act. The AML/CFT supervisors have issued guidance on how to interpret "ordinary course of business."[16] Whether an activity is in your "ordinary course of business" will always be a matter of judgement depending on the nature of your business. Some relevant factors to take into consideration would be whether the activity:

- Is normal or otherwise unremarkable for your business
- Is frequent
- Is regular (meaning predictable, consistent)
- Involves significant amounts of money
- Is a source of income
- Involves significant resources
- Involves a service offered to customers

It is likely that the activity is in the ordinary course of your business if one or more of these factors apply.

If you are conducting a captured activity in your personal capacity (as opposed to in your professional capacity) you are not captured by the AML/CFT Act. An example of this would be if you are a trustee for a registered charitable trust in your local community in your personal capacity.

If, after considering the AML/CFT Act and this guidance, you are still unsure as to whether you are a reporting entity, you should seek independent legal advice or contact us at amlphase2@dia.govt.nz.

What obligations are related to the captured activities

The AML/CFT Act requires you to know who your customers are (as well as who any beneficial owners of your customer are, and any person acting on behalf of your customer) by conducting customer due diligence (CDD) to the level required before you conduct a captured activity or establish a business relationship.

How to determine whether advice provided to your customer is captured

There will be circumstances where you give advice in relation to a captured activity (without necessarily then carrying out the activity). Generally, advice alone, in the absence of any actual captured activity on the lawyer or conveyancer's part, will not be caught by the definition of "designated non-financial business or profession".

16 Interpreting "Ordinary Course of Business" Guideline: http://bit.ly/2Bh3CEI

It may be that in practice you expect to provide a mixture of advice and captured activities for a customer over a period of time. In those circumstances, you would need to conduct CDD to the required level *prior* to establishing a business relationship with the customer (and prior to providing any advice).

You also need to be aware of your obligations to report suspicious activities, which can include requests or enquiries about particular services you offer from potential new customers (regardless of whether you ultimately provide those services).

Activities captured by the AML/CFT Act

This section outlines the activities that are captured by the AML/CFT Act and provides some examples of what these activities may look like for lawyers and conveyancers. The examples are indicative and not exhaustive. As we learn from our experiences regulating the legal and conveyancing professions, we will be able to provide more information about supervisor expectations in certain scenarios.

When in doubt about whether you undertake any of the activities described below, please look to the explanations. If you are still uncertain, contact DIA at amlphase2@dia.govt.nz or seek legal advice.

Activity: Acting as a formation agent for legal persons or legal arrangements

In the definition of "designated non-financial business or profession" a law firm, incorporated conveyancing firm or conveyancing practitioner who, in the ordinary course of business, acts as a formation agent of legal persons or legal arrangements, is captured by the AML/CFT Act as a reporting entity.

The term "legal arrangement" is defined in the AML/CFT Act[17] as meaning a trust, a partnership, a charitable entity (within the meaning of section 4(1) of the Charities Act 2005), and any other prescribed arrangements that involves a risk of ML/TF.[18]

Examples of this kind of activity in practice

- You register a company on behalf of a customer.
- You create a registered charitable trust for a customer.

17 Section 5(1), AML/CFT Act: http://bit.ly/2xHGfmy

18 As at December 2017, no arrangements have been prescribed.

ML/TF risks associated with this activity

When a lawyer is engaged to register a company or partnership, the actual ownership of the company or partnership being formed can be concealed or obscured – for example, where shell companies, multiple layers of ownership or other complex legal structures are used. Setting up a trust can also be a way to create a perception of distance between assets and their beneficial owners. International evidence shows that using charitable organisations (such as incorporated societies and charitable trusts) is also an identified method that criminals use to launder their money or to finance terrorism. (Please see section 6, case studies 5 and 6 in Appendix A, and the red flags in Appendix B.)

Activity: Acting as, or arranging someone to act as, a nominee director, nominee shareholder or trustee

In the definition of "designated non-financial business or profession" a law firm, incorporated conveyancing firm or conveyancing practitioner who, in the ordinary course of business, acts as, or arranges for a person to act as, a nominee director, nominee shareholder or trustee in relation to legal persons or legal arrangements, is captured by the AML/CFT Act as a reporting entity.

Examples of this kind of activity in practice

- You act as a nominee director of a company that is registered in New Zealand.
- You act as a trustee for a registered charitable trust in your local community.
- You arrange for a person to act as a nominee shareholder for a company.

ML/TF risks associated with this activity

If a lawyer is acting as a nominee director, nominee shareholder or a trustee for a company or other legal arrangement (such as a trust or charity), others may gain a false impression of legitimacy for the activities undertaken by the company or legal arrangements. This lack of visibility provides criminals with the opportunity to use their companies or other legal arrangements for money laundering or other financial crime without being detected. The possibility of detection is made less likely because they can do this while maintaining the impression of oversight by reputable New Zealand-based directors.

Lawyers who act or arrange for someone to act as a nominee director, nominee shareholder, or trustee need to establish the reason why this arrangement is required. We expect that lawyers establish that there is a legitimate economic purpose of the company or legal arrangement and know who its beneficial owners are. (Please see section 6 and the red flags in Appendix B.)

Activity: Providing an office or address for a company or legal arrangement

In the definition of "designated non-financial business or profession" a law firm, incorporated conveyancing firm or conveyancing practitioner who, in the ordinary course of business, provides a registered office or a business address, a correspondence address, or an administrative address for a company, or a partnership, or for any other legal persons or arrangement, is captured by the AML/CFT Act as a reporting entity.

The only exception to this is where the office or address is provided solely as an ancillary service to the provision of other services that are not otherwise captured by definition of "designated non-financial business or profession" in the AML/CFT Act.

Example of this kind of activity in practice

- You have assisted an offshore company to set up a subsidiary in New Zealand and allow the subsidiary to use your address as its registered office address.

ML/TF risks associated with this activity

For a person who is intent on money laundering or committing other financial crime, the use of an address that is not their physical location is attractive. It allows them to keep anonymity and distance from the transactions they are undertaking, and if it is the address of a lawyer, it adds a perception of legitimacy to their activities. It also makes it more difficult for law enforcement to track them down in person.

Activity: Managing client funds, accounts, securities, or other assets

In the definition of "designated non-financial business or profession" a law firm, incorporated conveyancing firm or conveyancing practitioner who, in the ordinary course of business, manages client funds (other than sums paid as fees for professional services), accounts, securities, or other assets, is captured by the AML/CFT Act as a reporting entity.

DIA's view is that managing payments to or from your customers' accounts is captured; and, with the exception of payments for professional fees, any instance where you receive or hold client funds and control the payment will also be captured.

Examples of this kind of activity in practice

- You hold customer funds for a property sale in your trust account until settlement date and then transfer those funds to the vendor.
- You make investments on behalf of customers in securities and/or other assets.
- You manage the sale and/or purchase of trust assets for your customer.
- You disburse the funds received into your trust account from a litigation settlement to your customer.
- You exercise the enduring power of attorney that you hold for a customer who has lost mental capacity by making payments from their personal account to meet their financial obligations.

ML/TF risks associated with this activity

Some people will try to avoid accessing banking services typically used in transactions to obscure the trail of money changing hands as a means to hide their criminal activities. One way to obscure this trail or to add an appearance of legitimacy is to try to use the trust accounts or professional services of legal and conveyancing professionals.

Activity: Providing real estate agency work to effect a transaction

In the definition of "designated non-financial business or profession" a law firm, incorporated conveyancing firm or conveyancing practitioner who, in the ordinary course of business, provides real estate agency work (within the meaning of the Real Estate Agents Act 2008) to effect a transaction (within the meaning of section 4(1) of the Real Estate Agents Act 2008), is captured by the AML/CFT Act as a reporting entity.

ML/TF risks associated with this activity

Property purchases are a recognised typology for money laundering. These purchases allow for large amounts of criminal proceeds to be stored in an asset that appreciates. Sales and purchases of property can provide the appearance of legitimacy for the acquisition and movement of large sums of money. Residential and commercial properties purchased for money laundering purposes can also be used as bases for other criminal operations – such as clandestine laboratories for the production of illicit drugs.

Activity: Engaging in or giving instructions on behalf of a customer to another person for a range of specified services (as below)

In the definition of "designated non-financial business or profession" a law firm, incorporated conveyancing firm or conveyancing practitioner who, in the ordinary course of business, does any of the activities listed in the next box is captured by the AML/CFT Act as a reporting entity.

The activities specified in the following box apply to situations where lawyers or conveyancers either engage in the following activities themselves, or give instructions on behalf of a customer to another person for those activities. This means that if you are instructing a third party to undertake activities on behalf of your customer, you are captured by the AML/CFT Act – as is the third party you instruct if they fall within the definition of either "designated non-financial business or profession" or "financial institution".[19]

Engaging in or giving instructions on behalf of a customer to another pers for –

A. any conveyancing (within the meaning of section 6 of the Lawyers and Conveyancers Act 2006)[20] to effect a transaction (within the meaning of section 4(1) of the Real Estate Agents Act 2008),[21] namely,—
   - the sale, the purchase, or any other disposal or acquisition of a freehold estate or interest in land:
   - the grant, sale, or purchase or any other disposal or acquisition of a leasehold estate or interest in land (other than a tenancy to which the Residential Tenancies Act 1986 applies):[22]
   - the grant, sale, or purchase or any other disposal or acquisition of a licence that is registrable under the Land Transfer Act 1952:[23]
   - the grant, sale, or purchase or any other disposal or acquisition of an occupation right agreement within the meaning of section 5 of the Retirement Villages Act 2003:[24]

B. a transaction (within the meaning of section 4(1) of the Real Estate Agents Act 2008);[25] or

C. the transfer of a beneficial interest in land or other real property; or

D. a transaction on behalf of any person in relation to the buying, transferring, or selling of a business or legal person (for example, a company) and any other legal arrangement; or

E. a transaction on behalf of a customer in relation to creating, operating, and managing a legal person (for example, a company) and any other legal arrangement"

19 Both of these terms are defined in section 5(1), AML/CFT Act: http://bit.ly/2xHGfmy

20 Section 6, Lawyers and Conveyancers Act 2006: http://bit.ly/2ztIqyK

21 Section 4(1), Real Estate Agents Act 2008: http:// bit.ly/2h79rQS

22 Residential Tenancies Act 1986: http://bit.ly/2iYKoQl

23 Land Transfer Act 1952: http://bit.ly/2iq9a8c

24 Section 5, Retirement Villages Act 2003: http:// bit.ly/2lJhJQv

25 Section 4(1), Real Estate Agents Act 2008: http:// bit.ly/2h79rQS

You should read both (D) and (E) to mean undertaking any one of the activities mentioned, not a combination of all activities at once.

ML/TF risks associated with this activity

The key risk with all the activities described in the box above is the anonymity and appearance of legitimacy that may be gained by the customer through the lawyer or conveyancing practitioner engaging in the activities, or giving instructions to another person on their behalf for those activities. The person being instructed by the lawyer or conveyancer will be unlikely to have any face-to-face contact with the actual customer. If the customer has criminal intentions, there would be a protective layer of the lawyer or conveyancer and the third person between the customer and the transaction they are instructing. (Please see section 6; case studies 3, 4 and 9 in Appendix A; and the red flags in Appendix B.)

3. Know how legal professional privilege applies

The Act does not require any person (lawyer or otherwise) to disclose any information that the person believes, on reasonable grounds, is a privileged communication.

The AML/CFT Act requires all reporting entities to report suspicious activities by filing suspicious activity reports (SARs) with the Financial Intelligence Unit (FIU). If it is possible for you to file an SAR without disclosing a privileged communication, you must do so. It is accepted that in some cases this will not be possible.

A "privileged communication" is defined in section 42 of the AML/CFT Act as:[26]

- A confidential communication between a lawyer and another lawyer or a lawyer and his or her client made for the purpose of obtaining or giving legal advice or assistance; or
- A communication that is subject to the general law governing legal professional privilege or is specified in sections 53–57 of the Evidence Act 2006[27]

A privileged communication can be oral or written, and it can include any information or opinion. It also includes communications between agents of lawyers and/or agents of customers.

However, the AML/CFT Act provides that a communication is not a privileged communication if:

26 Section 42, AML/CFT Act: http://bit.ly/2yj0ECT

27 Sections 53–57 of the Evidence Act 2006: http:// bit.ly/2Ah1n7T

- There is a prima facie case that it is made/ received/compiled or prepared for a dishonest purpose or to enable or aid the commission of an offence; or

- The information consists wholly or partly of (or relates to) receipts, payments, income, expenditure, or financial transactions of any person and is contained in (or comprises the whole or part of) any book, account, statement or other record kept by the lawyer in connection with the lawyer's trust account

It will be for lawyers to determine whether a "prima facie case" exists on the facts before them. This may involve considering whether there is some credible evidence that a communication is made for a dishonest purpose, or to enable the commission of a crime.[28]

28 Lawyers will note that the "prima facie" test also appears in section 136 of the Search and Surveillance Act 2012 (http://bit.ly/2jvrBZB) and section 67 of the Evidence Act 2006 (http://bit.ly/2zOkIgW).

Lawyers may find it helpful to ask the following questions when considering whether to file an SAR:

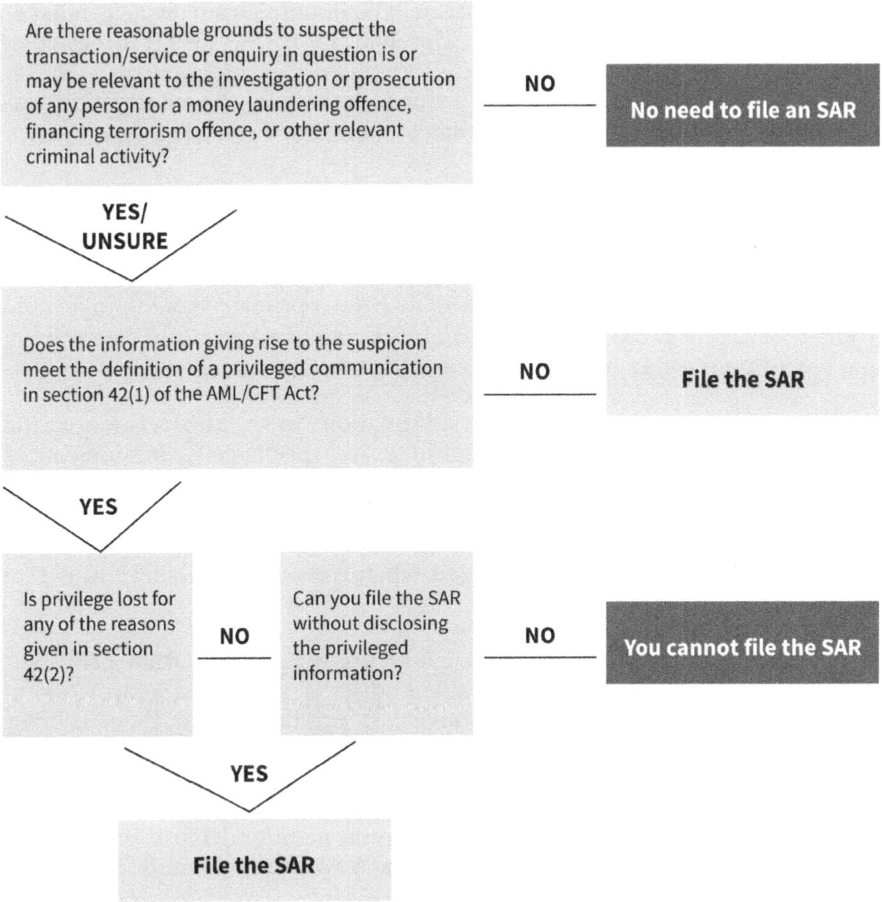

You should keep detailed records of any such assessment.

An SAR must be filed as soon as practicable, and no later than three working days after you become aware of facts that would objectively justify a suspicion (or by reasonable diligence would have become aware of).[29] The failure to do so is an offence (see section 92 of the Act).[30] It is not a defence if a reporting entity did not actually consider a transaction to be suspicious, when objectively it should have. It is a defence if a reporting entity believes on

29 DIA v Ping An Finance (Group) New Zealand Limited (2017) NZHC 2363, paragraphs 64–67: http://bit.ly/2kbWHtz

30 Section 92, AML/CFT Act: http://bit.ly/2hrFliB

reasonable grounds that the documents or information relating to the activity were privileged communications.

Generally, a person who makes an SAR will be immune from civil, criminal or disciplinary proceedings as a result. This will not be the case if information was disclosed in bad faith, or if the information was disclosed by a lawyer despite the existence of reasonable grounds to believe the information was privileged. This highlights the importance of making a considered assessment in every case.

AML/CFT supervisors and the Commissioner of Police have a range of powers to require the provision of information and documentation for the purpose of ensuring compliance with the AML/CFT Act. These powers cannot be used to compel any person to disclose a privileged communication. Your AML/ CFT programme should outline the procedure for determining and recording whether information is a privileged communication.

If a person refuses to disclose information to a supervisor or the Commissioner of Police on the grounds it is a privileged communication, either the person, the Commissioner of Police or the supervisor can apply to a District Court Judge to determine whether or not the claim of professional privilege is valid. This option is not available to a lawyer who is deciding whether a communication is privileged when considering whether to file an SAR.

Where the AML/CFT Act is silent about privilege, the normal principles apply. For example, you will not be able to disclose privileged information to any external auditor without a waiver of privilege from the customer concerned (bearing in mind the customer – not the lawyer – is the holder of privilege).

If you require additional support, you can access more detailed information and advice on professional privilege from the New Zealand Law Society.[31]

4. Know your compliance requirements

Any law firm, conveyancing practitioner or incorporated conveyancing firm, either existing or established after the introduction of the AML/CFT Act, that conducts captured activities will be a reporting entity and will have to comply with the Act. You will not be excused from compliance on the basis that to comply would breach any contract or agreement.[32]

31 Section 159A(1) and (2), AML/CFT Act: http://bit.ly/2xGq1Kv

32 Section 9, AML/CFT Act: http://bit.ly/2iR0JH3

Compliance requirements for reporting entities

Appoint a compliance officer - Section 56

Reporting entities must appoint a compliance officer who will have responsibility for administering and maintaining the AML/CFT Programme. An employee should be appointed to this role who reports to a senior manager. In the case of a sole practitioner, we would expect the sole practitioner to be the compliance officer. If that is not possible, an external person must be appointed as a compliance officer.

Conduct a risk assessment - Section 58

Reporting entities are required to undertake an assessment of the risks posed to their business by money laundering and financing of terrorism crimes. The risk assessment should be in writing and be informed by the *Phase 2 Sector Risk Assessment*, which is available on the DIA website.

Develop an AML/CFT programme - Section 57

The AML/CFT programme must be based on the risk assessment described above and be in writing. It should include procedures, policies and controls for ensuring all compliance obligations are adequately and effectively met.

Maintain your compliance programme

Conduct customer due diligence (CDD) - Part 2, Subpart 1

Reporting entities must conduct CDD when conducting an occasional transaction or activity or when establishing a business relationship with a client who is requesting assistance with a captured activity, or when an existing client makes this kind of request (if the reporting entity doesn't hold all the information required already). There are three levels of CDD depending on the circumstances.

Keep records - Sections 49–55

Reporting entities must keep records of transactions, suspicious activities, the documents verifying the identities of customers and other parties or beneficiaries, and any other related records that may be of interest to the supervisor. Records must be kept at least five years.

Ongoing customer due diligence and ongoing account monitoring - Section 31

Reporting entities are required to undertake ongoing CDD and ongoing account monitoring. This is to ensure that you have ongoing confidence that the business relationship and the transactions within the relationship are consistent with the customer's business and risk profile, and you can spot any suspicious activity early.

Review your compliance programme - Section 59

The supervisor expects reporting entities to conduct a regular review of their compliance programme. This is to ensure that any business changes or new risks in the operating environment are referenced in the programme and it remains fit-for-purpose.

Report and audit

Submit an annual report – Section 60

Reporting entities must submit an annual report. This report must be in the prescribed form and be submitted to the supervisor at the time set by the supervisor. The report must take into account the results and implications of the audit and any information prescribed in the regulations.

Audit your risk assessment and compliance programme every two years – Section 59A

At least every two years a reporting entity must review its risk assessment and compliance programme and have it audited by an independent person who is suitably qualified to conduct the audit. Supervisors may also require an audit to be undertaken on request at shorter notice.

Report to the FIU

Report to the Financial Intelligence Unit – Subparts 2 and 2A

When reporting entities identify suspicious activity, they must report it to the FIU. They should also submit prescribed transaction reports to the FIU as necessary. Lawyers will not be required to submit any privileged communication (as defined in the Act) in either report category.

Compliance requirements

This section provides guidance on:

- The risk-based approach that reporting entities need to take when developing their AML/CFT programme
- The range of procedures, policies and controls reporting entities must include in their AML/ CFT programme to comply with the AML/CFT Act
- Things to consider if you wish to establish a designated business group to share some aspects of your AML/CFT programme and its implementation

Section 5 provides more thorough detail about compliance requirements for CDD. Information on where to access other support to comply is noted in section 8.

Risk-based compliance

The AML/CFT regulatory system in New Zealand is "risk-based". This means each reporting entity must assess the risk its own business faces from money launderers and terrorist financers. You must then apply suitable procedures, policies and controls to effectively manage the risks you have identified. Compliance resources can then be targeted primarily at high-risk areas, which should reduce the overall compliance cost for your business.

You are the best judge of the risks your business is exposed to and how you can most effectively mitigate those risks in line with the requirements of the AML/CFT Act. As your supervisor, DIA expects you to genuinely and accurately assess the ML/TF risks to your business and then apply a suitable and proportionate AML/CFT programme.

AML/CFT programme – procedures, policies and controls

AML/CFT compliance cannot be achieved with a "set and forget" approach. The AML/CFT programme needs to be fully implemented within the business. It should be a living and adaptable programme. Your specific compliance obligations under the AML/CFT Act are summarised as follows.

Appoint a compliance officer

You must appoint an AML/CFT compliance officer to administer and maintain your compliance programme.[33] The compliance officer should be an employee of the business who reports to a senior manager or partner of the business. If practising on their own account, a lawyer or conveyancer would be expected to act as the compliance officer themselves and take full responsibility for all compliance requirements unless there is a reason why they cannot. In that case they should appoint a third party to take on this duty.[34]

When you have appointed your compliance officer, or if your compliance officer or other contact information changes, it is important that you advise us at amlphase2@dia.govt.nz. This enables us to communicate effectively with you and provide you with important information and updates.

Conduct a risk assessment

Your first step to compliance should be to conduct a risk assessment. All reporting entities must undertake a risk assessment, and it must be in writing. The specific requirements for a risk assessment are set out in section 58 of the AML/CFT Act.[35] The supervisors have provided guidance on how to conduct

33 Section 56, AML/CFT Act: http://bit.ly/2znn4Dd

34 This will only be possible where the business has no employees. The supervisor expects that if the person who is acting as a compliance officer is not part of the business, there should be a justifiable reason. The reporting entity should be able to demonstrate to the supervisor that the person selected has an appropriate level of access to business information and systems to discharge their duties and the authority to advise the senior management of the business about AML/CFT matters.

35 Section 58, AML/CFT Act: http://bit.ly/2ly11Dz

a risk assessment.[36] The AML/CFT Act requires that you have regard to guidance produced by the AML/CFT supervisors when developing your risk assessment.[37]

DIA has published its own assessment of the ML/TF risks in the sectors it is responsible for supervising, including in the legal and conveyancing professions.[38] DIA has also developed the *AML/CFT Risk Assessment and Programme: Prompts and Notes* (Prompts and Notes) guideline, which outlines the factors to be considered in a risk assessment along with some prompts for things to think about when completing a risk assessment and developing your AML/CFT programme.[39] It provides prompts to help businesses undertake their risk assessment in a way that reflects both the size of their business and their level of risk. In addition, the Financial Markets Authority has published a step-by-step guide for drafting a risk assessment.[40] Together, these resources will help businesses to conduct a realistic assessment of their ML/TF risks so that their AML/CFT programmes can be proportionate to the risks assessed.

You must review and update your risk assessment when there is any material change to the business, its service offerings, or its customer base, or when deficiencies in the effectiveness of the risk assessment are identified. As methods and techniques (known as "typologies") of ML/TF adapt and change, the nature of the risks posed to a business may change also. It is important that lawyers and conveyancers keep up-to-date with relevant changes in typologies. The Quarterly Typology Reports published by the FIU are a good source of typology information.[41]

Set up an AML/CFT programme

Once a risk assessment has been conducted, all reporting entities must develop an AML/CFT programme that includes internal procedures, policies and controls to detect and manage the risk of ML/TF.[42] The AML/CFT Act requires that you have regard to guidance produced by the supervisor when developing your AML/CFT programme.[43] The supervisors' guidance on developing an AML/CFT programme is available on the DIA website.[44]

The supervisors' guidance is generic in nature. It does not provide prescriptive instructions on how businesses can ensure they are compliant with the AML/CFT Act. This is because each business has unique

36 Risk Assessment Guideline: http://bit.ly/2iL7Spp
37 Section 58(2)(g), AML/CFT Act: http://bit.ly/2ly11Dz
38 Sector and National Risk Assessments: http:// bit.ly/2ik1tAu
39 Codes of Practice and Guidelines: http://bit.ly/2gQ3Iev
40 AML/CFT Guide for Small Financial Adviser Businesses: http://bit.ly/2nb1TyA
41 Financial Intelligence Unit assessments and reports: http://bit.ly/2xGSiAx
42 Sections 56 and 57, AML/CFT Act: http://bit.ly/2znn4Dd and http://bit.ly/2h2nN59
43 Section 57(2), AML/CFT Act: http://bit.ly/2h2nN59
44 AML/CFT Programme Guideline: http://bit.ly/2iS5I7k

circumstances that determine their exposure to ML/TF risks, which need to be understood and factored into their unique AML/CFT programme. Businesses will need to apply their own judgement, and where there are questions about compliance they can either ask the supervisor for general information, or seek independent legal advice.

Customer due diligence

Section 5 in this guideline is dedicated to explaining your CDD obligations.[45]

Record keeping

You must keep adequate records as outlined in sections 49 to 55 of the AML/CFT Act. This will enable you to operate your AML/CFT programme effectively and enable it to be audited by an independent auditor and reviewed by the supervisor on request. Records must either be kept in written form in English or be readily accessible and readily convertible into written form in English.

You must keep your records for at least five years. The supervisor or the Commissioner of Police may ask you to keep records for longer in some circumstances. After five years, the records can be destroyed unless there is a lawful reason why they should be retained – for example, the need to comply with another enactment or to enable you to carry on your business.

You must keep the following records:

Record type	Retention period
Transaction records sufficient to enable the transactions to be fully reconstructed at any time[46]	5 years from the completion of the transaction
Any reports of suspicious activities[47]	5 years after the report is made
Identity and verification evidence (as reasonably necessary to enable the nature of the evidence to be readily identified at any time)[48]	5 years from the end of the business relationship or the completion of the occasional transaction or activity

45 The CDD requirements are noted in Part 2, subpart 1, AML/CFT Act: http://bit.ly/2A5PJtA

46 Section 49, AML/CFT Act: http://bit.ly/2zEQkFA

47 Section 49A, AML/CFT Act: http://bit.ly/2iFJ1lM

48 Section 50, AML/CFT Act: http://bit.ly/2zdxog9

Record type	Retention period
Risk assessments, AML/CFT programmes and audits	5 years after the date on which they cease to be used on a regular basis
Information relevant to the establishment of a business relationship and any other records that explain the nature and purpose of a business relationship and the activities relating to that business relationship[49]	5 years from the end of the business relationship

You are also strongly advised to keep any detailed records of your assessment of whether an SAR is required, including any determinations of whether information is legally privileged.

Ongoing customer due diligence and ongoing account monitoring

When you have established a business relationship, you must conduct ongoing CDD and undertake ongoing account monitoring.[50] For more information, please see "Ongoing CDD and account monitoring" on page 39.

Review your AML/CFT programme

You must regularly review your risk assessment and AML/CFT programme to ensure it remains up-to-date and to identify and remedy any deficiencies.[51] Your records should show evidence of updates that address any identified deficiencies in its effectiveness. Ways to do this would be to keep a record of version history or retain evidence demonstrating reviews and updates.

Annual reporting to your supervisor

Like all reporting entities, you are required to submit an annual report each year covering the period July to June.[52] The date for submission is advised by the supervisor each year, and you will usually have two months to submit. This means the first annual report will be due approximately at the end of August 2019. A new annual report template has been designed for lawyers, conveyancers, accountants and real estate agents and is provided for by regulations.[53] Please go to the DIA website for more information.[54] All reporting entities are also expected to respond to any requests for subsequent information from the supervisor in a timely manner.

49 Section 51, AML/CFT Act: http://bit.ly/2znMDn8

50 Section 31, AML/CFT Act: http://bit.ly/2z1eCIX

51 Section 59, AML/CFT Act: http://bit.ly/2xJWm2P

52 Section 60, AML/CFT Act: http://bit.ly/2gQqiUa

53 AML/CFT Act and Regulations: http://bit.ly/2hsgYXt

54 General information about annual reporting is here: http://bit.ly/2kcI8WA

Independent audits of your risk assessment and AML/CFT programme

Every two years, you are required to have an independent audit of your risk assessment and AML/CFT programme.[55] An independent audit aims to ensure that documents remain up-to-date, that any deficiencies in programme effectiveness are identified, and that any necessary changes can be made. For guidance, please see the *Guideline for Audits of Risk Assessments and AML/CFT Programmes*, which is available on the DIA website.[56]

The AML/CFT Act requires you to appoint someone who is independent and suitably qualified to conduct the audit.[57] The audit cannot be undertaken by someone from within the business unless a sufficient degree of independence can be demonstrated. For instance, a very large firm with a dedicated audit function would likely be able to show a sufficient degree of independence. Someone who has been involved in the establishment of the compliance programme (such as completing the risk assessment and/or writing the AML/CFT programme) cannot conduct the audit.[58] The auditor does not need to be a chartered accountant or qualified to undertake financial audits.

To be suitably qualified we expect that your auditor would have a working knowledge of the AML/CFT Act and its complexities.

A copy of the independent audit must be provided to the supervisor on request. The supervisor can instruct a reporting entity to have a new independent audit undertaken at any time.

Reporting to the FIU

As a key part of your AML/CFT obligations, in specific circumstances you need to report certain information to the FIU. Each reporting entity will have visibility over different parts of any one chain of events leading to a transaction or following on from a transaction. Each type of report will provide the FIU with one set of information, complementing other types of reports providing further information. It may be that the report you provide will be the one crucial piece that brings enough of the puzzle together to lead the FIU to take appropriate action against a criminal.

55 Sections 59–59A, AML/CFT Act: http://bit.ly/2xJWm2P

56 Guideline for Audits of Risk Assessments and AML/CFT Programmes: http://bit.ly/2AfTf7m

57 It is up to you to decide if someone is suitably qualified to conduct an audit of your AML/CFT programme. You should be able to explain to the supervisor your rationale for this decision on request.

58 Section 59B, AML/CFT Act: http://bit.ly/2muArvE

When you need to report

From 1 July 2018, you will be required to submit suspicious activity reports[59] (SARs) and prescribed transaction reports (PTRs). From that date you will no longer be required to submit reports under the Financial Transactions Reporting Act 1996.

Suspicious activity reports

Section 39A of the AML/CFT Act defines a "suspicious activity", and section 40 of the Act requires a reporting entity to report a suspicious activity to the FIU as soon as practicable, but no later than three working days after forming its suspicion. This has been held to mean that a reporting entity must report a suspicious activity within three days of the point at which the reporting entity becomes aware of facts that would objectively justify a suspicion (or by reasonable diligence would have become aware of them).[60] It is not a defence that a reporting entity did not actually consider an activity to be suspicious in circumstances where it objectively should have. For further detail on making an assessment as to whether to file an SAR, please see section 3.

Prescribed transaction reports

A prescribed transaction is an international wire transfer of NZD $1,000 or more conducted through a reporting entity or a domestic physical cash transaction of a value equal to or above NZD $10,000.[61] Please refer to page 37 for more detail on wire transfers (including international wire transfers).

Only an ordering institution and a beneficiary institution are required to file a PTR in respect of an international wire transfer.

An "ordering institution" is defined as "any person who has been instructed by a payer to electronically transfer funds controlled by the payer to a payee via a "beneficiary institution". The ordering institution will be the first reporting entity to transfer the funds that are the subject of the international wire transfer – for instance, a law firm that holds customer funds in a trust account, and transfers those funds (including via the formal banking system) to an overseas beneficiary bank.

A reporting entity that simply passes on an instruction to transfer funds, without actually transacting, will not be required to file a PTR. A "beneficiary institution" (in relation to a wire transfer from an ordering institution) is defined as "any person who receives those funds and then makes those funds

59 The AML/CFT Amendment Act 2017 changed "suspicious transaction reports" to "suspicious activity reports".

60 DIA v Ping An Finance (Group) New Zealand Limited (2017) NZHC 2363, paragraphs 64–67: http://bit.ly/2kbWHtz

61 Section 5(1) of the AML/CFT Act (http:// bit.ly/2xHGfmy); regulation 5A, AML/CFT (Definitions) Regulations (http://bit.ly/2hbI5p6); Prescribed Transactions Reporting (http://bit.ly/2zkB9RJ)

available to a person (the payee) by crediting it to an account held by the payee or paying it to the payee". The beneficiary institution will be the last reporting entity in the chain that receives the funds before making them available to its customer (the beneficiary of the transaction).

Usually the bank will be a beneficiary institution; however, in some cases the beneficiary institution may be a different reporting entity, such as a law firm, depending on where the funds (intended for the customer) end up.

PTRs are intended to add further transparency to the financial system by making the range of methods of ML/TF even more difficult to hide. PTRs will also improve the detection and disruption of organised crime.

Suspicious property reports

You also need to be aware of your obligations to submit "suspicious property reports" (SPRs) under the Terrorism Suppression Act 2002. If you are in control of property that you suspect (on reasonable grounds) is property that is owned or controlled, directly or indirectly by a "designated terrorist entity" (or property derived or generated from that type of property), you must report that suspicion in accordance with sections 43 and 44 of the Terrorism Suppression Act (note that, like the AML/CFT Act, the Terrorism Suppression Act protects privileged communications).[62] The SPR must be submitted as soon as practicable after forming your suspicion. Designated terrorist entities are identified on a publicly available list that is updated by the New Zealand Police.[63] If you find a match on a list other than New Zealand's terrorist designation list, the reporting entity is required to submit an SAR to the FIU.

How to report

The FIU has issued guidance on how to submit reports using their goAML web-based reporting tool.[64] You must use the specific reporting format provided by the FIU. If you have reported on your customer, you must not disclose this information to your customer or to any person that is not entitled to receive this information.[65] If, after making a report, you are unsure if you need to end your existing relationship with your customer, you may wish to review the respective Conduct and Client Care Rules for lawyers and for conveyancers,[66] or consult the New Zealand Law Society, or seek independent advice. For further discussion on ending or declining business relationships, please see "What to do if you cannot complete CDD" on page 40.

62 Section 45, Terrorism Suppression Act 2002: http://bit.ly/2iI88oj

63 Designated terrorist entities: http://bit.ly/258MtKq

64 goAML – Financial Intelligence Unit reporting tool: http://bit.ly/2ygOri3

65 Section 46, AML/CFT Act: http://bit.ly/2xCrpxz

66 Lawyers and Conveyancers Act (Lawyers: Conduct and Client Care) Rules 2008 (http://bit.ly/2iQDGvZ) and Lawyers and Conveyancers Act (Conveyancers: Conduct and Client Care) Rules 2008 (http://bit.ly/2zJhM23)

Establishing a designated business group

In certain circumstances, law firms, conveyancing practitioners or conveyancing firms may be able to form a designated business group (DBG) with other entities (whether or not those entities are other law firms or conveyancers or even reporting entities). The term "designated business group" is defined in full in the AML/CFT Act and regulations.[67] In summary, it means a group of two or more persons who have elected (in writing) to form a group to enable some obligations under the AML/CFT Act to be met on a shared basis while the election is in force.

A member of a DBG can rely on another member to carry out certain obligations on their behalf, including CDD (in certain situations).[68] Members can also rely on specified parts of another member's AML/CFT programme, and another member's risk assessment (if relevant), as well as reporting to the FIU. Members may share information and rely on each other, but they still retain responsibility for their own compliance. Any decision to apply to become a DBG should include a thorough consideration of the risks and implications for all members.

The supervisor will consider all applications for DBGs. If you are not sure whether or not your proposed DBG meets the criteria in the definition in section 5(1) of the Act, you are welcome to contact us to discuss. We would prefer if reporting entities test their proposals with us rather than assume they could not apply. If you are interested in applying to form a DBG, we recommend you familiarise yourself with the two available guidelines to assist reporting entities to create DBGs, one on Scope and one on Formation, before you submit an application.[69] The application form is included in the Formation guideline.

5. Know your customer

This section provides information about:

- What a business relationship means and when it starts
- Who to conduct CDD on
- What the different levels of CDD are
- How to use the Amended Identity Verification Code of Practice
- When you can rely on others for CDD
- When to conduct CDD
- What to think about when participating in international transactions
- What to do if you cannot complete CDD

67 Section 5(1) of the AML/CFT Act: http://bit.ly/2xHGfmy

68 Section 32, AML/CFT Act: http://bit.ly/2hjDuF3

69 Designated Business Group – Scope Guideline and Designated Business Group – Formation Guideline: http://bit.ly/2y4KpFa

The requirements described in this section are contained in Part 2, subpart 1 of the AML/CFT Act.[70] The supervisors have prepared a range of guidelines that are likely to assist lawyers and conveyancers with undertaking CDD. The guidelines are available on the DIA website.[71]

When a business relationship starts

A business relationship is defined in section 5(1) of the Act as "a business, professional, or commercial relationship between a reporting entity and a customer that has an element of duration or that is expected by the reporting entity, at the time when contact is established, to have an element of duration". This has been held to capture situations where a reporting entity has, or expects to have, a relationship with a customer involving more than one interaction or the carrying out of multiple transactions.[72]

You will need to use your judgement to determine when a business relationship with a customer starts. This is likely to be after initial enquiries have been made, but before any work has commenced.

In the case of a property sale, the business relationship or occasional activity is assumed to have commenced at the point where the customer has engaged the lawyer or conveyancer to undertake the necessary work.

Who to conduct customer due diligence on

You must conduct CDD on:

- Your customer
- Any beneficial owner of a customer
- Any person acting on behalf of a customer

New customers

You may not have to conduct CDD on every new customer. You need to establish at the outset whether they are going to require you to conduct any activity captured by the AML/CFT Act. If they are, you will need to conduct CDD in line with the level of risk you anticipate and in accordance with the requirements in the Act. See further on in this section for the levels of CDD and further explanation of the compliance requirements. If your customer does not require you to conduct a captured activity initially, but over time you are instructed to carry out captured activities, you must ensure you have completed the necessary CDD before you carry out those captured activities.

70 Part 2, subpart 1, AML/CFT Act: http://bit.ly/2A5PJtA

71 Codes of Practice and Guidelines: http://bit.ly/2gQ3Iev

72 DIA v Ping An, paragraph 44: http://bit.ly/2kbWHtz Section 5(1), AML/CFT Act (http://bit.ly/2xHGfmy). "Existing customer" refers to any person who was in a business relationship with you immediately before the AML/CFT Act began to apply to the legal and conveyancing professions. The AML/CFT Act applies to lawyers and conveyancers from 1 July 2018.

Existing customers

The term "existing customer" is defined in the Act as a person who was in a business relationship with a reporting entity immediately before the Act began applying to the reporting entity.[73] You must conduct CDD on existing customers if there has been a material change in the nature or purpose of the business relationship with that customer, and you have insufficient information about that customer. When considering what information would be sufficient, you will need to assess the level of risk involved, and whether you hold the necessary identity information, verified to the appropriate level. You should not conduct any captured activity until these requirements are met.

Occasional customers

"Occasional activity" and "occasional transaction" are both defined in the Act.[74] The term "occasional" does not necessarily mean "single"; it also includes circumstances in which multiple transactions are so intermittent or infrequent that no business relationship is established.

The other people you must conduct CDD on

You must also complete CDD on:	For example:
Any beneficial owner[75] of a customer	Someone who owns more than 25% of a company that is your customer[76]
Any person acting on behalf of a customer	• A person exercising power of attorney for your customer • A legal guardian acting on behalf of a minor who is your customer • An employee of a company that is your customer

You need to have a good understanding of who your customers are and their circumstances and intentions. If you understand the sources of your customer's income and wealth and who else has an interest in their activities – ie, who else benefits – you can make a reasonable assessment about whether your customer's requests are typical, legitimate or potentially suspicious.

73 Section 5(1), AML/CFT Act: http://bit.ly/2xHGfmy

74 The term "beneficial owner" is defined in section 5(1), AML/CFT Act: http://bit.ly/2xHGfmy

75 More than 25% is the prescribed threshold for the definition of a beneficial owner. Regulation 5, AML/CFT (Definitions) Regulations: http://bit.ly/2yDVy49

76 CDD fact sheets: http://bit.ly/2Bxp2Pc

The DIA website provides a range of guidelines to help you conduct the appropriate level of CDD on different kinds of customers. There are fact sheets that cover the following CDD topics:[77]

- Acting on behalf of others
- Clubs and societies
- Companies
- Co-operatives
- Sole traders and partnerships
- Trusts

The supervisors have also provided specific guidance on beneficial ownership.[78] Customers that are individuals may be treated as the beneficial owner so long as you believe on reasonable grounds that the person is not acting on behalf of anyone else.[79]

The AML/CFT Act treats trusts as being capable of being customers in their own right, despite a trust not ordinarily having a legal personality. The supervisors have provided a fact sheet to help reporting entities

who engage with trusts as customers.[80]

Different levels of CDD

There are three levels of CDD. You will need to be sure you use the right level, which will depend on the unique factors of each business relationship, the characteristics of the customer(s), the nature of the activities and transactions you are facilitating, and the potential for ML/TF risk. The three levels are:

- **Standard CDD** – for most common situations
- **Simplified CDD** – for use with specific customers or customer types that are considered to be low risk for ML/TF – these customers are specified in section 18(2) of the AML/CFT Act[81]
- **Enhanced CDD** – for use when there are factors creating a higher level of ML/TF risk or are otherwise specified in the AML/CFT Act

You must use your own risk assessment and AML/CFT programme to establish the level of ML/TF risk. This will help you determine which kind of CDD to conduct before establishing the business relationship or conducting an occasional transaction or activity.

77 Beneficial Ownership Guideline: http://bit.ly/2Bxp2Pc

78 Section 11(2), AML/CFT Act: http://bit.ly/2gRumUg

79 Clarification of the position the AML/CFT supervisors are taking with respect of the AML/CFT Act interpretation of a trust as a customer: http://bit.ly/2Bxp2Pc

80 Section 18(2), AML/CFT Act: http://bit.ly/2gS5b3V

81 Amended Identity Verification Code of Practice 2013: http://bit.ly/2k13AxJ

How to use the Amended Identity Verification Code of Practice

Identity verification needs to be done by collecting and sighting documents, data, or information provided from a reliable and independent source. You are required to keep records of this information.

The Amended Identity Verification Code of Practice provides suggested best practice for anyone conducting name and date of birth identity verification on customers (who are natural persons) that have been assessed to be low to medium risk.[82] The Amended Identity Verification Code of Practice should be read in tandem with the Explanatory Note.[83]

Standard CDD

Lawyers and conveyancers must conduct standard CDD[84] if:

- They establish a business relationship with a new customer
- A customer seeks to conduct an occasional transaction or activity through the law firm, conveyancer or conveyancing practice; or
- In relation to an existing customer, and according to the level of risk involved, there has been a material change in the business relationship and there is insufficient information held about the customer (for example, they are a litigation customer you have dealt with prior to the Act taking effect who is now seeking legal assistance for establishing and managing a business enterprise)

Identity requirements

When standard CDD applies, the following identity information must be gathered about a customer, the beneficial owner(s), and a person acting on behalf of a customer:[85]

- Full name
- Date of birth
- If the person is not the customer, the person's relationship to the customer
- Address or registered office
- Company identifier or registration number
- You must also obtain information about the nature and purpose of the proposed business relationship with the customer, and sufficient information to determine whether enhanced CDD needs to be conducted on the customer[86]

82 Identity Verification Code of Practice – Explanatory Note: http://bit.ly/2k13AxJ
83 Section 14, AML/CFT Act: http://bit.ly/2z2zU99
84 Section 15, AML/CFT Act: http://bit.ly/2zDSNQt
85 Section 17, AML/CFT Act: http://bit.ly/2m1YSjC
86 Beneficial Ownership Guideline: http://bit.ly/2Bxp2Pc

Verification requirements

Lawyers and conveyancers are required to take reasonable steps to ensure that the information gathered is correct. According to the level of risk involved, you need to take reasonable steps to verify the identity of any beneficial owners, and to verify the identity and authority of any person who is seeking to act on behalf of your customer. The supervisors have published a *Beneficial Ownership Guideline* to help you.[87] Verification must be undertaken before the business relationship is established or before the occasional transaction or activity is conducted. There is an exception to this, which is described in "When to conduct CDD" on page 38.

The Amended Identity Verification Code of Practice allows lawyers (among other identified groups) to act as "trusted referees" to verify identity information. It is important to note that lawyers can only do this where they are not themselves party to the activity or transaction with the customer for whom the CDD is being conducted.

Example in practice – setting up a company

A new customer, Mr Kemal Dilan, approaches your law firm seeking assistance to set up a company that would operate as a social enterprise. The company would import sports gear to sell at very low cost to schools and sports clubs in underprivileged suburbs. Mr Dilan would also like you to be involved on an ongoing basis by providing a correspondence address for the company and ongoing advice on request. Your customer is an individual so cannot be on the list of entities where simplified CDD would apply. As you will be required to undertake captured activities for Mr Dilan, your CDD needs to be completed before you undertake any work for the customer. This includes asking a series of questions about the nature and purpose of the company and the people involved, which leads you to determine that there is no need for enhanced CDD.

Steps to complete standard CDD	How this applies to the example
Obtain identity information for all relevant persons and establish the nature and purpose of the intended business relationship.	Mr Dilan states he will be the sole director, shareholder and manager of the business. He provides you with the original of his current passport.
Obtain information about the nature and purpose of the proposed business relationship.	Mr Dilan explains his intention to establish the social enterprise as a way of giving back to his local community and to reduce barriers for children's participation sports activities.

87 Amended Identity Verification Code of Practice 2013 available at Codes of Practice and Guidelines: http://bit.ly/2gQ3Iev

Steps to complete standard CDD	How this applies to the example
Make a determination of the level of ML/TF risk involved.	After you establish there are no other people with a beneficial interest in the formation of the company (for instance, proposed shareholders) you assess the risk as low.
According to that level of risk, verify the identity of relevant persons, including natural persons using the Amended Identity Verification Code of Practice.[88]	You view and take a clear copy of the passport. You record the date on which you sighted the passport and made the copy.
If the identity information and verification requirements are satisfied, then you can proceed with the customer's instructions.	You provide advice to Mr Dilan about the best way to set up his company and register the company for him.

Simplified customer due diligence

You may complete simplified CDD if your customer is one of those listed in the AML/CFT Act. The list includes a range of organisations, including:

- Government departments
- Local authorities
- The New Zealand Police
- State-owned enterprises
- Crown entities
- Registered banks
- Licensed insurers
- Publicly listed companies

For the full list, please see section 18(2) of the AML/ CFT Act.[89]

Identity requirements

When simplified CDD applies, you need to record the full name of the entity in question and a brief explanation of how it falls within section 18(2) of the AML/CFT Act.

The following information needs to be gathered about the identity of a person acting on behalf of one of the entities listed in section 18(2) (eg, an employee of one of those organisations):

- Full name
- Date of birth
- The person's relationship to the customer

88 Section 18(2), AML/CFT Act: http://bit.ly/2gS5b3V

89 Section 21, AML/CFT Act: http://bit.ly/2zDTeu5

Appendix 9

You also need to obtain information about the nature and purpose of the proposed business relationship between you and the customer.[90]

Verification requirements

You must verify the identity of a person acting on behalf of a customer, and verify that person's authority to act so that you are satisfied you know who the person acting is and that they have the authority to act. Reasonable steps must be taken according to the level of risk involved. This verification must be undertaken before the business relationship is established (or before the occasional transaction or activity is conducted), or before the person acts on behalf of the customer.

Example in practice – forming and administering a scholarship fund

You are approached by Ms Sam Vacari, an employee of a local authority, to help with forming a scholarship fund for students who have been accepted to study law at university. The fund seed money will come directly from the local authority's Education Subcommittee budget. You would be engaged to form the scholarship fund as a legal entity and assist with its administration. You have not dealt with Ms Vacari before and you expect that you will be entering a business relationship of some duration with the local authority. The local authority is your customer and is listed in section 18(2) of the Act, so simplified CDD applies. You should assume for the purposes of this example that all other relevant legal obligations have been met.

Steps to complete simplified CDD	How this applies to the example
Identify whether your customer meets the criteria for simplified CDD.	You identify and record that the local authority meets the criteria for simplified CDD.
Obtain information about the nature and purpose of the proposed business relationship.	Ms Vacari explains the intention of the Education sub-committee to support students from the community to study law as this has been identified as a local skills shortage.

90 Amended Identity Verification Code of Practice 2013 available at Codes of Practice and Guidelines: http://bit.ly/2gQ3Iev

Steps to complete simplified CDD	How this applies to the example
Identify all relevant persons that need to be identified.	As the local authority meets criteria for simplified CDD, you only need to obtain information about the identity of the person acting on its behalf, Ms Vacari, as well as her authority to do so – in this case she shows you her New Zealand driver licence and credit card from a New Zealand registered bank with her name on it, and she also shows you a letter from the chair of the local authority's Education Sub-committee outlining her role in establishing the scholarship fund.
Make a determination of the level of ML/TF risk involved.	You determine that the risk is low, so you continue with applying simplified CDD.
According to that level of risk, verify the identity of Ms Vacari and her authority to act on behalf of the local authority using the Amended Identity Verification Code of Practice (IVCOP).[91]	To meet the requirements of the IVCOP, you sight Ms Vacari's drivers licence and credit card, and note her work email address is consistent with her working for the local authority. You decide that given the low risk you do not need to take any further action to verify her identity or the letter that shows she has authority to act on behalf of the local authority. You record this.
If the identity information and verification requirements are satisfied, then you can proceed with the customer's instructions.	You then proceed with forming the legal entity which would operate the scholarship fund.

Enhanced CDD

You must conduct enhanced CDD in specific circumstances:

1. If you are establishing a business relationship with, or looking to conduct an occasional transaction or activity for, a customer that is:
    - A trust or another vehicle for holding personal assets
    - A non-New Zealand resident who is from a country that has insufficient AML/CFT systems and measures in place;[92] or
    - A company with nominee shareholders or shares in bearer form

91 See "Compliance obligations when conducting international transactions" on page 39 for more discussion of how to assess whether a country is considered high risk.

92 Toogood J confirmed in paragraph 34 of DIA v Ping An that a transaction that is either complex or unusually large will trigger the enhanced CDD requirements. http://bit.ly/2kbWHtz

2. If a customer seeks your assistance to conduct a complex or unusually large transaction or an unusual pattern of transactions that have no apparent or visible economic or lawful purpose[93]
3. When you consider that the level of ML/TF risk involved means that enhanced CDD would be required
4. When you have had cause to submit an SAR to the FIU
5. When you determine that your customer is a politically exposed person
6. If you are an ordering institution, an intermediary institution, or a beneficiary institution in relation to a wire transfer; or
7. If you are undertaking an activity that involves the use of new and developing technologies that may favour anonymity

When conducting enhanced CDD you must obtain information about your customer's source of wealth or source of funds.[94] You must record this information and take reasonable steps, according to the level of risk involved, to verify this information using other reliable and independent sources.[95] Where you identify that the origin of your customer's funds or wealth has come from their beneficial owner(s), it may be necessary, according to the level of risk involved, for you to extend your level of verification to include the source of wealth or source of funds of these persons.

You will not need to obtain and verify source of wealth or source of funds for every beneficial owner where they have nothing to do with your customer's source of wealth or source of funds.

The supervisors have published guidance for all reporting entities on enhanced CDD.[96] The following examples have been tailored to suit lawyers and conveyancers. You should assume for the purposes of these examples that all other relevant legal obligations have been met.

Example in practice: Charitable trust entering into a property development

You are approached by a charitable trust that is looking to engage in a large-scale property development for affordable housing units on the outskirts of Christchurch. The property development is being funded with the assets of the trust and promised donations from other charitable organisations and the regional council. The charitable trust will on-sell each of the housing units at cost price to eligible applicants who meet a household income threshold. You

93 Section 23(1)(a) of the AML/CFT Act: http://bit.ly/2iFkDBE

94 Section 24(1)(a) of the AML/CFT Act: http://bit.ly/2zXSvDA

95 Section 24(1)(b) of the AML/CFT Act: http://bit.ly/2zXSvDA

96 Amended Identity Verification Code of Practice 2013 available at Codes of Practice and Guidelines: http://bit.ly/2gQ3Iev

97 Amended Identity Verification Code of Practice 2013 available at Codes of Practice and Guidelines: http://bit.ly/2gQ3Iev

are asked to help with conveyancing the land purchase (captured by the AML/CFT Act) and then to help with gaining all the required building consents (not captured).

Steps to complete enhanced CDD	How this applies to the example
Identify which criteria your customer meets to decide the level of CDD you must do.	You must complete enhanced CDD prior to establishing the business relationship because your customer is a trust.
Obtain information about the nature and purpose of the proposed business relationship.	The representative of the charitable trust advises you that the purpose of the property development is to enable low income families to purchase a home.
Determine the initial level of ML/TF risk.	You research the trust's history and determine that the trust has been in existence for a long time and has conducted large-scale charitable projects in the past. You identify that the charitable trust is registered under the Charities Act 2005 and listed on the Charities Register. You review the information on the Charities Register and identify that this is consistent with its involvement in the proposed property development. Your initial determination is that the ML/TF risk is medium.
Identify all relevant persons that need to be identified and gather information about the source of wealth/ source of funds.	You ask the representative of the charitable trust for proof of their identity. You identify that they are listed on the Charities Register as one of the trustees, along with two other persons. You ask to see the trust deed, copy this document and record the full name of the trust, its address and a description of the objects of the trust. You ask to see account documentation from their bank showing incoming donations and other income and outgoings of the charitable trust for a period of time you suggest. You also obtain documents showing the promised donations to the project from other charitable organisations, local businesses and the regional council.

Steps to complete enhanced CDD	How this applies to the example
Verify the information gathered, including using the Amended Identity Verification Code of Practice for the identity of individuals[97] (as risk is not deemed to be high).	You ask the trustee you are dealing with to show you his passport. You take a copy of this passport and record the date that you viewed the original. You retain the copy of the trustee's passport on your file. You advise the trustee that you are dealing with that you need to verify the identity of the other two trustees. One of them is based close by and you arrange for her to come and see you with a copy of her passport. You take a copy of this passport and record the date you viewed the original. The third trustee resides in a different town. You therefore request that a lawyer in that town, who is not involved with the charitable trust or their intended activities, certify a copy of the third trustee's passport. You arrange for the certified copy of this passport to be provided to you. To verify the charitable trust's address, you check the Charities Register online. You record that the stated address on the trust deed matches the address on the Charities Register. You review all the documents provided as proof of source of wealth/funds and determine them to be issued by reliable and independent sources (ie known organisations and the regional council). You therefore decide that no further third-party verification of source of funds/wealth is required.
If the identity information and verification requirements are satisfied, then you can proceed with the customer's instructions.	You assist with the purchase of land for the property development.

Example in practice: Winding up a family trust

Mr Ralph Swanson and Mrs Marjorie Swanson ask for your help to wind up their family trust in accordance with the trust deed. The Swanson family trust holds a commercial apple export business, an apple orchard, a packhouse, a residential home, five vehicles and other commercial machinery. Mr and Mrs Swanson have run the apple business but are now looking to retire. None of the beneficiaries (Mr and Mrs Swanson's five children) wish to take over the business. Mr and Mrs Swanson are the trustees of the family trust and decide to sell the apple business as a going concern on the open market. The sale will include the orchard, packhouse, the house and vehicles, and the commercial machinery (ie all the trust assets). The proceeds of the sale will be distributed in line with the trust deed.

Steps to complete enhanced CDD	How this applies to the example
Identify which criteria your customer meets to decide the level of CDD you must do.	You complete enhanced CDD because your customer is a trust.
Obtain information about the nature and purpose of the proposed business relationship.	Mr and Mrs Swanson outline their intentions to retire from the apple business and their need for the proceeds of the sale of trust assets to fund their retirement plans and to financially benefit their children who are beneficiaries named in the trust deed.
Determine the initial level of ML/TF risk.	You ask Mr and Mrs Swanson to provide a copy of the trust deed. You note that the trust was established many years ago by a previous local law firm that you had dealings with in the past and knew to be reputable. You determine that the beneficiaries of the trust are all immediate family members. Your initial determination is that the ML/TF risk is low.
Identify all relevant persons that need to be identified and gather information about the source of wealth/source of funds.	You ask to see the trust deed, and you copy this document and record the full name of the trust, its address and the names and dates of birth of the beneficiaries. You gather identity information for the two trustees (Mr and Mrs Swanson) and the beneficiaries (the five children). You check the trust deed and determine that there are no other beneficial owners. You also obtain documentation, such as bank records and accounts audited by an accountant to prove that the assets of the trust have been purchased from legitimate sources. In this case the source is the profits of the apple enterprise which have fully paid off a business mortgage.
Verify the information gathered, including using the Amended Identity Verification Code of Practice for the identity of individuals (as risk is not deemed to be high).	You ask Mr and Mrs Swanson to show you their passports so that you can verify their identities. Mrs Swanson is able to do this; however, Mr Swanson states that he does not have a passport. You ascertain that he does have a New Zealand driver licence and a credit card from a New Zealand registered bank with his name on it. You take copies of these documents and record the dates that you viewed the originals. You retain copies on your file.

Appendix 9

Steps to complete enhanced CDD	How this applies to the example
	You ascertain that four of the Swanson children live locally. You arrange for all of them to bring their passports and undertake the same process. You note that the biographical information on the passports matches the information on the trust documents. You find out that the fifth Swanson child currently lives in Scotland. You therefore request that a lawyer in Edinburgh, who has no connection to the fifth Swanson child or the Swanson Family Trust, certify a copy of his passport. You arrange for the certified copy of this passport to be provided to you. When it arrives, you note that the biographical information on the passport matches the information on the trust documents. You review all the documents provided as proof of source of wealth/funds and determine them to be issued by reliable and independent sources. You therefore decide that no further third party verification of source of funds/wealth is required. You also note that one of the trust bank statements was dated two weeks ago. You note that the address on the bank statement matches the address on the trust deeds. You record that you have verified the address on this basis.
If the identity information and verification requirements are satisfied, then you can proceed with the customer's instructions.	You help with winding up the family trust.

Example in practice: Assisting a company to acquire another company

The New Zealand-based director of ABC Limited, an architecture and design company, asks you to help the company purchase a competitor business, XYZ Limited, an interior design service, for $25m. You are interested in how ABC Limited can afford it given it is a medium-sized enterprise that is smaller than XYZ Limited, so you conduct enhanced CDD. You are informed by your customer that ABC Limited has gained some large-scale retirement village design contracts in the previous two years. Its annual turnover increased from $5m to $20m per annum and is expected to rise to $30m in the coming year with many more retirement village fit outs expected to be completed. ABC Limited aims to acquire XYZ to enable it to provide a more comprehensive interior design component for its retirement village fit outs. This would increase the income they can generate as the business expands and retirement village fit out becomes a significant source of income.[98]

Steps to complete enhanced CDD	How this applies to the example
Identify which criteria your customer meets to decide the level of CDD you must do.	ABC Limited is a new customer and has a director in New Zealand but some offshore ownership. You are unfamiliar with the company and it is seeking to undertake a large procurement.
Obtain information about the nature and purpose of the proposed business relationship.	The director describes the intention for horizontal and vertical expansion as outlined in the ABC Limited business plan.
Determine the initial level of ML/TF risk.	You identify that the offshore people with beneficial ownership are based in a country that poses a higher ML/TF risk. You determine the level of risk is high and that enhanced CDD must be conducted.
Identify all relevant persons that need to be identified and gather information about the source of wealth/source of funds.	You gather identity information on all those with a beneficial interest in ABC Limited, including the director in New Zealand and the shareholders offshore. You do some research to ensure that none of the beneficial owners are politically exposed persons; it turns out they are not. You also obtain business accounts audited by an accountant, bank records and tax payment records for the previous two years. You consider these documents to be issued by reliable and independent sources. You also sight and record the retirement village contracts showing expected fit outs and you research the business offering the retirement village fit out contracts to ensure it is a genuine company. To be sure of this, you contact them to ensure the contracts you hold remain valid.

98 Amended Identity Verification Code of Practice 2013: http://bit.ly/2k13AxJ
99 Section 17(b), AML/CFT Act: http://bit.ly/2m1YSjC

Steps to complete enhanced CDD	How this applies to the example
Verify the identity information gathered using more in-depth processes than those specified in the Amended Identity Verification Code of Practice[99] because you have determined the level of risk to be high.	You verify the identity of the director of ABC Limited in New Zealand by sighting his passport, his driver licence, a credit card with a New Zealand registered bank, a recent bank statement and a utility bill. For the overseas beneficial owners, you are concerned that obtaining a certified copy of their passports by a lawyer of their choosing does not provide you with the level of assurance you require. However, you are recommended a law firm in that same country that is known to be trustworthy. As a result, you arrange for the beneficial owners to visit and have their passports and other identity information certified by a lawyer in that law firm, who then provides you copies of the certified documents.
If the identity information and verification requirements are satisfied, then you can proceed with the customer's instructions.	You help ABC Limited to purchase XYZ Limited.

Identifying if a customer is a politically exposed person

As soon as possible after establishing a business relationship, or conducting an occasional transaction or activity, lawyers and conveyancers are required to take reasonable steps to identify whether their customer (or any beneficial owner) is a politically exposed person (PEP).[100] The Act requires reporting entities to conduct enhanced CDD if it establishes a business relationship with a customer or beneficial owner who is a PEP, or if a PEP seeks to conduct an occasional transaction or activity through the reporting entity.[101]

A PEP is defined in section 5(1) in the Act.[102] In summary, a PEP is a person, or an immediate family member or someone who has close business ties to that person, who holds or has held (in the preceding 12 months) a prominent public function in a foreign country. This may be because they are or were a head of state, senior politician, or an official with a public profile, such as a Supreme Court Judge, or a highly ranked military official. It could also be because they had authority and influence in a state enterprise in any country. PEPs can be exposed to bribery or corruption or their respected status may be misused (knowingly, or unknowingly) to legitimise otherwise suspect transactions.

100 Section 26(1), AML/CFT Act: http://bit.ly/2BKjPWO

101 See definition of "politically exposed person" in section 5(1), AML/CFT Act: http://bit.ly/2xHGfmy

102 Section 26(2)(a), AML/CFT Act: http://bit.ly/2A8liTh

If you determine that your customer or a beneficial owner is a PEP, you will require senior management approval to continue the business relationship.[103] Also, you must obtain information about the source of wealth or funds and verify that information.[104] If you have undertaken an occasional transaction or activity for someone who you didn't realise is a PEP, as soon as you can after the transaction you also need to obtain and verify information about their source of wealth or funds.

The *Enhanced Customer Due Diligence Guideline* has more information about how to manage compliance where customers are identified as PEPs.[105]

Wire transfers

The supervisors have published guidance on compliance matters when participating in wire transfers.[106]

A "wire transfer" is a transaction carried out on behalf of a person through a reporting entity by electronic means with a view to making an amount of money available to a beneficiary at another reporting entity (the person on whose behalf the transaction is conducted and the beneficiary can be the same person). An "international wire transfer" is a wire transfer where at least one of the ordering, intermediary or beneficiary institutions is in New Zealand, and at least one is outside New Zealand.

Section 27 of the Act places specific obligations on "ordering institutions" and "beneficiary institutions" when the wire transfer is equal to or above $1,000. Please refer to "Prescribed transaction reports" on page 23 for an explanation of these terms (both of which are defined in section 5(1) of the AML/CFT Act). It is possible that a lawyer could be either an ordering or a beneficiary institution, in which case they must complete identity and verification requirements in line with the AML/CFT Act.[107]

New or developing technologies, or products that might favour anonymity

People with criminal intentions value anonymity and will continually look for new ways to preserve it while conducting their activities. Section 30 of the AML/CFT[108] Act requires that if a customer is seeking assistance for an activity that involves new or developing technologies, or products, that might favour anonymity you must:

1. Complete standard CDD identity and verification requirements; and

103 Section 23(1)(a), AML/CFT Act: http://bit.ly/2ilUTJI

104 Section 26(2)(b), AML/CFT Act: http://bit.ly/2A8liTh

105 Wire Transfers: available at Codes of Practice and Guidelines: http://bit.ly/2gQ3Iev

106 Sections 27–28, AML/CFT Act: http://bit.ly/2hRYKyV

107 Section 30, AML/CFT Act: http://bit.ly/2gWmRLD

108 See the supervisors' Countries Assessment Guideline (http://bit.ly/2hOTHPk) or the Basel Index, which ranks countries by AML/CFT risk (https://index.baselgovernance.org/ranking).

2. Take any additional measures needed to mitigate the risk of the new or developing technology or product being used to commit ML/TF

Both steps must be done before you enter a business relationship or conduct an occasional transaction or activity for your customer.

When you can rely on others for CDD

In some specific circumstances, reporting entities can rely on others to conduct CDD if the other party is either:

- A member of the same DBG
- Another reporting entity in New Zealand or a person in another country that has sufficient AML/CFT systems and measures in place and who is regulated for AML/CFT purposes[109]
- An agent; or
- An approved entity

Relying on a member of your designated business group

A member of a DBG (Member A) can rely on another member of that same DBG (Member B) to conduct CDD if the information is given before Member A has established a business relationship or conducts an occasional transaction or activity for the customer. Any verification information must be able to be given to Member A by Member B as soon as practicable but within five working days of the request. In this scenario, Member A (not Member B) is responsible for ensuring that it is complying with the AML/CFT requirements.

Relying on another reporting entity or a suitably regulated person overseas

A reporting entity can rely on another person for CDD so long as the person:

1. Is either a reporting entity in New Zealand or is a person resident in a country which is regulated for AML/CFT purposes;[110] and
2. Has a business relationship with the customer concerned; and
3. Has conducted CDD to at least the standard required by the AML/CFT Act and:
    - Has provided the reporting entity the relevant identity information before it has established a business relationship or conducted an occasional transaction or activity; and

109 Please note that law firms and conveyancing practitioners in Australia are not specifically regulated for AML/CFT purposes.

110 Section 16(3), AML/CFT Act: http://bit.ly/2iTi1Da

- Can provide relevant verification information on request of the reporting entity as soon as practicable but within five working days; and

4. Consents to conducting the CDD and providing all relevant CDD information to the reporting entity

In this scenario, and as above, the reporting entity requesting the CDD remains responsible for ensuring the CDD is conducted in accordance with the AML/CFT Act.

Relying on an agent

A reporting entity may authorise a person to be its agent and rely on that agent to conduct CDD and obtain any information required for CDD records. "Agent" is not defined in the Act; instead, the ordinary principles of agency law will apply.

Relying on an approved entity

Section 33 of the Act enables a business to rely on an "approved entity". There are not yet any prescribed approved entities.

When to conduct CDD

You must conduct CDD (ie, obtain the required identity information and verify that information) on your customer before a business relationship with the customer is entered into, or an occasional transaction or activity is conducted.

The only exception to this timeframe, which would allow verification to be completed after the business relationship has been established, will be where all the following criteria apply:

- It is essential not to interrupt normal business practice
- ML/TF risks are effectively managed through appropriate risk management procedures; and
- Identity verification is completed as soon as practicable once the business relationship has been established[111]

Fast-paced scenarios may be common for some lawyers or conveyancers; however, instances of delaying the verification of customer identity information should be truly exceptional. The reasons for delaying verification should be fact-based, justifiable and recorded.

Ongoing CDD and account monitoring

Under section 31 of the AML/CFT Act, when you are in a business relationship with a customer, you are required to conduct ongoing CDD and ongoing account monitoring. You are required to regularly review any

111 Countries Assessment Guideline: http://bit.ly/2hOTHPk

information you hold about the customer and regularly review their account activity and transaction behaviour. The purpose of this is to ensure that the nature and purpose of the business relationship and any transactions relating to that business relationship are consistent with your knowledge of the customer and the customer's risk profile. This regular review will also help you to identify any grounds for reporting a suspicious activity.

Reporting entities are required to develop a process for ongoing CDD and account monitoring for their customers according to the level of risk each customer presents. You should think about the level of CDD that was previously undertaken, and consider the level of risk involved with that customer or their activities and transactions. This means higher-risk customers need to have more frequent and thorough account monitoring than customers deemed to be low or medium risk. The account monitoring conducted should enable you to identify any transaction behaviour that is out of character with your knowledge of the customer, their risk profile and the CDD you have previously conducted.

Compliance obligations when conducting international transactions

An area of general business practice that requires specific mention in your AML/CFT programme is your method of ensuring compliance when conducting or participating in international transactions with multiple parties. This is likely to be different for each firm. This section provides some basic information about how to comply with the Act when dealing with parties in other countries that may or may not have reputable AML/CFT regulation. The supervisors have published the *Countries Assessment Guideline* to help you determine whether a country you are dealing with has effective AML/CFT systems and measures.[112]

There is no definitive list of countries that are deemed not to have sufficient AML/CFT systems and measures, so reporting entities should consider a range of factors when determining the level of risk associated with engaging in a transaction with a country. For example, is the country:

- Subject to international sanctions, embargos or other measures?
- Identified by the FATF as lacking adequate AML/CFT systems and measures?[113]
- Recognised as having supporters of terrorism, or financing terrorism?
- Considered to have problems with corruption (eg, it has a low ranking on the Transparency International Corruption Perceptions Index)?[114]

112 High-risk and non-cooperative jurisdictions: http://bit.ly/1lTBG24

113 The Transparency International Corruption Perceptions Index for 2016 is available at: http:// bit.ly/2j3Y63K

114 The Basel Index, which ranks countries by AML/CFT risk, may also be useful: http://bit.ly/2djRNDR

- Known as a tax haven?
- Associated with production and/or transnational shipment of illicit drugs?

What to do if you cannot complete CDD

If you are not able to complete CDD for a customer, you must neither carry out an occasional transaction or activity for them nor establish a business relationship with them.[115] If you already have a business relationship with the customer, and that business relationship relates solely to captured activities, this must be terminated (you are free to continue providing non-captured services to the customer). This applies to all circumstances where a customer fails or refuses to provide information, data or documents that you have requested, including in relation to enhanced CDD. This also applies if the information, data or documents that the customer provides are inadequate.

You should always bear in mind your obligations under the Lawyers' Conduct and Client Care Rules or the Conveyancing Practitioners' Conduct and Client Care Rules (as applicable). These rules allow a lawyer or conveyancer to terminate a retainer for a range of specified reasons including where a customer gives instructions that would cause the lawyer or conveyancer to breach their professional obligations.[116]

If you are declining to enter into a business relationship or refusing an occasional transaction or activity, you are required to consider whether you need to file an SAR with the FIU.

6. Know the red flags

This section draws on available international information about the vulnerabilities of the legal and conveyancing professions to misuse by criminals. This information should assist your general awareness and your considerations of the risks your business may face from unwittingly facilitating ML/TF. In this section, the term "client" is used in preference to "customer" as the text is from open source material that uses the term "client".

Red flags identified by the Financial Action Task Force

The FATF is an inter-governmental body established in 1989 to set standards and promote effective implementation of legal, regulatory and operational measures for combating ML/TF and other related threats to the integrity of the international financial system.

115 Section 37, AML/CFT Act: http://bit.ly/2hydAdM

116 Rule 4.2.1(a), Lawyers and Conveyancers Act (Lawyers: Conduct and Client Care) Rules 2008 (http://bit.ly/2htoGR8) and rule 20.1(c), Lawyers and Conveyancers Act (Conveyancers: Conduct and Client Care) Rules 2008 (http://bit.ly/2jpl3iN)

The FATF provides a range of information and advice for the industries and professions that are affected by ML/TF. In June 2013, it published *Money Laundering and Terrorist Financing Vulnerabilities of Legal Professionals.*[117] The report identifies seven common ML/TF methods that require the assistance of a legal professional and present risk to lawyers who may be misused, even unwittingly, by criminals. Conveyancers also need to be mindful of the ML/TF risks they are exposed to.

The seven methods are:[118]

1. Misuse of client accounts
2. Purchase of real estate property
3. Creation of trusts and companies
4. Management of trusts and companies
5. Managing client affairs and making introductions
6. Undertaking certain litigation
7. Setting up and managing charities

1. Misuse of client accounts

Client accounts can be used as the first step in converting the cash proceeds of crime into other, less suspicious assets. This can permit access to financial institutions as it helps to hide the true source or ownership of the funds and assets and can facilitate buying property, setting up shell companies and onward transfer of the proceeds of crime to other parties. See case studies 1 and 2 in Appendix A.

Red flags to watch out for:

- Client actively avoids personal contact without good reason
- Client asks for unexplained speed
- Use of a disproportionate amount of cash
- Use of client account with no underlying legal work
- Willingness to pay fees when no legal work is undertaken
- Client is known to have connections with criminals
- Significant private funding and the transfers are structured so as to avoid the threshold of reporting requirements
- Aborted transactions after receipt of funds and there is an unexplained request to send funds to a third party

117 Money Laundering and Terrorist Financing Vulnerabilities of Legal Professionals: http://bit.ly/2z6i3ff

118 This section paraphrases content from Chapter 4 of the FATF report Money Laundering and Terrorist Financing Vulnerabilities of Legal Professionals. For more information, please see the full report.

2. Purchase of real estate property

Purchase of real estate is a common outlet for criminal proceeds as it appreciates and can provide a legitimate reason for the appearance and movement of funds. In addition, real estate gives criminals a place to live and enjoy the proceeds of their criminal activities or a place to set up new criminal enterprises. See case studies 3 and 4 in Appendix A.

Red flags to watch out for:

- Transaction involves a disproportionate amount of private funding/cash, which is inconsistent with the socio-economic profile of the client
- Funding from third parties requiring further consideration
- Requests to act for multiple parties without meeting them
- Back-to-back property transactions with rapidly increasing value
- Client changes legal advisor multiple times without good reason
- Parties to a transaction are connected without an apparent business reason

3. Creation of trusts and companies

Trusts and companies can be a convenient way to obscure the origin and ownership of assets, particularly if the trust or company is set up by a lawyer. This approach helps criminals retain control over criminally derived assets so they can enjoy the benefit of them while also distancing themselves from obvious ownership. See case studies 5 and 6 in Appendix A.

Red flags to watch out for:

- Use of an intermediary without good reason
- Attempts to disguise the real owner or parties to the transaction
- Involvement of structures in multiple countries where there is no apparent link to the client or transaction, or no other legitimate economic reason
- Client is known to have convictions or be under investigation for acquisitive crime[119]
- Transactions are unusual in terms of volume
- Involvement of high-risk countries[120]
- Mortgages are repeatedly repaid significantly prior to the initially agreed maturity date with no logical explanation

119 Acquisitive crime is any crime that produces proceeds of crime.

120 See "Compliance obligations when conducting international transactions" on page 39 for more discussion about high-risk countries.

4. Management of trusts and companies

Criminals will often seek the assistance of a lawyer to manage their trust or company to provide greater respectability and legitimacy to the entity and its activities. Techniques used by criminals include persuading a lawyer to act as a trustee to knowingly, or unknowingly, receive the proceeds of crime, or give the appearance of legitimacy and provide legal services that disguise criminal activities. See case studies 7 and 8 in Appendix A.

Red flags to watch out for:

- There are attempts to disguise the real owner or parties to the transaction
- Client is using false or fraudulent identity documents for the business entity
- Requests to make payments to third parties contrary to contractual obligations
- Client is known to have connections with criminals

5. Managing client affairs and making introductions

The involvement of a legal professional in a transaction or their referral of a client to other professionals or businesses can provide a veneer of legitimacy to criminal activities because of their ethical and professional obligations and general standing in society. See case study 9 in Appendix A.

Red flags to watch out for:

- Client requires an introduction to access banking facilities
- Private expenditure is being funded by a company, business or government
- Client is a politically exposed person[121] engaged in unusual private business given the frequency or characteristics involved
- There is an attempt to disguise the real owner or parties to the transaction
- Finance is being provided by a lender other than a credit institution, without a logical explanation or economic justification

6. Undertaking certain litigation

It is essential that lawyers act in a way to protect the right of access to justice by ensuring people have access to representation in litigation. There have been international cases where criminals have sought to exploit this protection mechanism by conducting sham litigation as a way to launder the proceeds of crime. Sham litigation is where, for example, the subject of the dispute is fabricated, or the subject of the dispute was a contract relating to a criminal

121 "Politically exposed person" is defined in section 5(1) of the AML/CFT Act: http://bit.ly/2xHGfmy

activity that no court would knowingly enforce. Funds received via a lawyer's trust account purporting to settle a debt or pay compensation could have the appearance of legitimacy sought by criminals. See case studies 10 and 11 in Appendix A.

Red flags to watch out for:

- Client with known convictions for acquisitive crime
- A party to the transaction has known links to organised crime
- Client and/or debtor are located at a distance from the legal professional
- The litigation is settled very quickly, sometimes before the legal professional has actually written to the debtor
- There is a request for the funds received from the debtor to be paid out very quickly, sometimes to third parties.
- Client is unconcerned about the level of fees

7. Setting up and managing charities

Some charities are set up as a vehicle for fraud while others could be used as a front for financing terrorism. In money laundering cases, the proceeds of crime are funnelled through the charity to launder the money and give the appearance of legitimacy. Legitimate funds can be given to a charity that then disguises the intended use and destination of the funds from authorities so that it can fund terrorist groups, activities and causes. See case study 12 in Appendix A.

Red flags to watch out for:

- Non-profit organisation engages in transactions not compatible with those declared and not typical for that body
- There are attempts to disguise the real owner or parties to the transactions
- Client is related to a person listed as having involvement with a known terrorist organisation

There will be other red flags that legal professionals should be on the lookout for when providing these services to a client. Please see Appendix B for the full list of the 42 red flags defined by the FATF.

Red flags identified by the International Bar Association, the American Bar Association and the Council of Bars and Law Societies of Europe

In October 2014, the International Bar Association, the American Bar Association and the Council of Bars and Law Societies of Europe published *A Lawyer's Guide to Detecting and Preventing Money Laundering*.[122] This report

122 A Lawyer's Guide to Detecting and Preventing Money Laundering: http://bit.ly/2hxRCrb

identifies a range of red flag indicators. They are included in Appendix B for your ease of reference.

How to keep up-to-date with changing methods of ML/TF

People with criminal intentions will always seek to stay ahead of authorities and the professionals whose services they wish to misuse. Over time new methods of ML/TF will develop and emerge. The FIU and DIA actively maintain a watch for these new methods and communicate them via the FIU's Quarterly Typology Reports[123] and DIA's newsletters.[124] Reporting entities are encouraged to look at these resources as well as media reports and information from the FATF and other jurisdictions to keep up-to-date with developments in ML/TF methods.

7. Know your AML/CFT supervisor

This section explains the regulatory approach you can expect from DIA.

The role of supervisors

DIA is the supervisor for law firms, conveyancing practitioners and incorporated conveyancing firms that are reporting entities under the AML/CFT Act. The Reserve Bank of New Zealand and the Financial Markets Authority both act as supervisors for other reporting entities. Our role includes monitoring reporting entities for compliance with the Act, providing guidance to reporting entities and investigating and enforcing compliance. This is to ensure that the AML/CFT system operates in a robust manner and that criminals seeking to launder money and finance terrorism are detected and deterred.

Our regulatory approach

We outline our regulatory approach for the AML/CFT system in two publications: the *AML/CFT Supervisory Framework*[125] and *Minimising Harm – Maximising Benefit*.[126] We apply a risk-based and responsive regulatory approach that promotes compliance through a mix of strategies, initiatives and tools. We aim to:

- Make it easy for reporting entities who want to comply
- Help reporting entities who are trying to comply
- Use the full force of the law on reporting entities that refuse to comply

We focus our efforts carefully and deliberately. We use our insight, knowledge and understanding to identify risks and determine interventions to most effectively ensure compliance. While we are fully prepared to escalate

123 Financial Intelligence Unit (FIU) assessments and reports: http://bit.ly/2xGSiAx

124 AML/CFT news: http://bit.ly/2z71Ad4

125 AML/CFT Supervisory Framework: http://bit.ly/2lHausc

126 Minimising Harm – Maximising Benefit: http:// bit.ly/2z669Sy

our response with enforcement action, we are equally prepared to work with reporting entities in a responsive and educative manner. We are a member of the National Co-ordination Committee, and we work with the other supervisors and the FIU, as well as with other government agencies, industry bodies and reporting entities, to apply a consistent approach to the AML/CFT system.

Monitoring and enforcement

We use a variety of regulatory tools to monitor a reporting entity's compliance with AML/CFT obligations. These include desk-based reviews of reporting entities' documents to test technical compliance, on-site inspections to test effectiveness of implementation of compliance programmes, analysis of annual reports and independent audits.

When we identify reporting entities that are not meeting their obligations under the AML/CFT Act, we consider a number of options. One of these options is a remediation plan with the reporting entity. A remediation plan includes a set of expected outcomes that the reporting entity must complete within a set timeframe. The timeframe includes measurable progress towards meeting the obligations under the AML/CFT Act. In most cases the timeframe and actions are met and the reporting entity progresses towards meeting the obligations.

In response to more serious or deliberate non-compliance, we may decide to issue a formal warning or to accept an enforceable undertaking. Alternatively, we may decide to seek an injunction, or a pecuniary penalty, from the High Court. In the most serious of cases, civil liability acts that are engaged in knowingly or recklessly are criminal offences. There are a number of further criminal offences – for example, failing to report or keep records relating to suspicious activities, structuring transactions to avoid AML/CFT requirements, and obstructing or misleading a supervisor. Where necessary, DIA will prosecute reporting entities for criminal offences under the Act.

Investigations of ML/TF

In New Zealand it is a criminal offence to knowingly and intentionally engage in, or facilitate any other person to engage in, money laundering[127] or the financing of terrorism.[128] The Police are responsible for investigating and prosecuting ML/TF offences, as well as forfeiture proceedings relating to the proceeds of crime. A robust AML/CFT system, in which reporting entities are conducting CDD, keeping customer and transaction records, and reporting suspicious activities, is an important tool in the collective fight against financial and organised crime.

127 Section 243, Crimes Act 1961: http://bit.ly/2zYeqXU

128 Section 8(1) and (2A), Terrorism Suppression Act 2002: http://bit.ly/2lZbZlE

Territorial scope of the AML/CFT Act

The supervisors have issued guidance outlining their interpretation of the territorial scope of the AML/ CFT Act.[129] Even though the AML/CFT Act only has jurisdiction in New Zealand, we strongly encourage reporting entities to report on suspicious activities and transactions that they are party to that occur entirely offshore. For more information about reporting suspicious activity, please see "Reporting to the FIU" on page 22.

8. Know where to get support

Reporting entities can access compliance support from a range of sources:

- Your AML/CFT programme and compliance officer
- DIA as the supervisor
- The New Zealand Law Society, the Auckland District Law Society and the New Zealand Society of Conveyancers
- Independent legal advice
- Open source information from relevant international bodies concerned with AML/CFT

Your AML/CFT programme and compliance officer

Where employees in your business have compliance questions, their first port of call should be your AML/ CFT programme. This document should be able to provide answers to basic questions that are likely to arise in your specific business context. As questions arise, it is likely that the AML/CFT programme will need to be updated to include provisions for resolving unanticipated issues and frequently asked questions.

Specific questions should be answered by your compliance officer. Where this approach does not resolve the question at hand, it is important to consider what would be the appropriate next step – seeking support from the relevant professional body, from your supervisor or from an independent lawyer.

Support from your supervisor

We recognise that this is a new compliance system to adjust to, and so we aim to provide proactive support to reporting entities. Examples of the support we provide range from general information and awareness promotion, all the way to specific support where a reporting entity is experiencing difficulty but has a genuine intention to comply. The DIA website provides a wide range of information about how to comply with the AML/CFT Act for reporting entities.[130]

129 Territorial Scope of the Anti-Money Laundering and Countering Financing of Terrorism Act 2009: http://bit.ly/2nf664p

130 Anti-money laundering and countering financing of terrorism: http://bit.ly/2zbaCoS

The AML/CFT Act allows supervisors to create codes of practice. A code of practice is a statement of practice that helps reporting entities to comply with the AML/CFT Act. So far, one code of practice has been developed: the Identity Verification Code of Practice. This was developed in 2011 and amended in 2013.[131] It should be read in tandem with the Explanatory Note.[132] There are no current plans to develop more codes of practice, but the supervisors are open to feedback from reporting entities on whether more would be helpful.

Support from your industry bodies

Lawyers and conveyancers are encouraged to keep abreast of the information and education on offer from their representative societies. Lawyers can expect a range of information and compliance support from the New Zealand Law Society. The Auckland District Law Society communicates with their members to raise awareness via articles in their publications and by hosting webinars on the topic. The New Zealand Society of Conveyancers also provides a range of information and support to conveyancers.

When to seek independent legal advice

There will be occasions where lawyers and conveyancers need to seek independent legal advice to ensure they remain compliant with the AML/CFT Act. Supervisors cannot provide legal advice to reporting entities. When you have specific compliance questions about unique circumstances that the supervisor or your professional body cannot reasonably answer, you may need to seek independent legal advice.

Other publicly available information

The Phase 2 Sector Risk Assessment (Phase 2 SRA) is essential reading for lawyers and conveyancers. This resource gives reporting entities the background understanding of the ways ML/TF poses risk to lawyers and conveyancers. The *AML/CFT Risk Assessment and Programme: Prompts and Notes* (Prompts and Notes) guideline outlines the factors to be considered in a risk assessment along with some prompts and things to think about when completing a risk assessment and developing your AML/CFT programme. The Phase 2 SRA and the Prompts and Notes are available on the DIA website.[133]

---

131 Amended Identity Verification Code of Practice 2013: http://bit.ly/2k13AxJ

132 Identity Verification Code of Practice – Explanatory Note: http://bit.ly/2k13AxJ

133 The Phase 2 SRA is available on the Sector and National Risk Assessments page (http://bit.ly/2ik1tAu) and the Prompts and Notes guideline is available on the Codes of Practice and Guidelines page (http://bit.ly/2gQ3Iev)

Appendix 9

The FATF has a range of information on its website, both specific to the legal sector[134] and to the New Zealand context.[135] You may be interested to read the FATF's 2013 report *Money Laundering and Terrorist Financing Vulnerabilities of Legal Professionals* and the International Bar Association, American Bar Association and the Council of Bars and Law Societies of Europe's 2014 report *A Lawyer's Guide to Detecting and Preventing Money Laundering.* [136] The red flags noted in Appendix B have been taken from these reports.

Support that may emerge in the future

As the AML/CFT system becomes established practice in the legal and conveyancing sectors, it is likely that relevant training establishments will begin to incorporate AML/CFT into curricula. Industry bodies will be a good source of information when new educational supports are in development.

Appendix A: Case studies

The case studies in this appendix provide illustrations of the seven common methods of money laundering identified by the FATF in their publication *Money Laundering and Terrorist Financing Vulnerabilities of Legal Professionals.* The case studies have been paraphrased and summarised for ease of reference. The case studies come from both the FATF report and other open source publications – references are provided in the footnotes. The purpose of including these case studies is to raise awareness of how lawyers and conveyancers have knowingly, or unknowingly, been involved with ML/TF both internationally and in New Zealand.

The seven common methods are:

1. Misuse of client accounts
2. Purchase of real estate property
3. Creation of trusts and companies
4. Managing trusts and companies
5. Managing client affairs and making introductions
6. Undertaking certain litigation
7. Setting up and managing charities

---

134 Money Laundering and Terrorist Financing Vulnerabilities of Legal Professionals: http://bit.ly/2z6i3ff

135 FATF evaluations of New Zealand: http://bit.ly/2nY08F1

136 A Lawyer's Guide to Detecting and Preventing Money Laundering: http://bit.ly/2hxRCrb

1. Misuse of client accounts

Case study 1: Aborted transactions and transfer of funds without underlying legal work[137]

A law firm was approached by a new client with instructions to assist on a number of asset purchases. The client was dealing with a junior lawyer at the firm who, at the request of the client, supplied her with the account details of the firm before completing CDD on the client or entering into an engagement letter with her. The client did not give any further instructions following the deposit of funds. Subsequently, the client explained that she no longer intended to purchase the relevant assets and asked for the deposited money to be provided to a third party, rather than returned to her personal account.

Case study 2: Use of client account to make a payment for ransom to terrorists[138]

Kidnapping for ransom is a growing source of revenue for terrorist groups, including ISIL. Cash often plays a significant role in kidnapping for ransom. Following the delivery of a ransom payment in physical cash, cash couriers move the cash to the terrorist group. Ransom payments can also be paid through financial institutions, such as banks, exchange houses, insurance companies, lawyers, or alternative remittance systems such as hawala. Kidnapping for ransom is particularly relevant to New Zealand as a kidnapping can occur in one jurisdiction and the ransom payment can be made in another. There have also been examples of funds that have been raised by relatives (on behalf of the victim), through the sale of assets and loans, and through the use of trusts to store the donation for a ransom payment.

2. Purchase of real estate property

Case study 3: Investment of proceeds in real estate[139]

A client deposited the total purchase price, in cash, with his lawyers at the very outset of the engagement with the law firm and well before final agreement was reached on the purchase price for the property. The lawyer's CDD indicated the sum that was deposited was a large amount relative to the client's employment income. The purchase of the property went ahead for a sum smaller than that deposited and the remaining funds were returned to a

137 International Bar Association, the American Bar Association and the Council of Bars and Law Societies of Europe, (October 2014), A Lawyer's Guide to Detecting and Preventing Money Laundering, p. 42.

138 Financial Intelligence Unit, (March 2016), Quarterly Typology Report Second Quarter (Q2) 2015/2016, Wellington, p. 13.

139 International Bar Association, the American Bar Association and the Council of Bars and Law Societies of Europe, (October 2014), A Lawyer's Guide to Detecting and Preventing Money Laundering, p. 42.

third party indicated by the client. It subsequently turned out the funds deposited were the proceeds of crime.

Case study 4: Misuse of legitimate businesses[140]

In 1998, Tom was looking to make a profitable property investment. He was told by Mariah, one of the directors of Lotos Ltd, that her company was looking to sell one of its buildings at a low price – US$275,000. Tom told Mariah that he wanted to purchase the property as soon as possible. Mariah had informed Tom that a co-director's name, Pete, would be on the contract as the seller of the building. When Tom went to his notary to sign the deed of purchase he did not question that Pete's name was there given his position as a co-director of the company.

Tom was unaware that the day before the sale, Mariah had already sold the building to Pete (in fact, he was her boyfriend and also a co-director of Lotos Ltd). That sale was for US$42,500, which meant that the resale to Tom had given her a profit of US$220,000, which had then gone into her and Pete's personal accounts. Even though Tom was unaware, his notary noticed that the land records showed the recent sale. In his experience the sale price and timing were very unusual and he decided to inform the FIU. The FIU questioned Mariah and the shareholders and found the shareholders had no knowledge of the first sale. Mariah had swindled the shareholders and the tax authorities and at the time of writing was due to face prosecution and asset confiscation.

3. Creation of trusts and companies

Case study 5: Creation of a private trust to disguise the proceeds of crime[141]

In Country A, an elderly female national from Country B with the appropriate visa consults with a trust lawyer. She found the lawyer's name through an internet search. She asks the lawyer to prepare a trust to handle an inheritance she has in Country B. The trust will be funded via wire transfer from Country B into the law firm's client account in Country A. Country B is a country that scores lowly on Transparency International's Corruption Perceptions Index and is subject to various sanctions programmes.

She will be the trustee and her children in Country A will be the beneficiaries. She asks for a memorandum on tax issues and filing requirements. She also

140 Egmont Group, (2002), FIUs in Action: 100 Cases from the Egmont Group, Egmont Group, Toronto, p. 59. This case study has been summarised by DIA for brevity and ease of reference.

141 International Bar Association, the American Bar Association and the Council of Bars and Law Societies of Europe, (October 2014), A Lawyer's Guide to Detecting and Preventing Money Laundering, p. 44.

wants an introduction to a certified public accountant and to a banker in Country A.

The type of trust requested by the client is a normal structure familiar to most trust lawyers. The goal of the client seems to be asset management for the benefit of the client's children. While the tax consequences may be complex, the plan is relatively typical and the lawyer agrees to act for the client.

Case study 6: Use of professional intermediaries to facilitate money laundering[142]

A criminal involved in smuggling into Great Britain set up a trust in order to launder the proceeds of his crime, with the assistance of a collusive independent financial adviser and a solicitor, who also appeared to be acting in the knowledge that the individual was a criminal. The trust was discretionary and therefore power over the management of the fund was vested in the trustees, namely the criminal, his wife and the independent financial adviser. This example illustrates the complexity of trusts used to hide the origins of funds from any law enforcement scrutiny.

One way in which funds were hidden was through the purchase of a garage. The criminal's daughter, who was a beneficiary of the trust, was given the property by her father and she in turn leased it to a company. The property was eventually sold to this company, the purchase funded by a loan provided by the trust. The company subsequently made repayments of several thousand pounds a month, ostensibly to the trust, but in practice to the criminal. Thus the criminal, who had originally owned the garage, probably maintained control despite his daughter's ownership. By controlling the trust the criminal was able to funnel funds back to himself through loaning funds from the trust and receiving payment on that loan.

4. Managing trusts and companies

Case study 7: Lawyer manages trusts used to perpetrate an advance-fee fraud scheme and launder the proceeds[143]

A lawyer at a Chicago law firm set up a trust that was used to perpetrate an advance-fee fraud scheme by his client, Mr Voigt. His client claimed it was a long-standing trust associated with the Catholic Church. He then solicited investments for phoney loans. The lawyer managed the trust and his credentials were publicised to add legitimacy to the trust. He may not have known the trust was fraudulent at first, but this soon became clear to him. Nevertheless, he continued to participate, even providing guarantees to borrowers and maintaining the client account where the advance fees were

142 Financial Intelligence Unit, (October 2014), Quarterly Typology Report Second Quarter (Q1) 2014/2015, Wellington, p. 7.

143 Financial Action Task Force, (June 2013), Money Laundering and Terrorist Financing Vulnerabilities of Legal Professionals, FATF, Paris, p. 61.

deposited. He distributed the funds to Mr Voigt and his associates. This was in violation of the contract's terms agreed with the loan applicants and the investors.

Case study 8: Tormex Limited[144]

The Tormex case, which was publicly reported overseas and in New Zealand, demonstrates the layers of people and entities that may be used in shell company formation. In this case foreign bank accounts in the shell company's name were used to move criminal proceeds under the guise of trade transactions with the shell company. Tormex Limited was a New Zealand shell company set up by a New Zealand trust and company service provider, GT Group, based in Vanuatu.

Tormex was registered on behalf of an unknown overseas client and nominees were used to hide the identity of the beneficial owners. The address listed on the companies register for Tormex was the same virtual office in Auckland listed for GT Group. The nominee director resided in Seychelles, and the nominee shareholder, Vicam (Auckland) Ltd, was a nominee shareholding company owned by GT Group. Vicam was itself substantially a shell company and had also been used as the nominee shareholder for hundreds of other shell companies registered by GT Group. For instance, one of the other shell companies that Vicam was used to facilitate was SP Trading Limited, which was used to charter an aircraft that was intercepted in December 2009 attempting to smuggle arms from North Korea.

The actual business of Tormex was not apparent and was not indicated by the company name. Unusual names that do not indicate the activity of the company is a common indicator of shell companies used to facilitate criminal activity. The Organized Crime and Corruption Reporting Project, a network of East European journalists, reported that, once Tormex was registered on the New Zealand companies register, a power of attorney document was used to transfer the directorship to a Russian national. A bank account was then opened at the Baltic International Bank in Latvia. Journalist enquiries with the man revealed he was unaware of either Tormex or its bank account. His identity had been used without his knowledge as he had sold his passport details. An ex-officer of the Russian tax police told journalists: "There are hundreds of law-firms in Moscow, which specialise in setting up ready-made shell companies for their clients, who want to remain in the shadows. Usually law firms use poor people, who sell them passport details. The sum for one passport may vary from US$100 to US$300."

When the journalists examined bank statements for the Latvian account held by Tormex obtained by lawyers in a Moldova court case, they discovered that during 2007 and 2008 US$680 million was transacted through the account.

144 Financial Intelligence Unit, (January 2015), Quarterly Typology Report Second Quarter (Q2) 2014/2015, Wellington, p. 9.

Analysis indicated the transactions were money laundering transactions carried out under the guise of trading contracts between Tormex Limited and several companies. Trade transactions were conducted with several Ukrainian companies including a state-owned weapons trader. The contracts were then cancelled after the funds had been transferred and refunds were made to different third-party offshore companies. The Organized Crime and Corruption Reporting Project journalists report that using transactions related to cancelled trade orders with legitimate companies is a common money laundering method amongst Russian organised crime.

Transactions were also made with three other New Zealand shell companies – Keronol Limited, Melide Limited, and Dorio Limited – which had also been registered by GT Group using the same nominee director, nominee shareholder and virtual office address as Tormex. The UK's *Guardian* newspaper reported that Tormex Limited, Keronol Limited, Melide Limited and Dorio Limited had been involved in laundering US$40 million for the Sinaloa Drug Cartel based in Mexico. Part of the money laundering process involved the New Zealand shell companies transferring funds to an account held at Wachovia Bank in London linked to the Sinaloa Cartel.

5. Managing client affairs and making introductions

Case study 9: Criminal defence lawyer introduces clients to other professionals to assist with laundering the proceeds of their crime[145]

A lawyer was instructed by his client, a drug trafficker, to deposit cash into the lawyer's trust account and then make routine payments to mortgages on properties beneficially owned by the drug trafficker. The lawyer received commissions from the sale of these properties and brokering the mortgages. While he later admitted to receiving the cash from the trafficker, depositing it into his trust account and administering payments to the trafficker's mortgages, the lawyer denied knowledge of the source of funds.

6. Undertaking certain litigation

Case study 10: Unexpectedly short procedure[146]

A foreign company retained a lawyer to file a claim against another foreign company. The defendant did not contest the claim, so a default judgement was entered. The defendant immediately paid the sum into the law firm's client account. The defendant even paid the amount in question twice – when the secondment was made, the defendant informed that the second payment

145 Financial Action Task Force, (June 2013), Money Laundering and Terrorist Financing Vulnerabilities of Legal Professionals, FATF, Paris, p. 67.

146 International Bar Association, the American Bar Association and the Council of Bars and Law Societies of Europe, (October 2014), A Lawyer's Guide to Detecting and Preventing Money Laundering, p. 45.

was made erroneously and asked the law firm to forward the funds to another subsidiary of the defendant company.

Case study 11: Legal practitioners receive requests for use of client account to recover debts with little or no legal services to be provided[147]

Australian legal practitioners have informed their supervisor, the Australian Transaction Reports and Analysis Centre, about receiving unusual requests from prospective clients particularly targeted at passing funds through solicitor's trust accounts.

This included a foreign company requesting legal services involving debt recovery, with the legal firm receiving substantial payments in its trust account from purported debtors (both in Australia and overseas) with little debt recovery work actually being required to be undertaken by the law firm.

7. Setting up and managing charities

Case study 12: Legal professional sets up a charity to provide funding to individuals convicted of terrorist activities[148]

In the Netherlands, a foundation was established by a person related to a member of an organisation whose purpose is committing terrorist offences. This person was not designated on international sanctions. The goal for the foundation was to provide funds to help people who were convicted of terrorist offences. Initially a notary refused to establish the foundation, but a second notary agreed to do so.

Appendix B: Red flags

Two key resources for red flag indicators have been compiled: one by the Financial Action Task Force (FATF) and one by the International Bar Association, the American Bar Association and the Council of Bars and Law Societies of Europe (IBA/ABA/CCBE). This appendix provides their lists out of context of their full reports. The References section on page 55 provides bibliographical details and web links to these resources if you wish further information.

FATF red flags

The FATF identifies 42 red flags in their publication *Money Laundering and Terrorist Financing Vulnerabilities of Legal Professionals.*[149] Lawyers and

147 Financial Action Task Force, (June 2013), Money Laundering and Terrorist Financing Vulnerabilities of Legal Professionals, FATF, Paris, p. 70.

148 Financial Action Task Force, (June 2013), Money Laundering and Terrorist Financing Vulnerabilities of Legal Professionals, FATF, Paris, p. 75.

149 Financial Action Task Force, (June 2013), Money Laundering and Terrorist Financing Vulnerabilities of Legal Professionals, FATF, Paris, pp 77–82.

conveyancers are encouraged to review this list to aid their understanding and future identification of suspicious activity.

- **Red flags about the client:**

  The client is overly secret about:

  - Who the client is
  - Who the beneficial owner is
  - Where the money is coming from
  - Why they are doing the transaction this way
  - What the big picture is

  The client:

  - Is using an agent or intermediary without good reason
  - Is actively avoiding personal contact without good reason
  - Is reluctant to provide or refuses to provide information, data and documents usually required in order to enable the transaction's execution
  - Holds or has previously held a public position (political or high-level professional appointment) or has professional or family ties to such an individual and is engaged in unusual private business given the frequency or characteristics involved
  - Provides false or counterfeited documentation
  - Is a business entity that cannot be found on the internet and/or uses an email address with a domain part such as Hotmail, Gmail, Yahoo etc., especially if the client is otherwise secretive or avoids direct contact
  - Is known to have convictions for acquisitive crime, known to be currently under investigation for acquisitive crime or have known connections to criminals
  - Is or is related to or is a known associate of a person listed as being involved or suspected of involvement with terrorist or terrorist financing related activities
  - Shows an unusual familiarity with respect to the ordinary standards provided for by the law in the matter of satisfactory customer identification, data entries, and suspicious transaction reports[150] – that is, asks repeated questions on the procedures for applying the ordinary standards

150 Please note that since the FATF published this information we have moved from "suspicious transaction reports" to "suspicious activity reports".

The parties:

- The parties or their representatives (and, where applicable, the real owners or intermediary companies in the chain of ownership of legal entities) are native to, resident in, or incorporated in a high-risk country
- The parties to the transaction are connected without an apparent business reason
- The ties between the parties of a family, employment, corporate or any other nature generate doubts as to the real nature or reason for the transaction
- There are multiple appearances of the same parties in transactions over a short period of time
- The age of the executing parties is unusual for the transaction, especially if they are under legal age, or the executing parties are incapacitated, and there is no logical explanation for their involvement
- There are attempts to disguise the real owner or parties to the transaction
- The person actually directing the operation is not one of the formal parties to the transaction or the representative
- The natural person acting as the director or representative does not appear to be a suitable representative

▶ **Red flags in the source of funds:**

- The transaction involves a disproportionate amount of private funding, bearer cheques or cash, especially if it is inconsistent with the socio-economic profile of the individual or the company's economic profile
- The client or third party is contributing a significant sum in cash as collateral provided by the borrower/debtor rather than simply using those funds directly, without logical explanation
- The source of funds is unusual, eg:
  - Third party funding either for the transaction or for the fees taxes involved with no apparent connection or legitimate explanation
  - Funds received from or sent to a foreign country when there is no apparent connection between the country and the client
  - Funds received from or sent to high-risk countries
  - The client is using multiple bank accounts or foreign accounts without good reason
  - Private expenditure is funded by a company, business, or government

- Selecting the method of payment has been deferred to a date very close to the time of notarisation, in a jurisdiction where the method of payment is normally included in the contract, particularly if no guarantee securing the payment is established, without logical explanation
- An unusually short repayment period has been set without logical explanation
- Mortgages are repeatedly repaid significantly prior to the initially agreed maturity date, with no logical explanation
- The asset is purchased with cash and then rapidly used as collateral for a loan
- There is a request to change the payment procedures previously agreed upon without logical explanation, especially when payment instruments are suggested that are not appropriate for the common practice used for the ordered transaction
- Finance is provided by a lender, either a natural or legal person, other than a credit institution, with no logical explanation or economic justification
- The collateral being provided for the transaction is currently located in a high-risk country
- There has been a significant increase in capital for a recently incorporated company or successive contributions over a short period of time to the same company, with no logical explanation
- There has been an increase in capital from a foreign country, which either has no relationship to the company or is high risk
- The company receives an injection of capital or assets in kind that is notably high in comparison to the business, size or market value of the company performing, with no logical explanation
- There is an excessively high or low price attached to the securities transferred, with regard to any circumstance indicating such an excess (eg, volume of revenue, trade or business; premises; size; knowledge of declaration of systematic losses or gains) or with regard to the sum declared in another operation
- There are large financial transactions, especially if requested by recently created companies, where these transactions are not justified by the corporate purpose, the activity of the client or the possible group of companies to which it belongs or other justifiable reasons

- **Red flags in the choice of lawyer:**
  - Instruction of a legal professional at a distance from the client or transaction without legitimate or economic reason
  - Instruction of a legal professional without experience in a particular speciality or without experience in providing services in complicated or especially large transactions
  - The client is prepared to pay substantially higher fees than usual, without legitimate reason
  - The client has changed advisor a number of times in a short space of time or engaged multiple legal advisors without legitimate reason
  - The required service was refused by another professional or the relationship with another professional was terminated
- **Red flags in the nature of the retainer:**

  The transaction is unusual, eg:
  - The type of operation being notarised is clearly inconsistent with the size, age, or activity of the legal entity or natural person acting
  - The transactions are unusual because of their size, nature, frequency, or manner of execution
  - There are remarkable and highly significant differences between the declared price and the approximate or actual values in accordance with any reference that could give an approximate idea of this value or in the judgement of a legal professional
  - A non-profit organisation requests services for purposes or transactions not compatible with those declared or not typical for that body

  The client:
  - Is involved in transactions that do not correspond to his/her normal professional or business activities
  - Shows he/she does not have a suitable knowledge of the nature, object or the purpose of the professional performance requested
  - Wishes to establish or take over a legal person with a dubious description of the aim, or a description of the aim that is not related to their normal professional or commercial activities, or their other activities, or with a description of the aim for which a licence is required, while the customer does not have an intention to obtain such a licence
  - Frequently changes legal structures and/or managers of legal persons
  - Asks for short cuts or unexplained speed in completing a transaction
  - Appears very disinterested in the outcome of the retainer

- Requires introduction to financial institutions to help secure banking facilities
- Creation of complicated ownership structures when there is no legitimate or economic reason
- Involvement of structures with multiple countries where there is no apparent link to the client or transaction, with no legitimate or economic reason
- Incorporation and/or purchase of stock or securities of several companies, enterprises or legal entities within a short space of time with elements in common (one or several partners or shareholders, director, registered company office, corporate purpose etc.) with no logical explanation
- There is an absence of documentation to support the client's story, previous transactions, or company activities
- There are several elements in common between a number of transactions in a short period of time without logical explanations
- Back-to-back (or ABC) property transactions, with rapidly increasing value or purchase price
- Abandoned transactions with no concern for the fee level or after receipt of funds
- There are unexplained changes in instructions, especially at the last minute
- The retainer exclusively relates to keeping documents or other goods, holding large deposits of money or otherwise using the client account without the provision of legal services
- There is a lack of sensible commercial/financial/ tax or legal reason for the transaction
- There is increased complexity in the transaction or the structures used for the transaction that results in higher taxes and fees than apparently necessary
- A power of attorney is sought for the administration or disposal of assets under conditions that are unusual, where there is no logical explanation
- Investment in immovable property, in the absence of any links with the place where the property is located and/or of any financial advantage from the investment
- Litigation is settled too easily or quickly, with little/no involvement by the legal professional retained
- Requests for payments to third parties without substantiating reason or corresponding transaction

Appendix 9

IBA/ABA/CCBE red flags

- **Country/Geographic risk:**
  - Countries subject to sanctions, embargoes or similar measures issued by, for example, the United Nations
  - Countries identified by credible sources (ie, well-known bodies that are regarded as reputable (eg, International Monetary Fund, the World Bank) as:
    - Generally lacking appropriate AML laws, regulations and other measures
    - Being in a location from which funds or support are provided to terrorist organisations, or
    - Having significant levels of corruption or other criminal activity
- **Client risk:**
  - Domestic and international PEPs
  - Entity, structure or relationships of client make it difficult to identify its beneficial owner or controlling interests (eg, the unexplained use of legal persons or legal instruments)
  - Charities and "not-for-profit" organisations that are not monitored or supervised by authorities
  - Use of financial intermediaries that are neither subject to adequate AML laws nor adequately supervised by authorities
  - Clients who:
    - Conduct their business relationship or request services in unconventional circumstances
    - Are cash-intensive businesses (eg, money-service businesses and casinos), that are not usually cash-rich but generate substantial amounts of cash
    - Have no address, or multiple addresses; or
    - Change settlement or execution instructions
- **Service risk:**
  - Where lawyers, acting as financial intermediaries, actually handle the receipt and transmission of funds through accounts they control
  - Services to conceal improperly beneficial ownership from competent authorities
  - Services requested by the client for which the lawyer does not have expertise (unless the lawyer is referring the request to an appropriately training professional for advice)
  - Transfer of real estate between parties in an unusually short time period

- Payments from un-associated or unknown third parties and payments for fees in cash where this would not be typical
- Consideration is inadequate or excessive
- Clients who offer to pay extraordinary fees for services that would not warrant such a premium

▶ **Client's behaviour or identity:**

- Client is secretive or evasive about:
  - Its identity or that of its beneficial owner
  - The source of funds or money; or
  - Why it is doing the transaction in the way it is
- Client is:
  - Known to have convictions or to be currently under investigation for acquisitive crime, or has known connections with criminals
  - Related to or a known associate of a person listed as being involved or suspected of involvement with terrorists or terrorist financing operations
  - Involved in a transaction that engages a highly technical or regulatory regime that imposes criminal sanctions for breaches (increasing the risk of a predicate offence being committed); or
  - Unusually familiar with the ordinary standards provided for by the law in satisfactory customer identification, data entries and suspicious transaction reporting or asks repeated questions on related procedures

▶ **Concealment techniques:**

- Use of intermediaries without good reason
- Avoidance of personal contact for no good reason
- Reluctance to disclose information, data and documents that are necessary to enable the execution of the transaction
- Use of false or counterfeited documentation
- The client is a business entity that cannot be found on the internet

▶ **The relationship between the client and the counterparties:**

- Ties between the parties of a family, employment, corporate or any other nature generate doubts as to the real nature/reason for connection
- Multiple appearances of the same parties in transactions over a short period of time

- The parties attempt to disguise the real owner or parties to the transaction
- The natural person acting as a director or representative does not appear to be a suitable representative
- The parties are:
  - Native to, resident in, or incorporated in a higher-risk country
  - Connected without apparent business reason
  - Of an unusual age for executing parties
  - Not the same as the persons actually directing the operation

▶ **Size of funds:**

- There is no legitimate explanation for:
- A disproportionate amount of private funding, bearer cheques or cash (consider individual's socio-economic, or company's economic, profile)
- A significant increase in capital for a recently incorporated company or successive contributions over a short period of time to the same company
- Receipt by the company of an injection of capital or assets that is high in comparison with the business, size or market value of the company performing
- An excessively high or low price attached to securities being transferred
- A large financial transaction, especially if requested by a recently created company, where it is not justified by the corporate purpose, the activity of the client or its group companies; or
- The client or third party contributing a significant sum in cash as collateral provided by the borrower/debtor rather than simply using those funds directly

▶ **Source of funds:**

The source of funds is:

- Third party funding either for the transaction or for fees/taxes involved with no apparent connection or legitimate explanation
- Funds are received from or sent to a foreign country when there is no apparent connection between the country and the client
- Funds are received from or sent to higher-risk countries
- The client is using multiple bank accounts or foreign accounts without good reason
- Private expenditure is funded by a company, business or government; or

- The collateral being provided for the transaction is currently located in a higher-risk country

▶ **Mode of payment:**

- The asset is purchased with cash and then rapidly used as collateral for a loan
- There is no legitimate explanation for:
  - An unusually short repayment period having been set
  - Mortgages being repeatedly repaid significantly prior to the initially agreed maturity date; or
  - Finance being provided by a lender, either a natural or legal person, other than a credit institution

References

Courts of New Zealand, (28 September 2017), *Department of Internal Affairs v Ping An Finance (Group) New Zealand Company Limited* [2017] NZHC 2363. http://www.courtsofnz.govt.nz/cases/department-of-internal-affairs-v-ping-an-finance-group-new-zealand-company-limited/?searchterm=Ping An

Department of Internal Affairs, Reserve Bank of New Zealand, Financial Markets Authority, (July 2011), *Supervisory Framework*, DIA, RBNZ & FMA, Wellington. https://www.dia.govt.nz/Pubforms.nsf/URL/AMLCFT_SupervisoryFramework_FINAL_updated28July2011.pdf/$file/AMLCFT_SupervisoryFramework_FINAL_updated28July2011.pdf

Egmont Group, (2002), *FIUs in Action: 100 Cases from the Egmont Group*, Egmont Group, Toronto. https://www.u4.no/recommended-reading/fius-in-action-100-cases-from-the-egmont-group/

Financial Action Task Force, (June 2013), *Money Laundering and Terrorist Financing Vulnerabilities of Legal Professionals*, FATF, Paris. http://www.fatf-gafi.org/publications/methodsandtrends/documents/mltf-vulnerabilities-legal-professionals.html

Financial Intelligence Unit, (October 2014), *Quarterly Typology Report First Quarter (Q1) 2014/2015*, FIU, Wellington. http://www.police.govt.nz/sites/default/files/publications/fiu-quarterly-typology-report-q1-2014-15.pdf

Financial Intelligence Unit, (January 2015), *Quarterly Typology Report Second Quarter (Q2) 2014/2015*, FIU, Wellington. http://www.police.govt.nz/sites/default/files/publications/fiu-quarterly-typology-report-q2-2014-2015.pdf

Financial Intelligence Unit, (March 2016), *Quarterly Typology Report Second Quarter (Q2) 2015/2016*, FIU, Wellington. http://www.police.govt.nz/sites/default/files/publications/fiu-quarterly-typology-report-q1-2015-16-terrorist-financing.pdf

International Bar Association, the American Bar Association and the Council of Bars and Law Societies of Europe, (October 2014), *A Lawyer's Guide to Detecting and Preventing Money Laundering*. https://www.anti-money laundering.org/Document/Default.aspx?DocumentUid=3DBCE981-598E-45E 6-8723-CC89C89E8086.

Appendix 10 Guideline: Accountants Complying with the Anti-Money Laundering and Countering Financing of Terrorism Act 2009 (March 2018)

Executive summary

It is likely that money laundering is currently going on undetected in New Zealand. Money laundering is the method by which people disguise and conceal the proceeds of crime and protect and enjoy their assets. Some people in New Zealand may also be financing the activities of terrorists and known terrorist organisations. Financers of terrorism use similar techniques to money launderers to avoid detection by authorities and to protect the identity of those providing and receiving the funds.

People with criminal intentions value anonymity and are looking for ways to distance themselves from their activities while still enjoying the proceeds of their crime. Both domestic and international evidence suggests that using gatekeepers, such as accountants, is a way for criminals to create a false perception of legitimately acquired wealth. The recent changes to the Anti-Money Laundering and Countering Financing of Terrorism Act 2009 (the AML/CFT Act or the Act) included accountants in the AML/CFT system.[1]

The AML/CFT Act is activities-based. Professionals offering accounting services who undertake activities captured by the AML/CFT Act will need to undertake an assessment of their money laundering and terrorist financing (ML/TF) risk and develop a programme to ensure they comply with the requirements in the Act. This includes accountants, bookkeepers and tax agents – hereafter referred to collectively as "accountants". The flow chart in the '"At a glance"' section of this guideline can help you determine if you are captured by the AML/CFT Act.

This guideline helps you to determine whether your business must comply with the AML/CFT Act and, if so, what you must do to ensure you comply with the Act. You must comply with the AML/CFT Act by ensuring you identify, understand and assess the risks of ML/TF to your business, and manage those risks in your day to day business via a dedicated AML/CFT programme. AML/CFT programmes will vary from business to business according to professional judgements about how to best manage specific risks.

1 The recent changes were made by the AML/CFT Amendment Act 2017 (http://bit.ly/2Cy5p8Q).

You need to know your customers. Before conducting captured activities, you need to conduct customer due diligence (CDD) according to the level of risk posed by your customers. CDD is not optional. When you are not able to complete CDD, you must not undertake a captured activity or transaction for that customer. To do so would be a breach of the AML/CFT Act.

The Department of Internal Affairs (DIA) is the supervisor charged with monitoring your compliance with the AML/CFT Act. We recognise that adjusting to the new AML/CFT system will take time and effort. This guideline, and other existing guidelines, can help you develop awareness of the risks posed by ML/TF and provide prompts on what to think about when developing programmes to manage these risks. We are available to respond to queries, and we are working with accountants' professional bodies to ensure you are well supported to meet your obligations under the AML/CFT Act.

Disclaimer

This guideline is provided for information only and cannot be relied on as evidence of complying with the requirements of the AML/CFT Act. It does not constitute legal advice and cannot be relied on as such. After reading this guideline, if you do not fully understand your obligations, you should seek legal advice or contact your AML/CFT supervisor. DIA can be contacted at amlphase2@dia.govt.nz.

Glossary

Accountants	The use of the term "accountants" in this guideline refers to Chartered Accountants, accountants, bookkeepers, tax agents and anyone else who is providing professional accounting services.
Accounting practice	Defined in section 5(1) of the AML/CFT Act as "an accountant in public practice on his or her own account in sole practice; or, in relation to two or more accountants in public practice, and practising in partnership, the partnership; or an incorporated accounting practice". This definition includes businesses referring to themselves as "bookkeepers" and "tax agents" if they are undertaking activities captured by the Act.
AML/CFT Act	Anti-Money Laundering and Countering Financing of Terrorism Act 2009

Captured activities	Activities that are specified under the definition of "designated non-financial business or profession" in the AML/CFT Act
CDD	Customer due diligence
Compliance officer	An individual (usually an employee) appointed to administer and maintain the AML/CFT compliance programme
Customers/Clients	While the term "clients" is more commonly used, the term "customers" is used throughout the AML/CFT Act. In this guideline the terms "customers" and "clients" are used interchangeably.
DBG	Designated business group
DIA	Department of Internal Affairs
DNFBP	Designated non-financial business or profession
FATF	Financial Action Task Force
FIU	New Zealand Police Financial Intelligence Unit
Financing terrorism offence	As defined in section 8(1) of the Terrorism Suppression Act 2002
goAML	FIU reporting portal
ML/TF	Money laundering or terrorist financing
Money laundering offence	As defined in section 243 of the Crimes Act 1961
PEP	Politically exposed person
PTR	Prescribed transaction report
Reporting entities	Casinos; designated non-financial businesses or professions; financial institutions; high-value dealers; and the New Zealand Racing Board
SAR	Suspicious activity report
SPR	Suspicious property report
STR	Suspicious transaction report
Supervisors	Supervisors have responsibility for monitoring compliance with the AML/CFT Act. DIA is the supervisor for reporting entities in the accounting profession among other sectors. The Reserve Bank of New Zealand and the Financial Markets Authority supervise other sectors.

TCSP	Trust and company service provider. A person (other than a law firm, a conveyancing practitioner, an incorporated conveyancing firm, an accounting practice, or a real estate agent) who carries out any of the activities described in the definition of DNFBP (see section 5(1) of the AML/CFT Act).

Introduction

This guideline is for accounting practices that have compliance obligations under the Anti-Money Laundering and Countering Financing of Terrorism Act 2009 (the AML/CFT Act or the Act) from 1 October 2018.[2] Those that do are "reporting entities" for the purposes of the Act. The Department of Internal Affairs (DIA) is the supervisor for accounting practices.[3] This guideline uses the term "accountants" to refer to accounting practices – please see the Glossary for definitions.

The terms "accountant" or "accounting practice" are not protected in New Zealand. Nor is there a requirement for individuals or businesses providing accounting services to be members of a professional body. Tax agents and bookkeepers may be captured by the Act, even if they do not refer to themselves as accountants. The determining factor will be whether, in the ordinary course of business, one or more of a number of specific activities are conducted. These activities are described in Section 5(1) of the Act in the definition of "designated non-financial business or profession" (DNFBP) and are referred to in this guide as "captured activities".

If you do not consider your business to be an "accounting practice", but you are conducting activities captured by the definition of DNFBP, you will still be a reporting entity under the AML/CFT Act under the definition of trust and company service provider (TCSP). If you are a TCSP your business will need to comply with the Act from 1 July 2018 rather than 1 October 2018. In either case, this guideline provides you with the information you need to ensure you can comply in the required timeframe, and from this point in the document you should consider any reference to "accountant" to include TCSP also (please see the Glossary for the definition of this term).

2 "Accounting practice" is defined in section 5(1) of the AML/CFT Act: http://bit.ly/2xHGfmy

3 Section 130(1)(c), AML/CFT Act (http://bit.ly/2A2AKj7). There are two other supervisors for other reporting entities: the Reserve Bank of New Zealand and the Financial Markets Authority. References to "the supervisors" in this document refer to all three agencies collectively.

Accountants will have obligations under the AML/CFT Act when they conduct certain activities (referred to throughout this guidance as "captured activities").

As your supervisor, DIA expects accountants to:

1. Know your ML/TF risks
2. Know your AML/CFT supervisor
3. Know how to apply the AML/CFT Act to your business
4. Know your compliance requirements
5. Know your customer
6. Know the red flags of ML/TF
7. Know where to get support.

This guideline will help reporting entities in the accounting profession to meet each of the expectations identified above and is structured in that order. The AML/CFT Act requires that reporting entities have regard to any guidance produced by the AML/CFT supervisor and the Commissioner of Police when developing their risk assessment and AML/CFT programme.[4]

This guideline does not provide a "how to" guide or additional prescription to complement the AML/CFT Act. A one-size-fits-all approach will not work well for most reporting entities. Instead, this guideline will help accountants increase their awareness of money laundering and terrorist financing (ML/TF) risks, and provide prompts for how to manage your compliance.

Where the terms "must" or "required" are used, this means that the information is referring directly to an obligation that is specified in legislation. Where we have used the term "should" we are making a recommendation which is your choice to accept or not. While the term "customers" is used throughout the AML/CFT Act, the term "clients" is more commonly used in the accounting profession. The terms "customers" and "clients" are used interchangeably in this guideline.

This guideline may be updated periodically to make minor changes as new information and feedback is assessed. As such, we recommend that instead of printing this guideline in hard copy, you should bookmark the webpage and refer to it online to ensure you have the most up-to-date information to hand.

Over time new case law may become available, new regulations may be made, or existing regulations may be amended and this guideline will be updated. The DIA website provides a reference page to find the relevant regulations.[5] DIA will inform reporting entities of any new regulations or updates to existing guidance. The AML/CFT supervisors have already produced a wide

4 Sections 58(2)(g) http://bit.ly/2ly11Dz and 57(2) http://bit.ly/2h2nN59 of the AML/CFT Act.

5 AML/CFT Act and Regulations: http://bit.ly/2hpGU5V

range of guidance, much of which accountants are likely to find useful. The guidelines are all available on the DIA website and are referred to throughout this guideline where relevant.[6] Other guidelines may be produced in the future as needed.

We can be contacted at amlphase2@dia.govt.nz if you have further questions.

At a glance

How to know if you are captured by the AML/CFT Act

The following flow chart provides a quick way to check if you are captured under the AML/CFT Act.

6 Codes of Practice and Guidelines: http://bit.ly/2gQ3Iev

Am I captured by the AML/CFT Act as a DNFBP?

Are you a law firm, a conveyancing practitioner, an incorporated conveyancing firm, an accounting practice, a real estate agent, or a trust and company service provider?

YES

NO

Do you do any of the following activities in the ordinary course of business?

Act as a formation agent of legal persons or legal arrangements

OR

Act as, or arrange for a person to act as, a nominee director, nominee shareholder or trustee in relation to legal persons or legal arrangements

OR

Manage client funds (other than sums paid for professional services), accounts, securities or other assets

OR

Provide real estate agent work to effect a transaction

OR

Provide a registered office or a business address, a correspondence address, or an administrative address for a company or partnership, or for any legal person or legal arrangement (unless that service is provided solely as an ancillary service to the provision of other services that are not captured by the definition of a DNFBP)

OR

Engage in or give instructions on behalf of a customer to another person for:

- Any conveyancing to effect a transaction (see section 5(1) for more detail)
- A transaction within the meaning of section 4(1) of the Real Estate Agents Act 2008
- A transfer of beneficial interest in land or other real property
- A transaction on behalf of any person for buying or selling or transferring of a business or legal person and any other legal arrangement; or
- A transaction on behalf of a customer in relation to creating, operating, and managing a legal person, and any other legal arrangement

YES

You are captured and must comply with the AML/CFT Act

NO

There is an exemption which excludes your business from compliance requirements

NO

You are not captured

NB: If in the future you are asked to conduct any activity described above, you will need to determine if you are captured by the Act

What you need to do to comply

Step 1: Establish a compliance programme

Appoint a compliance officer – Section 56

Reporting entities must appoint a compliance officer who will have responsibility for administering and maintaining the AML/CFT programme. An employee should be appointed to this role who reports to a senior manager. In the case of a sole practitioner, we would expect the sole practitioner to be the compliance officer. If that is not possible, an external person must be appointed as a compliance officer.

Conduct a risk assessment – Section 58

Reporting entities are required to undertake an assessment of the risks posed to their business by money laundering and financing of terrorism crimes. The risk assessment should be in writing and have regard to the applicable guidance material, which is available on the DIA website.

Develop an AML/CFT programme – Section 57

The AML/CFT programme must be based on the risk assessment described above and be in writing. It should include procedures, policies and controls for ensuring all compliance obligations are adequately and effectively met and must have regard to the applicable guidance material.

Step 2: Maintain your compliance programme

Conduct customer due diligence (CDD) – Part 2, Subpart 1

Reporting entities must conduct CDD when conducting an occasional transaction or activity or when establishing a business relationship with a client who is requesting assistance with a captured activity, or when an existing client makes this kind of request (if the reporting entity doesn't hold all the information required already). There are three levels of CDD depending on the circumstances.

Keep records – Sections 49–55

Reporting entities must keep records of transactions, suspicious activities, the documents verifying the identities of customers and other parties or beneficiaries, and any other related records that may be of interest to the supervisor. Records must be kept at least five years.

Ongoing customer due diligence and ongoing account monitoring – Section 31

Reporting entities are required to undertake ongoing CDD and ongoing account monitoring. This is to ensure that you have ongoing confidence that the business relationship and the transactions within the relationship are consistent with the customer's business and risk profile, and you can spot any suspicious activity early.

Review your compliance programme - Section 59

The supervisor expects reporting entities to conduct a regular review of their compliance programme. This is to ensure that any business changes or new risks in the operating environment are referenced in the programme and it remains fit-for-purpose.

Step 3: Report and audit

Submit an annual report - Section 60

Reporting entities must submit an annual report. This report must be in the prescribed form and be submitted to the supervisor at the time set by the supervisor. The report must take into account the results and implications of the audit and any information prescribed in the regulations.

Audit your risk assessment and compliance programme every two years - Section 59(2)

At least every two years a reporting entity must review its risk assessment and compliance programme and have it audited by an independent person who is suitably qualified to conduct the audit. Supervisors may also require an audit to be undertaken on request at shorter notice.

Report to the FIU

Report to the Financial Intelligence Unit - Part 2 subparts 2 and 2A

When reporting entities identify suspicious activity, they must report it to the FIU. They should also submit prescribed transaction reports to the FIU as necessary. No one will be required to submit any privileged communication (as defined in the Act) in either report category.

1. Do you know your ML TF risks?

Undetected financial crime reduces the integrity of national and international financial systems, distorts the economy and diminishes opportunities for legitimate economic activities. The Government loses tax revenue, while people are rewarded for criminal behaviour. New Zealand is at risk of being targeted by international criminal networks to inject the proceeds of crime into the international financial system. Money laundering and financing of terrorism are not solely international crimes. Domestic criminals use a variety of methods to conceal the proceeds of their criminal activities from authorities in New Zealand.

The Financial Action Task Force (FATF) is an intergovernmental body that sets standards for combating ML/TF and other related threats to the integrity of the international financial system. New Zealand has included accountants in the AML/CFT system in response to recommendations made by the FATF in its country review of New Zealand in 2009.[7]

Using accounting professionals is attractive to some criminals because these professionals are required for the completion of certain kinds of transactions and because their specialist skills can be misused to assist the laundering of criminal proceeds or funding terrorism. Accountants can add respectability and a veneer of legitimacy to transactions.

When gatekeeper professionals, such as accountants and trust and company service providers, lack ML/ TF awareness, they are more at risk of inadvertently helping criminals. For example, it is important to understand that even small transactions can be indicative of ML/TF. Offenders have been known to conduct a series of continuous, seemingly immaterial, transactions which, when added up, can conceal and disguise a significant amount of criminal proceeds. It is not enough to simply understand the ML/TF risks inherent in accounting practices.

We encourage accountants and other professionals to develop an understanding of the ML/TF risks in the wider sectors and industries that they have business dealings with as well. Given these risks, and the FATF recommendations, the Government has chosen to engage gatekeeper professions in the collective efforts to deter and detect these crimes. The more eyes and ears attuned to the indicators (or red flags) of these crime types, the more likely people will struggle to benefit financially from criminal activities. By expanding the AML/CFT system to include the gatekeeper professions, the Government intends that gatekeepers will be better able to protect themselves from customers who launder money and finance terrorism. FATF has provided the following diagram to describe the two potential trajectories of legal professionals' involvement in ML/TF.[8] These two trajectories can be applied to any of the gatekeeper professions.

The AML/CFT system has been designed to help businesses achieve the level of compliance required to assist authorities to deter and detect criminal customers. Compliance also has a value for business risk management. Professionals closely guard their reputations. It is in their interest to avoid relationships with customers who will cause them disrepute in the community or censure by their professional bodies or government authorities. Businesses that fail to comply and are misused by criminals risk negative media coverage both in New Zealand and internationally. This also diminishes New Zealand's international reputation as a safe place to do business.

7 *Mutual Evaluation of New Zealand*: http://bit.ly/2EBoTyn

8 Financial Action Task Force, (June 2013), *Money Laundering and Terrorist Financing Vulnerabilities of Legal Professionals*, FATF, Paris, p. 35. Please note, where it refers to STR in the diagram, it means "suspicious transaction report". We now refer to these as "suspicious activity reports" (SARs).

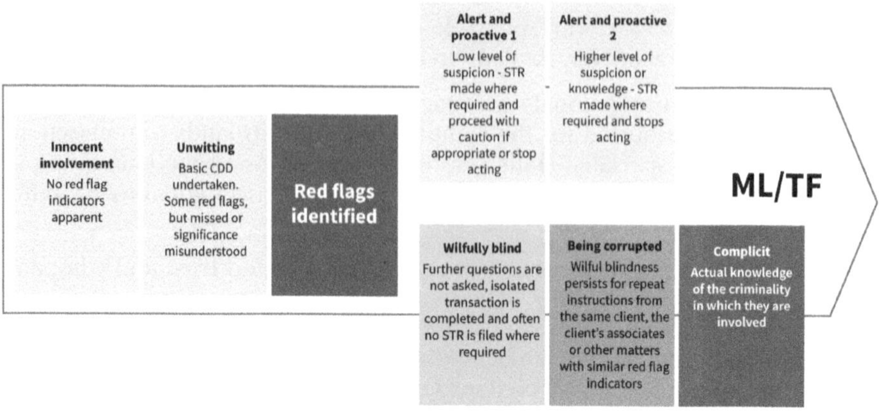

2. Do you know what to expect from your AML/ CFT supervisor?

This section explains the regulatory approach you can expect from DIA.

The role of supervisors

DIA is the supervisor for accountants, the other DNFBPs, and a range of financial institutions, such as money remitters, that are reporting entities under the AML/CFT Act. The Reserve Bank of New Zealand and the Financial Markets Authority both act as supervisors for other reporting entities. Our role includes monitoring reporting entities for compliance with the Act, providing guidance to reporting entities and investigating and enforcing compliance. This is to ensure that the AML/CFT system operates in a robust manner and that criminals seeking to launder money and finance terrorism are detected and deterred.

Our regulatory approach

We outline our regulatory approach for the AML/CFT system in two publications: the *AML/CFT Supervisory Framework*[9] and *Minimising Harm – Maximising Benefit.*[10] We apply a risk-based and responsive regulatory approach that promotes compliance through a mix of strategies, initiatives and tools. We aim to:

- Make it easy for reporting entities who want to comply
- Help reporting entities who are trying to comply
- Use the full force of the law on reporting entities that refuse to comply

We focus our efforts carefully and deliberately. We use our insight, knowledge and understanding to identify risks and determine interventions to most effectively ensure compliance. While we are fully prepared to escalate

9 *AML/CFT Supervisory Framework*: https://bit.ly/2J2FyKL

10 *Minimising* Harm – *Maximising* Benefit: http://bit.ly/2z669Sy

our response with enforcement action, we are equally prepared to work with reporting entities in a responsive and educative manner. We are a member of the National Co-ordination Committee, and we work with the other supervisors and the FIU, as well as with other government agencies, industry bodies and reporting entities to apply a consistent approach to the AML/CFT system.

Monitoring and enforcement

We use a variety of regulatory tools to monitor a reporting entity's compliance with AML/CFT obligations. These include desk-based reviews of reporting entities' documents to test technical compliance; on-site inspections to test effectiveness of implementation of compliance programmes; analysis of annual reports; and independent audits.

When we identify reporting entities that are not meeting their obligations under the AML/CFT Act we consider a number of options. One of these options is a remediation plan with the reporting entity. A remediation plan includes a set of expected outcomes that the reporting entity must complete within a set timeframe. The timeframe includes measurable progress towards meeting the obligations under the AML/CFT Act. In most cases the timeframe and actions are met and the reporting entity progresses towards meeting the obligations.

In response to more serious or deliberate non-compliance, we may decide to issue a formal warning or to accept an enforceable undertaking. Alternatively, we may decide to seek an interim, performance or restraining injunction, or a pecuniary penalty, from the High Court.

In the most serious of cases, civil liability acts that are engaged in knowingly or recklessly are criminal offences. There are a number of further criminal offences; for example, failing to report or keep records relating to suspicious activities, structuring transactions to avoid AML/CFT requirements, and obstructing or misleading a supervisor. Where necessary, DIA will prosecute reporting entities for criminal offences under the Act.

Investigations of ML/TF

In New Zealand it is a criminal offence to knowingly and intentionally engage in, or facilitate any other person to engage in, money laundering[11] or the financing of terrorism[12]. The Police are responsible for investigating and prosecuting ML/TF offences, as well as forfeiture proceedings relating to the proceeds of crime. A robust AML/CFT system, in which reporting entities are conducting CDD, keeping customer and transaction records, and reporting suspicious activities, is an important tool in the collective fight against financial and organised crime.

11 Section 243, Crimes Act 1961: http://bit.ly/2zYeqXU

12 Section 8(1) and (2A), Terrorism Suppression Act 2002: http://bit.ly/2lZbZlE

Territorial scope of the AML/CFT Act

The supervisors have issued guidance outlining their interpretation of the territorial scope of the AML/ CFT Act.[13] Even though the AML/CFT Act only has jurisdiction in New Zealand, we strongly encourage reporting entities to report on suspicious activities and transactions that they are party to that occur offshore. For more information about reporting suspicious activity, please see "Suspicious activity reports" in section 4.

3. Do you know how to apply the AML/CFT Act to your business?

The AML/CFT Act is activities-based. This section provides more detail about captured activities and why they are included in the Act. In addition, accountants need to develop a thorough understanding of:

- Exclusions to and exemptions from the AML/ CFT Act
- What conducting captured activities "in the ordinary course of business" means
- What obligations are related to the captured activities
- How to determine whether advice to a customer is captured in an activity
- The nature of each of the activities that are captured by the AML/CFT Act

This section elaborates on the captured activities that accountants may perform. The AML/CFT Act imposes obligations only for these captured activities.[14] The obligations of the AML/CFT Act do not apply to any other activities that an accountant carries out in the ordinary course of business.

Exclusions to and exemptions from the AML/CFT Act

There are a number of ways in which entities, transactions or activities can be exempt from the Act's requirements. For instance, the AML/CFT (Definitions) Regulations 2011[15] provide a number of specific exclusions to the definition of "reporting entity", and the AML/CFT (Exemptions) Regulations 2011[16] provide a range of exemptions for specific classes of transactions and services. There are also Ministerial exemptions, which can exempt (from any or all of the provisions of the Act) either specific reporting entities, or classes of reporting entities, as well as transactions or classes of transactions.[17] The

13 *Territorial Scope of the Anti-Money Laundering and* Countering Financing *of Terrorism Act 2009*: http://bit.ly/2nf664p

14 For the full text of the activities please see section 5(1) of the AML/CFT Act under the definition of "designated non-financial business or profession". http://bit.ly/2xIIGfmy

15 AML/CFT (Definitions) Regulations 2011: http://bit.ly/2hrFYy3

16 AML/CFT (Exemptions) Regulations 2011: http://bit.ly/2lAImH6

17 AML/CFT Ministerial exemptions: http://bit.ly/2xCmQU6

AML/CFT (Class Exemptions) Notice 2014[18] provides further detail about class exemptions.

The Ministry of Justice handles Ministerial exemption applications and provides advice to the appropriate Minister who makes the final decisions. Exemptions may be granted by the Minister subject to sections 157 to 159 of the AML/CFT Act.[19] Please review these sections if you are considering making an application.

Interpreting "ordinary course of business"

Activities must be done in the ordinary course of business to be captured by the Act. The AML/CFT supervisors have issued guidance on how to interpret "ordinary course of business".[20] Whether an activity is in your "ordinary course of business" will always be a matter of judgement depending on the nature of your business. Some relevant factors to take into consideration would be whether the activity:

- is normal or otherwise unremarkable for your business
- is frequent
- is regular (meaning predictable, consistent)
- involves significant amounts of money
- is a source of income
- involves significant resources
- involves a service offered to customers

It is likely that the activity is in the ordinary course of your business if one or more of these factors apply.

If you are conducting a captured activity in your personal capacity (as opposed to in your professional capacity) you are not captured by the AML/CFT Act. An example of this would be if you are a trustee for a registered charitable trust in your local community in your personal capacity.

If, after considering the AML/CFT Act and this guideline, you are still unsure as to whether you are a reporting entity, you should seek independent professional advice or contact us at amlphase2@dia.govt.nz.

What obligations are related to the captured activities?

The AML/CFT Act requires you to know who your customers are (as well as who any beneficial owners of your customer are, and any person acting on behalf of your customer) by conducting customer due diligence (CDD) to the

18 AML/CFT (Class Exemptions) Notice 2014: http://bit.ly/2zly18h

19 Sections 157–159 AML/CFT Act: http://bit.ly/2aFZRjN

20 *Interpreting* "Ordinary Course of Business" Guideline: http://bit.ly/2Bh3CEI

level required before you conduct a captured activity or establish a business relationship.

How to determine whether advice provided to your customer is captured

There will be circumstances where you give advice in relation to a captured activity (without necessarily then carrying out the activity). Generally, advice alone, in the absence of any actual captured activity on the accountant's part, will not be captured by the definition of "designated non-financial business or profession".

It may be that in practice you expect to provide a mixture of advice and captured activities for a client over a period of time. In those circumstances, you would need to conduct CDD to the required level *prior* to establishing a business relationship with the client (and prior to providing any advice).

If you regularly provide advice to a client about captured activities, such as providing advice about payments they should make (eg, for tax or payroll), but you never directly control the flow of their funds yourself, you should consider whether there is an apparent ML/TF risk. If you think there is a risk you need to mitigate you should do so in line with your professional obligations.

You also need to be aware of your obligations to report suspicious activities, which can include requests or enquiries about particular services you offer from potential or current clients (regardless of whether you ultimately provide those services).

Activities captured by the AML/CFT Act

This section outlines the activities which are captured by the AML/CFT Act and provides some examples of what these activities may look like for accountants. The examples are illustrative and not exhaustive. As we learn from our experiences regulating the accounting profession we will be able to provide more information about supervisor expectations in certain scenarios.

When in doubt about whether you undertake any of the activities described below, please look to the explanations. If you are still unclear, contact DIA at amlphase2@dia.govt.nz or seek advice.

Activity: Acting as a formation agent for legal persons or legal arrangements

In the definition of "designated non-financial business or profession" an accounting practice which, in the ordinary course of business, acts as a formation agent of legal persons or legal arrangements, is captured by the AML/CFT Act as a reporting entity.

The term "legal arrangement" is defined in the AML/CFT Act as meaning a trust, a partnership, a charitable entity (within the meaning of section 4(1) of the Charities Act 2005), and any other prescribed arrangements that involves a risk of ML/TF.[21]

This activity refers to forming a legal person (such as a company) or legal arrangement on behalf of a client; for example, registering a company on the Companies Office website. The activity does not include instances where you simply provide advice about formation of a legal person that is acted on by either your client themselves or a third party. In the case of forming a trust, if your client asks a lawyer to do that for them the captured activity would be undertaken by the lawyer and they would have to apply their AML/CFT compliance programme to that activity.

If you were to engage a lawyer to form a trust on behalf of your client, then both you and the lawyer would be conducting a captured activity (ie, the activity of forming a company) and would both need to apply your AML/CFT compliance programmes' policies, procedures and controls, including the appropriate level of CDD. Please see further on in this section for discussion about captured activities that involve engaging in, or giving instructions on behalf of a client to another person.

Examples of this kind of activity in practice

- You register a company with the Companies Office on behalf of a client.
- You form an incorporated society on behalf of a client.

ML/TF risks associated with this activity

When an accountant is engaged to register a company or partnership, the actual ownership of the company or partnership being formed may be concealed or obscured; for example, where shell companies, multiple layers of ownership, or other complex legal structures are used. Setting up a trust can also be a way to create a perception of distance between assets and their beneficial owners. International evidence shows that criminals use charitable organisations (such as incorporated societies and charitable trusts) to launder their money or to finance terrorism.

Activity: Acting as, or arranging someone to act as a nominee director, nominee shareholder or trustee

In the definition of "designated non-financial business or profession" an accounting practice which, in the ordinary course of business, acts as, or arranges for a person to act as, a nominee director or nominee shareholder or trustee in relation to legal persons or legal arrangements, is captured by the AML/CFT Act as a reporting entity.

21 As at 29 March 2018, no arrangements have been prescribed. Section 5(1), AML/CFT Act: http://bit.ly/2xHGfmy

If you are acting as a nominee director, nominee shareholder or a trustee in your personal capacity (as opposed to in your professional capacity) the AML/ CFT Act does not apply. An example would be if you were volunteering your time to act as a trustee on a community trust board that funds sports events in your local area.

Examples of this kind of activity in practice

- You act as a nominee director of a company.
- You act as a trustee for a trust.
- You arrange for a person to act as a nominee shareholder for a company.

ML/TF risks associated with this activity

If an accountant is acting as a nominee director, nominee shareholder or a trustee for a company or other legal arrangement (such as a trust or charity), this may provide a false impression of legitimacy for the activities undertaken by the company or legal arrangement. This facade provides criminals with the opportunity to use their companies or other legal arrangements for laundering money or other crime without being detected. The possibility of detection is made less likely because they can do this while maintaining the impression of oversight by reputable New Zealand-based directors.

Accountants who act or arrange for someone to act as a nominee director, nominee shareholder, or trustee need to establish the reason why this arrangement is required. We expect that accountants establish that there is a legitimate economic purpose of the company or other legal arrangement and to know who its beneficial owners are.

Activity: Providing an office or address for a company or legal arrangement

In the definition of "designated non-financial business or profession" an accounting practice which, in the ordinary course of business, provides a registered office or a business address, a correspondence address, or an administrative address for a company, or a partnership, or for any other legal persons or arrangement, is captured by the AML/CFT Act as a reporting entity. The only exception to this is where the office or address is provided solely as an ancillary service to the provision of other services that are not otherwise captured by the definition of "designated non-financial business or profession" in the AML/CFT Act.

Example of this kind of activity in practice

- You allow a small company to use your business address as its registered office address but you do not provide them with any other services.

ML/TF risks associated with this activity

For a person who is intent on laundering money or committing other crime, the use of an address that is not their physical location is attractive. It allows them to keep anonymity and distance from the transactions and activities they are undertaking, and if it is the address of an accountant, it adds a perception of legitimacy to their activities. It also makes it more difficult for law enforcement to track them down in person.

Activity: Managing client funds, accounts, securities, or other assets

In the definition of "designated non-financial business or profession" an accounting practice which, in the ordinary course of business, manages client funds (other than sums paid as fees for professional services), accounts, securities, or other assets, is captured by the AML/CFT Act as a reporting entity.

Managing payments to or from your clients' accounts is captured; and, with the exception of payments for professional fees, any instance where you receive or hold client funds and control the payment of those funds will also be captured. The key determining factor is whether you have control over the flow of funds – if you do have control, your activity is captured. Taking a payroll situation, for example, if you are loading payments that are then actioned by your client, you are not controlling the funds, your client is. However, if you are authorising wage and salary payments from your client's account directly into their staff's personal accounts, then this is a captured activity.

Examples of this kind of activity in practice

- You have the authority to make payments on behalf of your client's business directly from their bank accounts.
- You make investments on behalf of a client in securities and/or other assets using funds from their bank accounts which you have the authority to transfer.
- You manage the sale and/or purchase of trust assets for your customer using funds from their bank accounts which you have the authority to transfer.
- You disburse the funds generated from a company's insolvency liquidation to a creditor in line with the relevant administration requirements.

- You exercise the enduring power of attorney which you hold for a client who has lost mental capacity by making payments from their personal account to meet their financial obligations, such as medical bills.
- You operate a trust account to receive tax refunds from Inland Revenue on behalf of your clients and you repay those funds to your clients.

ML/TF risks associated with this activity

Some people will try to avoid accessing banking services typically used in transactions to obscure the trail of funds changing hands as a means to hide their criminal activities. One way to obscure this trail or to add an appearance of legitimacy is to use the trust accounts or other professional services of accountants.

Activity: Engaging in, or giving instructions on behalf of a customer to another person, for a range of specified services (as below)

In the definition of "designated non-financial business or profession" an accounting practice which, in the ordinary course of business, does any of the activities listed in the box below (in italics) is captured by the AML/CFT Act as a reporting entity.

The activities specified in the following box apply to situations where accountants either engage in the activities themselves, or give instructions on behalf of a client to another person for those activities. This means that if you are instructing a third party to undertake activities on behalf of your client, you are captured by the AML/CFT Act – as is the third party you instruct if they fall within the definition of either "designated non-financial business or profession" or "financial institution".[22]

Engaging in or giving instructions on behalf of a customer to another pers for—

a. *any conveyancing (within the meaning of section 6 of the Lawyers and Conveyancers Act 2006[23]) to effect a transaction (within the meaning of section 4(1) of the Real Estate Agents Act 2008[24]), namely,—*
   - *the sale, the purchase, or any other disposal or acquisition of a freehold estate or interest in land:*
   - *the grant, sale, or purchase or any other disposal or acquisition of a leasehold estate or interest in land (other than a tenancy to which the Residential Tenancies Act 1986 applies[25]):*

22 Both these terms are defined in section 5(1), AML/CFT Act: http://bit.ly/2xHGfmy

23 Section 6, Lawyers and Conveyancers Act 2006: http://bit.ly/2ztIqyK

24 Section 4(1), Real Estate Agents Act 2008: http://bit.ly/2h79rQS

25 Residential Tenancies Act 1986: http://bit.ly/2iYKoQl

- *the grant, sale, or purchase or any other disposal or acquisition of a licence that is registrable under the Land Transfer Act 1952:* [26]
- *the grant, sale, or purchase or any other disposal or acquisition of an occupation right agreement within the meaning of section 5 of the Retirement Villages Act 2003:*[27]

Note: Only lawyers and conveyancers are able to engage in conveyancing work but an accountant might give conveyancing instructions to a lawyer or conveyancer.

b. *a transaction (within the meaning of section 4(1) of the Real Estate Agents Act 2008); or*

c. *the transfer of a beneficial interest in land or other real property; or*

d. *a transaction on behalf of any person in relation to the buying, transferring, or selling of a business or legal person (for example, a company) and any other legal arrangement; or*

e. *a transaction on behalf of a customer in relation to creating, operating, and managing a legal person (for example, a company) and any other legal arrangement"*

You should read both (D) and (E) to mean undertaking any one of the activities mentioned, not a combination of all activities at once. "Transaction" is defined in section 6 of the AML/CFT Act and means any deposit, withdrawal, exchange or transfer of funds whether (i) in cash; (ii) by cheque, payment order or other instrument; or (iii) by electronic or other non-physical means. There are some inclusions and exclusions specified in the definition.

Examples of these kinds of activities in practice

- You instruct a conveyancer to effect the sale of a house owned by your client.
- You purchase farm land as a trustee (together with the other trustees) for your client's family trust.
- You give instructions to a nominee overseas to purchase a company for your client in that country with funds provided by the client.
- You instruct a trust and company service provider to transfer funds provided by your client to the bank accounts of a newly formed company of which your client is the sole shareholder.

ML/TF risks associated with this activity

The key risk with all the activities described in the previous box is the anonymity and appearance of legitimacy that may be gained by the customer

26 Land Transfer Act 1952: http://bit.ly/2iq9a8c

27 Section 5, Retirement Villages Act 2003: http://bit.ly/2lJhJQv

through the accountant engaging in the activities, or giving instructions to another person on their behalf for those activities. The person being instructed by the accountant may be unlikely to have any face-to-face contact with the actual client. If the client has criminal intentions, there would be a protective layer of other people between the client and the transaction they are instructing.

Auditing, and other assurance activities, are not captured by the AML/CFT Act

In general, financial auditing and other assurance services are not captured by the AML/CFT Act, so you will not be required to apply your compliance programme to clients who are only requesting these kinds of services. You may be requested to provide AML/CFT auditing services to businesses which, by virtue of their being either a financial institution or a DNFBP, are required to comply with the AML/CFT Act. Similarly, this activity is not captured by the AML/CFT Act and you will not have to apply your compliance programme to it.

If, however, in the course of your (financial or AML/ CFT) auditing or other assurance procedures you have reasonable grounds to suspect that an activity is relevant to the potential investigation or prosecution of any person for a money laundering or other offence, you should consider your obligations to report that activity to the FIU.[28]

4. Do you know your compliance obligations?

Any accounting practice, either existing or established after the introduction of the AML/CFT Act, that conducts captured activities, will be a reporting entity and will have to comply with the Act. You will not be excused from compliance on the basis that to comply would breach any contract or agreement.[29]

Compliance requirements

This section provides guidance on:

- The risk-based approach that reporting entities need to take when developing their AML/CFT programme
- The range of policies, procedures and controls reporting entities must include in their AML/ CFT programme to comply with the AML/CFT Act
- Things to consider if you wish to establish a designated business group to share some aspects of your AML/CFT programme and its implementation

28 Section 43, AML/CFT Act: http://bit.ly/2og1BEW

29 Section 9, AML/CFT Act: http://bit.ly/2iR0JH3

Section 5 provides more detail about compliance requirements for CDD. Information on where to access other support to comply is noted in section 7.

Risk-based compliance

The AML/CFT regulatory system in New Zealand is "risk-based". This means your business must assess the risk it is exposed to from money launderers and terrorist financers. You must then apply suitable policies, procedures and controls to effectively manage the risks you have identified for your business. Compliance resources can then be targeted primarily at high-risk areas, which should reduce the overall compliance cost for your business.

You are the best judge of the risks your business is exposed to and how you can most effectively mitigate those risks in line with the requirements of the AML/CFT Act. As your supervisor, DIA expects you to genuinely and accurately assess the ML/TF risks to your business and then apply a suitable and proportionate AML/CFT programme.

AML/CFT programme – policies, procedures and controls

AML/CFT compliance cannot be achieved with a "set and forget" approach. The AML/CFT programme needs to be fully implemented within the business. It should be a living and adaptable programme. Your specific compliance obligations under the AML/CFT Act are summarised below.

Appoint a compliance officer

You must appoint an AML/CFT compliance officer to administer and maintain your compliance programme.[30] The compliance officer should be an employee of the business who reports to a senior manager or partner of the business. If practising on their own account, an accounting professional would be expected to act as the compliance officer themselves and take full responsibility for all compliance requirements unless there is a reason why they cannot. In that case they should appoint a third party to take on this duty.[31]

When you have appointed your compliance officer, or if your compliance officer or other contact information changes, it is important that you advise us at amlphase2@dia.govt.nz. This enables us to communicate effectively with you and provide you with important information and updates.

30 Section 56, AML/CFT Act: http://bit.ly/2znn4Dd

31 This will only be possible where the business has no employees. The supervisor expects that if the person who is acting as a compliance officer is not part of the business, there should be a justifiable reason. The reporting entity should be able to demonstrate to the supervisor that the person selected has an appropriate level of access to business information and systems to perform their duties and the authority to advise the senior management of the business about AML/CFT matters.

Conduct a risk assessment

All reporting entities must undertake a risk assessment, and it must be in writing. The specific requirements for a risk assessment are set out in section 58 of the AML/CFT Act.[32] The supervisors have provided guidance on how to conduct a risk assessment.[33] The AML/CFT Act requires that you have regard to guidance produced by the AML/CFT supervisors when developing your risk assessment.[34]

DIA has published its own assessment of the ML/TF risks in the sectors it is responsible for supervising, including in the accounting, bookkeeping and tax agency professions.[35] DIA has also developed a "Prompts and Notes" guideline (*AML/CFT Risk Assessment and Programme: Prompts and Notes for DIA Reporting Entities*), which outlines the factors to be considered in a risk assessment along with some prompts for things to think about when completing a risk assessment and developing your AML/CFT programme.[36] It provides prompts to help businesses undertake their risk assessment in a way that reflects both the size of their business and their level of risk. In addition, the Financial Markets Authority has published a step-by-step guide for drafting a risk assessment.[37] Together, these resources will help businesses to conduct a realistic assessment of their ML/TF risks, so that their AML/CFT programme is proportionate to the risks assessed.

Risk assessments are required to be regularly reviewed and updated where there is any material change to the business, its service offerings, or its client base, or where deficiencies in the effectiveness of the risk assessment are identified. As methods and techniques (known as "typologies") of ML/TF adapt and change, the nature of the risks posed to a business may change also. It is important for accountants, particularly compliance officers in accounting practices, to keep up-to-date with relevant changes in typologies. The Quarterly Typology Reports published by the FIU are an excellent source of typology information.[38]

32 Section 58, AML/CFT Act: http://bit.ly/2ly11Dz

33 Risk Assessment Guideline: http://bit.ly/2sdlv83

34 Section 58(2)(g), AML/CFT Act: http://bit.ly/2ly11Dz

35 Sector and National Risk Assessments: http://bit.ly/2ik1tAu

36 AML/CFT Risk Assessment and Programme: Prompts and Notes for DIA Reporting Entities: http://bit.ly/2EBUMXy

37 Guide for Small Financial Adviser Businesses: http://bit.ly/2z18hNI

38 FIU assessments and reports: http://bit.ly/2xGSiAx

Good times to think about updating your business's risk assessment are when:

- The FIU publish a National Risk Assessment for ML/TF or a Quarterly Typology Report about ML/TF issues that highlights the potential for vulnerabilities in your business activities
- DIA updates its Sector Risk Assessment
- You have become aware of an increased ML/ TF risk to your business due to a change in the nature of or demand in your services
- International ML or TF-related events trigger you to reconsider your risk assessment

Set up an AML/CFT programme

Once a risk assessment has been conducted, all reporting entities must develop an AML/CFT programme that includes internal procedures, policies and controls to detect and manage the risk of ML/TF.[39] The AML/CFT Act requires that you have regard to guidance produced by the supervisor when developing your AML/CFT programme.[40] The supervisors' guidance on developing an AML/CFT programme is available on the DIA website.[41]

The supervisors' guidance is generic in nature. It does not provide prescriptive instructions on how businesses can ensure they are compliant with the AML/CFT Act. This is because each business has unique circumstances that determine their exposure to ML/TF risks, which they need to understand and factor into their unique AML/CFT programme. Businesses will need to apply their own judgement, and where there are questions about compliance they can either ask the supervisor for general information, or seek independent advice.

Customer due diligence (CDD)

Section 5 in this guideline is dedicated to explaining your CDD obligations.[42]

Record keeping

You must keep adequate records as outlined in sections 49 to 55 of the AML/CFT Act. This will enable you to operate your AML/CFT programme effectively and enable it to be audited by an independent auditor and reviewed by the supervisor on request. Records must either be kept in written form in English or be readily accessible and readily convertible into written form in English.

39 Sections 56 and 57, AML/CFT Act: http://bit.ly/2znn4Dd and http://bit.ly/2h2nN59

40 Section 57(2), AML/CFT Act: http://bit.ly/2h2nN59

41 AML/CFT Programme Guideline: http://bit.ly/2iS5I7k

42 The CDD requirements are noted in Part 2, subpart 1, AML/CFT Act: http://bit.ly/2A5PJtA

You must keep your records for at least five years. The supervisor or the FIU may ask you to keep records for longer in some circumstances. After five years, the records must be destroyed unless there is a lawful reason why they should be retained, such as the need to comply with another enactment or to enable you to carry on your business.

You must keep the following records.

Record Type	Retention period
Transaction records sufficient to enable the transactions to be fully reconstructed at any time[43]	5 years from the completion of the transaction
Any reports of suspicious activities[44]	5 years after the report is made
Identity and verification evidence (as reasonably necessary to enable the nature of the evidence to be readily identified at any time)[45]	5 years from the end of the business relationship or the completion of the occasional transaction or activity
Risk assessments, AML/CFT programmes and audits	5 years after the date on which they cease to be used on a regular basis
Information relevant to the establishment of a business relationship and any other records that explain the nature and purpose of a business relationship and the activities relating to that business relationship[46]	5 years from the end of the business relationship

You are also strongly advised to keep any detailed records of your assessment of whether a suspicious activity report (SAR) is required, including any determinations of whether information you hold is legally privileged.

Ongoing customer due diligence and account monitoring

When you have established a business relationship, you must conduct ongoing CDD and undertake account monitoring.[47] For more information about what this means in practice, please see "Ongoing CDD and account monitoring" in section 5.

Review your AML/CFT programme

You must regularly review your risk assessment and AML/CFT programme to ensure it remains up-to-date and to identify and remedy any deficiencies.[48]

43 Section 49, AML/CFT Act: http://bit.ly/2zEQkFA

44 Section 49A, AML/CFT Act: http://bit.ly/2iFJ1lM

45 Section 50, AML/CFT Act: http://bit.ly/2zdxog9

46 Section 51, AML/CFT Act: http://bit.ly/2znMDn8

47 Section 31, AML/CFT Act: http://bit.ly/2z1eCIX

48 Section 59, AML/CFT Act: http://bit.ly/2xJWm2P

Your records should show evidence of updates that address any identified deficiencies in its effectiveness. Ways to do this would be to keep a record of version history or retain evidence demonstrating reviews and updates.

Annual reporting to your supervisor

Like all reporting entities, you are required to submit an annual report each year covering the period July to June.[49] The date for submission is advised by the supervisor each year, and you will usually have two months to submit. This means the first annual report will likely be due at the end of August 2019. Given the Act applies to accounting practices from 1 October 2018, your first annual report will be for the nine month period 1 October 2018 to 30 June 2019. A new set of annual report questions has been designed for lawyers, conveyancers, accountants and real estate agents and is provided for by Regulations, and a user guide for the new annual report for DNFPBs has been published by DIA.[50] All reporting entities are also expected to respond to any requests for subsequent information from the supervisor in a timely manner.

Independent audits of your risk assessment and AML/CFT programme

Every two years, you are required to have an independent audit of your risk assessment and AML/CFT programme.[51] An independent audit aims to ensure that documents remain up-to-date, that any deficiencies in programme effectiveness are identified, and that any necessary changes are made. For guidance, please see the *Guideline for Audits of Risk Assessments and AML/CFT Programmes*, which is available on the DIA website.[52]

The AML/CFT Act requires you to appoint someone who is independent and suitably qualified to conduct the audit.[53] The audit cannot be undertaken by someone from within the business unless a sufficient degree of independence can be demonstrated. For instance, a very large firm with a dedicated audit function would likely be able to show a sufficient degree of independence. Someone who has been involved in the establishment of the compliance programme (such as completing the risk assessment and/or writing the AML/CFT programme) cannot conduct the audit. The auditor does not need to be a Chartered Accountant or qualified to undertake financial audits.[54] To

49 Section 60, AML/CFT Act: http://bit.ly/2gQqiUa

50 *User Guide: Annual AML/CFT Report by Designated Non-Financial Businesses and Professions*: available at Codes of Practice and Guidelines: http://bit.ly/2gQ3Iev

51 Sections 59–59A, AML/CFT Act: http://bit.ly/2xJWm2P

52 *Guideline for Audits of Risk Assessments and AML/ CFT Programmes*: http://bit.ly/2AfTf7m

53 It is up to you to decide if someone is suitably qualified to conduct an audit of your AML/CFT programme. You should be able to explain to the supervisor your rationale for this decision on request.

54 Section 59B, AML/CFT Act: http://bit.ly/2muArvE

be suitably qualified we expect that your auditor would have a working knowledge of the AML/CFT Act and its complexities.

A copy of the independent audit must be provided to the supervisor on request. The supervisor can instruct a reporting entity to have a new independent audit undertaken at any time.

You may be asked to conduct an independent audit as a professional service to a client who is a financial institution or a DNFBP. Auditing and assurance services are not captured under the AML/ CFT Act, so you do not have to apply your compliance programme to independent audits that assist a client to meet their own AML/CFT compliance requirements.

Reporting to the FIU

As a key part of your AML/CFT obligations, in specific circumstances you need to report certain information to the FIU. Each reporting entity will have visibility over different parts of any one chain of events leading to an activity or transaction or following on from an activity or transaction. Each report will provide the FIU with information, complementing other types of reports providing further information. It may be that the report you provide will be the one crucial piece that brings enough of the puzzle together to lead the FIU to take appropriate action against a criminal.

When you need to report

From 1 October 2018, you will be required to submit suspicious activity reports (SARs; previously known as "suspicious transaction reports"[55]) and prescribed transaction reports. From that date you will no longer be required to submit suspicious transaction reports under the Financial Transactions Reporting Act 1996.

Suspicious activity reports (SARs)

Section 39A of the AML/CFT Act defines a "suspicious activity" and section 40 of the Act requires you to report suspicious activity to the FIU as soon as practicable, but no later than three working days after forming its suspicion. This has been held to mean that a reporting entity must report a suspicious activity within three days of the point at which the reporting entity becomes aware of facts that would objectively justify a suspicion (or by reasonable diligence would have become aware of them).[56] It is not a defence that a reporting entity did not actually consider an activity to be suspicious, in circumstances where it objectively should have.

55 The AML/CFT Amendment Act 2017 changed "suspicious transaction reports" to "suspicious activity reports".

56 *DIA v Ping An Finance (Group) New Zealand Limited* (2017) NZHC 2363, at paragraphs 64-67.

Prescribed transaction reports (PTRs)

A prescribed transaction is an international wire transfer of NZ$1,000 or more conducted through a reporting entity or a domestic physical cash transaction of a value equal to or above NZ$10,000.[57] The requirement to submit PTRs came into force on 1 November 2017. Please refer to "Wire transfers" in section 5 for more detail on wire transfers (including international wire transfers).

Only an ordering institution and a beneficiary institution are required to file a PTR in respect of an international wire transfer.

An "ordering institution" is defined as "any person who has been instructed by a payer to electronically transfer funds controlled by the payer to a payee via a "beneficiary institution". The ordering institution will be the first reporting entity to transfer the funds that are the subject of the international wire transfer to another jurisdiction – for instance, an accountant that holds client funds in a trust account or has authority to move funds from a client's own bank account, and transfers those funds (including via the formal banking system) to an overseas beneficiary bank.

A reporting entity that simply passes on an instruction to transfer funds, without actually transacting, will not be required to file a PTR. A "beneficiary institution" (in relation to a wire transfer from an ordering institution) is defined as "any person who receives those funds and then makes those funds available to a person (the payee) by crediting it to an account held by the payee or paying it to the payee". The beneficiary institution will be the last reporting entity in the chain that receives the funds before making them available to its customer (the beneficiary of the transaction).

Usually a bank will be a beneficiary institution; however, in some cases the beneficiary institution may be a different reporting entity, such as an accounting practice, depending on where the funds (intended for the customer) end up.

PTRs are intended to add further transparency to the financial system by making the range of methods of ML/TF even more difficult to hide. PTRs will also improve the detection and disruption of organised crime.

Suspicious property reports

You also need to be aware of your obligations to submit "suspicious property reports" (SPRs) under the Terrorism Suppression Act 2002. If you are in control of property that you suspect (on reasonable grounds) is property that is owned or controlled, directly or indirectly by a "designated terrorist entity" (or property derived or generated from that type of property), you must

57 Section 5(1), AML/CFT Act (http://bit.ly/2xHGfmy); Regulation 5A, AML/CFT (Definitions) Regulations (http://bit.ly/2hbI5p6). Also see the FIU's Prescribed Transactions Reporting web page: http://bit.ly/2zkB9RJ

report that suspicion in accordance with sections 43 and 44 of the Terrorism Suppression Act. You must submit the SPR as soon as practicable after forming your suspicion. Designated terrorist entities are identified on a publicly available list that is updated by the New Zealand Police.[58] If you find a match on a list other than New Zealand's terrorist designation list, you must submit an SAR (as opposed to an SPR) to the FIU.

How to report

The FIU has issued guidance on how to submit reports using their goAML web-based reporting tool.[59] You must use the specific reporting format provided by the FIU. If you have reported on your customer, you must not disclose this information to your customer or to any person that is not entitled to receive this information.[60] If, after making a report, you are unsure if you need to end your existing relationship with your customer, you may wish to consider your professional obligations and any code of ethics that you have signed up to, consult your professional body, or seek independent advice. For further discussion on ending or declining business relationships, please see "What to do if you cannot complete CDD" in section 5.

What to do if you hold legally professionally privileged information

There may be occasions where you hold customer information that is protected by legal professional privilege (which the AML/CFT Act refers to as a "privileged communication"). For example, while acting as a tax agent for your customer you may receive tax-related legal advice as an agent for your customer.

The Act does not require any person (lawyer or otherwise) to disclose any information that the person believes, on reasonable grounds, is a privileged communication.[61]

A "privileged communication" is defined in section 42 of the AML/CFT Act as:[62]

- A confidential communication between a lawyer and another lawyer or a lawyer and his or her client made for the purpose of obtaining or giving legal advice or assistance; or
- A communication that is subject to the general law governing legal professional privilege or is specified in sections 53–57 of the Evidence Act 2006[63]

58 Designated terrorist entities: http://bit.ly/258MtKq

59 goAML – Financial Intelligence Unit reporting tool: http://bit.ly/2ygOri3

60 Section 46, AML/CFT Act: http://bit.ly/2xCrpxz

61 Section 40(4), AML/CFT Act: http://bit.ly/2CB4DYH

62 Section 42, AML/CFT Act: http://bit.ly/2yj0ECT

63 Sections 53–57 of the Evidence Act 2006: http://bit.ly/2Ah1n7T

The AML/CFT Act requires all reporting entities to report suspicious activities by filing SARs with the FIU. If it is possible for you to file an SAR without disclosing a privileged communication, you must do so. It is accepted that in some cases this will not be possible. A privileged communication may lose the protection of privilege if prepared for a dishonest purpose or to enable or aid the commission of an offence – in which case, it can be included in an SAR.

Establishing a Designated Business Group

In certain circumstances, accountants may be able to form a designated business group (DBG) with other entities (whether or not those entities are other law firms or accountants or even reporting entities). The term "designated business group" is defined in full in the AML/CFT Act and regulations.[64] In summary, it means a group of two or more persons who have elected (in writing) to form a group to enable some obligations under the AML/CFT Act to be met on a shared basis while the election is in force.

A member of a DBG can rely on another member to carry out certain obligations on their behalf, including CDD (in certain situations[65]). Members can also rely on specified parts of another member's AML/CFT programme, and another member's risk assessment (if relevant), as well as reporting to the FIU. Members may share information and rely on each other but they still retain responsibility for their own compliance. Any decision to apply to become a DBG should include a thorough consideration of the risks and implications for all members.

The supervisor will consider all applications for DBGs. If you are not sure whether or not your proposed DBG meets the criteria in the definition in section 5(1) of the Act, you are welcome to contact DIA to discuss. We would prefer if reporting entities test their proposals with us rather than assume they could not apply. If you are interested in applying to form a DBG, we recommend you familiarise yourself with the two available guidelines to assist reporting entities to create DBGs, one on Scope and one on Formation, before you submit an application.[66] The application form is included in the Formation guideline.

5. Do you know your customer?

This section provides information about:

- What a business relationship means and when it starts
- Who to conduct CDD on

64 Section 5(1) of the AML/CFT Act: http://bit.ly/2xHGfmy

65 Section 32, AML/CFT Act: http://bit.ly/2hjDuF3

66 Designated Business Group Guidelines: http://bit.ly/2y4KpFa

- What the different levels of CDD are, and scenario-based examples of each level
- How to use the Identity Verification Code of Practice
- When you can rely on others for CDD
- When to conduct CDD
- What to think about when participating in international transactions
- What to do if you cannot complete CDD

The requirements described in this section are contained in Part 2, subpart 1 of the AML/CFT Act.[67] The supervisors have prepared a range of fact sheets that are likely to assist accountants with undertaking CDD. The fact sheets are available on the DIA website.[68]

When a business relationship starts

A business relationship is defined in section 5(1) of the Act as "a business, professional, or commercial relationship between a reporting entity and a customer that has an element of duration or that is expected by the reporting entity at the time when contact is established, to have an element of duration". This captures situations where a reporting entity has, or expects to have, a relationship with a customer involving more than one interaction or the carrying out of multiple transactions.[69]

You will need to use your judgement to determine when a business relationship with a customer starts. This is likely to be after initial inquiries have been made, but before any work has commenced.

Who to conduct CDD on

You must conduct CDD on:

- Your customer
- Any beneficial owner of a customer
- Any person acting on behalf of a customer

New customers

You may not have to conduct CDD on every new customer. You need to establish at the outset whether they are going to require you to conduct any activity captured by the AML/CFT Act. If they are, you will need to conduct CDD in line with the level of risk you anticipate and in accordance with the requirements in the Act. See below for the levels of CDD and further explanation of the compliance requirements. If your customer does not require you to conduct a captured activity initially, but over time you are instructed to

67 Part 2, subpart 1, AML/CFT Act: http://bit.ly/2A5PJtA

68 Customer Due Diligence Fact Sheets: http://bit.ly/2Bxp2Pc

69 *DIA v Ping An*, paragraph 44.

carry out captured activities, you must ensure you have completed the necessary CDD before you carry out those captured activities.

Existing customers

The term "existing customer" is defined in the Act as a person who was in a business relationship with a reporting entity immediately before the Act began applying to the reporting entity.[70] You must conduct CDD on existing customers if there has been a material change in the nature or purpose of the business relationship with that customer, and you have insufficient information about that customer.[71] When considering what information would be sufficient, you will need to assess the level of risk involved, and whether you hold the necessary identity information, verified to the appropriate level. You should not conduct any captured activity until these requirements are met.

Occasional customers

"Occasional activity" and "occasional transaction" are both defined in the Act.[72] The term "occasional" does not necessarily mean "single"; it also includes circumstances in which multiple transactions are so intermittent or infrequent that no business relationship is established.

The other people you must conduct CDD on

You must also complete CDD on:	For example:
Any beneficial owner[73] of a customer	Someone who owns more than 25 percent of a company that is your customer[74]
Any person acting on behalf of a customer	A person exercising a power of attorney for your customer A legal guardian acting on behalf of a minor who is your customer An employee who has the authority to act on behalf of a company that is your customer

70 Section 5(1), AML/CFT Act: http://bit.ly/2xHGfmy. For accountants, "existing customer" refers to any person who was in a business relationship with you immediately before 1 October 2018.

71 Section 11(4), AML/CFT Act https://bit. ly/2gRumUg. The term "material change" has been defined in the Enhanced Customer Due Diligence Guideline (available here: http://bit.ly/2GrKaHV) as "an event, activity or situation that you identify during interactions with your customer (or via ongoing customer due diligence and account monitoring) that could change their level of ML/TF risk".

72 Section 5(1), AML/CFT Act: http://bit.ly/2xHGfmy

73 The term "beneficial owner" is defined in section 5(1), AML/CFT Act: http://bit.ly/2xHGfmy

74 More than 25% is the prescribed threshold for the definition of a beneficial owner. Regulation 5, AML/CFT (Definitions) Regulations: http://bit.ly/2yDVy49

The DIA website provides a range of fact sheets to help you. They cover the following topics[75]:

- Acting on behalf of others
- Clubs and societies
- Companies
- Co-operatives
- Sole traders and Partnerships
- Trusts

The supervisors have also provided specific guidance on beneficial ownership.[76] Customers that are individuals may be treated as the beneficial owner so long as you believe on reasonable grounds that the person is not acting on behalf of anyone else.[77]

The AML/CFT Act treats trusts as being capable of being customers in their own right, despite a trust not ordinarily having a legal personality. The supervisors have provided a factsheet to help reporting entities who engage with trusts as customers.[78]

Different levels of CDD requirements

There are three levels of CDD. You will need to be sure you use the right level, which will depend on the unique factors of each business relationship, the characteristics of the customer(s), the nature of the activities and transactions you are facilitating, and the potential for ML/TF risk. The three levels are:

- ***Standard CDD*** – for most common situations
- ***Simplified CDD*** – for use with specific customers or customer types that are considered to be low risk for ML/TF. These customers are specified in section 18(2) of the AML/CFT Act[79]
- ***Enhanced CDD*** – for use when there are factors creating a higher level of ML/TF risk or are otherwise specified in the AML/CFT Act

You must use your own risk assessment and AML/CFT programme to establish the level of ML/TF risk. This will help you determine which kind of CDD to conduct before establishing the business relationship or conducting an occasional transaction or activity.

75 Customer Due Diligence Fact Sheets: http://bit.ly/2Bxp2Pc

76 *Beneficial Ownership Guideline*: http://bit.ly/2Bxp2Pc

77 Section 11(2), AML/CFT Act: http://bit.ly/2gRumUg

78 *Clarification of the position the AML/CFT supervisors are taking with respect of the AML/ CFT Act interpretation of a trust as a customer*: http://bit.ly/2Bxp2Pc

79 Section 18(2), AML/CFT Act: http://bit.ly/2gS5b3V

Other CDD requirements

Regardless of the level of CDD you are conducing on your client, you must seek information about the nature and purpose of the proposed business relationship or occasional transaction or activity.[80] This means you need to have a good understanding of your client's circumstances and intentions and who else has an interest in their activities; ie, who else benefits. If you are conducting standard CDD you also must obtain sufficient information to allow you to determine whether you should conduct enhanced CDD.[81] Enhanced CDD generally requires you to ascertain the sources of your customer's wealth and/ or funds (for more information see the "Enhanced CDD" section further on in this section). With this information you can make an assessment about whether your client's requests are typical, legitimate or suspicious.

Scenario-based examples

This section includes a series of scenario-based examples to demonstrate the process of compliance based on a range of fictional circumstances. Most of the examples focus on the captured activity "managing client funds", which many accountants do in their day-to-day work. You should assume for the purposes of these examples that all other relevant legal obligations have been met.

Standard CDD

Accountants must conduct standard CDD[82] if:

- They establish a business relationship with a new customer
- A customer seeks to conduct an occasional transaction or activity through the accounting practice, or
- In relation to an existing customer, and according to the level of risk involved, there has been a material change in the business relationship and there is insufficient information held about the customer (for example, they are a customer that you have dealt with prior to the Act taking effect who is now seeking assistance with captured activities and you are informed there are new investors (beneficial owners) that you do not have any CDD information about)

80 Sections 17, 21 and 25, AML/CFT Act: http://bit.ly/2m1YSjC

81 Section 17, AML/CFT Act: http://bit.ly/2m1YSjC

82 Section 14, AML/CFT Act: http://bit.ly/2z2zU99

Identity requirements

When standard CDD applies, the following identity information must be gathered about a customer, the beneficial owner(s), and a person acting on behalf of a customer:[83]

- Full name
- Date of birth
- If the person is not the customer, the person's relationship to the customer
- Address or registered office
- Company identifier or registration number

You must also obtain information about the nature and purpose of the proposed business relationship with the customer, and sufficient information to determine whether enhanced CDD needs to be conducted on the customer.[84]

Verification requirements

Accountants are required to take reasonable steps to ensure that the information gathered is correct.[85] According to the level of risk involved, you need to take reasonable steps to verify the identity of any beneficial owners, and to verify the identity and authority of any person who is seeking to act on behalf of your customer. The supervisors have published a *Beneficial Ownership Guideline* to help you.[86] Verification must be undertaken before the business relationship is established or before the occasional transaction or activity is conducted. There is an exception to this which is described in "When to conduct CDD" later in this section.[87]

The Amended Identity Verification Code of Practice allows Chartered Accountants (among other identified groups) to act as "trusted referees" to verify identity information. It is important to note that Chartered Accountants can only do this where they are not themselves party to the activity or transaction with the customer for whom the CDD is being conducted.

83 Section 15, AML/CFT Act: http://bit.ly/2zDSNQt

84 Section 17, AML/CFT Act: http://bit.ly/2m1YSjC

85 Section 16, AML/CFT Act: http://bit.ly/2HAmByd

86 *Beneficial Ownership Guideline*: http://bit.ly/2Bxp2Pc

87 Section 16(3), AML/CFT Act: http://bit.ly/2HAmByd

Example in practice (low risk): Managing payroll for a small brewery

Customer:	Ms Genevieve Mills, owner of Mills Brewing Limited
Captured activity:	Managing client funds – making payroll payments to staff
Level of CDD required:	Standard CDD
Steps to complete standard CDD	**How this applies to the example**
1. Obtain identity information for all relevant persons	Ms Mills shows you her current passport. You check the Companies Office records online and you see that Ms Mills is listed as the sole director and shareholder of your customer (Mills Brewing), and the company address and business number match those that have been provided by Ms Mills. There are no indicators that enhanced CDD is required.
2. Obtain information about the nature and purpose of the proposed business relationship	Ms Mills explains that with the business growing, it is the right time to obtain professional accounting services for making payroll payments directly to staff.
3. Make a determination of the level of ML/TF risk involved	Based on the information that Ms Mills has provided you and your review of Companies Office records, you establish there are no other people with a beneficial interest in Mills Brewing Limited. You also assess the level of ML/TF risk associated with Mills Brewing Limited as low.
4. According to that level of risk, verify the identity of relevant persons, including natural persons, using the Amended Identity Verification Code of Practice	You view and take a clear copy of Ms Mills' passport. You record the date on which you sighted the passport and made the copy. You print a copy of the Mills Brewing Limited records from the Companies Office website and record the date on which you did.
5. If the identity information and verification requirements are satisfied, then you can proceed with the customer's instructions.	You on-board Mills Brewing Limited as a customer and set up systems to support the payroll operation.

If there were any number of changes to the range of facts in the fictional scenario above, the level of CDD required may have been different. For example, if there had been a range of beneficial owners, then you would have had to do CDD on all of them, and the level of CDD would depend on their characteristics and associated levels of ML/ TF risk. Or, if the business was receiving investment funds from offshore, then you would have had to consider whether the originating countries have sufficient AML/CFT systems in place and whether they were countries known for ML/TF risks, such as known tax havens.

Example in practice (medium risk): Managing a small farm business's accounts payment

Customer:	Mr Randall Marsh and Mrs Stacy Evans – dairy farm owners
Captured activity:	Managing client funds – making payments from a customer's accounts
Level of CDD required:	Standard CDD
Steps to complete standard CDD	**How this applies to the example**
1. Obtain identity information for all relevant persons	Mr Marsh and Mrs Evans do not have passports so they provide you with their driver licences and birth certificates. Mr Marsh and Mrs Evans explain they have inherited their land from Mrs Evans' parents and there are no investors in their dairy farm business. At this stage, you note there are no indicators that enhanced CDD is required.
2. Obtain information about the nature and purpose of the proposed business relationship	Mr Marsh and Mrs Evans are looking for your assistance to ensure they make the right payments at the right time to keep their dairy farm business operating well.
3. Make a determination of the level of ML/TF risk involved	You note that Mr Marsh and Mrs Evans host occasional hunting and tramping events on their farm and some of the participants are tourists from the United States and Canada who give a gift for the hospitality; these are often large sums in cash. You determine the ML/TF risk is medium.
4. According to that level of risk, verify the identity of relevant persons, including natural persons using the Amended Identity Verification Code of Practice	You take copies of Mr Marsh's and Mrs Evans' driver licences and birth certificates and you use the Companies Register to confirm they are the sole owners of the farm and gain reliable information about the farm's address and business registration number.
5. If the identity information and verification requirements are satisfied, then you can proceed with the customer's instructions.	You set up systems to support the business account and payment management services for Mr Marsh and Mrs Evans' dairy farm business.

If there were any number of changes to the range of facts in the fictional scenario above, the level of CDD required may have been different. For example, if it was unclear to you how Mr Marsh and Mrs Evans came to own the dairy farm, you may have had to ask further questions about the source of their wealth. Or, if the occasional hunting and tramping events were a specific business enterprise that was attracting investors, you would have had to identify all people with beneficial ownership.

Simplified CDD

You may complete simplified CDD if your customer is one of those listed in the AML/CFT Act. The list includes a range of organisations such as:

- Government departments
- Local authorities
- The New Zealand Police
- State owned enterprises
- Crown entities
- Registered banks
- Licensed insurers
- Publicly listed companies

For the full list, please see section 18(2) of the AML/ CFT Act.[88]

Identity requirements

When simplified CDD applies, you need to record the full name of the entity in question and a brief explanation of how it falls within section 18(2) of the AML/CFT Act.

The following information needs to be gathered about the identity of a person acting on behalf of one of the entities listed in section 18(2) (for instance, an employee of one of those organisations):

- Full name
- Date of birth
- The person's relationship to the customer

You also need to obtain information about the nature and purpose of the proposed business relationship between you and the customer.[89]

Verification requirements

You must verify the identity of a person acting on behalf of a customer, and verify that person's authority to act so that you are satisfied you know who the person acting is and that they have the authority to act. Reasonable steps

88 Section 18(2), AML/CFT Act: http://bit.ly/2gS5b3V

89 Section 21, AML/CFT Act: http://bit.ly/2zDTeu5

must be taken according to the level of risk involved. This verification must be undertaken before the business relationship is established (or before the occasional transaction or activity is conducted), or before the person acts on behalf of the customer.

Example in practice (low risk): Provision of tax services for a licensed insurance company

Customer:	A small-scale life insurance provider, Pura Vida Insurance Limited
Captured activity:	Manage client funds – making tax payments to Inland Revenue directly from the customer's business accounts
Level of CDD required:	Simplified CDD
Steps to complete simplified CDD	**How this applies to the example**
1. Identify whether your customer meets the criteria for simplified CDD	Your customer is a licensed insurer which is a category listed in section 18(2) of the Act; so, you check the Financial Service Providers Register online and identify and record that Pura Vida Insurance Limited meets the criteria for simplified CDD.
2. Obtain information about the nature and purpose of the proposed business relationship	The Chief Executive, Mrs Elena Ortiz, explains the tax accounting and payment services she would like your accounting practice to undertake for the business. Her explanation demonstrates an intention for an ongoing business relationship.
3. Identify all relevant persons that need to be identified	Because Pura Vida Insurance Limited meets the criteria for simplified CDD, you only need to obtain information about the identity of the person acting on its behalf, Mrs Ortiz. Mrs Ortiz shows you her New Zealand passport, her employee identification card and a business card that states her to be Chief Executive.
4. Make a determination of the level of ML/TF risk involved	You determine that the risk is low, so you continue with applying simplified CDD.

5. According to that level of risk, verify the identity of relevant persons, including natural persons using the Amended Identity Verification Code of Practice	You take a copy of Mrs Ortiz's passport. You record the date on which you sighted the passport and made the copy. You also take a copy of Mrs Ortiz's Employment ID card and one of her business cards. You also check the Pura Vida Insurance website and record your belief that the chief executive you met with is the same person whose profile and photo is posted and that she has the authority to act on behalf of the customer – Pura Vida Insurance Limited.
6. If the identity information and verification requirements are satisfied, then you can proceed with the customer's instructions	You set up the necessary arrangements to provide accounting services to Pura Vida Life Insurance Limited.

If there were any number of changes to the range of facts in the fictional scenario above, the level of CDD required may have been different. For example, if Pura Vida Insurance Limited was an overseas based company that was opening a subsidiary in New Zealand and you were being asked to provide accounting services that are captured activities to the subsidiary, you would need to consider the ownership arrangements of the parent company and whether the country where the parent company resides has sufficient AML regulations in place and whether it is a country known for ML/TF risks.

Enhanced CDD

You must conduct enhanced CDD in specific circumstances:

- If you are establishing a business relationship with, or looking to conduct an occasional transaction or activity for, a customer that is:
  - A trust or another vehicle for holding personal assets; or
  - A non-New Zealand resident who is from a country that has insufficient AML/CFT systems and measures in place[90]; or
  - A company with nominee shareholders or shares in bearer form
- If a customer seeks your assistance to conduct a complex, or unusually large transaction or an unusual pattern of transactions that have no apparent or visible economic or lawful purpose[91]

90 See "Compliance obligations when conducting international transactions" in section 4 for more discussion of how to assess whether a country is considered high risk.

91 Toogood J confirmed in paragraph 34 of *DIA v Ping An* that a transaction that is either complex or unusually large will trigger the enhanced CDD requirements.

- When you consider that the level of ML/TF risk involved means that enhanced CDD would be required
- When you have had cause to submit an SAR to the FIU

When conducting enhanced CDD, in the above circumstances, you must obtain information about your customer's source of wealth or source of funds.[92] You must record this information and take reasonable steps, according to the level of risk involved, to verify this information using other reliable and independent sources.[93] Where you identify that the origin of your customer's funds or wealth has come from their beneficial owner(s), it may be necessary, according to the level of risk involved, for you to extend your level of verification to include the source of wealth or source of funds of these persons. You will not need to obtain and verify source of wealth or source of funds for every beneficial owner if they have nothing to do with your customer's source of wealth or source of funds.

You must **also** conduct enhanced CDD in the following circumstances, which have specific prescribed identity and verification requirements:

- When you determine that your customer is a politically exposed person[94]; or
- If you are an ordering institution, an intermediary institution, or a beneficiary institution in relation to a wire transfer[95]; or
- If you are undertaking an activity that involves the use of new and developing technologies that may favour anonymity[96]

The supervisors have published guidance for all reporting entities on enhanced CDD.[97] The following examples have been tailored to suit accountants. Again, you should assume for the purposes of these examples that all other relevant legal obligations have been met.

Example in practice (low risk): Account management for a charitable trust

Customer:	A church that operates as a charitable trust
Captured activity:	Acting as a trustee – you are asked to act as a trustee
Level of CDD required:	Enhanced CDD

92 Section 23(1)(a) of the AML/CFT Act: http://bit.ly/2iFkDBE
93 Section 24(1)(b) of the AML/CFT Act: http://bit.ly/2zXSvDA
94 Section 26 of the AML/CFT Act: http://bit.ly/2BKjPWO
95 Sections 27–28 of the AML/CFT Act: http://bit.ly/2onXXbh
96 Section 30 of the AML/CFT Act: http://bit.ly/2CcOpcE
97 *Enhanced Customer Due Diligence Guideline*: http://bit.ly/2GrKaHV

Steps to complete enhanced CDD	How this applies to the example
1. Identify which criteria your customer meets to decide the level of CDD you must do	You must complete enhanced CDD because your customer is a trust.
2. Obtain information about the nature and purpose of the proposed business relationship	The religious leader requests you to act as a trustee for the charitable trust.
3. Determine the initial level of ML/TF risk	While recognising that donations from the congregation represent a cash-based income, you determine that the risk is low given your knowledge that this church has been operating for a very long time and is well-regarded in the community.
4. Identify all relevant persons that need to be identified and gather information about the source of wealth/source of funds	You ask the religious leader for proof of their identity. You identify that they are listed on the Charities Register as one of the trustees, along with five other people. You ask to see the trust deed, copy this document and record the full name of the trust, its address and a description of the objects of the trust. You ask to see account documentation from their bank showing incoming donations and other income and outgoings for a period of time that you specify. In this case, you select the previous three months.
5. Verify the information gathered, including using the Amended Identity Verification Code of Practice for the identity of individuals[98] (as risk is not deemed to be high)	You take a copy of the religious leader's passport and record the date that you viewed the original. You advise them that you need to verify the identity of the other five trustees. You arrange to attend an upcoming meeting to meet them in person and take photos of their passports. You record the date and save copies of the photos. You review the bank statements provided as proof of source of funds/wealth. They are from a New Zealand-registered bank, which you determine to be a reliable and independent source. The accounts demonstrate prudent spending of income in line with the trust deed. You decide that no third-party verification of source of funds/ wealth is required.

98 *Amended Identity Verification Code of Practice* 2013: http://bit.ly/2k13AxJ

6. If the identity information and verification requirements are satisfied, then you can proceed with the customer's instructions	You set up the necessary arrangements to act as a trustee for the church.

If there were any number of changes to the range of facts in the fictional scenario above, the level of CDD required may have been different. For example, if the charitable trust had a cash-based income stream and was sending funds to undisclosed offshore locations, you would need to consider the risks associated with terrorism financing, as this is an established typology for terrorism financing activity globally, as well as considering any ML risks with each destination country and the level of AML/CFT regulation in those countries.

Example in practice (medium risk): Voluntary liquidation of a solvent company

Customer:	Nail salon business in liquidation
Captured activity:	Managing client funds – return of funds to beneficial owners
Level of CDD required:	Enhanced CDD
Steps to complete enhanced CDD	**How this applies to the example**
1. Obtain information about the nature and purpose of the proposed business relationship	You meet the director, Mr Poole. He explains to you that the nail salon business has not been as profitable as estimated. He is looking to liquidate as a means to recoup funds that can be redirected to more profitable enterprises. He assures you the company is solvent.
2. Determine the initial level of ML/TF risk	You determine the level of risk is medium based on your knowledge of ML/TF typologies; specifically, proceeds of crime may have been mixed with legitimate revenues, and customers of the business pay cash and are anonymous.
3. Identify which criteria your customer meets to decide the level of CDD you must do	You decide to undertake enhanced CDD because you recognise that nail salons feature in money laundering cases and typologies internationally and carry a risk due to their cash-based nature and potential for links to organised crime.

4.	Identify all relevant persons that need to be identified and gather information about the source of wealth/source of funds	Mr Poole explains the ownership arrangements of the nail salon business. There are four individual investors with equal shares. You request the financial records for the past few years that demonstrate the volume and frequency of funds invested in the business by each investor. You request identity information for each investor. You request from Mr Poole copies of the contracts with each investor to show you the terms and conditions of each investment – including the provisions related to company liquidation. You then request information from each investor about the source of the funds that they have invested in the nail salon. They each come back to you with statements from their own accounting practices to show that the sources of funds are either profits from other investments or income gained from their ownership of specific businesses. The statements are each certified by those accounting practices.
5.	Verify the information gathered, including using the Amended Identity Verification Code of Practice for the identity of individuals[99] (as risk is not deemed to be high)	You use the Companies Register to confirm that Mr Poole is the director of the nail salon business and you see that the investors' names match the list of shareholders on the Companies Register. The Companies Register also provides you with reliable information about the business number, the physical address of each salon, and the physical address of the head office where Mr Poole manages the salons. At your request, Mr Poole provides you with copies of each investor's passport and his own passport all of which have been certified by a trusted referee. You keep these as a record. You do internet searches on Mr Poole and all of the named investors to see if there is any information that would raise the ML/TF risk – such as whether any are politically exposed persons or are known associates of criminals. You find no such information. Instead you find information which confirms that the investors are involved in a range of legitimate business activities in the Auckland region such as property development, and other commercial investments in hospitality and retail businesses.

99 *Amended Identity Verification Code of Practice 2013*: http://bit.ly/2k13AxJ

6. If the identity information and verification requirements are satisfied, then you can proceed with the customer's instructions	You set up the necessary arrangements to liquidate the nail salon business

In this fictional example, the liquidator looks through the corporate entity to understand the beneficial ownership of the payments. If there were any changes to the range of facts in the fictional scenario above, the level of CDD required may have been different. For example, if the company had become insolvent, there would be a lower risk of ML/TF. In that case, there is less risk of abuse of the corporate structure for the personal gain of the beneficial owners.

Example in practice (high risk): Accounting services for a tech start-up company

Customer:	Mr Michele Soto, who is launching a start-up company
Captured activity:	Forming a company and providing a registered address – you are asked to form a company for a customer to develop a smartphone application, and you are asked to provide a registered address for that company
Level of CDD required:	Enhanced CDD
Steps to complete enhanced CDD	**How this applies to the example**
1. Identify which criteria your customer meets to decide the level of CDD you must do	Mr Soto's proposed business would be part funded by an investor, his uncle, who lives in a country that is associated with corruption, so you decide to conduct enhanced CDD.
2. Obtain information about the nature and purpose of the proposed business relationship	Mr Soto explains that the purpose of his start-up business is to generate income from the smartphone application. Users will make subscription payments via an online platform for using the application. Mr Soto explains that he would like your advice on how best to set up this company and your assistance to form it. He explains that he also requires you to offer a registered address for the company as he frequently moves homes. Mr Soto explains that 50% of the seed funding is coming from his parents, with a further 50% from his uncle who lives overseas.

3.	Determine the initial level of ML/TF risk	You ask Mr Soto about his uncle. He states that his uncle has various investments in new and developing technology businesses and has offered to top up the seed funding. Mr Soto's reference to using the online payment platform raises your perception of risk as these platforms can enable anonymous payments. You decide that the level of ML/TF risk is such that enhanced CDD is required.
4.	Identify all relevant persons that need to be identified and gather information about the source of wealth/source of funds	You ask Mr Soto to provide you with identity information about himself (including proof of his address), his parents and his uncle and information about the sources of his seed funding.
5.	Verify the information gathered using a higher level of vigour than provided for by the Amended Identity Verification Code of Practice for the identity of individuals[100] (as risk is deemed to be high)	Mr Soto provides his original passport and you view and take a clear copy. You record the date you sighted the passport and made the copy. Mr Soto also provides you with bank statements that show his home address and show lump sum payments from two sources: his parents and his uncle. You can see from the bank statement that the uncle's contribution originated by wire transfer from the overseas country. However, this does not fully enable you to identify the actual source of the funds. Mr Soto's parents live locally and bring their driver licenses, birth certificates and a recent sale and purchase agreement that shows they have a profit from a property sale – some of which has been given to their son for the seed money. You also ask to see Mr Soto's birth certificate to confirm the relationship and ask whether the funds provided are a gift or a loan. Mr Soto's parents advise that they are a gift, in lieu of future inheritance, and that appropriate paperwork has been filed via their lawyer with the IRD to confirm this. They have this paperwork with them. You make copies of all these documents. You ask to see further documents relating to the source of the uncle's funds and verifiable evidence of his identity. You are provided with a copy of a five-year term deposit bank statement held at a bank in the overseas country, which has been certified by one of the bank's in-house lawyers. This shows that the term deposit concluded shortly before the date

100 *Amended Identity Verification Code of Practice 2013*: http://bit.ly/2k13AxJ

		on which Mr Soto received funds in New Zealand. There are certified copies of accompanying bank records showing the instruction to send the balance by wire transfer to Mr Soto in New Zealand. You are also provided with a copy of the uncle's New Zealand passport, which has been certified by a suitable professional in the overseas country. So that you can confirm that this person is genuinely Mr Soto's uncle, you also request a certified copy of his New Zealand birth certificate. You receive this, compare it against his parents' birth certificates to ensure there is a relationship, and file it.
6.	If the identity information and verification requirements are satisfied, then you can proceed with the customer's instructions	You decide that this customer and activity is not suspicious and does not require an SAR to be filed. You then set up the necessary arrangements to form the company for Mr Soto and you record the business number the company is issued.

If there were any number of changes to the range of facts in the fictional scenario above, the level of CDD required may have been different. For example, if you had been unable to identify the source of funds for the seed money and/or if the online payment platform proposed to be used by the smartphone application was known for anonymity, you may have established the risk to be so high as to not be able to be mitigated and you would have considered how to end your engagement with Mr Soto.

Identifying if a customer is a politically exposed person

As soon as possible after establishing a business relationship, or conducting an occasional transaction or activity, accountants are required to take reasonable steps to identify whether their customer (or any beneficial owner) is a politically exposed person (PEP).[101] The Act requires reporting entities to conduct enhanced CDD if they establish a business relationship with a customer or beneficial owner who is a PEP, or if a PEP seeks to conduct an occasional transaction or activity through the reporting entity.[102]

A PEP is defined in section 5(1) of the Act.[103] In summary, a PEP is a person, or an immediate family member or someone who has close business ties to that person, who holds or has held (in the preceding 12 months) a prominent public function in a *foreign* country. This may be because they are or were a head of state, senior politician, or an official with a public profile, such as a

101 Section 26(1), AML/CFT Act: http://bit.ly/2BKjPWO

102 Section 22(2), AML/CFT Act: http://bit.ly/2zYaTbY

103 See definition of "politically exposed person" in section 5(1), AML/CFT Act: http://bit.ly/2xHGfmy

Supreme Court Judge, or a highly ranked military official. It could also be because they had authority and influence in a state enterprise in any country. PEPs can be exposed to bribery or corruption or their respected status may be misused (knowingly, or unknowingly) to legitimise otherwise suspect transactions.

If you determine that your customer or a beneficial owner is a PEP, you will require senior management approval to continue the business relationship.[104] Also, you must obtain information about the source of wealth or funds and verify that information.[105] If you have undertaken an occasional transaction or activity for someone who you didn't realise is a PEP, as soon as you can after the transaction you also need to obtain and verify information about their source of wealth or funds.

The *Enhanced Customer Due Diligence Guideline* has more information about how to manage compliance where customers are identified as PEPs.[106]

Wire transfers

The supervisors have published guidance on compliance matters when participating in wire transfers.[107]

A "wire transfer" is a transaction carried out on behalf of a person through a reporting entity by electronic means with a view to making an amount of money available to a beneficiary at another reporting entity (the person on whose behalf the transaction is conducted and the beneficiary can be the same person).

An "international wire transfer" is a wire transfer where at least one of the ordering, intermediary or beneficiary institutions is in New Zealand, and at least one is outside New Zealand.

Section 27 of the Act places specific obligations on "ordering institutions" and "beneficiary institutions" when the wire transfer is equal to or above NZ$1,000. It is possible that an accountant could be either an ordering or a beneficiary institution, in which case they must complete identity and verification requirements in line with the AML/CFT Act.[108]

New or developing technologies, or products that might favour anonymity

People with criminal intentions value anonymity and will continually look for new ways to preserve it while conducting their activities. Section 30 of the

104 Section 26(2)(a), AML/CFT Act: http://bit.ly/2A8liTh

105 Section 26(2)(b), AML/CFT Act: http://bit.ly/2A8liTh

106 Enhanced Customer Due Diligence Guideline: http://bit.ly/2GrKaHV

107 Wire Transfers: http://bit.ly/2ERdQBp

108 Sections 27–28, AML/CFT Act: http://bit.ly/2hRYKyV

AML/CFT Act[109] requires that if a customer is seeking assistance for an activity that involves new or developing technologies, or products that might favour anonymity, you must:

- Complete standard CDD identity and verification requirements; and
- Take any additional measures needed to mitigate the risk of the new or developing technology or product being used to commit ML/TF. Depending on the technology and the product, and the ways in which they might favour anonymity, you will need to determine what additional measures are required[110]

Both steps must be done before you enter a business relationship or conduct an occasional transaction or activity for your customer.

How to use the Amended Identity Verification Code of Practice

Identity verification needs to be done by collecting and sighting documents, data, or information provided from a reliable and independent source. You are required to keep records of this information. The Amended Identity Verification Code of Practice provides suggested best practice for anyone conducting name and date of birth identity verification on customers (that are natural persons) who have been assessed to be low to medium risk.[111] The Amended Identity Verification Code of Practice should be read in tandem with the Explanatory Note.[112]

When you can rely on others for CDD

In some specific circumstances, reporting entities can rely on others to conduct CDD if the other party is either:

- A member of the same DBG[113]
- Another reporting entity in New Zealand or a person in another country that has sufficient AML/CFT systems and measures in place and who is regulated for AML/CFT purposes[114]

---

109 Section 30, AML/CFT Act: http://bit.ly/2gWmRLD

110 Section 22(5), AML/CFT Act: http://bit.ly/2zYaTbY

111 *Amended Identity Verification Code of Practice 2013*: http://bit.ly/2k13AxJ

112 *Identity Verification Code of Practice – Explanatory Note*: http://bit.ly/2k13AxJ

113 Section 32(1), AML/CFT Act: http://bit.ly/2hjDuF3

114 Section 33(1), AML/CFT Act (http://bit.ly/2nQNm8F), and see the supervisors' *Countries Assessment Guideline* (http://bit.ly/2Fc2upe) or the Basel Index (https://index.basel governance.org/ranking), which ranks countries by AML/CFT risk.

- An agent[115]; or
- An approved entity[116]

Relying on a member of your Designated Business Group

A member of a DBG (Member A) can rely on another member of that same DBG (Member B) to conduct CDD if the information is given before Member A has established a business relationship or conducts an occasional transaction or activity for the customer. Any verification information must be able to be given to Member A by Member B as soon as practicable but within five working days of the request. In this scenario, Member A (not Member B) is responsible for ensuring that it is complying with the AML/CFT requirements.

Relying on another reporting entity or a suitably regulated person overseas

A reporting entity can rely on another person for CDD so long as the person:

- Is either a reporting entity in New Zealand or is a person resident in a country which is regulated for AML/CFT purposes[117]; and
- Has a business relationship with the customer concerned; and
- Has conducted CDD to at least the standard required by the AML/CFT Act and:
  - Has provided the reporting entity the relevant identity information before it has established a business relationship or conducted an occasional transaction or activity; and
  - Can provide relevant verification information on request of the reporting entity as soon as practicable but within five working days; and
- Consents to conducting the CDD and providing all relevant CDD information to the reporting entity

In this scenario, and as above, the reporting entity requesting the CDD remains responsible for ensuring the CDD is conducted in accordance with the AML/CFT Act.

115 Section 34, AML/CFT Act: http://bit.ly/2HDbWTl

116 Please note that the option of relying on an approved entity provided by section 33(3A) in the AML/CFT Act has not yet been made operational and is not available for use by reporting entities.

117 Please note that neither law firms, conveyancing practices, nor accounting practices in Australia are specifically regulated for AML/CFT purposes.

Relying on an agent

A reporting entity may authorise a person to be its agent and rely on that agent to conduct CDD and obtain any information required for CDD records. "Agent" is not defined in the Act; instead, the ordinary principles of agency law will apply.

Relying on an approved entity

Section 33 of the Act enables a business to rely on an "approved entity". There are not as yet any prescribed approved entities.

When to conduct CDD

You must conduct CDD (ie, obtain the required identity information and verify that information) on your customer *before* a business relationship with the customer is entered into, or an occasional transaction or activity is conducted.

The only exception to this timeframe, which would allow verification to be completed after the business relationship has been established, will be where all the following criteria apply:

- It is essential not to interrupt normal business practice; and
- ML/TF risks are effectively managed through appropriate risk management procedures; and
- Identity verification is completed as soon as practicable once the business relationship has been established[118]

Fast-paced scenarios may be common for some accountants; however, instances of delaying the verification of customer identity information should be rare. The reasons for delaying verification should be fact-based, justifiable and recorded.

Ongoing CDD and account monitoring

Under section 31 of the AML/CFT Act, when you are in a business relationship with a customer, you are required to conduct ongoing CDD and account monitoring. This means that you are required to regularly review any information about their account activity and transactions *you hold* about your customer to ensure it remains current. The purpose of this is to ensure that the nature and purpose of the business relationship and any activities or transactions relating to that business relationship are consistent with your knowledge of the customer and the customer's risk profile. This regular review will also help you to identify any grounds for reporting a suspicious activity.

Reporting entities are required to develop a process for ongoing CDD and account monitoring for their customers according to the level of risk each customer presents. You should think about the level of CDD that was

118 Section 16(3), AML/CFT Act: http://bit.ly/2iTi1Da

previously undertaken, and consider the level of risk involved with that customer or their activities and transactions. This means higher-risk customers need to have more frequent and thorough account monitoring than customers deemed to be low or medium risk. The account monitoring conducted should assist you to identify any activity or transaction behaviour that is not consistent with the expected activity of the customer, their risk profile and the CDD you have previously conducted.

Compliance obligations when conducting international transactions

An area of general business practice that requires specific mention in your AML/CFT programme is your method of ensuring compliance when you are engaged by other professionals on behalf of their customers, when conducting or participating in international transactions with multiple parties, or when you are otherwise engaging with parties in other countries. This is likely to be different for each firm.

Accountants are often engaged by other professionals, such as lawyers, to conduct accounting work that is required by *the other professional's* customer. In these instances it may be difficult to figure out who is *your* customer – the lawyer or their customer? Your answer to this question will be based on the particular circumstances.

Often, the lawyer's customer will be your customer, with the lawyer being a person acting on their behalf in their engagement with you. Alternatively, the lawyer's customer could be a party to an activity or transaction that is being conducted by you for your customer, the lawyer. In practice, this means that you will often need to conduct CDD on both the lawyer and their customer, unless you already hold sufficient CDD information on them and there has been no material change in your business relationship with them. You will then need to consider the level of CDD required depending on the particular circumstances. In some cases, a lawyer or other professional instructing you on behalf of their customer will themselves be a reporting entity (or equivalent in an overseas jurisdiction). For example, the law firm in New Zealand instructing you on behalf of their customer is captured as a reporting entity under the Act. This means that they must do their own CDD on their customer at the time their business relationship started. When you are subsequently engaged by this law firm to conduct captured activities for their customer, you can choose to rely on the CDD that they have conducted on their customer so long as the criteria set out in section 33(2) are met (including obtaining permission and relevant identity and verification information from the law firm). **If you rely on a third party to conduct CDD, you remain responsible for ensuring that the required CDD is conducted in accordance with the AML/CFT Act.**

Conducting CDD in a multi-party international transaction

The above requirements apply whether you are being engaged by another professional in New Zealand or from another country. DIA recognises that this may be challenging when dealing with professionals who operate in countries where a high standard of AML/ CFT regulation is not the norm.Also, there may be instances where there are multiple beneficiaries in multiple countries on whom you require CDD information to allow you to proceed. In such instances you have two options:

1. consider whether it will be possible to obtain the identity and verification information you need via other professionals involved, remembering you remain accountable for completing CDD in accordance with the AML/ CFT Act; or
2. conclude your engagement without conducting activities that are captured by the AML/CFT Act. For more information about concluding engagements when CDD cannot be conducted, please see further on in this section.

Dealing with other countries

The supervisors have published the *Countries Assessment Guideline* to help you determine whether a country you are dealing with has effective AML/CFT systems and measures.[119]

There is no definitive list of countries that are deemed not to have sufficient AML/CFT systems and measures, so reporting entities should consider a range of factors when determining the level of risk associated with engaging in a transaction with a country.

For example, is the country:

- Subject to international sanctions, embargos or other measures?
- Identified by the FATF as lacking adequate AML/CFT systems and measures?[120]
- Recognised as having supporters of terrorism, or financing terrorism?
- Considered to have problems with corruption (eg, does it have a low ranking on the Transparency International Corruption Perceptions Index[121])?
- Known as a tax haven[122]?

119 *Countries Assessment Guideline*: http://bit.ly/2Fc2upe

120 High-risk and other monitored jurisdictions: http://bit.ly/1lTBG24

121 The Transparency International Corruption Perceptions Index for 2016 is available at: http://bit.ly/2j3Y63K The Basel Index, which ranks countries by AML/CFT risk, may also be useful: http://bit.ly/2djRNDR

122 The Council of the European Union has developed a list of non-cooperative jurisdictions for tax purposes: http://bit.ly/2Flrv4A

- Associated with production and/or transnational shipment of illicit drugs?

You must develop an understanding of the ML/TF risks associated with any countries that you deal with.[123]

What to do if you cannot complete CDD

If you are not able to complete CDD for a customer, you must neither carry out an occasional transaction or activity for them nor establish a business relationship with them.[124] If you already have a business relationship with the customer, and that business relationship relates solely to captured activities, this must be terminated (you are free to continue providing non-captured services to the customer). This applies to all circumstances where a customer fails or refuses to provide information, data or documents that you have requested, including in relation to enhanced CDD. This also applies if the information, data or documents that the customer provides are inadequate.

If you are declining to enter into a business relationship or refusing an occasional transaction or activity, you are required to consider whether you need to file an SAR with the FIU.

6. Do you know the red flags?

This section draws on available international information about the vulnerabilities of the accounting profession to misuse for ML/TF purposes by their customers. This information should assist your general AML/CFT awareness and your consideration of the risks your business may face from ML/TF activity.

Red flags identified by the Financial Action Task Force

The Financial Action Task Force (FATF) is an intergovernmental body established in 1989 to set global standards and promote effective implementation of legal, regulatory and operational measures for combating money laundering, terrorist financing and other related threats to the integrity of the international financial system.

The FATF provides a range of information and advice for the industries and professions that are affected by money laundering and terrorism financing. The FATF published *Guidance on the Risk-Based Approach to Combating Money Laundering and Terrorism Financing: High Level Principles and Procedures for Accountants*[125] in 2008 and *Money Laundering Using Trust and Company Service Providers* [126] in 2010. These documents aim to support the development of a

123 Section 58, AML/CFT Act: http://bit.ly/2ly11Dz

124 Section 37, AML/CFT Act: http://bit.ly/2hydAdM

125 *Guidance on the Risk-Based Approach to Combating Money Laundering and Terrorism Financing: High Level Principles and Procedures for Accountants*: http://bit.ly/29OakqM

126 *Money Laundering Using Trust and Company Service Providers*: http://bit.ly/2FJRwHU

common understanding of what a risk-based approach involves; outline the high level principles in applying this approach, and suggest some best practice in designing and implementing a risk-based approach.

The document *Guidance on the Risk-Based Approach to Combating Money Laundering and Terrorism Financing: High Level Principles and Procedures for Accountants* highlights the activities conducted by the accounting profession that are vulnerable to potential misuse by those who wish to launder the proceeds of crime or fund terrorist activities. These vulnerable activities can be summarised as follows:

- Management of client money, securities and other assets
- Management of bank, savings or securities accounts
- Creation, operation or management of legal persons or arrangements, and buying and selling of business entities
- Organisation of contributions for the creation, operation and management of companies
- Buying and selling of real estate

These activities correspond closely with the captured activities in the AML/CFT Act that are outlined in section 3 of this guideline. Section 3 also identifies the ML/TF risks with each of the captured activities.

This section provides more detail on the "red flags" to be on the lookout for when you are conducting these activities for your customers. The red flags described below have been taken from a range of open source publications (which are noted in the References section) and professional judgements of subject matter experts. They can be categorised in the following manner:

- Customer risk
- Product, service or delivery method risk
- Country/Geographic risk
- Other risk factors

Customer risk

There are a range of risks that relate to the nature of your customer that you should consider. When thinking about the risks posed by your customers, have regard to whether:

- The business relationship is conducted in a unusual circumstances
- The customer is a resident in a geographical area that is considered to be high risk (see also the "Country/Geographic risk" section below)
- The customer is a legal person or arrangement that is a vehicle for holding personal assets
- The customer is a company that has nominee shareholders or shares in bearer form

- The customer is a business that is cash-intensive
- The corporate structure of the customer is unusual or excessively complex given the nature of the company's business
- You do not have a face-to-face introduction to your customer
- There is a subsequent lack of contact, where contact would be expected normally
- Beneficial ownership of the customer is unclear
- There are inexplicable changes in the ownership of your customer
- The position of intermediaries is unclear
- The activities of the company are unclear
- The legal structure of the customer is frequently altered, including name changes and transfers of ownership, and location of headquarters
- The people who manage the customer appear to be acting according to the instructions of unknown or inappropriate persons
- The reason for the customer using your firm is unclear given the firm's size, location or specialisation
- The customer is reluctant to provide all the relevant information, or you have a reasonable doubt that the information provided is correct or sufficient
- The customer is a politically exposed person, a relative or close associate of a politically exposed person, a head of an international organisation, or a high net worth individual
- The customer works in an industry or occupation that has a high risk of ML/TF

Product, service or delivery method risk

Particular products or services or transaction delivery methods can be vulnerable to misuse by those wishing to launder money or finance terrorism. When considering the risks associated with a product or service or transaction delivery method, have regard to whether:

- The product involves private banking
- The product, service or transaction delivery channel might favour anonymity
- The situation prevents face-to-face business relationships or transactions without certain safeguards, such as electronic signatures
- Payments will be received from unknown or un-associated third parties
- New products and new business practices are involved, including new delivery mechanisms and the use of new or developing technologies for both new or pre-existing products

- The service involves the provision of nominee directors, nominee shareholders, or shadow directors, or the formation of companies in third countries
- The service is open to misuse of pooled client (or trust) accounts or provides safe custody of customer money or assets
- The service requested is for introductions to other financial institutions, where this is not otherwise necessary or ordinary
- The service requested is for advice on setting up legal arrangements that may be used to obscure ownership or real economic purpose (including setting up trusts, companies, or change of name/ corporate seat or other complex group structures)

Country/Geographic risk

Moving money from country to country is a key typology for obscuring the criminal origins of funds and/or the true intended destination for funds. There are particular countries that represent higher ML/TF risks and these will change over time in the dynamic AML/CFT environment. When considering the risks associated with dealing with customers or transactions that relate to other countries or geographic regions, have regard to whether the countries are:

- Identified by credible sources as not having effective systems to counter money laundering and terrorist financing
- Identified by credible sources as having significant levels of corruption or other criminal activity, such as terrorism, money laundering, and the production and supply of illicit drugs
- Subject to sanctions, embargos or similar measures issued by, for example, the United Nations or the European Union
- Identified by credible sources to have provided funding or support for terrorism

There are a wide variety of credible sources and it is up to your judgement what information you access and how you perceive the credibility of that information. Generally, sources with expertise in AML/ CFT are deemed to be credible, such as the FATF, the Asia/Pacific Group (the FATF-style regional body New Zealand is a member of), and other international organisations such as the United Nations, International Monetary Fund, and the Financial Intelligence Units of countries with strong AML/CFT systems in place.

Other risk factors

These are some factors to consider that can either increase or decrease your perception of risk:

- Involvement of financial institutions or other DNFBPs
- Unexplained urgency of assistance required

- Sophistication of the customer, including the complexity of the control environment (ie, the overall attitude, awareness and actions of directors and management regarding the internal control system and its importance to the entity)
- Sophistication of transaction/scheme
- Country location of accountant
- Working environment/structure of the accountant (eg, sole practitioner or large firm)
- Role or oversight of another regulator
- The regularity or duration of a business relationship (long-standing relationships involving frequent customer contact throughout the relationship present less risk)
- The purpose of the business relationship and the need for an accountant to provide services
- The reputation of customers in the local community
- Whether private companies are transparent and well known in the public domain
- The familiarity of the accountant with a country, including knowledge of local laws and regulations as well as the structure and extent of regulatory oversight

These factors may indicate a higher ML/TF risk:

- Customer instructions or access to funds is out of sync with their business or personal profile
- Your customer conducts individual or classes of transactions that are outside their business profile and are unexpected activities in terms of what you know about your customer
- Your customer's employee numbers or structure is out of keeping with the size and nature of the business (eg, the turnover of a company is unreasonably high considering the number of employees and assets used)
- Sudden activity from a previously dormant customer
- Your customer starts or develops an enterprise with an unexpected profile or early results (ie, unexpected profits)
- Indicators that your customer does not wish to obtain the necessary government approvals or licences
- Your customer offers to pay extraordinary fees for services that would not ordinarily warrant such a premium

- Payments received from un-associated or unknown third parties and payments for fees in cash where this would not be a typical method of payment

The nature of the business activities of your customer may be a risk factor. You should seek to understand whether:

- Your customer is an entity with a high level of transactions in cash or readily transferable assets, among which illegitimate funds could be obscured
- There are any politically exposed persons engaged in or with your customer
- Your customer invests in real estate at higher or lower prices than expected by the market
- Your customer conducts unusual financial transactions with unknown source(s)
- Your customer has multijurisdictional operations that do not have adequate centralised corporate oversight
- Your customer is incorporated in countries that permit bearer shares

If you have a customer who engages in trade or the provision of goods and services, you should be on the lookout for whether there are instances where there is:

- Over- and/or under-invoicing of goods/services
- Multiple invoicing of the same goods/services
- Falsely described goods/services, such as over- or under-shipments
- Multiple trading of goods/services

There are some red flags you should be looking for when engaging with other professionals in your sector. For example, you may need to be wary of instances where:

- Accounts and/or facilities are opened and/or operated by company formation agents
- Gatekeepers (eg, lawyers, other accountants) appear to have full control
- Known or suspected corrupt professionals are offering services to criminal entities
- Accounts are operated by someone other than the account holder

How to keep up-to-date with changing methods of ML/TF

People with criminal intentions will seek to stay ahead of authorities and the professionals whose services they wish to misuse. Over time new methods of ML/TF will develop and emerge. The FIU and DIA actively maintain a watch for these new methods and communicate them via the FIU's Quarterly

Typology Reports[127] and DIA's newsletters.[128] Reporting entities, their compliance officers in particular, are encouraged to look at these resources as well as media reports and information from the FATF and other jurisdictions to keep up-to-date with developments in ML/TF methods.

7. Do you know where to get support?

- Reporting entities can access compliance support from a range of sources:
- Your AML/CFT programme and compliance officer
- DIA as the supervisor
- Your professional body if you have membership with one
- Independent professional advice
- Open source information from relevant international bodies concerned with AML/CFT

Your AML/CFT programme and compliance officer

Where employees in your business have compliance questions, their first port of call should be your AML/ CFT programme. The programme documentation should be able to provide answers to basic questions that are likely to arise in your specific business context. As questions arise, it is likely that the AML/ CFT programme will need to be updated to include provisions for resolving unanticipated issues and frequently asked questions.

Specific questions should be answered by your compliance officer. Where this approach does not resolve the question at hand, it is important to consider what would be the appropriate next step – seeking support from the relevant professional body, from your supervisor, or from an independent lawyer or other suitable professional.

Support from your supervisor

We recognise that this is a new compliance system to adjust to, and so we aim to provide proactive support to reporting entities. Examples of the support we provide range from general information and awareness promotion, all the way to specific support where a reporting entity is experiencing difficulty but has a genuine intention to comply. The DIA website provides a wide range of information about how to comply with the AML/CFT Act for reporting entities.[129] The AML/CFT Act allows supervisors to create codes of practice. A code of practice is a statement of practice that helps reporting entities to comply with the AML/CFT Act. So far, one code of practice has been

127 FIU assessments and reports: http://bit.ly/2xGSiAx

128 AML/CFT news: http://bit.ly/2z7lAd4

129 *Anti-money laundering and countering financing of terrorism*: http://bit.ly/2zbaCoS

developed: the Identity Verification Code of Practice.[130] This was developed in 2011 and amended in 2013. It should be read in tandem with the Explanatory Note.[131] There are no current plans to develop more codes of practice, but the supervisors are open to feedback from reporting entities on whether more would be helpful.

Support from your professional bodies

Accountants are encouraged to keep abreast of the information and education on offer from the professional bodies they have a membership with. The following professional bodies offer support to accountants:

- Chartered Accountants Australia and New Zealand raises awareness via articles and by hosting webinars on AML/CFT topics.
- The Accountants and Tax Agents Institute of New Zealand ensures that AML/CFT topics are well covered in conferences to inform their members.
- The New Zealand Bookkeepers Association Incorporated ensures that AML/CFT topics are covered via membership meetings, conferences, newsletters and social media to keep its members well informed.

When to seek independent advice

There will be occasions where accountants need to seek independent advice to ensure they remain compliant with the AML/CFT Act. Supervisors cannot provide legal advice to reporting entities. When you have specific compliance questions about unique circumstances that the supervisor or your professional body cannot reasonably answer, you may need to seek independent legal advice or advice from an otherwise suitable professional.

Other publicly available information

The Phase 2 Sector Risk Assessment (Phase 2 SRA) is important reading for accountants. This resource gives reporting entities the background understanding of the ways ML/TF poses risk to accountants. The Prompts and Notes guideline outlines the factors to be considered in a risk assessment along with some prompts and questions to think about when completing a risk assessment and developing your AML/CFT programme. The Phase 2 SRA and the Prompts and Notes guideline are available on the DIA website.[132] The FATF has a range of information on its website, both specific to

130 *Amended Identity Verification Code of Practice 2013*: http://bit.ly/2k13AxJ

131 *Identity Verification Code of Practice – Explanatory Note*: http://bit.ly/2k13AxJ

132 *Phase 2 AML/CFT Sector Risk Assessment* (http://bit.ly/2o155u8) and *AML/CFT Risk Assessment and Programme: Prompts and Notes for DIA Reporting Entities* (http://bit.ly/2EBUMXy).

accounting and other gatekeeper professions[133] and to the New Zealand context.[134]

Support that may emerge in the future

As the AML/CFT system becomes established practice among accountants it is likely that relevant training establishments will begin to incorporate AML/CFT into curricula. Professional bodies will be a good source of information when new educational supports are in development. Supervisors are responsible for updating and creating new guidance in line with sector needs. You will be advised when new guides are made available.

Appendix A:Case studies

The case studies come from open source publications – references are provided in the endnotes. The purpose of including these case studies is to raise awareness of how accountants have knowingly, or unknowingly, been involved with ML/TF.

Case study 1: Accountant received funds on behalf of criminal[135]

A methamphetamine manufacturer and dealer in the Waikato region used an accountant to receive cash from his drug dealing and convert it into various purchases of farm land over a number of years. He used two of his farm employees to collect and take cash from drug sales to the accountant's office. The accountant had 12 accounts held at different banks in which he would bank the cash. The accounts were held for his accounting practice, a gift shop he and his wife owned, his personal accounts and a company account he was nominee director and shareholder of on behalf of the methamphetamine manufacturer.

The accountant went to different branches across the Waikato region and banked the cash into the various accounts. Some excuses he gave about the source of the cash were "it was cash takings from a client who owned a bar" or "it was his cash takings from a stall he operated at a market". The deposited cash would then be electronically transferred to his accounting practice to be held on behalf of the methamphetamine manufacturer. With his accumulated wealth, the methamphetamine manufacturer purchased farm land in the name of his family trust. The trustee of his trust was a corporate trustee company that the accountant was the director and shareholder of. This trust arrangement enabled the methamphetamine manufacturer to hide the fact he owned the farm land. It was estimated that, over ten years, he had accumulated NZ$4.8 million from his drug offending. He was sentenced to 12

133 FATF – All publications: http://bit.ly/2Ff66He

134 FATF evaluations of New Zealand: http://bit.ly/2nY08F1

135 Financial Intelligence Unit, (May 2014), *Quarterly Typology Report Third Quarter (Q3) 2013/2014*, FIU, Wellington http://bit.ly/2zijNkM

years prison and his farm land (valued at approximately NZ$5million) was forfeited to the Crown. Whilst it was clear the accountant had engaged in money laundering, he was used as a witness against the methamphetamine manufacturer in exchange for immunity from prosecution.

Case study 2: Using an accountant as an intermediary in the legal structure of a business[136]

In Operation Ark, the New Zealand Police investigated a case where drug offenders had engaged an accountant to set up a complex structure of legal entities, including a trust. This case demonstrates many of the principal ways trusts are used to launder proceeds – in particular, layering entities to hide the beneficial control of companies controlling assets; use of a professional service provider to access complex structures and act as an intermediary; and use of a trust to hide criminal involvement in transactions.

The drug offender used the trust to buy shares in a fitness magazine business and a company with the proceeds of drug offending. Vehicles owned by the drug offender were then registered in the name of the company, ostensibly distancing the offender from ownership of the vehicles. The offender also used his accountant as an intermediary and additional layer in the legal structure of his finances. Ultimately, as was the case in his layering of entities to hide ownership of the magazine and vehicles, the offender used the accountant and the trust to hide his own beneficial ownership of property. For example, the offender's house was put in the name of a company whose nominee shareholder was the accountant's trust company. The accountant's trust company was in turn holding the shares on behalf of the offender's trust.

Case study 3: Accountant facilitated a round-robin tax evasion scheme[137]

"Round robin" tax evasion schemes essentially aim to make funds movements appear as payments to other parties while, in reality, the funds ultimately return to the original beneficiary. In this case enquiries identified that the principal promoter and operator of a tax evasion scheme was a senior partner of an accounting firm based in Vanuatu. Analysis of Australian Transaction Reports and Analysis Centre (AUSTRAC) information uncovered the round robin tax evasion scheme, which involved the transfer of funds between Australia-based individuals and bank accounts of companies in other countries to evade tax in Australia.

---

136 Financial Intelligence Unit, (October 2014), *Quarterly Typology Report First Quarter (Q1) 2014/2015*, FIU, Wellington (available to reporting entities via goAML portal https://fiu.police.govt.nz).

137 Financial Intelligence Unit, (May 2014), *Quarterly Typology Report Third Quarter (Q3) 2013/2014*, FIU, Wellington (available to reporting entities via goAML portal https://fiu.police.govt.nz)

The method used to facilitate tax evasion was:

1. Suspects in Australia transferred funds from their companies' accounts to the bank accounts of companies in New Zealand. The New Zealand companies and the bank accounts were controlled by the Vanuatu-based accountant, who was a signatory to the bank accounts.

2. The payments were falsely described in the suspects' companies' records as expenses in the form of "management and consultancy fees". False invoices were created for the fictitious expenses. No evidence was available to show that any consulting work had been carried out. The invoice amounts matched the amounts paid to the bank accounts in New Zealand.

3. The false expense payments were claimed as deductible expenses in the tax returns of the Australian companies, fraudulently reducing the companies' taxable income and the amount of tax they were assessed as liable to pay.

4. The accountant then transferred the funds under the guise of international "loans" through a series of round robin international transactions, through accounts held in the name of companies owned and operated by the accountant.

5. The accountant transferred the funds into the personal bank accounts of the suspects in Australia. The funds were transferred via an overseas company controlled by the accountant, separate to the companies in New Zealand that received the funds originally.

6. In order to disguise the funds as loans, false documents were created purporting to be international loan agreements with a foreign lender. Loans are not assessable income and are tax-free.

7. The funds, disguised as international loans, were not disclosed in the suspects' personal tax returns. The suspects were thus assessed as liable for less tax than they should have been, thereby avoiding income tax obligations.

8. Effectively, the "loans" paid to the suspects were funds from their respective companies but were disguised by the scheme, allowing them to evade approximately AU$750,000 in company and personal tax.

Both suspects in Australia were ultimately convicted of tax evasion and fraud offences and sentenced to three years imprisonment. The suspects also became liable to pay penalties and interest to the Australian Taxation Office of more than AU$1 million and AU$900,000 respectively. The accountant was convicted of conspiring to defraud the Commonwealth and was sentenced to 8 years and 11 months imprisonment.

Case Study 4: Assets forfeited from dishonest accountant in New Zealand[138]

In March 2014, assets valued at an estimated NZ$1.4 million were forfeited from an accountant who used funds stolen from the trust accounts of his clients to fund a lavish lifestyle. For years the Hamilton-based accountant siphoned off funds and used them to build a mansion complete with hydro-slide and to fund purchases such as vehicles, company shares, boats, and a holiday home in Fiji. His actions were concealed by a complex set of entities that were used to hide his fraud, often under the guise of legitimate transactions. The accountant was caught when Inland Revenue noted discrepancies between his assets and his declared income. He has been sentenced to more than five years imprisonment and his status as a Chartered Accountant has been suspended by the Institute of Chartered Accountants.

Case Study 5: Using shell businesses as a front for drug supply network[139]

In 2013 the High Court restrained around NZ$1.8 million worth of assets related to a drug supply network connected to a roading contractor. The Crown alleges that the principal offender and a number of associates were involved in a national drug supply network that used the roading contractor's roading and forestry businesses as a front to facilitate offending. The businesses provided ideal fronts for drug distribution and/or manufacture, providing the principal offender with a reason for local and domestic travel required for drug related transactions.

The offenders also appear to have used these companies to commingle the proceeds of the offending. Such businesses provide an opportunity to explain the illicit earnings from drug supply. The principal offender ensured that his businesses maintained good records of apparent earnings by using professional accountants. In addition to facilitation of predicate offending, the nationally dispersed business interests also would have provided an opportunity to select professional service providers which may have allowed the offenders to select professionals who would be unable to detect illicit activity. These types of arrangements could also allow criminals to seek remote professional services and/or to change professional service providers so as to prevent professionals gaining a full appreciation of any unusual business activity.

138 Financial Intelligence Unit, (May 2014), *Quarterly Typology Report Third Quarter (Q3) 2013/2014*, FIU, Wellington (available to reporting entities via goAML portal https://fiu.police.govt.nz).

139 Financial Intelligence Unit, (July 2014), *Quarterly Typology Report Fourth Quarter (Q4) 2013/2014*, FIU, Wellington (available to reporting entities via goAML portal https://fiu.police.govt.nz). (The text in the case study uses some updated information.)

In this case, maintaining professionally facilitated business records and declaring earnings for tax helped the offenders to maintain an air of legitimacy.

Using such businesses as fronts for criminal activity may also make law enforcement investigation to establish illicit earnings more complex. However, despite the extensive and well documented earnings, corresponding legitimate business had not been established, giving a strong indication that the illegitimate earnings from drug supply were commingled with whatever legitimate earnings the businesses made. It was concluded that in this case, the offenders' accountants were unwittingly involved in commingling the proceeds of the drug supply business with the legitimate business activity earnings.

Case study 6: Transnational drug dealing[140]

Operation Major involved Asian organised crime using New Zealand-registered companies to act as a cover for the facilitation of drug smuggling into New Zealand. Multiple companies and bank accounts were established for the sole purpose of being able to import legitimate goods that concealed illicit drugs within them (crystal methamphetamine and precursor chemicals). The companies purported to be in the business of international trading and supply of materials relating to polymer technologies. In May 2006, a New Zealand Customs drug seizure found 95kg of crystal methamphetamine concealed in the bottom of 95 paint tins. A few days later a second drug seizure found 150kg of pseudo ephedrine tablets in amongst a shipment of bags of block plaster. Both drug seizures had a combined potential total street value of NZ$135 million. This was the largest and most significant illicit synthetic drug seizure in New Zealand's history. The shell companies involved were registered by accountants and the individuals involved in the drug importations.

References

Consultative Committee of Accountancy Bodies (CCAB), (Published in draft in August 2017, final version expected in mid-2018), *Anti-Money Laundering Guidance for the Accountancy Sector*, CCAB, United Kingdom. https://www.ccab.org.uk/documents/TTCCABGuidance2017regsAugdraftforpublication.pdf

Courts of New Zealand, (28 September 2017), *Department of Internal Affairs v Ping An Finance (Group) New Zealand Company Limited* [2017] NZHC 2363. https://forms.justice.govt.nz/search/Documents/pdf/jdo/15/alfresco/service/api/node/content/workspace/SpacesStore/916f5146-d0bb-4c1f-9fda-979cd3d122f0/916f5146-d0bb-4c1f-9fda-979cd3d122f0.pdf

140 Financial Intelligence Unit, (January 2015), *Quarterly Typology Report Second Quarter (Q2) 2014/2015*, FIU, Wellington (available to reporting entities via goAML portal https://fiu.police.govt.nz).

Department of Internal Affairs, Reserve Bank of New Zealand, Financial Markets Authority, (July 2011), *Supervisory Framework*, DIA, RBNZ & FMA, Wellington. https://www.dia.govt.nz/Pubforms.nsf/URL/Supervisory-Framework-FINAL-updated-28-July-2011.pdf/$file/Supervisory-Framework-FINAL-updated-28-July-2011.pdf

Financial Intelligence Unit, (May 2014), *Quarterly Typology Report Third Quarter (Q3) 2013/2014*, FIU, Wellington. (available to reporting entities via goAML portal https://fiu.police.govt.nz).

Financial Intelligence Unit, (July 2014), *Quarterly Typology Report Fourth Quarter (Q4) 2013/2014*, FIU, Wellington. (available to reporting entities via goAML portal https://fiu.police.govt.nz)

Financial Intelligence Unit, (October 2014), *Quarterly Typology Report First Quarter (Q1) 2014/2015*, FIU, Wellington. (available to reporting entities via goAML portal https://fiu.police.govt.nz).

Financial Intelligence Unit, (January 2015), *Quarterly Typology Report Second Quarter (Q2) 2014/2015*, FIU, Wellington. (available to reporting entities via goAML portal https://fiu.police.govt.nz).

Financial Action Task Force, (16 October 2009), *Mutual Evaluation Report: New Zealand*, FATF, Paris. http://www.fatf-gafi.org/countries/n-r/newzealand/documents/mutualevaluationofnewzealand.html Financial Action Task Force, (17 June 2008), *Guidance on the Risk-Based Approach to Combatting Money Laundering and Terrorism Financing: High Level Principles and Procedures for Accountants*, FATF, Paris. http://www.fatf-gafi.org/publications/fatfrecommendations/documents/fatfguidanceontherisk-basedapproachforaccountants.html

Institute of Singapore Chartered Accountants, (November 2014), *Anti-Money Laundering and Countering the Financing of Terrorism – Requirements and Guidelines for Professional Accountants in Singapore*, Singapore. https://isca.org.sg/ethics/anti-money-laundering-and-countering-the-financing-of-terrorism/

Appendix 11
Anti-Money Laundering and Countering Financing of Terrorism Act 2009

[Legislation details]

[Reprint changes]

[**CCH note:** The official reprint of this Act includes editorial changes as set out in the Legislation Act 2012. Those changes may affect the format and style of the wording but do not affect the meaning of the legislation as originally enacted. Any differences between legislation reproduced in CCH publications and the official reprint are likely to be of a minor nature and the result of different drafting styles.]

TABLE OF SECTIONS

Section	
48	Disclosure of personal information relating to employees or senior managers
	Subpart 2A — Prescribed transaction reports
48A	Reporting entities to report certain prescribed transactions
48B	Prescribed transaction reports
48C	Sections 43 to 48 apply to prescribed transactions
	Subpart 3 — Record keeping
49	Obligation to keep transaction records
49A	Obligation to keep reports of suspicious activities
50	Obligation to keep identity and verification records
51	Obligation to keep other records
52	How records to be kept
53	When records need not be kept
54	Destruction of records
55	Other laws not affected
	Subpart 4 — Compliance with AML/CFT requirements
56	Reporting entity must have AML/CFT programme and AML/CFT compliance officer
57	Minimum requirements for AML/CFT programmes
58	Risk assessment
59	Review and audit of risk assessment and AML/CFT programmes
59A	Audit of compliance with AML/CFT obligations
59B	Who carries out audit
60	Annual AML/CFT report
61	Reporting entities to ensure that branches and subsidiaries comply with AML/CFT requirements
	Subpart 5 — Codes of practice
62	Interpretation
63	AML/CFT supervisors to prepare codes of practice for relevant sectors
64	Procedure for approval and publication of codes of practice
65	Amendment and revocation of codes of practice
66	Proof of codes of practice
67	Legal effect of codes of practice
	Subpart 6 — Cross-border transportation of cash
68	Reports about movement of cash into or out of New Zealand
69	Reports about receipt of cash from outside New Zealand
70	Reporting requirements
71	Information to be forwarded to Commissioner

ANTI-MONEY LAUNDERING AND COUNTERING FINANCING OF TERRORISM ACT 2009

2009, No 35

[**CCH note:** No 69 of 2013 includes the following transitional provision, effective on a date to be appointed by Governor-General by Order in Council, or 1 April 2017:

"**52 Transitional provision for offences and contravention under repealed, revoked, or amended enactments**

52(1) This section applies to an offence committed under, or a contravention of, any of the enactments repealed or revoked by section 4 or 5 of the Financial Markets (Repeals and Amendments) Act 2013, or amended by the Financial Markets (Repeals and Amendments) Act 2013, before the commencement of the provision that repealed, revoked, or amended that enactment.

52(2) The enactments repealed or revoked by section 4 or 5 of the Financial Markets (Repeals and Amendments) Act 2013, or amended by the Financial Markets (Repeals and Amendments) Act 2013, continue to have effect as if they had not been repealed, revoked, or amended for the purpose of—

(a) investigating an offence or a contravention to which this section applies:

(b) commencing or completing proceedings for an offence or a contravention to which this section applies:

(c) imposing a penalty or other remedy, or making an order, in relation to an offence or a contravention to which this section applies."]

[**CCH note:** No 24 of 2012 provides:

"**351 TRANSITIONAL PROVISION RELATING TO PROVISIONS BROUGHT INTO FORCE UNDER SECTION 2**

351(1) Despite any amendment in Part 5 of this Act,—

(a) where an application has been made under an authorising Act before the relevant commencement, and the application is not finally determined before that date, the provisions of that Act continue to apply to the application and to any matter or obligation relating to the application in all respects as if this Act (other than this section and any provisions in force immediately before the relevant commencement) had not been enacted; and

(b) those provisions continue to apply to a continuing warrant and to any matter relating to the warrant in all respects as if this Act (other than this section and any provisions in force immediately before the relevant commencement) had not been enacted; and

(c) those provisions continue to apply to any other proceeding, matter, or thing commenced and not completed before the relevant commencement as if this Act (other than this section and any provisions in force immediately before the relevant commencement) had not been enacted.

351(2) Subsection (1)(c) does not limit the provisions of the Interpretation Act 1999.

351(3) In this section,—

authorising Act means an Act amended by Part 5

continuing warrant means a warrant or other authority issued under an authorising Act—

(a) before the relevant commencement; or

(b) on or after that date on an application made before that date

relevant commencement , in relation to an authorising Act, means the commencement of a provision in Part 5 that amends an authorising Act."]

[*16 October 2009*]

The Parliament of New Zealand enacts as follows:

SECTION 1 TITLE

1 This Act is the Anti-Money Laundering and Countering Financing of Terrorism Act 2009.

SECTION 2 COMMENCEMENT

2(1) Parts 1 and 4 (except section 162) come into force on the day after the date that this Act receives the Royal assent.

2(2) Sections 68 to 71, 106 to 115, and 163 come into force 12 months after the date on which this Act receives the Royal assent.

2(3) Except as provided in subsection (5), the rest of this Act comes into force on a date to be appointed by the Governor-General by Order in Council.

2(4) One or more Orders in Council may be made appointing different dates for the commencement of different provisions.

2(5) However, section 162 may not be brought into force unless every provision of Part 2 has been brought into force.

[**CCH Note:** SR 2011/221 provides:

2 Commencement of certain provisions of Anti-Money Laundering and Countering Financing of Terrorism Act 2009

"(1) Subpart 5 of Part 2 of the Anti-Money Laundering and Countering Financing of Terrorism Act 2009 (the Act) comes into force on 30 June 2011.

(2) The rest of the Act (except section 162) that is not in force immediately after the commencement of subpart 5 of Part 2 of the Act comes into force on 30 June 2013.

(3) Section 162 of the Act comes into force immediately after the rest of the Act is commenced by subclause (2).]"

2(6) An order under this section is secondary legislation (*see* Part 3 of the Legislation Act 2019 for publication requirements)

History

S 2(6) inserted by No 7 of 2021, s 3 and sch 16, **effective 28 October 2021** (LI 2021/250).

PART 1 — PRELIMINARY PROVISIONS

SECTION 3 PURPOSE

3(1) [Main purposes] The purposes of this Act are—

(a) to detect and deter money laundering and the financing of terrorism; and

(b) to maintain and enhance New Zealand's international reputation by adopting, where appropriate in the New Zealand context, recommendations issued by the Financial Action Task Force; and

(c) to contribute to public confidence in the financial system.

3(2) [Facilitation] Accordingly, this Act facilitates co-operation amongst reporting entities, AML/CFT supervisors, and various government agencies, in particular law enforcement and regulatory agencies.

SECTION 4 OVERVIEW

4(1) [General guide] This section is a guide to the general scheme and effect of this Act, but does not affect the interpretation or application of the other provisions of the Act.

4(2) [Preliminary matters] Part 1 deals with preliminary matters such as definitions of terms used in the Act. It sets out the purpose of the Act and the extent to which it applies to reporting entities.

4(3) [Requirements and compliance] Part 2 deals with AML/CFT requirements and compliance and has 7 subparts, as follows:

(a) subpart 1 includes provisions dealing with requirements on reporting entities to conduct due diligence on customers and certain other persons, the ability of reporting entities to rely on third parties to carry out customer due diligence and other AML/CFT functions, and prohibitions on establishing or continuing business relationships and setting up facilities in certain circumstances:

(b) subpart 2 includes provisions dealing with requirements on reporting entities to report suspicious activities and protection of persons making suspicious activity reports:

(ba) subpart 2A sets out requirements on reporting entities to report certain prescribed transactions:

(c) subpart 3 sets out requirements on reporting entities to keep records and includes provisions concerning the storage and destruction of records:

(d) subpart 4 deals with reporting entities' internal policies and procedures relating to the prevention of money laundering and the financing of terrorism, including provisions setting out requirements for reporting entities to have an AML/CFT programme for detecting and managing the risk of money laundering and the financing of terrorism, to carry out a risk assessment before conducting customer due diligence or establishing an AML/CFT programme, and to review, audit, and report on their risk assessment and AML/CFT programmes:

(e) subpart 5 deals with codes of practice and includes provisions relating to the preparation of codes by AML/CFT supervisors, approval of codes of practice, and their legal effect:

(f) subpart 6 contains provisions relating to the reporting of certain movements of cash into and out of New Zealand.

History

S 4(3) amended by No 35 of 2017, s 4(1), by replacing para (b); **effective 11 August 2017**. Former para (b) read:

"(b) subpart 2 includes provisions dealing with requirements on reporting entities to report suspicious transactions, protection of persons making suspicious transaction reports, and disclosure of information relating to such reports:".

S 4(3) amended by No 96 of 2015, s 4(1) and (2), by (i) replacing "6 subparts" with "7 subparts"; and (ii) inserting para (ba); **effective 1 July 2017**.

4(4) [Enforcement] Part 3 deals with enforcement and contains provisions relating to civil liability acts, offences, search and seizure, penalties, and immunity of certain persons from civil and criminal proceedings.

4(5) [Institutional arrangements] Part 4 deals with institutional arrangements and miscellaneous matters and has 2 subparts, as follows:

(a) subpart 1 includes provisions that identify the AML/CFT supervisors and their functions, powers, and ability to delegate supervisory functions; the financial intelligence functions of the Commissioner of Police and a requirement on that person to issue guidelines relating to the reporting of suspicious activities and prescribed transactions; the roles and responsibilities of the Ministry, the AML/CFT co-ordination committee required to be established by the chief executive of the Ministry, and other agencies concerning monitoring, evaluating, and advising on the operation of the AML/CFT regulatory system:

(b) subpart 2 includes regulation-making powers and provisions relating to the Minister's power to grant exemptions from the requirements of the Act.

History

S 4(5) amended by No 35 of 2017, s 4(2), by replacing in para (a) "suspicious transaction reports" with "the reporting of suspicious activities and prescribed transactions"; **effective 11 August 2017**.

SECTION 5 INTERPRETATION

5(1) In this Act, unless the context otherwise requires,—

accounting practice means—

(a) an accountant in public practice on his or her own account in sole practice:

(b) in relation to 2 or more accountants in public practice, and practising in partnership, the partnership:

(c) an incorporated accounting practice

History

Definition of "accounting practice" inserted by No 35 of 2017, s 5(1), **effective 11 August 2017**.

AML/CFT means anti-money laundering and countering the financing of terrorism

AML/CFT programme means a compliance programme established under section 56(1)

AML/CFT requirements means the requirements set out in Part 2

AML/CFT supervisor, in relation to a reporting entity, means the person referred to in section 130(1) that is responsible for supervising the reporting entity under Parts 3 and 4

applicable threshold value means the threshold value that—

(a) is prescribed in regulations; and

(b) applies to a particular person, class of persons, transaction, class of transactions, financial activity, or class of financial activities prescribed in regulations

approved entity means an entity—

(a) that is prescribed by regulations as an approved entity; or

(b) that comes within a class of entities prescribed by regulations as a class of approved entities

History

Definition of "approved entity" inserted by No 35 of 2017, s 5(1), **effective 11 August 2017**.

bearer-negotiable instrument means—

(a) a bill of exchange; or

(b) a cheque; or

(c) a promissory note; or

(d) a bearer bond; or

(e) a traveller's cheque; or

(f) a money order, postal order, or similar order; or

(g) any other instrument prescribed by regulations

beneficial owner means the individual who—

(a) has effective control of a customer or person on whose behalf a transaction is conducted; or

(b) owns a prescribed threshold of the customer or person on whose behalf a transaction is conducted

beneficiary institution, in relation to a wire transfer from an ordering institution, means any person who receives those funds and then makes those funds available to a person (the **payee**) by—

(a) crediting it to an account held by the payee; or

(b) paying it to the payee

business relationship means a business, professional, or commercial relationship between a reporting entity and a customer that has an element of duration or that is expected by the reporting entity, at the time when contact is established, to have an element of duration

cash means—

(a) physical currency:

(b) bearer-negotiable instruments

cash report means a report made under subpart 6 of Part 2

casino means the holder of a casino operator's licence under the Gambling Act 2003

chief executive means the chief executive of the Ministry

civil liability act has the meaning set out in section 78

code of practice and **proposed code of practice** have the meanings set out in section 62

Commissioner means the Commissioner of Police

constable has the same meaning as in section 4 of the Policing Act 2008

conveyancing practitioner has the meaning given to it by section 6 of the Lawyers and Conveyancers Act 2006

History

Definition of "conveyancing practitioner" inserted by No 35 of 2017, s 5(1), **effective 11 August 2017**.

correspondent banking relationship has the meaning set out in section 29(3)

country includes any State, territory, province, or other part of a country

customer—

(a) means a new customer or an existing customer; and

(b) includes—

(i) a facility holder:

(ii) a person conducting or seeking to conduct an occasional transaction or activity through a reporting entity:

(iii) a junket organiser as defined in section 4(1) of the Gambling Act 2003:

(iv) a person or class of persons declared by regulations to be a customer for the purposes of this Act; but

(c) excludes a person or class of persons that is declared by regulations not to be a customer for the purposes of this Act

History

Definition of "customer" amended by No 35 of 2017, s 68 and sch 2, by replacing in para (b)(ii) "occasional transaction" with "occasional transaction or activity"; **effective 11 August 2017**.

Customs officer has the same meaning as in section 5(1) of the Customs and Excise Act 2018

History

Definition of "Customs officer" amended by No 4 of 2018, s 443(3) and sch 9, by replacing "section 2(1) of the Customs and Excise Act 1996" with "section 5(1) of the Customs and Excise Act 2018"; **effective 1 October 2018** (LI 2018/148).

designated business group means a group of 2 or more persons in which—

(a) each member of the group has elected, in writing, to be a member of the group and the election is in force; and

(b) each election was made in accordance with regulations (if any); and

(c) no member of the group is a member of another designated business group; and

(d) each member of the group is—

(i) related to each other member of the group within the meaning of section 2(3) of the Companies Act 1993 and is—

(A) a reporting entity resident in New Zealand; or

(B) a person that is resident in a country that has sufficient AML/CFT systems and is supervised or regulated for AML/CFT purposes; or

(ii) providing a service under a joint venture agreement to which each member of the group is a party; or

(iii) a public service agency as defined in section 5 of the Public Service Act 2020, a State enterprise under the State-Owned Enterprises Act 1986, or a Crown entity under section 7 of the Crown Entities Act 2004; or

(iv) related to 1 or more of the entities referred to in subparagraph (iii) through the provision of common products or services; or

(v) a body corporate that is—

(A) either a company (within the meaning of section 2(1) of the Companies Act 1993) or an overseas company within the meaning of that section; and

(B) related (within the meaning of section 12(2) of the Financial Markets Conduct Act 2013) to every body corporate in the designated business group or proposed designated business group; and

(C) either a reporting entity resident in New Zealand or a person who is resident in a country that has sufficient AML/CFT systems and that is supervised or regulated for AML/CFT purposes; or

(vi) a related law firm, or a subsidiary of a law firm, that is a reporting entity in New Zealand (or the equivalent body in another country that has sufficient AML/CFT systems and that is supervised or regulated for AML/CFT purposes); or

(vii) a related conveyancer, or a subsidiary of a conveyancer, that is a reporting entity in New Zealand (or the equivalent body in another country that has sufficient AML/CFT systems and that is supervised or regulated for AML/CFT purposes); or

(viii) a related accounting practice, or a subsidiary of an accounting practice, that is a reporting entity in New Zealand (or the equivalent body in another country that has sufficient AML/CFT systems and that is supervised or regulated for AML/CFT purposes); or

(ix) a related trust and company service provider, or a subsidiary of a trust and company service provider, that is a reporting entity in New Zealand (or the equivalent body in another country that has sufficient AML/CFT systems and that is supervised or regulated for AML/CFT purposes); or

(x) a related real estate agent, or a subsidiary of a real estate agent, that is a reporting entity in New Zealand (or the equivalent in another country that has sufficient AML/CFT systems and that is supervised or regulated for AML/CFT purposes); or

(xi) a related high-value dealer, or a subsidiary of a high-value dealer, that is a reporting entity in New Zealand (or an equivalent person resident outside New Zealand in a country that has sufficient AML/CFT systems and that is supervised or regulated for AML/CFT purposes); or

(xii) a group of reporting entities, if the entities are each money transfer agents or sub-agents and each entity is related to every other entity in the designated business group or proposed designated business group in either of the following ways:

(A) one of those entities is a money transfer agent and the other entities are the sub-agents of those agents:

(B) those entities are each sub-agents of the same money transfer agent; or

(xiii) an entity or a class of entities prescribed by regulations; and

(e) each member of the group satisfies any conditions in subsection (3) that apply to that member

History

Definition of ''designated business group'' amended by No 40 of 2020, s 135 and sch 11, by replacing in para (d)(iii) ''a government department named in Schedule 1 of the State Sector Act 1988'' with ''a public service agency as defined in section 5 of the Public Service Act 2020''; **effective 7 August 2020**.

Definition of ''designated business group'' replaced by No 35 of 2017, s 5(2), **effective 11 August 2017**. Former definition read:

''**designated business group** means a group of 2 or more persons where—

(a) each member of the group has elected, in writing, to be a member of the group and the election is in force; and

(b) each election was made in accordance with regulations (if any); and

(c) no member of the group is a member of another designated business group; and

(d) each member of the group is—

(i) related to each other member of the group within the meaning of section 2(3) of the Companies Act 1993 and is—

(A) a reporting entity resident in New Zealand; or

(B) a person that is resident in another country with sufficient anti-money laundering and countering the financing of terrorism systems and is supervised or regulated for anti-money laundering and countering the financing of terrorism purposes; or

Sec 5(1)

(ii) providing a service under a joint venture agreement, to which each member of the group is a party; or

(iii) a government department named in Schedule 1 of the State Sector Act 1988, a State enterprise under the State-Owned Enterprises Act 1986, or a Crown entity under section 7 of the Crown Entities Act 2004; or

(iv) related to 1 or more of the entities in subparagraph (iii) through the provision of common products or services; or

(v) an entity or class of entities prescribed by regulations; and

(e) each member of the group satisfies any conditions that may be prescribed by regulations and that apply to that member''.

Definition of ''designated business group'' amended by No 98 of 2012, s 4, by omitting in para (d)(v) ''to be a member of a designated entity''; **effective 12 December 2012.**

designated non-financial business or profession means—

(a) a law firm, a conveyancing practitioner, an incorporated conveyancing firm, an accounting practice, a real estate agent, or a trust and company service provider, who, in the ordinary course of business, carries out 1 or more of the following activities:

(i) acting as a formation agent of legal persons or legal arrangements:

(ii) acting as, or arranging for a person to act as, a nominee director or nominee shareholder or trustee in relation to legal persons or legal arrangements:

(iii) providing a registered office or a business address, a correspondence address, or an administrative address for a company, or a partnership, or for any other legal person or arrangement, unless the office or address is provided solely as an ancillary service to the provision of other services (being services that do not constitute an activity listed in this subparagraph or subparagraphs (i), (ii), and (iv) to (vi)):

(iv) managing client funds (other than sums paid as fees for professional services), accounts, securities, or other assets:

(v) providing real estate agency work (within the meaning of section 4(1) of the Real Estate Agents Act 2008) to effect a transaction (within the meaning of section 4(1) of the Real Estate Agents Act 2008):

(vi) engaging in or giving instructions on behalf of a customer to another person for—

(A) any conveyancing (within the meaning of section 6 of the Lawyers and Conveyancers Act 2006) to effect a transaction (within the meaning of section 4(1) of the Real Estate Agents Act 2008), namely,—

- the sale, the purchase, or any other disposal or acquisition of a freehold estate or interest in land:
- the grant, sale, or purchase or any other disposal or acquisition of a leasehold estate or interest in land (other than a tenancy to which the Residential Tenancies Act 1986 applies):
- the grant, sale, or purchase or any other disposal or acquisition of a licence that is registrable under the Land Transfer Act 1952:
- the grant, sale, or purchase or any other disposal or acquisition of an occupation right agreement within the meaning of section 5 of the Retirement Villages Act 2003:

(B) a transaction (within the meaning of section 4(1) of the Real Estate Agents Act 2008); or

(C) the transfer of a beneficial interest in land or other real property; or

(D) a transaction on behalf of any person in relation to the buying, transferring, or selling of a business or legal person (for example, a company) and any other legal arrangement; or

(E) a transaction on behalf of a customer in relation to creating, operating, and managing a legal person (for example, a company) and any other legal arrangement; and

(b) includes a person or class of persons declared by regulations to be a designated non-financial business or profession for the purposes of this Act; but

(c) excludes a person or class of persons declared by regulations not to be a designated non-financial business or profession for the purposes of this Act

History

Definition of "designated non-financial business or profession" inserted by No 35 of 2017, s 5(1), **effective 11 August 2017**.

domestic physical cash transaction means a transaction in New Zealand involving the use of physical currency

History

Definition "domestic physical cash transaction" inserted by No 96 of 2015, s 5(1), **effective 1 July 2017**.

domestic wire transfer has the meaning set out in section 27(7)

existing customer, in relation to a reporting entity, means a person who was in a business relationship with the reporting entity immediately before any provisions of this Act began to apply to the reporting entity

History

Definition of "existing customer" replaced by No 35 of 2017, s 5(3), **effective 11 August 2017**. Former definition read:

> "**existing customer**, in relation to a reporting entity, means a person who was in a business relationship with the reporting entity immediately before the commencement of Part 2"

facility—

(a) means any account or arrangement—

(i) that is provided by a reporting entity; and

(ii) through which a facility holder may conduct 2 or more transactions; and

(b) without limiting paragraph (a), includes—

(i) a life insurance policy:

(ii) membership of a superannuation scheme, workplace savings scheme, or KiwiSaver scheme:

(iii) the provision, by a reporting entity, of facilities for safe custody, including (without limitation) a safety deposit box:

(iv) an account or arrangement declared by regulations to be a facility for the purposes of this Act; but

(c) excludes an account or arrangement declared by regulations not to be a facility for the purposes of this Act

History

Definition of "facility" amended by No 70 of 2013, s 150 and sch, by replacing para (b)(ii); **effective 1 December 2014** (LI 2014/325). Former para (b)(ii) read:

"(ii) membership of a superannuation scheme:"

facility holder, in relation to a facility,—

(a) means the person in whose name the facility is established; or

(b) if that facility is a life insurance policy, means any person who for the time being is the legal holder of that policy; or

(c) if that facility consists of membership of a superannuation scheme, workplace savings scheme, or KiwiSaver scheme, means the product holder of the managed investment product in the scheme (within the meanings of product holder and managed investment product in section 6(1) of the Financial Markets Conduct Act 2013)

History

Definition of "facility holder" amended by No 70 of 2013, s 150 and sch, by replacing para (c); **effective 1 December 2014** (LI 2014/325). Former para (c) read:

"(c) if that facility consists of membership of a superannuation scheme, means any person who is a member of the scheme within the meaning of member in section 2(1) of the Superannuation Schemes Act 1989"

financial institution—

(a) means a person who, in the ordinary course of business, carries on 1 or more of the following financial activities:

(i) accepting deposits or other repayable funds from the public:

(ii) lending to or for a customer, including consumer credit, mortgage credit, factoring (with or without recourse), and financing of commercial transactions (including forfeiting):

(iii) financial leasing (excluding financial leasing arrangements in relation to consumer products):

(iv) transferring money or value for, or on behalf of, a customer:

(v) issuing or managing the means of payment (for example, credit or debit cards, cheques, traveller's cheques, money orders, bankers' drafts, or electronic money):

(vi) undertaking financial guarantees and commitments:

(vii) trading for, or on behalf of, a customer in any of the following using the person's account or the customer's account:

(A) money market instruments (for example, cheques, bills, certificates of deposit, or derivatives):

(B) foreign exchange:

(C) exchange, interest rate, or index instruments:

(D) transferable securities:

(E) commodity futures trading:

(viii) participating in securities issues and the provision of financial services related to those issues:

(ix) managing individual or collective portfolios:

(x) safe keeping or administering of cash or liquid securities on behalf of other persons:

(xi) investing, administering, or managing funds or money on behalf of other persons:

(xii) issuing, or undertaking liability under, life insurance policies as an insurer:

(xiii) money or currency changing; and

(b) includes a person or class of persons declared by regulations to be a financial institution for the purposes of this Act; but

(c) excludes a person or class of persons declared by regulations not to be a financial institution for the purposes of this Act

History

Definition of "financial institution" amended by No 35 of 2017, s 5(4), by replacing in para (a)(vii) "for the person's own account or for the accounts of customers in any of the following:" with "for, or on behalf of, a customer in any of the following using the person's account or the customer's account:"; **effective 11 August 2017**.

Definition of "financial institution" amended by No 111 of 2010, s 241(2) and sch 3, by substituting para (a)(xii); **effective 1 February 2011**. Former para (a)(xii) read:

"(xii) underwriting or placement of life insurance or other investment related insurance:".

financing of terrorism has the same meaning as in section 4(1) of the Terrorism Suppression Act 2002

gambling inspector has the same meaning as in section 4(1) of the Gambling Act 2003

government agency means—

(a) a public service agency as defined in section 5 of the Public Service Act 2020; or

(b) a Crown entity under section 7 of the Crown Entities Act 2004; or

(c) the Reserve Bank, the Parliamentary Counsel Office, and the New Zealand Police; or

(d) any overseas country's counterpart of any of the entities in paragraphs (a) to (c)

History

Definition of "government agency" amended by No 40 of 2020, s 135 and sch 11, by replacing para (a); **effective 7 August 2020**. Former para (a) read:

"(a) a government department named in Schedule 1 of the State Sector Act 1988; or".

Definition of "government agency" amended by No 10 of 2017, s 335 and sch 4, by replacing para (c); **effective 28 September 2017**. Former para (c) read:

"(c) the Reserve Bank, the Parliamentary Counsel Office, the New Zealand Police, and the New Zealand Security Intelligence Service; or".

Definition of "government agency" amended by No 106 of 2013, s 4, by replacing para (d); **effective 5 December 2013**. Former para (d) read:

"(d) any international counterpart of the entities in paragraphs (a) to (c)".

high-value dealer—

(a) means a person who is in trade and in the ordinary course of business, buys or sells all or any of the following articles by way of a cash transaction or a series of related cash transactions, if the total value of that transaction or those transactions is equal to or above the applicable threshold value:

(i) jewellery:

(ii) watches:

(iii) gold, silver, or other precious metals:

(iv) diamonds, sapphires, or other precious stones:

(v) paintings:

(vi) prints:

(vii) protected foreign objects (within the meaning of section 2(1) of the Protected Objects Act 1975):

(viii) protected New Zealand objects (within the meaning of section 2(1) of the Protected Objects Act 1975):

(ix) sculptures:

(x) photographs:

(xi) carvings in any medium:

(xii) other artistic or cultural artefacts:

(xiii) motor vehicles (within the meaning of section 6(1) of the Motor Vehicle Sales Act 2003):

(xiv) ships (within the meaning of section 2(1) of the Maritime Transport Act 1994); and

(b) includes any person who carries out the activities referred to in paragraph (a) as a registered auctioneer (within the meaning of section 4(1) of the Auctioneers Act 2013); but

(c) does not include any person, to the extent that the person is engaged in providing services other than the buying or selling of articles referred to in paragraph (a), including the following services:

(i) mining precious metals or precious stones:

(ii) manufacturing jewellery:

(iii) crafting or polishing precious stones; and

(d) does not include any person to the extent that the person is engaged in the buying or selling of precious metals or precious stones for industrial purposes

History

Definition of ''high-value dealer'' inserted by No 35 of 2017, s 5(1), **effective 11 August 2017**.

identity information means information obtained under sections 15, 19, 23, and 27(1) and (2) and any other information relating to identity prescribed by sections 29(2)(g) and 30(b)

incorporated conveyancing firm has the meaning given to it by section 6 of the Lawyers and Conveyancers Act 2006

History

Definition of ''incorporated conveyancing firm'' inserted by No 35 of 2017, s 5(1), **effective 11 August 2017**.

incorporated law firm has the meaning given to it by section 6 of the Lawyers and Conveyancers Act 2006

History

Definition of "incorporated law firm" inserted by No 35 of 2017, s 5(1), **effective 11 August 2017**.

individual means a natural person, other than a deceased natural person

intermediary institution, in relation to a wire transfer, is a person that participates in a transfer of funds that takes place through more than 1 institution but is not an ordering institution or a beneficiary institution

international wire transfer means a wire transfer where—

(a) at least 1 of the following institutions is in New Zealand:

  (i) the ordering institution:

  (ii) the intermediary institution:

  (iii) the beneficiary institution; and

(b) at least 1 of the following institutions is outside New Zealand:

  (i) the ordering institution:

  (ii) the intermediary institution:

  (iii) the beneficiary institution

History

Definition "international wire transfer" inserted by No 96 of 2015, s 5(1), **effective 1 July 2017**.

KiwiSaver scheme has the same meaning as in section 6(1) of the Financial Markets Conduct Act 2013

History

Definition of "KiwiSaver scheme" inserted by No 70 of 2013, s 150 and sch, **effective 1 December 2014** (LI 2014/325).

law enforcement purposes means—

(a) the prevention, disruption, detection, investigation, and prosecution of—

  (i) any offence under this Act; or

  (ii) a money laundering offence; or

  (iii) any offence within the meaning of that term in section 243(1) of the Crimes Act 1961; or

  (iv) an offence under the Terrorism Suppression Act 2002:

(b) the enforcement and administration of—

  (i) this Act:

  (ii) the Criminal Proceeds (Recovery) Act 2009:

  (iii) the Misuse of Drugs Act 1975:

  (iv) the Terrorism Suppression Act 2002:

  (v) the Mutual Assistance in Criminal Matters Act 1992:

  (vi) the Customs and Excise Act 1996:

(c) the performance by the New Zealand Security Intelligence Service or the Government Communications Security Bureau of its functions under the Intelligence and Security Act 2017:

(d) the detection and prevention of the harms specified in section 58(2) of the Intelligence and Security Act 2017:

(e) any purpose or action referred to in paragraphs (a) to (d) relating to, or taken in respect of, legislation of an overseas jurisdiction that is broadly equivalent to the enactments referred to in those paragraphs

History

Definition of "law enforcement purposes" replaced by No 35 of 2017, s 5(5), **effective 11 August 2017**. Former definition read:

"**law enforcement purposes** means—

(a) the administration of this Act:

(b) the detection, investigation, and prosecution of—

(i) any offence under this Act; or

(ii) a money laundering offence; or

(iii) any offence under section 143B of the Tax Administration Act 1994; or

(iv) an offence within the meaning of section 243(1) of the Crimes Act 1961:

(c) the enforcement of the Proceeds of Crime Act 1991 or the Criminal Proceeds (Recovery) Act 2009:

(d) the enforcement of the Misuse of Drugs Act 1975:

(e) the enforcement of the Terrorism Suppression Act 2002:

(f) the administration of the Mutual Assistance in Criminal Matters Act 1992:

(g) the performance by the New Zealand Security Intelligence Service or the Government Communications Security Bureau of its function under section 10 or 11 of the Intelligence and Security Act 2017:

(h) any action referred to in paragraphs (a) to (g) taken in respect of legislation of an overseas jurisdiction that is broadly equivalent to the enactments listed in those paragraphs"

Definition of "law enforcement purposes" amended by No 10 of 2017, s 335 and sch 4, by replacing para (g); **effective 28 September 2017**. Former para (g) read:

"(g) the investigation of matters relating to security under the New Zealand Security Intelligence Service Act 1969:".

Definition of "law enforcement purposes" amended by No 96 of 2015, s 5(2), by replacing para (b)(iv); **effective 1 July 2017**. Former para (b)(iv) read:

"(iv) any serious offence (within the meaning of section 243(1) of the Crimes Act 1961)".

law firm means—

(a) a barrister or a barrister and solicitor who is practising on the barrister's or barrister and solicitor's own account in sole practice:

(b) in relation to 2 or more barristers and solicitors practising law in partnership, the partnership:

(c) an incorporated law firm

History

Definition of "law firm" inserted by No 35 of 2017, s 5(1), **effective 11 August 2017**.

lawyer has the meaning given to it by section 6 of the Lawyers and Conveyancers Act 2006

History

Definition of "lawyer" inserted by No 35 of 2017, s 5(1), **effective 11 August 2017**.

legal arrangement means—

(a) a trust:

(b) a partnership:

(c) a charitable entity (within the meaning of section 4(1) of the Charities Act 2005):

(d) any other prescribed arrangement (being an arrangement that involves a risk of money laundering or the financing of terrorism)

History

Definition of "legal arrangement" inserted by No 35 of 2017, s 5(1), **effective 11 August 2017**.

life insurance policy means a life policy within the meaning of section 6(1) of the Insurance (Prudential Supervision) Act 2010

History

Definition of "life insurance policy" inserted by No 111 of 2010, s 241(2) and sch 3, **effective 1 February 2011**.

Minister means the Minister who is, with the authority of the Prime Minister, for the time being responsible for the administration of this Act

Ministry means the department of State that, with the authority of the Prime Minister, is for the time being responsible for the administration of this Act

money laundering offence means an offence against section 243 of the Crimes Act 1961 or section 12B of the Misuse of Drugs Act 1975 or any act committed overseas that, if committed in New Zealand, would be an offence under those sections of those Acts

non-bank deposit taker has the meaning given to NBDT by section 5 of the Non-bank Deposit Takers Act 2013

History

Definition of "non-bank deposit taker" inserted by No 35 of 2017, s 5(1), **effective 11 August 2017**.

occasional activity—

(a) means an activity—

  (i) that is specified in section 6(4) in relation to a reporting entity (other than an occasional transaction); and

  (ii) that does not involve a business relationship between the reporting entity and the reporting entity's customer; and

(b) includes an activity or a class of activities declared by regulations to be an occasional activity for the purposes of this Act; but

(c) excludes an activity or a class of activities declared by regulations not to be an occasional activity for the purposes of this Act

History

Definition of "occasional activity" inserted by No 35 of 2017, s 5(1), **effective 11 August 2017**.

occasional transaction—

(a) means a cash transaction that occurs outside of a business relationship and is equal to or above the applicable threshold value (whether the transaction is carried out in a single operation or several operations that appear to be linked); and

(b) includes a transaction or class of transactions declared by regulations to be an occasional transaction for the purposes of this Act; but

(c) excludes—

(i) cheque deposits; and

(ii) a transaction or class of transactions declared by regulations not to be an occasional transaction for the purposes of this Act

History

Definition of ''occasional transaction'' amended by No 35 of 2017, s 5(6), by replacing in para (a) ''over'' with ''equal to or above''; **effective 11 August 2017**.

occasional transaction or activity means—

(a) an occasional transaction:

(b) an occasional activity

History

Definition of ''occasional transaction or activity'' inserted by No 35 of 2017, s 5(1), **effective 11 August 2017**.

ordering institution—

(a) means any person who has been instructed by a person (the **payer**) to electronically transfer funds controlled by the payer to a person (the **payee**) who may or may not be the payer on the basis that the transferred funds will be made available to the payee by a beneficiary institution; and

(b) includes a person declared by regulations to be an ordering institution for the purposes of this Act; but

(c) excludes a person or class of persons declared by regulations not to be an ordering institution for the purposes of this Act

physical currency means the coin and printed money (whether of New Zealand or of a foreign country) that—

(a) is designated as legal tender; and

(b) circulates as, and is customarily used and accepted as, a medium of exchange in the country of issue

Police employee has the same meaning as in section 4 of the Policing Act 2008

politically exposed person means—

(a) an individual who holds, or has held at any time in the preceding 12 months, in any overseas country the prominent public function of—

(i) Head of State or head of a country or government; or

(ii) government minister or equivalent senior politician; or

(iii) Supreme Court Judge or equivalent senior Judge; or

(iv) governor of a central bank or any other position that has comparable influence to the Governor of the Reserve Bank of New Zealand; or

(v) senior foreign representative, ambassador, or high commissioner; or

(vi) high-ranking member of the armed forces; or

(vii) board chair, chief executive, or chief financial officer of, or any other position that has comparable influence in, any State enterprise; and

(b) an immediate family member of a person referred to in paragraph (a), including—

(i) a spouse; or

(ii) a partner, being a person who is considered by the relevant national law as equivalent to a spouse; or

(iii) a child and a child's spouse or partner; or

(iv) a parent; and

(c) having regard to information that is public or readily available,—

(i) any individual who is known to have joint beneficial ownership of a legal entity or legal arrangement, or any other close relationship, with a person referred to in paragraph (a); or

(ii) any individual who has sole beneficial ownership of a legal entity or legal arrangement that is known to exist for the benefit of a person described in paragraph (a)

prescribed transaction, in relation to a reporting entity, means a transaction conducted through the reporting entity in respect of—

(a) an international wire transfer of a value equal to or above the applicable threshold value; or

(b) a domestic physical cash transaction of a value equal to or above the applicable threshold value

History

Definition ''prescribed transaction'' amended by No 35 of 2017, s 5(7), by replacing in para (a) and (b) ''value greater than'' with ''value equal to or above''; **effective 11 August 2017**.

Definition ''prescribed transaction'' inserted by No 96 of 2015, s 5(1), **effective 1 July 2017**.

prescribed transaction report means a report made under section 48A

History

Definition ''prescribed transaction report'' inserted by No 96 of 2015, s 5(1), **effective 1 July 2017**.

privileged communication has the meaning set out in section 42

History

Definition of ''privileged communication'' inserted by No 35 of 2017, s 5(1), **effective 11 August 2017**.

real estate agent has the same meaning as the definition of agent in section 4(1) of the Real Estate Agents Act 2008

History

Definition of ''real estate agent'' inserted by No 35 of 2017, s 5(1), **effective 11 August 2017**.

real estate agency work has the same meaning as in the definition of that term in section 4(1) of the Real Estate Agents Act 2008

History

Definition of ''real estate agency work'' inserted by No 35 of 2017, s 5(1), **effective 11 August 2017**.

[Effective on a date to be appointed, or 1 October 2022]

registered bank has the same meaning as in section 2(1) of the Banking (Prudential Supervision) Act 1989

History

Definition of "registered bank" amended by No 31 of 2021, s 300(1) and sch 4, by replacing "Reserve Bank of New Zealand Act 1989" with "Banking (Prudential Supervision) Act 1989"; **effective on a date to be appointed by the Governor-General by Order in Council, or 1 October 2022, whichever is earlier**.

registered bank has the same meaning as in section 2(1) of the Reserve Bank of New Zealand Act 1989

regulations means regulations made under this Act

regulator—

(a) means a professional body responsible under any New Zealand enactment for enforcing the regulatory obligations of a particular industry or profession whose members are subject to this Act; and

(b) includes any other body prescribed in regulations

History

Definition of "regulator" inserted by No 35 of 2017, s 5(1), **effective 11 August 2017**.

reporting entity—

(a) means—

(i) a casino:

(ii) a designated non-financial business or profession:

(iii) a financial institution:

(iv) a high-value dealer:

(v) TAB NZ; and

(b) includes—

(i) a person or class of persons declared by regulations to be a reporting entity for the purposes of this Act; and

(ii) any other person that is required by any enactment to comply with this Act as if it were a reporting entity; but

(c) excludes a person or class of persons declared by regulations not to be a reporting entity for the purposes of this Act

History

Definition of "reporting entity" amended by No 28 of 2020, s 129 and sch 5, by replacing in para (a)(v) "the Racing Industry Transition Agency" with "TAB NZ"; **effective 1 August 2020**.

Definition of "reporting entity" amended by No 32 of 2019, s 25(2) and sch 3, by replacing in para (a)(v) "New Zealand Racing Board" with "Racing Industry Transition Agency"; **effective 1 July 2019**.

Definition of "reporting entity" amended by No 35 of 2017, s 5(8), by replacing para (a); **effective 11 August 2017**. Former para (a) read:

"(a) means—

(i) a financial institution; and

(ii) a casino; and".

search warrant means a warrant issued under section 117

History

Definition of "search warrant" inserted by No 35 of 2017, s 5(1), **effective 11 August 2017**.

security (*repealed*)

History

Definition of "security" repealed by No 10 of 2017, s 335 and sch 4, **effective 28 September 2017**. Former definition read:

"**security** has the same meaning as in section 2(1) of the New Zealand Security Intelligence Service Act 1969".

senior manager (and **senior management** correspondingly) means,—

(a) in relation to a reporting entity that is a company, a director within the meaning of section 126 of the Companies Act 1993; and

(b) in relation to a reporting entity that is not a company, a person who occupies a position comparable to that of a director (for example, a trustee or partner); and

(c) any other person who occupies a position within a reporting entity that allows that person to exercise an influence over the management or administration of the reporting entity (for example, a chief executive or a chief financial officer)

shell bank has the meaning set out in section 39(2)

superannuation scheme has the same meaning as in section 6(1) of the Financial Markets Conduct Act 2013

History

Definition of "superannuation scheme" inserted by No 70 of 2013, s 150 and sch, **effective 1 December 2014** (LI 2014/325).

suspicious activity report—

(a) means a report made under section 40:

(b) includes—

  (i) a suspicious transaction report made under this Act; and

  (ii) a suspicious transaction report made under the Financial Transactions Reporting Act 1996

History

Definition of "suspicious activity report" inserted by No 35 of 2017, s 5(1), **effective 11 August 2017**.

suspicious property report has the same meaning as in section 4(1) of the Terrorism Suppression Act 2002

suspicious transaction report (*repealed*)

History

Definition of "suspicious transaction report" repealed by No 35 of 2017, s 5(9), **effective 11 August 2017**. Former definition read:

"**suspicious transaction report** means a report made under section 40".

transaction—

(a) means any deposit, withdrawal, exchange, or transfer of funds (in any denominated currency), whether—

  (i) in cash; or

  (ii) by cheque, payment order, or other instrument; or

  (iii) by electronic or other non-physical means; and

(b) without limiting paragraph (a), includes—

(i) any payment made in satisfaction, in whole or in part, of any contractual or other legal obligation; and

(ii) a transaction or class of transactions declared by regulations to be a transaction for the purposes of this Act; but

(c) excludes the following:

(i) the placing of any bet unless authorised under the Racing Industry Act 2020:

(ii) participation in gambling (as defined in section 4(1) of the Gambling Act 2003) unless authorised under the Racing Industry Act 2020:

(iii) a transaction or class of transactions declared by regulations not to be a transaction for the purposes of this Act

History

Definition of "transaction" amended by No 28 of 2020, s 129 and sch 5, by replacing in para (c)(i) and (ii) "Racing Act 2003" with "Racing Industry Act 2020"; **effective 1 August 2020**.

Definition of "transaction" amended by No 35 of 2017, s 5(10), by replacing para (c); **effective 11 August 2017**. Former para (c) read:

"(c) excludes the following:

(i) the placing of any bet:

(ii) participation in gambling as defined in section 4(1) of the Gambling Act 2003:

(iii) a transaction or class of transactions declared by regulations not to be a transaction for the purposes of this Act".

trust and company service provider means a person (other than a law firm, a conveyancing practitioner, an incorporated conveyancing firm, an accounting practice, or a real estate agent) who carries out any of the activities described in paragraphs (a)(i) to (vi) of the definition of designated non-financial business or profession

History

Definition of "trust and company service provider" inserted by No 35 of 2017, s 5(1), **effective 11 August 2017**.

trustee has the same meaning as in section 9 of the Trusts Act 2019

History

Definition of "trustee" amended by No 38 of 2019, s 161 and sch 4, by replacing "section 2(1) of the Trustee Act 1956" with "section 9 of the Trusts Act 2019"; **effective 30 January 2021**.

verification information means information obtained under sections 16, 20, 24, and 28

wire transfer—

(a) means a transaction carried out on behalf of a person (the **originator**) through a reporting entity by electronic means with a view to making an amount of money available to a beneficiary (who may also be the originator) at another reporting entity; and

(b) includes a transfer or transaction, or class of transfers or transactions, declared by regulations to be a wire transfer for the purposes of this Act; but

(c) excludes—

(i) transfers and settlements between financial institutions or other reporting entities if both the originator and the beneficiary are financial institutions or other reporting entities acting on their own behalf; and

(ii) credit and debit card transactions if the credit or debit card number accompanies the transaction; and

(iii) any other transfer or transaction or class of transfers or transactions declared by regulations not to be a wire transfer for the purposes of this Act.

History

Definition of "wire transfer" replaced by No 35 of 2017, s 5(11), **effective 11 August 2017**. Former definition read:

"**wire transfer** —

(a) means a transaction carried out on behalf of a person (the **originator**) through a reporting entity by electronic means with a view to making an amount of money available to a beneficiary (who may also be the originator) at another financial institution; and

(b) includes a transfer or transaction, or class of transfers or transactions, declared by regulations to be a wire transfer for the purposes of this Act; but

(c) excludes—

(i) transfers and settlements between financial institutions if both the originator and the beneficiary are financial institutions acting on their own behalf; and

(ii) credit and debit card transactions if the credit or debit card number accompanies the transaction; and

(iii) any other transfer or transaction or class of transfers or transactions declared by regulations not to be a wire transfer for the purposes of this Act."

workplace savings scheme has the same meaning as in section 6(1) of the Financial Markets Conduct Act 2013

History

Definition of "workplace savings scheme" inserted by No 70 of 2013, s 150 and sch, **effective 1 December 2014** (LI 2014/325).

5(2) For the purposes of paragraph (d)(xii) of the definition of **designated business group** in subsection (1),—

money transfer agent, in relation to a money transfer provider, means a reporting entity that has a representation agreement with a money transfer provider

money transfer provider means a person who, under a representation agreement, authorises a money transfer agent to carry on money transfer services on behalf of the money transfer provider and to engage sub-agents for the purpose of carrying on those services in New Zealand

money transfer services means the provision of remittance services that are carried on, otherwise than by a bank, under a single brand, trade mark, or business name

representation agreement means a written agreement between a money transfer provider and a money transfer agent, or between a money transfer agent and a sub-agent, that states the terms on which the money transfer agent, or the subagent, carries on money transactions for customers relating to creating, operating, and managing companies

sub-agent means a reporting entity that has a representation agreement with a money transfer agent.

History

S 5(2) inserted by No 35 of 2017, s 5(12), **effective 11 August 2017**.

5(3) For the purposes of paragraph (e) of the definition of **designated business group** in subsection (1), a condition of membership is that the contact person of a designated business group must notify the relevant AML/CFT supervisor, in writing within 30 days, of any of the following:

(a) the withdrawal of a member from the designated business group:

(b) the termination of the designated business group:

(c) any other change in the details previously notified to any AML/CFT supervisor in respect of the designated business group.

History

S 5(3) inserted by No 35 of 2017, s 5(12), **effective 11 August 2017**.

5(4) For the purpose of applying the definitions of **designated non-financial business or profession** and **designated business group**, a reporting entity must take into account guidance (if any) on the application of those definitions issued by the relevant AML/CFT supervisor.

History

S 5(4) inserted by No 35 of 2017, s 5(12), **effective 11 August 2017**.

SECTION 6 APPLICATION OF THIS ACT TO REPORTING ENTITIES

6(1) Subject to subsections (2) and (3) and to Schedule 1, this Act (as amended by the Anti-Money Laundering and Countering Financing of Terrorism Amendment Act 2017) applies to any reporting entity that is in existence at the commencement of this section or that comes into existence on or after the commencement of this section.

6(2) Sections 39A to 41 and 43 to 47 (as inserted by section 25 of the Anti-Money Laundering and Countering Financing of Terrorism Amendment Act 2017) do not apply until 1 July 2018 or an earlier date appointed by the Governor-General by Order in Council.

6(3) This Act—

(a) does not apply to a law firm, a conveyancing practitioner, or an incorporated conveyancing firm until 1 July 2018 or an earlier date set by the Governor-General by Order in Council:

(b) does not apply to an accounting practice until 1 October 2018 or an earlier date set by the Governor-General by Order in Council:

(c) does not apply to a real estate agent until 1 January 2019 or an earlier date set by the Governor-General by Order in Council:

(d) does not apply to TAB NZ or a high-value dealer until 1 August 2019 or an earlier date set by the Governor-General by Order in Council:

(e) in the case of a trust and company service provider that immediately before the commencement of this section was a reporting entity under regulation 17 of the Anti-Money Laundering and Countering Financing of Terrorism (Definitions) Regulations 2011, applies on and after the date on which this section comes into force:

(f) in the case of a trust or company service provider to which paragraph (e) does not apply, applies on 1 July 2018 or an earlier date set by the Governor-General by Order in Council.

History

S 6(3) amended by No 28 of 2020, s 129 and sch 5, by replacing in para (d) "the Racing Industry Transition Agency" with "TAB NZ"; **effective 1 August 2020**.

S 6(3) amended by No 32 of 2019, s 25(2) and sch 3, by replacing in para (d) "New Zealand Racing Board" with "Racing Industry Transition Agency"; **effective 1 July 2019**.

6(4) This Act applies to a reporting entity only to the extent that,—

(a) in the case of a reporting entity that is a financial institution, the financial activities undertaken by that entity fall within the activities described in the definition of financial institution in section 5(1):

(b) in the case of TAB NZ, it carries out the following:

(i) the conduct of betting under section 74 of the Racing Industry Act 2020:

(ii) the operation of accounts or provision of vouchers:

(c) in the case of a law firm, conveyancer, incorporated conveyancing firm, accounting practice, real estate agent, or other designated non-financial business or profession, the activities carried out by that reporting entity are activities described in the definition of designated non-financial business or profession in section 5(1):

(d) in the case of a high-value dealer,—

(i) the high-value dealer carries out activities described in the definition of high-value dealer in section 5(1); and

(ii) if subparagraph (i) applies, the high-value dealer—

(A) must conduct standard customer due diligence under sections 14(1)(b), 15, and 16:

(B) may rely on third parties under sections 32 to 34:

(C) must comply with the prohibitions under section 37 if the high-value dealer is unable to conduct standard customer due diligence:

(D) may report suspicious activities to the Commissioner under section 40(5) (in which case sections 44 to 46 (which relate to suspicious activities) apply to the high-value dealer):

(E) must report prescribed transactions equal to or above the applicable cash threshold under sections 48A and 48B:

(F) must keep records of any suspicious activity reports under section 49A:

(G) must keep identity and verification records under section 50 when standard customer due diligence is conducted:

(H) must keep records of any audits under section 51(1)(b), (2), and (3):

(I) must audit its AML/CFT compliance obligations under section 59A if requested by an AML/CFT supervisor:

(e) in the case of a casino, the casino carries out activities that may give rise to a risk of money laundering or financing of terrorism.

History

S 6(4) amended by No 28 of 2020, s 129 and sch 5, by replacing (i) in para (b) "the Racing Industry Transition Agency" with "TAB NZ"; and (ii) in para (b)(i) "section 50 of the Racing Act 2003" with "section 74 of the Racing Industry Act 2020"; **effective 1 August 2020**.

S 6(4) amended by No 32 of 2019, s 25(2) and sch 3, by replacing in para (b) "New Zealand Racing Board" with "Racing Industry Transition Agency"; **effective 1 July 2019**.

6(5) An order under this section is secondary legislation (*see* Part 3 of the Legislation Act 2019 for publication requirements).

History

S 6(5) inserted by No 7 of 2021, s 3 and sch 16, **effective 28 October 2021** (LI 2021/250).

History

S 6 replaced by No 35 of 2017, s 6, **effective 11 August 2017**. Former s 6 read:

"**SECTION 6 APPLICATION OF THIS ACT TO REPORTING ENTITIES**

6 This Act applies to a reporting entity only to the extent that—

(a) in the case of a reporting entity that is a financial institution, the financial activities undertaken by that entity fall within the activities described in the definition of financial institution; or

(b) a reporting entity, that is not a financial institution, is carrying out activities that may give rise to a risk of money laundering or financing of terrorism."

SECTION 7 AMOUNTS NOT IN NEW ZEALAND CURRENCY

7(1) [When this section applies] This section applies if, for the purposes of this Act or regulations, it is necessary to determine whether the amount of any cash (whether alone or together with any other amount of cash)—

(a) is equal to or above the applicable threshold value; and

(b) is denominated in a currency other than New Zealand currency.

History

S 7(1) amended by No 35 of 2017, s 7(1) and (2), by (i) inserting "or regulations" after "Act"; and (ii) replacing in para (a) "exceeds" with "is equal to or above"; **effective 11 August 2017**.

7(2) [Exchange rate calculation] If this section applies, the amount of the cash is taken to be the equivalent in New Zealand currency,—

(a) calculated at the rate of exchange on the date of the determination; or

(b) if there is more than 1 rate of exchange on that date, calculated at the average of those rates.

7(3) [Evidence of rate of exchange] For the purposes of this section, a written certificate purporting to be signed by an officer of any bank in New Zealand that a specified rate of exchange prevailed between currencies on a specified day, and that at such rate a specified sum in a particular currency is equivalent to a specified sum in terms of the currency of New Zealand, is sufficient evidence of the rate of exchange so prevailing and of the equivalent sums in terms of the respective currencies.

Compare: 1996 No 9 s 4

SECTION 7A TRANSITIONAL, SAVINGS, AND RELATED PROVISIONS

7A The transitional, savings, and related provisions set out in Schedule 1 have effect according to their terms.

History

S 7A inserted by No 35 of 2017, s 8, **effective 11 August 2017**.

SECTION 8 ACT BINDS THE CROWN

8 This Act binds the Crown.

PART 2 — AML/CFT REQUIREMENTS AND COMPLIANCE

SECTION 9 NON-COMPLIANCE NOT EXCUSED BY CONTRACTUAL OBLIGATIONS

9(1) [No contracting out] This Act has effect despite anything to the contrary in any contract or agreement.

9(2) [Breach of contract no excuse] No person is excused from compliance with any requirement of this Act or regulations by reason only that compliance with that requirement would constitute breach of any contract or agreement.

Subpart 1 — Customer due diligence

SECTION 10 DEFINITIONS

10 In this subpart, unless the context otherwise requires,—

enhanced customer due diligence means customer due diligence in accordance with the requirements set out in sections 23 to 30 and any other requirements prescribed by regulations

simplified customer due diligence means customer due diligence in accordance with the requirements set out in sections 19 to 21 and any other requirements prescribed by regulations

standard customer due diligence means customer due diligence in accordance with the requirements set out in sections 15 to 17 and any other requirements prescribed by regulations.

SECTION 11 CUSTOMER DUE DILIGENCE

11(1) [Persons for whom required] A reporting entity must conduct customer due diligence on—

(a) a customer:

(b) any beneficial owner of a customer:

(c) any person acting on behalf of a customer.

11(2) [Individuals assumed to be beneficial owners] For the purposes of subsection (1)(b), a customer who is an individual and who the reporting entity believes on reasonable grounds is not acting on behalf of another person is to be treated as if he or she were also the beneficial owner unless the reporting entity has reasonable grounds to suspect that that customer is not the beneficial owner.

11(3) [Type of customer due diligence to be performed] The type of customer due diligence that must be conducted by a reporting entity is,—

(a) in the circumstances described in section 14, at least standard customer due diligence:

(b) in the circumstances described in section 18, at least simplified customer due diligence:

(c) in the circumstances described in section 22, enhanced customer due diligence.

11(4) [No requirement to obtain previously verified information unless doubts] A reporting entity that is required to conduct customer due diligence in the circumstances described in sections 14, 18, and 22 is not required to obtain or verify any documents, data, or information that it has previously obtained and verified for the purposes of carrying out customer due diligence in accordance with this Act, unless there are reasonable grounds for the reporting entity to doubt the adequacy or veracity of the documents, data, or information previously obtained.

11(5) [Obligation to conduct ongoing due diligence not affected] Nothing in subsection (4) affects the obligation to conduct ongoing customer due diligence in accordance with section 31.

11(6) [Where no effect] Subsections (1) and (3) and sections 14 to 31 do not apply in relation to the provision of services by a reporting entity to a customer that, in relation to that reporting entity, are not, under section 6(4), activities to which this Act applies.

History

S 11(6) inserted by No 35 of 2017, s 9, **effective 11 August 2017**.

SECTION 12 RELIANCE ON RISK ASSESSMENT WHEN ESTABLISHING LEVEL OF RISK

12 When establishing the level of risk involved for the purposes of this subpart, a reporting entity must rely on its AML/CFT programme and its risk assessment undertaken in accordance with section 58.

SECTION 13 BASIS FOR VERIFYING IDENTITY

13 Verification of identity must be done on—

(a) the basis of documents, data, or information issued by a reliable and independent source; or

(b) any other basis applying to a specified situation, customer, product, service, business relationship, or transaction prescribed by regulations.

Standard customer due diligence

SECTION 14 CIRCUMSTANCES WHEN STANDARD CUSTOMER DUE DILIGENCE APPLIES

14(1) [Standard diligence required] A reporting entity must conduct standard customer due diligence in the following circumstances:

(a) if the reporting entity establishes a business relationship with a new customer:

(b) if a customer seeks to conduct an occasional transaction or activity through the reporting entity:

(c) if, in relation to an existing customer, and according to the level of risk involved,—

  (i) there has been a material change in the nature or purpose of the business relationship; and

  (ii) the reporting entity considers that it has insufficient information about the customer:

(d) any other circumstances specified in subsection (2) or in regulations.

History

S 14(1) amended by No 35 of 2017, s 10(1), 68 and sch 2, by replacing (i) para (d); and (ii) in para (b) "occasional transaction" with "occasional transaction or activity"; **effective 11 August 2017**. Former para (d) read:

"(d) any other circumstances specified in regulations."

14(2) [Anonymous accounts] For the purposes of subsection (1)(d), as soon as practicable after a reporting entity becomes aware that an existing account is anonymous, the reporting entity must conduct standard customer due diligence in respect of that account.

History

S 14(2) inserted by No 35 of 2017, s 10(2), **effective 11 August 2017**.

14(3) [Real estate agents] Despite subsections (1) and (2), a real estate agent must conduct standard customer due diligence at the times, and with any other modifications, specified in regulations.

History

S 14(3) inserted by No 35 of 2017, s 10(2), **effective 11 August 2017**.

SECTION 15 STANDARD CUSTOMER DUE DILIGENCE: IDENTITY REQUIREMENTS

15 A reporting entity must obtain the following identity information in relation to the persons referred to in section 11(1):

(a) the person's full name; and

(b) the person's date of birth; and

(c) if the person is not the customer, the person's relationship to the customer; and

(d) the person's address or registered office; and

(e) the person's company identifier or registration number; and

(f) any information prescribed by regulations.

SECTION 16 STANDARD CUSTOMER DUE DILIGENCE: VERIFICATION OF IDENTITY REQUIREMENTS

16(1) [Requirements for reporting entities] A reporting entity must—

(a) take reasonable steps to satisfy itself that the information obtained under section 15 is correct; and

(b) according to the level of risk involved, take reasonable steps to verify any beneficial owner's identity so that the reporting entity is satisfied that it knows who the beneficial owner is; and

(c) if a person is acting on behalf of the customer, according to the level of risk involved, take reasonable steps to verify the person's identity and authority to act on behalf of the customer so that the reporting entity is satisfied it knows who the person is and that the person has authority to act on behalf of the customer; and

(d) verify any other information prescribed by regulations.

History

S 16(1) amended by No 106 of 2013, s 5, by replacing in para (a) "provided" with "obtained"; **effective 5 December 2013**.

16(2) [Verification to be prior to business relationship] Except as provided in subsection (3), a reporting entity must carry out verification of identity before establishing a business relationship or conducting an occasional transaction or activity.

History

S 16(2) amended by No 35 of 2017, s 68 and sch 2, by replacing "occasional transaction" with "occasional transaction or activity"; **effective 11 August 2017**.

16(3) [Exceptions to the prior verification requirement] Verification of identity may be completed after the business relationship has been established if—

(a) it is essential not to interrupt normal business practice; and

(b) money laundering and financing of terrorism risks are effectively managed through procedures of transaction limitations and account monitoring or (if the reporting entity is not a financial institution) through other appropriate risk management procedures; and

(c) verification of identity is completed as soon as is practicable once the business relationship has been established.

History

S 16(3) amended by No 35 of 2017, s 11, by replacing in para (b) "and account monitoring" with "and account monitoring or (if the reporting entity is not a financial institution) through other appropriate risk management procedures"; **effective 11 August 2017**.

SECTION 17 STANDARD CUSTOMER DUE DILIGENCE: OTHER REQUIREMENTS

17 A reporting entity must also obtain—

(a) information on the nature and purpose of the proposed business relationship between the customer and the reporting entity; and

(b) sufficient information to determine whether the customer should be subject to enhanced customer due diligence.

Simplified customer due diligence

SECTION 18 CIRCUMSTANCES WHEN SIMPLIFIED CUSTOMER DUE DILIGENCE APPLIES

18(1) A reporting entity may conduct simplified customer due diligence if—

(a) it establishes a business relationship with one of the customers specified in subsection (2); or

(b) one of the customers specified in subsection (2) conducts an occasional transaction or activity through the reporting entity; or

(c) a customer conducts a transaction or obtains a product or service specified in regulations through the reporting entity.

History

S 18(1) amended by No 35 of 2017, s 68 and sch 2, by replacing in para (b) "occasional transaction" with "occasional transaction or activity"; **effective 11 August 2017**.

S 18(1) amended by No 106 of 2013, s 6, by replacing in para (c) "provides" with "obtains"; **effective 5 December 2013**.

18(2) The following are customers for the purposes of subsection (1):

(a) a listed issuer (within the meaning of section 6(1) of the Financial Markets Conduct Act 2013) that is the issuer of quoted voting products (within the meaning of that Act):

(b) a public service agency as defined in section 5 of the Public Service Act 2020:

(c) a local authority, as defined in section 5(2) of the Local Government Act 2002:

(d) the New Zealand Police:

(e) a State enterprise (within the meaning of section 2 of the State-Owned Enterprises Act 1986) and a new State enterprise (as listed in Schedule 2 of that Act):

(f) a body that—

(i) corresponds to a State enterprise or a new State enterprise (as defined in paragraph (e); and

(ii) is located in a country that has sufficient AML/CFT systems:

(g) (*repealed*)

(h) a person licensed to be a supervisor or statutory supervisor under the Financial Markets Supervisors Act 2011, when the person acts for itself:

(i) a trustee corporation, within the meaning of section 2(1) of the Administration Act 1969, when the trustee corporation acts for itself:

(j) a Crown entity, as defined in section 7(1) of the Crown Entities Act 2004:

(k) an organisation named in Schedule 4 of the Public Finance Act 1989:

(l) a company named in Schedule 4A of the Public Finance Act 1989:

(m) a government body that—

(i) corresponds to a public service agency as defined in section 5 of the Public Service Act 2020; and

(ii) is located in an overseas jurisdiction that has sufficient AML/CFT systems:

[Effective on a date to be appointed, or 1 October 2022]

(n) a registered bank within the meaning of section 2(1) of the Banking (Prudential Supervision) Act 1989:

(n) a registered bank within the meaning of section 2(1) of the Reserve Bank of New Zealand Act 1989:

(o) a licensed insurer within the meaning of section 6(1) of the Insurance (Prudential Supervision) Act 2010:

(p) a company, or a subsidiary (within the meaning of section 5(1) of the Companies Act 1993) of that company,—

(i) whose equity securities are listed in New Zealand or on an overseas stock exchange that has sufficient disclosure requirements; and

(ii) that is located in a country that has sufficient AML/CFT systems in place:

(q) any other entity or class of entities specified in regulations.

History

S 18(2) amended by No 31 of 2021, s 300(1) and sch 4, by replacing in para (n) "Reserve Bank of New Zealand Act 1989" with "Banking (Prudential Supervision) Act 1989"; **effective on a date to be appointed by the Governor-General by Order in Council, or 1 October 2022, whichever is earlier**.

S 18(2) amended by No 40 of 2020, s 135 and sch 11, by replacing (i) para (b); and (ii) in para (m)(i) "a government department named in Schedule 1 of the State Sector Act 1988" with "a public service agency as defined in section 5 of the Public Service Act 2020"; **effective 7 August 2020**. Former para (b) read:

"(b) a government department named in Schedule 1 of the State Sector Act 1988:".

S 18(2) amended by No 10 of 2017, s 335 and sch 4, by repealing para (g); **effective 28 September 2017**. Former para (g) read:

"(g) the New Zealand Security Intelligence Service:".

S 18(2) replaced by No 35 of 2017, s 12(1), **effective 11 August 2017**. Former s 18(2) read:

"18(2) [Specified customers] The following are customers for the purposes of subsection (1):

(a) a listed issuer (within the meaning of the Financial Markets Conduct Act 2013) that is the issuer of quoted voting products (within the meaning of that Act):

(b) a government department named in Schedule 1 of the State Sector Act 1988:

(c) a local authority as defined in section 5 of the Local Government Act 2002:

(d) the New Zealand Police:

(e) (*repealed*)

(f) any other entity or class of entities specified in regulations."

S 18(2) amended by No 70 of 2013, s 150 and sch, by replacing para (a); **effective 1 December 2014** (LI 2014/325). Former para (a) read:

"(a) a company that is listed on an exchange registered under Part 2B of the Securities Markets Act 1988:"

18(3) A reporting entity may also conduct simplified customer due diligence on a person who purports to act on behalf of a customer when—

(a) the reporting entity already has a business relationship with the customer at the time the person acts on behalf of the customer; and

(b) the reporting entity has conducted one of the specified types of customer due diligence on the customer in accordance with this Act and regulations (if any).

18(3A) Despite subsections (1) to (3), a real estate agent must conduct simplified customer due diligence at the times, and with any other modifications, specified in regulations.

History

S 18(3A) inserted by No 35 of 2017, s 12(2), **effective 11 August 2017**.

18(4) For the avoidance of doubt, nothing in this subpart requires identification or verification of identity of a beneficial owner of a customer in respect of whom a reporting entity may conduct simplified customer due diligence.

SECTION 19 SIMPLIFIED CUSTOMER DUE DILIGENCE: IDENTITY REQUIREMENTS

19 A reporting entity must obtain the following identity information in relation to a person acting on behalf of the customer:

(a) the person's full name; and

(b) the person's date of birth; and

(c) the person's relationship to the customer; and

(d) any information prescribed by regulations.

SECTION 20 SIMPLIFIED CUSTOMER DUE DILIGENCE: VERIFICATION OF IDENTITY REQUIREMENTS

20(1) [Verification of identity and authority to act] A reporting entity must, according to the level of risk involved, verify the identity of a person acting on behalf of a customer and that person's authority to act for the customer so that it is satisfied it knows who the person is and that the person has authority to act on behalf of the customer.

20(2) [Verification to be prior to business relationship] Verification of identity must be carried out before the business relationship is established or the occasional transaction or activity is conducted or the person acts on behalf of the customer.

History

S 20(2) amended by No 35 of 2017, s 68 and sch 2, by replacing "occasional transaction" with "occasional transaction or activity"; **effective 11 August 2017**.

20(3) [Reporting entity may rely on an authority to act] For the purposes of verifying a person's authority to act in the circumstances described in section 18, a reporting entity may rely on an authority provided in an application form or other document provided to the reporting entity that shows a person's authority to act or transact on an account.

SECTION 21 SIMPLIFIED CUSTOMER DUE DILIGENCE: OTHER REQUIREMENTS

21 In the circumstances described in section 18(1)(a), a reporting entity must also obtain information on the nature and purpose of the proposed business relationship between the customer and the reporting entity.

Enhanced customer due diligence

SECTION 22 CIRCUMSTANCES WHEN ENHANCED CUSTOMER DUE DILIGENCE APPLIES

22(1) [List of circumstances] A reporting entity must conduct enhanced customer due diligence in accordance with sections 23 and 24 in the following circumstances:

(a) if the reporting entity establishes a business relationship with a customer that is—

- (i) a trust or another vehicle for holding personal assets:
- (ii) a non-resident customer from a country that has insufficient anti-money laundering and countering financing of terrorism systems or measures in place:
- (iii) a company with nominee shareholders or shares in bearer form:

(b) if a customer seeks to conduct an occasional transaction or activity through the reporting entity and that customer is—

- (i) a trust or another vehicle for holding personal assets:
- (ii) a non-resident customer from a country that has insufficient anti-money laundering and countering financing of terrorism systems or measures in place:
- (iii) a company with nominee shareholders or shares in bearer form:

(c) if a customer seeks to conduct, through the reporting entity, a complex, unusually large transaction or unusual pattern of transactions that have no apparent or visible economic or lawful purpose:

(d) when a reporting entity considers that the level of risk involved is such that enhanced due diligence should apply to a particular situation:

(e) any other circumstances specified in section 22A or regulations.

History

S 22(1) amended by No 35 of 2017, s 13(1), 68 and sch 2, by replacing (i) in para (e) "regulations" with "section 22A or regulations"; and (ii) in para (b) "occasional transaction" with "occasional transaction or activity"; **effective 11 August 2017**.

22(2) [Requirement when politically exposed persons] A reporting entity must conduct enhanced customer due diligence in accordance with section 26 if—

(a) it establishes a business relationship with a customer who it has determined is a politically exposed person; or

(b) a customer who it has determined is a politically exposed person seeks to conduct an occasional transaction or activity through the reporting entity.

History

S 22(2) amended by No 35 of 2017, s 68 and sch 2, by replacing in para (b) "occasional transaction" with "occasional transaction or activity"; **effective 11 August 2017**.

22(3) [Requirement in respect of a wire transfer] A reporting entity must conduct enhanced customer due diligence in accordance with sections 27 and 28 if it is an ordering institution, an intermediary institution, or a beneficiary institution in relation to a wire transfer.

22(4) [Requirement in respect of a correspondent banking relationship] A reporting entity must conduct enhanced customer due diligence in accordance with section 29 if it has, or proposes to have, a correspondent banking relationship.

22(5) [New or developing technologies and products that might favour anonymity] A reporting entity must conduct enhanced due diligence in accordance with section 30 if—

(a) it establishes a business relationship with a customer that involves new or developing technologies, or new or developing products, that might favour anonymity; or

(b) a customer seeks to conduct an occasional transaction or activity through the reporting entity that involves new or developing technologies, or new or developing products, that might favour anonymity.

History

S 22(5) amended by No 35 of 2017, s 68 and sch 2, by replacing in para (b) "occasional transaction" with "occasional transaction or activity"; **effective 11 August 2017**.

22(6) [Real estate agents] Despite subsections (1) to (5), a real estate agent must conduct enhanced customer due diligence at the times, in the circumstances, and with any other modifications specified in regulations.

History

S 22(6) inserted by No 35 of 2017, s 13(2), **effective 11 August 2017**.

SECTION 22A ENHANCED CUSTOMER DUE DILIGENCE REQUIRED FOR CERTAIN ACTIVITIES REQUIRING SUSPICIOUS ACTIVITIES REPORT

22A(1) [Where this section applies] This section applies to an activity—

(a) that the reporting entity concerned (other than a high-value dealer) is required to report to the Commissioner under section 40; and

(b) that is not otherwise exempt from the customer due diligence requirements or from all the requirements of the Act; and

(c) that is conducted, or sought to be conducted,—

(i) by an existing customer; or

(ii) by a customer engaging in an occasional transaction or activity.

22A(2) [Application] For the purposes of section 22(1)(e), as soon as practicable after a reporting entity becomes aware that the reporting entity must report the suspicious activity under section 40, a circumstance occurs in which the reporting entity must conduct enhanced customer due diligence in respect of that activity.

History

S 22A inserted by No 35 of 2017, s 14, **effective 11 August 2017**.

SECTION 23 ENHANCED CUSTOMER DUE DILIGENCE: IDENTITY REQUIREMENTS

23(1) [General obligations] A reporting entity must, in relation to a person referred to in section 11(1), obtain the information required under section 15 and the following additional information:

(a) information relating to the source of the funds or the wealth of the customer; and

(b) the additional information referred to in subsection (2) and any additional information prescribed by regulations.

History

S 23(1) amended by No 35 of 2017, s 15(1), by replacing para (b); **effective 11 August 2017**. Former para (b) read:

"(b) any additional information prescribed by regulations."

23(2) [Obligations for trusts] For the purposes of subsection (1)(b), a reporting entity must obtain,—

(a) in the case of a trust other than a trust to which paragraph (b) applies, the name and the date of birth of each beneficiary of the trust:

(b) in the case of a customer that is a discretionary trust or a charitable trust or a trust that has more than 10 beneficiaries, a description of—

(i) each class or type of beneficiary:

(ii) if the trust is a charitable trust, the objects of the trust.

History

S 23(2) inserted by No 35 of 2017, s 15(2), **effective 11 August 2017**.

SECTION 24 ENHANCED CUSTOMER DUE DILIGENCE: VERIFICATION OF IDENTITY REQUIREMENTS

24(1) [What a reporting entity must do] A reporting entity must—

(a) conduct the verification of identity requirements for standard customer due diligence set out in section 16; and

(b) according to the level of risk involved, take reasonable steps to verify the information obtained under section 23(a); and

(c) verify any other information prescribed by regulations.

24(2) [Verification must be prior to business relationship] Except as provided in subsection (3), a reporting entity must carry out verification of identity before establishing a business relationship or conducting an occasional transaction or activity.

History

S 24(2) amended by No 35 of 2017, s 68 and sch 2, by replacing "occasional transaction" with "occasional transaction or activity"; **effective 11 August 2017**.

24(3) [Exceptions to the prior verification requirement] Verification of identity may be completed after the business relationship has been established if—

(a) it is essential not to interrupt normal business practice; and

(b) money laundering and financing of terrorism risks are effectively managed through procedures of transaction limitations and account monitoring or (if the reporting entity is not a financial institution) through other appropriate risk management procedures; and

(c) verification of identity is completed as soon as is practicable once the business relationship has been established.

History

S 24(3) amended by No 35 of 2017, s 16, by replacing in para (b) "and account monitoring" with "and account monitoring or (if the reporting entity is not a financial institution) through other appropriate risk management procedures"; **effective 11 August 2017**.

SECTION 25 ENHANCED CUSTOMER DUE DILIGENCE: OTHER REQUIREMENTS

25 In the circumstances described in section 22(1)(a), 22(2)(a), and 22(5)(a), a reporting entity must also obtain information on the nature and purpose of the proposed business relationship between the customer and the reporting entity.

SECTION 26 POLITICALLY EXPOSED PERSON

26(1) [Requirement to determine whether a politically exposed person] The reporting entity must, as soon as practicable after establishing a business relationship or conducting an occasional transaction or activity, take reasonable steps to determine whether the customer or any beneficial owner is a politically exposed person.

History

S 26(1) amended by No 35 of 2017, s 68 and sch 2, by replacing "occasional transaction" with "occasional transaction or activity"; **effective 11 August 2017**.

26(2) [Steps required if found to be a politically exposed person] If a reporting entity determines that a customer or beneficial owner with whom it has established a business relationship is a politically exposed person, then—

(a) the reporting entity must have senior management approval for continuing the business relationship; and

(b) the reporting entity must obtain information about the source of wealth or funds of the customer or beneficial owner and take reasonable steps to verify the source of that wealth or those funds.

26(3) [Requirement to establish source of wealth or funds] If a reporting entity determines that a customer or beneficial owner with whom it has conducted an occasional transaction or activity is a politically exposed person, then the reporting entity must, as soon as practicable after conducting that transaction or other activity, take reasonable steps to obtain information about the source of wealth or funds of the customer or beneficial owner and verify the source of that wealth or those funds.

History

S 26(3) amended by No 35 of 2017, s 68 and sch 2, by (i) replacing "occasional transaction" with "occasional transaction or activity"; and (ii) inserting "or other activity" after "that transaction"; **effective 11 August 2017**.

SECTION 27 WIRE TRANSFERS: IDENTITY REQUIREMENTS

27(1) [Requirement to identify originator of a wire transfer] A reporting entity that is an ordering institution must identify the originator of a wire transfer that is equal to or above the applicable threshold value by obtaining the following information:

(a) the originator's full name; and

(b) the originator's account number or other identifying information that may be prescribed and allows the transaction to be traced back to the originator; and

(c) one of the following:

(i) the originator's address:

(ii) the originator's national identity number:

(iii) the originator's customer identification number:

(iv) the originator's place and date of birth; and

(d) any information prescribed by section 27A or regulations.

History

S 27(1) amended by No 35 of 2017, s 17(1) and (2), by replacing (i) "over" with "equal to or above"; and (ii) in para (d) "regulations" with "section 27A or regulations"; **effective 11 August 2017**.

27(2) [Identification in respect of domestic wire transfers] However, if the wire transfer is a domestic wire transfer, a reporting entity that is an ordering institution may identify the originator by obtaining the originator's account number or other identifying information that may be prescribed and allows the transaction to be traced back to the originator if the reporting entity that is the ordering institution is able to provide the information specified in subsection (1)(a), (c), and (d) within 3 working days of a request being made by the beneficiary institution.

27(3) [Exemption under regulations] Regulations may be made under section 154(1)(c) exempting the reporting entity from the obligation to obtain some or all of the information set out in subsection (1) in relation to a specified transfer or transaction.

27(4) [Information must accompany wire transfer] The information obtained by the reporting entity (the ordering institution under subsection (1) or (2), as the case may be) must accompany the wire transfer.

27(5) [Requirements for beneficiary institutions] A reporting entity that is a beneficiary institution must—

(a) use effective risk-based procedures for handling wire transfers that are not accompanied by all the information specified in subsection (1); and

(b) consider whether the wire transfers constitute a suspicious activity.

History

S 27(5) amended by No 35 of 2017, s 17(3), by replacing in para (b) "suspicious transaction" with "suspicious activity"; **effective 11 August 2017**.

27(6) [Requirements for intermediary institutions] Any information about the originator obtained by a reporting entity that is an intermediary institution must be provided by that reporting entity to the beneficiary institution as soon as practicable.

History

S 27(6) replaced by No 106 of 2013, s 7, **effective 5 December 2013**. Former s 27(6) read:

"27(6) [Requirements for intermediary institutions] Any information obtained by a reporting entity that is an intermediary institution must be maintained by that reporting entity with the wire transfer accompanying the information."

27(7) [Definition of domestic wire transfer] For the purposes of this section, a **domestic wire transfer** is a wire transfer where the ordering institution, the intermediary institution, and the beneficiary institution are all in New Zealand.

SECTION 27A OTHER IDENTIFYING INFORMATION PRESCRIBED IN RELATION TO WIRE TRANSFERS

27A(1) [Name and account number] Information that gives the name of the beneficiary of a wire transfer and the account number of that beneficiary or any unique transaction reference that allows the transaction to be traced is prescribed for the purposes of section 27(1)(d).

27A(2) [Domestic wire transfers] In the case of a domestic wire transfer, any information that enables the transaction itself to be identified and traced to the originator is prescribed to be other identifying information for the purposes of section 27(2).

History

S 27A inserted by No 35 of 2017, s 18, **effective 11 August 2017**.

SECTION 28 WIRE TRANSFERS: VERIFICATION OF IDENTITY REQUIREMENTS

28(1) [Requirement of ordering institution to verify identity] The ordering institution must, according to the level of risk involved,—

(a) verify the originator's identity so that the reporting entity is satisfied that the information obtained under section 27 is correct; and

(b) verify any other information prescribed by regulations.

History

S 28(1) amended by No 106 of 2013, s 8, by replacing para (a); **effective 5 December 2013**. Former para (a) read:

"(a) verify the originator's identity so that the reporting entity is satisfied that the information provided under section 27 is current and correct; and".

28(2) [Verification must be before wire transfer] Verification of the originator's identity must be carried out before the wire transfer is ordered.

SECTION 29 CORRESPONDENT BANKING RELATIONSHIPS

29(1) [Requirement to conduct due diligence in respect of correspondent banking relationships] A financial institution (the **correspondent**) that has, or proposes to have, a correspondent banking relationship with a respondent financial institution (the **respondent**) must, according to the level of risk involved, conduct enhanced customer due diligence as set out in subsection (2) in relation to correspondent accounts that are used, or are proposed to be used, for payments to, or receipts from, foreign financial institutions.

29(2) [Requirements for correspondent institution] The correspondent must—

(a) gather enough information about the respondent to understand fully the nature of the respondent's business; and

(b) determine from publicly available information the reputation of the respondent and whether and to what extent the respondent is supervised for AML/CFT purposes, including whether the respondent has been subject to a money laundering or financing of terrorism investigation or regulatory action; and

(c) assess the respondent's anti-money laundering and countering financing of terrorism controls to ascertain that those controls are adequate and effective; and

(d) have approval from its senior management before establishing a new correspondent banking relationship; and

(e) document the respective AML/CFT responsibilities of the correspondent and the respondent; and

(f) be satisfied that, in respect of those of the respondent's customers who have direct access to accounts of the correspondent, the respondent—

  (i) has verified the identity of, and conducts ongoing monitoring in respect of, those customers; and

  (ii) is able to provide to the correspondent, on request, the documents, data, or information obtained when conducting the relevant customer due diligence and ongoing customer due diligence; and

(g) meet any other requirements prescribed by regulations and that apply to correspondent banking relationships.

29(3) [Definition of correspondent banking relationship] For the purposes of this Act or regulations, a **correspondent banking relationship** means a relationship that involves the provision of banking services by a financial institution (the **correspondent**) to another financial institution (the **respondent**) if—

(a) the correspondent carries on an activity or business at or through a permanent establishment of the correspondent in a particular country; and

(b) the respondent carries on an activity or business at or through a permanent establishment of the respondent in another country; and

(c) the correspondent banking relationship relates, in whole or in part, to those permanent establishments; and

(d) the relationship is not of a kind specified in regulations; and

(e) the banking services are not of a kind specified in regulations.

History

S 29(3) amended by No 35 of 2017, s 19, by inserting "or regulations" after "Act"; **effective 11 August 2017**.

SECTION 30 NEW OR DEVELOPING TECHNOLOGIES, OR PRODUCTS, THAT MIGHT FAVOUR ANONYMITY

30 Before a reporting entity establishes a business relationship or conducts an occasional transaction or activity that involves new or developing technologies, or new or developing products, that might favour anonymity, the reporting entity must, in addition to the requirements in sections 15 and 16,—

(a) take any additional measures that may be needed to mitigate and manage the risk of new or developing technologies, or new or developing products, that might favour anonymity from being used in the commission of a money laundering offence or for the financing of terrorism; and

(b) meet any other requirements prescribed by regulations and that apply to the particular technology or product.

History

S 30 amended by No 35 of 2017, s 68 and sch 2, by replacing "occasional transaction" with "occasional transaction or activity"; **effective 11 August 2017**.

Ongoing customer due diligence and account monitoring

SECTION 31 ONGOING CUSTOMER DUE DILIGENCE AND ACCOUNT MONITORING

31(1) [Ongoing business relationship] This section applies to a business relationship between a reporting entity and a customer.

31(2) [Requirement to conduct ongoing customer due diligence] A reporting entity must conduct ongoing customer due diligence and undertake account monitoring in order to—

(a) ensure that the business relationship and the transactions relating to that business relationship are consistent with the reporting entity's knowledge about the customer and the customer's business and risk profile; and

(b) identify any grounds for reporting a suspicious activity under paragraph (b) of the definition of that term in section 39A.

History

S 31(2) amended by No 35 of 2017, s 20, by replacing in para (b) "suspicious transaction under section 40(1)(b)" with "suspicious activity under paragraph (b) of the definition of that term in section 39A"; **effective 11 August 2017**.

31(3) [Relevant considerations] When conducting ongoing customer due diligence and undertaking account monitoring, the reporting entity must have regard to—

(a) the type of customer due diligence conducted when the business relationship with the customer was established; and

(b) the level of risk involved.

31(4) [Minimum regular review requirements] When conducting ongoing customer due diligence and undertaking account monitoring, a reporting entity must do at least the following:

(a) regularly review the customer's account activity and transaction behaviour; and

(b) regularly review any customer information obtained under sections 15, 17, 19, 21, 23, 25, 26, 27, 29, and 30, or, in relation to an existing customer, any customer information the reporting entity holds about the customer; and

(c) anything prescribed by regulations.

Reliance on third parties

SECTION 32 RELIANCE ON MEMBER OF DESIGNATED BUSINESS GROUP

32(1) [Ways reporting entities may rely on members of a designated business group] A reporting entity (**member A**) that is a member of a designated business group may—

(a) rely on another member of the group (**member B**) to conduct any customer due diligence procedures required for customer due diligence under this Act or regulations as long as—

  (i) any identity information is given to member A by member B before member A establishes a business relationship or an occasional transaction or activity is conducted; and

  (ii) any verification information is given to member A by member B as soon as practicable on request by the reporting entity, but within 5 working days of the request, after the business relationship is established or the occasional transaction or activity is conducted:

(b) adopt that part of an AML/CFT programme of another member of the group that relates to record keeping, account monitoring, ongoing customer due diligence, and annual reporting and share and use the procedures, policies, and controls relating to those parts of the programme subject to any conditions prescribed by regulations:

(c) use another member of the group's risk assessment if that risk assessment is relevant to member A's business:

(d) make a suspicious activity or prescribed transaction report on behalf of any other member or all members of the designated business group.

History

S 32(1) amended by No 35 of 2017, s 21(1), (2), 68 and sch 2, by replacing (i) in para (a)(ii) ", but no later than 5 working days," with "on request by the reporting entity, but within 5 working days of the request,"; (ii) in para (d) "suspicious transaction" with "suspicious activity or prescribed transaction"; and (iii) in para (a)(i) and (ii) "occasional transaction" with "occasional transaction or activity"; **effective 11 August 2017**.

32(1A) [Reliance on other group members] A reporting entity (**member A**) that is a member of a designated business group may rely on another member of the group (**member B**) to make prescribed transaction reports under this Act or regulations.

History

S 32(1A) inserted by No 35 of 2017, s 21(3), **effective 11 August 2017**.

32(2) [Still responsible for ensuring compliance] Despite subsection (1), a reporting entity, and not the member of the designated business group relied on by the reporting entity, is responsible for ensuring that it is complying with this Act and regulations.

32(3) [Supervisor may require risk assessment if reliance not appropriate] An AML/CFT supervisor for a reporting entity that is part of a designated business group may require the reporting entity to undertake its own risk assessment or develop its own AML/CFT programme if the AML/CFT supervisor is of the view that the risk assessment or AML/CFT programme being, or proposed to be, relied on by the reporting entity is not appropriate for that entity.

32(4) [Subject to s 36] This section is subject to section 36, which relates to the protection of personal information.

Compare: Anti-Money Laundering and Counter-Terrorism Financing Act 2006 s 36(4) (Aust)

SECTION 33 RELIANCE ON OTHER REPORTING ENTITIES OR PERSONS IN ANOTHER COUNTRY

33(1) [A reporting entity may rely on another person to conduct procedures] Subject to the conditions in subsection (2), a reporting entity may rely on another person (who is not an agent) to conduct the customer due diligence procedures required for customer due diligence under this Act or regulations.

33(2) [Conditions on application of this section] The conditions are that—

(a) the person being relied on is either—

(i) a reporting entity; or

(ii) a person who is resident in a country with sufficient anti-money laundering and countering financing of terrorism systems and measures in place and who is supervised or regulated for AML/CFT purposes; and

(b) the person has a business relationship with the customer concerned; and

(c) the person has conducted relevant customer due diligence procedures to at least the standard required by this Act and regulations and has provided to the reporting entity—

(i) relevant identity information before the reporting entity establishes a business relationship or an occasional transaction or activity is conducted; and

(ii) relevant verification information as soon as practicable on request by the reporting entity, but within 5 working days of the request; and

(d) the person consents to conducting the customer due diligence procedures for the reporting entity and to providing all relevant information to the reporting entity; and

(e) any other conditions prescribed by regulations are complied with.

History

S 33(2) amended by No 35 of 2017, s 22(1), 68 and sch 2, by replacing (i) in para (c)(ii) ", but no later than 5 working days, after the business relationship is established or the occasional transaction is conducted" with "on request by the reporting entity, but within 5 working days of the request"; and (ii) in para (c)(i) "occasional transaction" with "occasional transaction or activity"; **effective 11 August 2017**.

33(3) [Reporting entity remains responsible for ensuring compliance] Despite subsection (1), a reporting entity relying on a third party to conduct the customer due diligence procedure, and not the person carrying out the customer due diligence procedure, is responsible for ensuring that customer due diligence is carried out in accordance with this Act.

33(3A) [Reliance on third party] However, a reporting entity relying on a third party to conduct the customer due diligence procedure is not responsible for ensuring that customer due diligence is carried out in accordance with this Act if the following conditions are met:

(a) the reporting entity is acting in good faith when relying on a third party; and

(b) the reporting entity has reasonable cause to believe the reporting entity that is relied on has conducted relevant customer due diligence procedures to at least the standard required by this Act and regulations; and

(c) the reporting entity being relied on is an approved entity or is within an approved class of entities; and

(d) the conditions (if any) prescribed by regulations are complied with.

History

S 33(3A) inserted by No 35 of 2017, s 22(2), **effective 11 August 2017**.

SECTION 34 RELIANCE ON AGENTS

34 Subject to any conditions that may be prescribed by regulations, a reporting entity may authorise a person to be its agent and rely on that agent to conduct the customer due diligence procedures and obtain any information required for customer due diligence under this Act or regulations.

SECTION 35 USE OF INFORMATION OBTAINED FROM THIRD PARTY CONDUCTING CUSTOMER DUE DILIGENCE

35 Information obtained by a third party conducting customer due diligence under sections 32 to 34 for a reporting entity may only be used by that third party for the purpose of complying with this Act and regulations.

SECTION 36 PROTECTION OF PERSONAL INFORMATION AND DESIGNATED BUSINESS GROUPS

36(1) This section applies to personal information that is either—

(a) identity or verification information received for the purposes of section 32(1)(a); or

(b) information received for the purposes of section 32(1)(b).

36(2) Any information supplied by any member of a designated business group to another member of that group must be subject to privacy protections at least equivalent to those set out in information privacy principles 5 to 12 set out in section 22 of the Privacy Act 2020.

History

S 36(2) amended by No 31 of 2020, s 217 and sch 9, by replacing "privacy principles 5 to 11 in section 6 of the Privacy Act 1993" with "information privacy principles 5 to 12 set out in section 22 of the Privacy Act 2020"; **effective 1 December 2020**.

36(3) Each member of the designated business group must agree, in writing, to comply with information privacy principles 5 to 12 set out in section 22 of the Privacy Act 2020 or their equivalent if the member is resident overseas.

History

S 36(3) amended by No 31 of 2020, s 217 and sch 9, by replacing "privacy principles 5 to 11 in section 6 of the Privacy Act 1993" with "information privacy principles 5 to 12 set out in section 22 of the Privacy Act 2020"; **effective 1 December 2020**.

36(4) The entity that provides information to another member of its designated business group remains responsible for the use or disclosure of that information.

36(5) A reporting entity may use or disclose information to which this section applies only as follows:

(a) it may use identity and verification information received for the purposes of section 32(1)(a) in a suspicious activity report:

(b) it may disclose information for the purposes of section 32(1)(b) to another member of the designated business group unless such disclosure is likely to result in a suspicious activity report being filed in an overseas jurisdiction by the member to whom the information is disclosed.

History

S 36(5) amended by No 35 of 2017, s 23(1) and (2), by replacing (i) in para (a) "suspicious transactions report" with "suspicious activity report"; and (ii) in para (b) "suspicious transaction" with "suspicious activity"; **effective 11 August 2017**.

Prohibitions

SECTION 37 PROHIBITIONS IF CUSTOMER DUE DILIGENCE NOT CONDUCTED

37(1) [General prohibitions] If, in relation to a customer, a reporting entity is unable to conduct customer due diligence in accordance with this subpart, the reporting entity—

(a) must not establish a business relationship with the customer; and

(b) must terminate any existing business relationship with the customer; and

(c) must not carry out an occasional transaction or activity with or for the customer; and

(d) must consider whether to make a suspicious activity report; and

(e) may disclose the possibility of making a suspicious activity report only to a person referred to in section 46(2).

History

S 37(1) amended by No 35 of 2017, s 24(1), (2), 68 and sch 2, by replacing (i) in para (d) ''suspicious transactions report'' with ''suspicious activity report''; (ii) in para (e) ''suspicious transaction'' with ''suspicious activity''; and (iii) in para (c) ''occasional transaction'' with ''occasional transaction or activity''; **effective 11 August 2017**.

37(2) [Allowed business relationships] A reporting entity is not prohibited by subsection (1)(a) or (b) from establishing or continuing a business relationship with a customer in respect of an activity that is not specified in section 6(4) in relation to that reporting entity.

History

S 37(2) inserted by No 35 of 2017, s 24(3), **effective 11 August 2017**.

SECTION 38 PROHIBITION ON FALSE CUSTOMER NAMES AND CUSTOMER ANONYMITY

38(1) A reporting entity must not,—

(a) knowingly or recklessly, set up a facility for a customer on the basis of customer anonymity:

(b) without lawful justification or reasonable excuse, set up a facility for a customer under a false customer name.

38(2) Subsection (1) does not apply to a facility—

(a) that has a number or other identifier allocated to it and the customer and any person who is authorised to act on behalf of the customer in respect of the facility has had their identity verified in accordance with the relevant customer due diligence requirements; or

(b) that has been set up for the Commissioner or for the New Zealand Security Intelligence Service or for the Government Communications Security Bureau for law enforcement purposes.

History

S 38(2) amended by No 56 of 2019, s 4, by inserting in para (b) ''or for the Government Communications Security Bureau'' after ''New Zealand Security Intelligence Service''; **effective 24 October 2019**.

S 38(2) amended by No 98 of 2012, s 5, by replacing in para (a) ''or the'' with ''and any''; **effective 12 December 2012**.

SECTION 39 PROHIBITION ON ESTABLISHING OR CONTINUING BUSINESS RELATIONSHIP INVOLVING SHELL BANK

39(1) [Business relationships with shell banks prohibited] A reporting entity must not establish or continue a business relationship with, or allow an occasional transaction or activity to be conducted through it by,—

(a) a shell bank; or

(b) a financial institution that has a correspondent banking relationship with a shell bank.

History

S 39(1) amended by No 35 of 2017, s 68 and sch 2, by replacing ''occasional transaction'' with ''occasional transaction or activity''; **effective 11 August 2017**.

39(2) [Definition of shell bank] For the purposes of subsection (1), a **shell bank** is a corporation that—

(a) is incorporated in a foreign country; and

(b) is authorised to carry on banking business in its country of incorporation; and

(c) does not have a physical presence in its country of incorporation; and

(d) is not an affiliate of another corporation that—

(i) is incorporated in a particular country; and

(ii) is authorised to carry on banking business in its country of incorporation; and

(iii) is sufficiently supervised and monitored in carrying on its banking business; and

(iv) has a physical presence in its country of incorporation.

39(3) [Definition of affiliated] For the purposes of paragraph (d) of the definition of **shell bank** in subsection (2), a corporation is affiliated with another corporation only if—

(a) the corporation is a subsidiary of the other corporation; or

(b) both corporations are under common effective control; or

(c) both corporations are declared to be affiliated in accordance with regulations (if any).

39(4) [Definition of physical presence] For the purposes of the definition of **shell bank** in subsection (2), a corporation has a physical presence in a country if, and only if,—

(a) the corporation carries on banking business at a place in that country; and

(b) banking operations of the corporation are managed and conducted from that place.

Compare: Anti-Money Laundering and Counter-Terrorism Financing Act 2006 ss 15, 95 (Aust)

Subpart 2 — Suspicious activity reports

History

Pt 2, subpart 2, replaced by No 35 of 2017, s 25, **effective 11 August 2017**. Former subpart 2 heading read: "Subpart 2 — Suspicious transaction reports".

SECTION 39A INTERPRETATION

39A For the purposes of this subpart,—

service—

(a) means an activity that is carried out by a reporting entity; but

(b) does not include an activity unless section 6(4) applies this Act to the reporting entity in relation to the activity

suspicious activity means an activity undertaken in circumstances—

(a) in which—

(i) a person conducts or seeks to conduct a transaction through a reporting entity; or

(ii) a reporting entity provides or proposes to provide a service to a person; or

(iii) a person requests a reporting entity to provide a service or makes an inquiry to the reporting entity in relation to a service; and

(b) where the reporting entity has reasonable grounds to suspect that the transaction or proposed transaction, the service or proposed service, or the inquiry, as the case may be, is or may be relevant to—

(i) the investigation or prosecution of any person for a money laundering offence; or

(ii) the enforcement of the Misuse of Drugs Act 1975; or

(iii) the enforcement of the Terrorism Suppression Act 2002; or

(iv) the enforcement of the Proceeds of Crime Act 1991 or the Criminal Proceeds (Recovery) Act 2009; or

(v) the investigation or prosecution of an offence (within the meaning of section 243(1) of the Crimes Act 1961).

History

Pt 2, subpart 2, s 39A, inserted by No 35 of 2017, s 25, **effective 11 August 2017**.

SECTION 40 REPORTING ENTITIES TO REPORT SUSPICIOUS ACTIVITIES

40(1) [Non-high value dealers] Subsections (3) and (4) apply to reporting entities other than high-value dealers.

40(2) [High-value dealers] Subsection (5) applies to high-value dealers.

40(3) [Time limit] If this subsection applies, the reporting entity must, as soon as practicable but no later than 3 working days after forming its suspicion, report the activity, or suspicious activity, to the Commissioner in accordance with section 41.

40(4) [Privileged communications] Nothing in subsection (3) requires any person to disclose any information that the person believes on reasonable grounds is a privileged communication.

40(5) [Report to Commissioner] A high-value dealer may report a suspicious activity to the Commissioner.

History

Pt 2, subpart 2, s 40, replaced by No 35 of 2017, s 25, **effective 11 August 2017**. Former s 40 read:

"**SECTION 40 REPORTING ENTITIES TO REPORT SUSPICIOUS TRANSACTIONS**

40(1) [Application] Despite any other enactment or any rule of law, but subject to section 42 of this Act and to section 44(4) of the Terrorism Suppression Act 2002, this section applies if—

(a) a person conducts or seeks to conduct a transaction through a reporting entity; and

(b) the reporting entity has reasonable grounds to suspect that the transaction or proposed transaction is or may be—

(i) relevant to the investigation or prosecution of any person for a money laundering offence; or

(ii) relevant to the enforcement of the Misuse of Drugs Act 1975; or

(iii) relevant to the enforcement of the Terrorism Suppression Act 2002; or

(iv) relevant to the enforcement of the Proceeds of Crime Act 1991 or the Criminal Proceeds (Recovery) Act 2009; or

(v) relevant to the investigation or prosecution of an offence within the meaning of section 243(1) of the Crimes Act 1961.

[S 40(1) amended by No 96 of 2015, s 6, by replacing in para (b)(v) "a serious offence" with "an offence"; **effective 1 July 2017**.]

40(2) [Reporting requirement] If this section applies, the reporting entity must, as soon as practicable, but no later than 3 working days after forming its suspicion, report the transaction or proposed transaction to the Commissioner, in accordance with section 41.

40(3) [Protection for privileged communications] Nothing in subsection (2) requires any lawyer to disclose any privileged communication (as defined in section 42).

Compare: 1996 No 9 ss 15(1), 19(1)''.

SECTION 41 NATURE OF SUSPICIOUS ACTIVITY REPORT

41(1) [Form of report] Except as provided in subsection (2), a report under section 40 must—

(a) be in the prescribed form (if any); and

(b) contain the details prescribed by regulations; and

(c) contain a statement of the grounds on which the reporting entity holds the suspicions referred to in paragraph (b) of the definition of suspicious activity in section 39A; and

(d) be signed by a person authorised by the reporting entity to sign suspicious activity reports (unless the report is forwarded by electronic means); and

(e) be forwarded, in writing, to the Commissioner—

(i) by way of secure electronic transmission by a means specified or provided by the Commissioner for that purpose; or

(ii) by another means (including, without limitation, by way of transmission by fax or email) that may be agreed from time to time between the Commissioner and the reporting entity concerned.

41(2) [Reporting under urgency] If the urgency of the situation requires, a suspicious activity report may be made orally to any Police employee authorised for the purpose by the Commissioner, but in any such case the reporting entity must, as soon as practicable but no later than 3 working days after forming its suspicions, forward to the Commissioner a suspicious activity report that complies with the requirements in subsection (1).

41(3) [May confer authority] The Commissioner may confer the authority to receive a suspicious activity report under subsection (2) on—

(a) any specified Police employee; or

(b) Police employees of any specified rank or class; or

(c) any Police employee or Police employees for the time being holding any specified office or specified class of offices.

History

Pt 2, subpart 2, s 41, replaced by No 35 of 2017, s 25, **effective 11 August 2017**. Former s 41 read:

"**SECTION 41 NATURE OF SUSPICIOUS TRANSACTION REPORT**

41(1) [Reporting requirements] Except as provided in subsection (2), a report under section 40 must—

(a) be in the prescribed form (if any); and

(b) contain the details prescribed by regulations; and

(c) contain a statement of the grounds on which the reporting entity holds the suspicions referred to in section 40(1)(b); and

(d) be signed by a person authorised by the reporting entity to sign suspicious transaction reports (unless the report is forwarded by email or another similar means of communication); and

(e) be forwarded, in writing, to the Commissioner—

(i) by way of secure electronic transmission by a means specified or provided by the Commissioner for this purpose; or

(ii) by another means (including, without limitation, by way of transmission by fax or email) that may be agreed from time to time between the Commissioner and the reporting entity concerned.

41(2) [Oral reporting in urgent circumstances] However, if the urgency of the situation requires, a suspicious transaction report may be made orally to any Police employee authorised for the purpose by the Commissioner, but in any such case the reporting entity must, as soon as practicable, but no later than 3 working days, forward to the Commissioner a suspicious transaction report that complies with the requirements in subsection (1).

41(3) [Authority to receive reports] The Commissioner may confer the authority to receive a suspicious transaction report under subsection (2) on—

(a) any specified Police employee; or

(b) Police employees of any specified rank or class; or

(c) any Police employee or Police employees for the time being holding any specified office or specified class of offices.

Compare: 1996 No 9 s 15(2)–(4)''.

SECTION 42 PRIVILEGED COMMUNICATION DEFINED

42(1) [Where privileged] A communication is a **privileged communication** if—

(a) it is a confidential communication (oral or written) (including any information or opinion)—

(i) that passes between—

(A) a lawyer and another lawyer in their professional capacity; or

(B) a lawyer in his or her professional capacity and his or her client; or

(C) any person described in subsubparagraph (A) or (B) and the agent of the other person described in that subsubparagraph (or between the agents of both the persons described) either directly or indirectly; and

(ii) that is made or brought into existence for the purpose of obtaining or giving legal advice or assistance; or

(b) it is a communication (including any information or opinion) that—

(i) is subject to the general law governing legal professional privilege; or

(ii) is specified in section 53, 54, 55, 56, or 57 of the Evidence Act 2006.

42(2) [No privilege] However, a communication is not a privileged communication—

(a) if there is a prima facie case that the communication or information is made or received, or compiled or prepared,—

(i) for a dishonest purpose; or

(ii) to enable or aid the commission of an offence; or

(b) if, where the information wholly or partly consists of, or relates to, the receipts, payments, income, expenditure, or financial transactions of any specified person, it is contained in (or comprises the whole or a part of) any book, account, statement, or other record prepared or kept by the lawyer in connection with a trust account of the lawyer within the meaning of section 6 of the Lawyers and Conveyancers Act 2006.

42(3) [Interpretation] For the purposes of this section, references to a **lawyer** include a firm in which the lawyer is a partner or is held out to be a partner.

History

Pt 2, subpart 2, s 42, replaced by No 35 of 2017, s 25, **effective 11 August 2017**. Former s 42 read:

"**SECTION 42 PRIVILEGED COMMUNICATION DEFINED**

42(1) [When a communication is privileged] For the purposes of sections 40(3) and 48A(2), a communication is a **privileged communication** only if—

(a) it is a confidential communication, whether oral or written, passing between—

(i) a lawyer in his or her professional capacity and another lawyer in that capacity:

(ii) a lawyer in his or her professional capacity and his or her client:

(iii) any person described in subparagraph (i) or (ii) and the agent of the other person described in that subparagraph, or between the agents of both the persons described, either directly or indirectly; and

(b) it is made or brought into existence for the purpose of obtaining or giving legal advice or assistance; and

(c) it is not made or brought into existence for the purpose of committing or furthering the commission of some illegal or wrongful act.

[S 42(1) amended by No 96 of 2015, s 7, by replacing "section 40(3)" with "sections 40(3) and 48A(2)"; **effective 1 July 2017**.]

42(2) [Information comprising financial transactions excluded] However, where the information consists wholly or partly of, or relates wholly or partly to, the receipts, payments, income, expenditure, or financial transactions of a specified person (whether a lawyer, his or her client, or any other person), it is not a privileged communication if it is contained in, or comprises the whole or part of, any book, account, statement, or other record prepared or kept by the lawyer in connection with a trust account of the lawyer within the meaning of section 6 of the Lawyers and Conveyancers Act 2006.

42(3) [References to a lawyer include a firm] For the purposes of this section, references to a lawyer include a firm in which he or she is a partner or is held out to be a partner.

Compare: 1996 No 9 s 19(2)–(4)".

SECTION 43 AUDITORS MAY REPORT SUSPICIOUS ACTIVITIES

43(1) [Suspicions by auditor] Despite any other enactment or any rule of law, this section applies to a person who, in the course of carrying out the duties of that person's occupation as an auditor, has reasonable grounds to suspect, in relation to any activity, that the activity is relevant to—

(a) the investigation or prosecution of any person for a money laundering offence; or

(b) the enforcement of the Misuse of Drugs Act 1975; or

(c) the enforcement of the Terrorism Suppression Act 2002; or

(d) the enforcement of the Proceeds of Crime Act 1991 or the Criminal Proceeds (Recovery) Act 2009; or

(e) the investigation or prosecution of an offence (within the meaning of section 243(1) of the Crimes Act 1961).

43(2) [Report to Commissioner] A person may report an activity referred to in subsection (1) to the Commissioner.

History

Pt 2, subpart 2, s 43, replaced by No 35 of 2017, s 25, **effective 11 August 2017**. Former s 43 read:

"**SECTION 43 AUDITORS MAY REPORT SUSPICIOUS TRANSACTIONS**

43(1) [When this section applies] Despite any other enactment or any rule of law, this section applies to a person who, in the course of carrying out the duties of that person's occupation as an auditor, has reasonable grounds to suspect, in relation to any transaction, that the transaction is—

(a) relevant to the investigation or prosecution of any person for a money laundering offence; or

(b) relevant to the enforcement of the Misuse of Drugs Act 1975; or

(c) relevant to the enforcement of the Terrorism Suppression Act 2002; or

(d) relevant to the enforcement of the Proceeds of Crime Act 1991 or the Criminal Proceeds (Recovery) Act 2009; or

(e) relevant to the investigation or prosecution of an offence within the meaning of section 243(1) of the Crimes Act 1961.

[S 43(1) amended by No 96 of 2015, s 8, by replacing in para (e) "a serious offence" with "an offence"; **effective 1 July 2017**.]

43(2) [Reporting to Commissioner] A person may report a transaction referred to in subsection (1) to the Commissioner.

Compare: 1996 No 9 s 16".

SECTION 44 PROTECTION OF PERSONS REPORTING SUSPICIOUS ACTIVITIES

44(1) [Application] Subsection (2) applies to a person who—

(a) discloses or supplies any information in any suspicious activity report; or

(b) supplies any information in connection with any suspicious activity report, whether at the time the report is made or afterwards.

44(2) [No proceedings against person] No civil, criminal, or disciplinary proceedings lie against a person to whom subsection (1) applies—

(a) in respect of the disclosure or supply, or the manner of the disclosure or supply, by that person of the information referred to in that subsection; or

(b) for any consequences that follow from the disclosure or supply of that information.

44(3) [Reporting to Police] If any information is reported under section 43 to any Police employee by any person, no civil, criminal, or disciplinary proceedings lie against that person—

(a) in respect of the disclosure or supply, or the manner of the disclosure or supply, of that information by that person; or

(b) for any consequences that follow from the disclosure or supply of that information.

44(4) [Where bad faith or privilege] However, subsections (2) and (3) do not apply—

(a) if the information was disclosed or supplied in bad faith; or

(b) if, in the case of information disclosed or supplied by a lawyer, there were reasonable grounds to believe that the information was a privileged communication but the lawyer disclosed it or supplied it despite the existence of those grounds.

44(5) [Application of ss 92 to 97] Nothing in this section applies in respect of proceedings for an offence under any of sections 92 to 97.

History

Pt 2, subpart 2, s 44, replaced by No 35 of 2017, s 25, **effective 11 August 2017**. Former s 44 read:

"**SECTION 44 PROTECTION OF PERSONS REPORTING SUSPICIOUS TRANSACTIONS**

44(1) [Application to a person supplying information regarding a suspicious transaction] Subsection (2) applies to a person who—

(a) discloses or supplies any information in any suspicious transaction report; or

(b) supplies any information in connection with any suspicious transaction report, whether at the time the report is made or afterwards.

44(2) [Protection against civil, criminal or disciplinary proceedings] No civil, criminal, and disciplinary proceedings lie against a person to whom subsection (1) applies—

(a) in respect of the disclosure or supply, or the manner of the disclosure or supply, by that person of the information referred to in that subsection; or

(b) for any consequences that follow from the disclosure or supply of that information.

44(3) [Protection for disclosure by auditors] If any information is reported under section 43 to any Police employee by any person, no civil, criminal, or disciplinary proceedings lie against that person—

(a) in respect of the disclosure or supply, or the manner of the disclosure or supply, of that information by that person; or

(b) for any consequences that follow from the disclosure or supply of that information.

44(4) [Exclusion for disclosures in bad faith] However, subsections (2) and (3) do not apply if the information was disclosed or supplied in bad faith.

44(5) [Exclusion where disclosure gives rise to offences under ss 92 to 97] Nothing in this section applies in respect of proceedings for an offence under any of sections 92 to 97.

Compare: 1996 No 9 s 17".

SECTION 45 IMMUNITY FROM LIABILITY FOR DISCLOSURE OF INFORMATION RELATING TO MONEY LAUNDERING TRANSACTIONS

45(1) [Where this section applies] This section applies if—

(a) a person does any act that would constitute, or that the person believes would constitute, an offence against section 243(2) or (3) of the Crimes Act 1961; and

(b) in respect of the doing of that act, that person would have, by virtue of section 244 of the Crimes Act 1961, a defence to a charge under section 243(2) or (3) of that Act; and

(c) that person discloses to any Police employee any information relating to a money laundering transaction (within the meaning of section 243(4) of the Crimes Act 1961), being a money laundering transaction that constitutes (in whole or in part), or is connected with or related to, the act referred to in paragraph (a); and

(d) that information is so disclosed, in good faith, for the purpose of, or in connection with, the enforcement or intended enforcement of any enactment or provision referred to in section 244(a) of the Crimes Act 1961; and

(e) that person is otherwise under any obligation (whether arising by virtue of any enactment or any rule of law or any other instrument) to maintain secrecy in relation to, or not to disclose, that information.

45(2) [No breach of obligation] If this section applies, then, without limiting section 44 and despite the fact that the disclosure would otherwise constitute a breach of that obligation of secrecy or non-disclosure, the disclosure by that person, to that Police employee, of that information is not a breach of that obligation of secrecy or non-disclosure or (where applicable) of any enactment by which that obligation is imposed.

History

Pt 2, subpart 2, s 45, replaced by No 35 of 2017, s 25, **effective 11 August 2017**. Former s 45 read:

"**SECTION 45 IMMUNITY FROM LIABILITY FOR DISCLOSURE OF INFORMATION RELATING TO MONEY LAUNDERING TRANSACTIONS**

45(1) [Application in respect of s 243 of the Crimes Act 1961] This section applies if—

(a) a person does any act that would constitute, or the person believes would constitute, an offence against section 243(2) or (3) of the Crimes Act 1961; and

(b) in respect of the doing of that act, that person would have, by virtue of section 244(a) of the Crimes Act 1961, a defence to a charge under section 243(2) or (3) of that Act; and

(c) that person discloses, to any Police employee, any information relating to a money laundering transaction (within the meaning of section 243(4) of the Crimes Act 1961), being a money laundering transaction that constitutes (in whole or in part), or is connected with or related to, the act referred to in paragraph (a); and

(d) that information is so disclosed, in good faith, for the purpose of, or in connection with, the enforcement or intended enforcement of any enactment or provision referred to in section 244(a) of the Crimes Act 1961; and

(e) that person is otherwise under any obligation (whether arising by virtue of any enactment or any rule of law or any other instrument) to maintain secrecy in relation to, or not to disclose, that information.

45(2) [Disclosure is deemed not to be a breach of obligations of secrecy] If this section applies, then, without limiting section 44 and despite that the disclosure would otherwise constitute a breach of that obligation of secrecy or non-disclosure, the disclosure by that person, to that Police employee, of that information is not a breach of that obligation of secrecy or non-disclosure or (where applicable) of any enactment by which that obligation is imposed.

Compare: 1996 No 9 s 18".

SECTION 46 DISCLOSURE OF INFORMATION RELATING TO SUSPICIOUS ACTIVITY REPORTS

46(1) [Relevant information] This section and section 47 apply in respect of the following information:

(a) any suspicious activity report:

(b) any information the disclosure of which will identify, or is reasonably likely to identify, any person—

(i) as a person who, in his or her capacity as an officer or employee of a reporting entity, has handled a transaction in respect of which a suspicious activity report was made; or

(ii) as a person who has prepared a suspicious activity report; or

(iii) as a person who has made a suspicious activity report:

(c) any information that discloses, or is reasonably likely to disclose, the existence of a suspicious activity report.

46(2) [Limits on disclosure] A reporting entity must not disclose information to which this section relates to any person except—

(a) a Police employee who is authorised by the Commissioner to receive the information; or

(b) the reporting entity's AML/CFT supervisor; or

(c) an officer or employee of the reporting entity, for any purpose connected with the performance of that person's duties; or

(d) a lawyer, for the purpose of obtaining legal advice or representation in relation to the matter; or

(e) another member of a designated business group of which the reporting entity is a member, to the extent necessary for the reporting entity to decide whether to make a suspicious activity report.

46(3) [Police employee] A Police employee may disclose information to which this section applies only for law enforcement purposes.

46(4) [AML/CFT supervisor] An AML/CFT supervisor may disclose information to which this section applies only to the Police for law enforcement purposes.

46(5) [Person with delegated power] A person to whom a function or power has been delegated under section 134 may disclose information to which this section applies only to the AML/CFT supervisor that made the delegation.

46(6) [Employee of reporting entity] A person (**person A**) referred to in subsection (2)(c) to whom disclosure of any information to which that subsection applies has been made must not disclose that information except to another person of the kind referred to in that subsection for the purpose of—

(a) the performance of person A's duties; or

(b) obtaining legal advice or representation in relation to the matter.

46(7) [Lawyer] A person referred to in subsection (2)(d) to whom disclosure of any information to which that subsection applies has been made must not disclose that information except to a person of the kind referred to in that subsection for the purpose of giving legal advice or making representations in relation to the matter.

46(8) [Disclosure by any other person] Any other person who has information to which this section applies may disclose that information only to the Police for law enforcement purposes.

History

Pt 2, subpart 2, s 46, replaced by No 35 of 2017, s 25, **effective 11 August 2017**. Former s 46 read:

"SECTION 46 DISCLOSURE OF INFORMATION RELATING TO SUSPICIOUS TRANSACTION REPORTS

46(1) [Application] This section and section 47 apply in respect of the following information:

(a) any suspicious transaction report:

(b) any information the disclosure of which will identify, or is reasonably likely to identify, any person—

(i) as a person who, in his or her capacity as an officer or employee of a reporting entity, has handled a transaction in respect of which a suspicious transaction report was made; or

(ii) as a person who has prepared a suspicious transaction report; or

(iii) as a person who has made a suspicious transaction report:

(c) any information that discloses, or is reasonably likely to disclose, the existence of a suspicious transaction report.

46(2) [Persons to whom suspicious transactions may be disclosed] A reporting entity must not disclose information to which this section relates to any person except—

(a) a Police employee who is authorised by the Commissioner to receive the information; or

(b) the reporting entity's AML/CFT supervisor; or

(c) an officer or employee of the reporting entity, for any purpose connected with the performance of that person's duties; or

(d) a barrister or solicitor, for the purpose of obtaining legal advice or representation in relation to the matter; or

(e) another member of a designated business group of which the reporting entity is a member to the extent necessary to decide whether to make a suspicious transaction report.

46(3) [Police disclosure limited to law enforcement] A Police employee may only disclose information to which this section applies for law enforcement purposes.

46(4) [Supervisor reports to police] An AML/CFT supervisor may only disclose information to which this section applies to the Police for law enforcement purposes.

46(5) [Disclosure under delegated powers] A person to whom a function or power has been delegated under section 134 may disclose information to which this section applies only to the AML/CFT supervisor that made the delegation.

46(6) [Disclosure by employee receiving information] A person (**person A**) referred to in subsection (2)(c) to whom disclosure of any information to which that subsection applies has been made must not disclose that information except to another person of the kind referred to in that subsection for the purpose of—

(a) the performance of person A's duties; or

(b) obtaining legal advice or representation in relation to the matter.

46(7) [Restrictions on disclosure by lawyers] A person referred to in subsection (2)(d) to whom disclosure of any information to which that subsection applies has been made must not disclose that information except to a person of the kind referred to in that subsection for the purpose of giving legal advice or making representations in relation to the matter.

46(8) [Other disclosures only to police] Any other person who has information to which this section applies may only disclose that information to the Police for law enforcement purposes.

Compare: 1996 No 9 s 20".

SECTION 47 DISCLOSURE OF INFORMATION IN PROCEEDINGS

47(1) [Interests of justice] No person may disclose, in any judicial proceeding (within the meaning of section 108(4) of the Crimes Act 1961), any information contained in a suspicious activity report unless the Judge or, as the case requires, the person presiding at the proceeding is satisfied that the disclosure of the information is necessary in the interests of justice.

47(2) [Application] Nothing in this section prohibits the disclosure of any information for the purposes of the prosecution of any offence against section 93 or 94.

History

Pt 2, subpart 2, s 47, replaced by No 35 of 2017, s 25, **effective 11 August 2017**. Former s 47 read:

"**SECTION 47 DISCLOSURE OF INFORMATION IN PROCEEDINGS**

47(1) [Restriction on disclosure in judicial proceedings] No person may disclose, in any judicial proceeding (within the meaning of section 108 of the Crimes Act 1961), any information to which this section applies unless the Judge or, as the case requires, the person presiding at the proceeding is satisfied that the disclosure of the information is necessary in the interests of justice.

47(2) [Disclosure in respect of prosecutions not limited] Nothing in this section prohibits the disclosure of any information for the purposes of the prosecution of any offence against section 93 or 94.

Compare: 1996 No 9 s 21".

SECTION 48 DISCLOSURE OF PERSONAL INFORMATION RELATING TO EMPLOYEES OR SENIOR MANAGERS

48 An AML/CFT supervisor that has, in the performance and exercise of its functions and powers under this Act, obtained personal information about employees or senior managers may disclose that information to another government agency for the following purposes if the AML/CFT supervisor is satisfied that the agency has a proper interest in receiving the information:

(a) law enforcement purposes:

(b) the detection, investigation, and prosecution of any offence under the following Acts:

(i) the Companies Act 1993:

(ii) (*repealed*)

(iii) the Financial Service Providers (Registration and Dispute Resolution) Act 2008:

(iv) the Gambling Act 2003:

[Effective on a date to be appointed, or 1 October 2022]

(v) the Reserve Bank of New Zealand Act 2021 and the Acts that are prudential legislation (within the meaning of section 5 of that Act):

(v) the Reserve Bank of New Zealand Act 1989:

(vi) the Financial Markets Conduct Act 2013.

History

S 48 amended by No 31 of 2021, s 300(1) and sch 4, by replacing para (b)(v); **effective on a date to be appointed by the Governor-General by Order in Council, or 1 October 2022, whichever is earlier**.

S 48 amended by No 8 of 2019, s 98 and sch 4, by repealing para (b)(ii); **effective 15 March 2021** (LI 2020/131). Former para (b)(ii) read:

"(ii) the Financial Advisers Act 2008:".

Pt 2, subpart 2, s 48, replaced by No 35 of 2017, s 25, **effective 11 August 2017**. Former s 48 read:

"**SECTION 48 DISCLOSURE OF PERSONAL INFORMATION RELATING TO EMPLOYEES OR SENIOR MANAGERS**

48 An AML/CFT supervisor that has, in the performance and exercise of its functions and powers under this Act, obtained personal information about employees or senior managers may disclose that information to another government agency for the following purposes if the AML/CFT supervisor is satisfied that the agency has a proper interest in receiving the information:

(a) law enforcement purposes:

(b) the detection, investigation, and prosecution of any offence under the following Acts:

(i) the Companies Act 1993:

(ii) the Financial Advisers Act 2008:

(iii) the Financial Service Providers (Registration and Dispute Resolution) Act 2008:

(iv) the Gambling Act 2003:

(v) the Reserve Bank of New Zealand Act 1989:

(vi) the Financial Markets Conduct Act 2013.

(vii) (*repealed*)".

S 48 amended by No 70 of 2013, s 150 and sch, by replacing para (b)(vi) and (vii) with para (b)(vi); **effective 1 December 2014** (LI 2014/325). Former para (b)(vi) and (vii) read:

"(vi) the Securities Act 1978:

(vii) the Securities Markets Act 1988."

Subpart 2A — Prescribed transaction reports

History

Subpart 2A inserted by No 96 of 2015, s 9, **effective 1 July 2017**.

SECTION 48A REPORTING ENTITIES TO REPORT CERTAIN PRESCRIBED TRANSACTIONS

48A(1) [Application of s 48B] Despite any other enactment or rule of law, but subject to any regulations made under section 154, if a person conducts a prescribed transaction through a reporting entity, the reporting entity must (as soon as practicable, but not later than 10 working days after the transaction) report the transaction to the Commissioner in accordance with section 48B.

48A(2) [Privileged communications] Nothing in subsection (1) requires any lawyer to disclose any privileged communication (as defined in section 42).

History

Subpart 2A, s 48A, inserted by No 96 of 2015, s 9, **effective 1 July 2017**.

SECTION 48B PRESCRIBED TRANSACTION REPORTS

48B(1) [Form of report] Except as provided in subsection (2), a report made under section 48A(1) must—

(a) be in the form or forms (if any) prescribed by regulations made under section 153(c); and

(b) contain the following information:

(i) a description of the nature of the transaction:

(ii) the amount of the transaction and the currency in which it was denominated:

(iii) the date on which the transaction was conducted:

(iv) the parties to the transaction:

(v) if applicable, the name of the facility through which the transaction was conducted, and any other facilities (whether or not provided by the reporting entity) directly involved in the transaction:

(vi) any other information prescribed by regulations made under section 153(c); and

(c) be signed by a person authorised by the reporting entity to sign prescribed transaction reports (unless the report is provided by electronic means other than an electronic copy of the signed report); and

(d) be forwarded, in writing, to the Commissioner—

(i) by way of secure electronic transmission specified or provided by the Commissioner for this purpose; or

(ii) by another means (including, without limitation, by way of transmission by post, fax, or email) that may be agreed from time to time between the Commissioner and the reporting entity concerned.

48B(2) [Delegation] The Commissioner may confer the authority to receive a prescribed transaction report under subsection (1) on—

(a) any specified Police employee; or

(b) Police employees of any specified rank or class; or

(c) any Police employee or Police employees for the time being holding any specified office or specified class of offices.

History

Subpart 2A, s 48B, inserted by No 96 of 2015, s 9, **effective 1 July 2017**.

SECTION 48C SECTIONS 43 TO 48 APPLY TO PRESCRIBED TRANSACTIONS

48C Sections 43 to 48 apply, with all necessary modifications, to prescribed transactions.

History

Subpart 2A, s 48C, inserted by No 96 of 2015, s 9, **effective 1 July 2017**.

Subpart 3 — Record keeping

SECTION 49 OBLIGATION TO KEEP TRANSACTION RECORDS

49(1) [Records necessary to enable transaction reconstruction] In relation to every transaction that is conducted through a reporting entity, the reporting entity must keep those records that are reasonably necessary to enable that transaction to be readily reconstructed at any time.

49(2) [Required information] Without limiting subsection (1), records must contain the following information:

(a) the nature of the transaction:

(b) the amount of the transaction and the currency in which it was denominated:

(c) the date on which the transaction was conducted:

(d) the parties to the transaction:

(e) if applicable, the facility through which the transaction was conducted, and any other facilities (whether or not provided by the reporting entity) directly involved in the transaction:

(f) the name of the officer or employee or agent of the reporting entity who handled the transaction, if that officer, employee, or agent—

  (i) has face-to-face dealings in respect of the transaction with any of the parties to the transaction; and

  (ii) has formed a suspicion (of the kind referred to in section 40(1)(b)) about the transaction:

(g) any other information prescribed by regulations.

49(3) [Retention of records] A reporting entity must retain the records kept by that reporting entity, in accordance with this section, in relation to a transaction for—

(a) a period of at least 5 years after the completion of that transaction; or

(b) any longer period that the AML/CFT supervisor for the reporting entity, or the Commissioner, specifies.

Compare: 1996 No 9 s 29

SECTION 49A OBLIGATION TO KEEP REPORTS OF SUSPICIOUS ACTIVITIES

49A(1) [Retain copy of report] If a reporting entity reports a suspicious activity to the Commissioner, the reporting entity must keep a copy of that report.

49A(2) [Retention period] The reporting entity must keep a copy of the report for—

(a) a period of at least 5 years after the report is made; or

(b) any longer period that the AML/CFT supervisor for the reporting entity, or the Commissioner, specifies.

History

S 49A inserted by No 35 of 2017, s 26, **effective 11 August 2017**.

SECTION 50 OBLIGATION TO KEEP IDENTITY AND VERIFICATION RECORDS

50(1) [Keeping records as to the nature of identification and verification] In respect of each case in which a reporting entity is required, under subpart 1 of this Part, to identify and verify the identity of a person, the reporting entity must keep those records that are reasonably necessary to enable the nature of the evidence used for the purposes of that identification and verification to be readily identified at any time.

50(2) [Nature of records to be kept] Without limiting subsection (1), those records may comprise—

(a) a copy of the evidence so used; or

(b) if it is not practicable to retain that evidence, any information as is reasonably necessary to enable that evidence to be obtained.

50(3) [Retention periods] A reporting entity must retain the records kept by that reporting entity for,—

(a) in the case of records relating to the identity and verification of the identity of a person in relation to establishing a business relationship, a period of at least 5 years after the end of that business relationship; or

(b) in the case of records relating to the identity and verification of the identity of a person in relation to conducting an occasional transaction or activity, a period of at least 5 years after the completion of that occasional transaction or activity; or

(c) in the case of records relating to the identity and verification of the identity of an originator in relation to a wire transfer,—

(i) if the wire transfer is conducted by a customer with whom the reporting entity has a business relationship, a period of at least 5 years after the end of that business relationship; or

(ii) if the wire transfer is an occasional transaction or activity, a period of at least 5 years after the completion of the wire transfer.

History

S 50(3) amended by No 35 of 2017, s 68 and sch 2, by replacing (i) in para (b) "occasional transaction" with "occasional transaction or activity" wherever occurring; and (ii) in para (c)(ii) "occasional transaction" with "occasional transaction or activity"; **effective 11 August 2017**.

Compare: 1996 No 9 s 30

SECTION 51 OBLIGATION TO KEEP OTHER RECORDS

51(1) [Other records to be retained] A reporting entity must keep the following records in addition to the records referred to in sections 49 and 50:

(a) records that are relevant to the establishment of the business relationship; and

(b) records relating to risk assessments, AML/CFT programmes, and audits; and

(c) any other records (for example, account files, business correspondence, and written findings) relating to, and obtained during the course of, a business relationship that are reasonably necessary to establish the nature and purpose of, and activities relating to, the business relationship; and

(d) any other records prescribed by regulations made under section 153.

History

S 51(1) amended by No 35 of 2017, s 27(1) and (2), by inserting (i) in para (c) "; and" after "the business relationship"; and (ii) para (d); **effective 11 August 2017**.

51(2) [Retention period] The records relating to risk assessment, AML/CFT programmes, and audits must be kept for a period of at least 5 years after the date on which they ceased to be used on a regular basis.

History

S 51(2) replaced by No 35 of 2017, s 27(3), **effective 11 August 2017**. Former s 51(2) read:

> "51(2) [Period after end of business relationship] The records must be kept in accordance with section 52 for a period of at least 5 years after the end of the business relationship."

51(3) [Records to be available to supervisor] A reporting entity must make records relating to risk assessments, AML/CFT programmes, and audits available to its AML/CFT supervisor on request.

Compare: 1996 No 9 s 31

SECTION 52 HOW RECORDS TO BE KEPT

52 Records required by this subpart to be kept by a reporting entity must—

(a) be kept either in written form in the English language, or so as to enable the records to be readily accessible and readily convertible into written form in the English language; and

(b) be kept in the manner prescribed by regulations (if any).

Compare: 1996 No 9 s 32

SECTION 53 WHEN RECORDS NEED NOT BE KEPT

53(1) [Retention not required by liquidated entities] Nothing in this subpart requires the retention of any records kept by a reporting entity that has been liquidated and finally dissolved except as provided in subsection (2).

53(2) [Except when ordered by the High Court] The High Court may, in relation to a reporting entity that is being or has been liquidated, make an order requiring that any or all of the records referred to in sections 50 and 51 be kept for any period it thinks fit.

Compare: 1996 No 9 s 33

SECTION 54 DESTRUCTION OF RECORDS

54(1) [Destruction required after retention period] Subject to subsection (2), a reporting entity must take all practicable steps to ensure that every record retained by that reporting entity under this subpart, and every copy of that record, is destroyed as soon as practicable after the expiry of the period for which the reporting entity is required to retain that record.

54(2) [Except when lawful reason] Nothing in this section requires the destruction of any record, or any copy of any record, in any case where there is a lawful reason for retaining that record.

54(3) [Specific lawful reasons] Without limiting subsection (2), there is a lawful reason for retaining a record if the retention of that record is necessary—

(a) in order to comply with the requirements of any other enactment; or

(b) to enable a reporting entity to carry on its business; or

(c) for the purposes of the detection, investigation, or prosecution of any offence.

Compare: 1996 No 9 s 34

SECTION 55 OTHER LAWS NOT AFFECTED

55 Nothing in this subpart limits or affects any other enactment that requires any reporting entity to keep or retain a record.

Compare: 1996 No 9 s 35

Subpart 4 — Compliance with AML/CFT requirements

SECTION 56 REPORTING ENTITY MUST HAVE AML/CFT PROGRAMME AND AML/CFT COMPLIANCE OFFICER

56(1) [Requirement for compliance programme] A reporting entity must establish, implement, and maintain a compliance programme (an **AML/CFT programme**) that includes internal procedures, policies, and controls to—

(a) detect money laundering and the financing of terrorism; and

(b) manage and mitigate the risk of money laundering and financing of terrorism.

56(2) [Designation of compliance officer] A reporting entity must designate an employee as an AML/CFT compliance officer to administer and maintain its AML/CFT programme.

56(3) [When no employees] In the case of a reporting entity that does not have employees, the reporting entity must appoint a person to act as its AML/CFT compliance officer.

56(4) [Compliance officer reporting] The AML/CFT compliance officer must report to a senior manager of the reporting entity.

56(5) [Application] Despite subsections (2) to (4), if a reporting entity is a partnership,—

(a) the partnership may designate one of the partners as an AML/CFT compliance officer to administer and maintain its AML/CFT programme, irrespective of whether the partnership has or does not have employees; and

(b) the partner so designated must report to another partner designated for the purpose of receiving those reports by the partnership.

History

S 56(5) inserted by No 27 of 2018, s 6, **effective 8 September 2018**.

SECTION 57 MINIMUM REQUIREMENTS FOR AML/CFT PROGRAMMES

57(1) [Programme features] A reporting entity's AML/CFT programme must be in writing and be based on the risk assessment undertaken in accordance with section 58 and include adequate and effective procedures, policies, and controls for—

(a) vetting—

(i) senior managers:

(ii) the AML/CFT compliance officer:

(iii) any other employee that is engaged in AML/CFT related duties; and

(b) training on AML/CFT matters for the following employees:

(i) senior managers:

(ii) the AML/CFT compliance officer:

(iii) any other employee that is engaged in AML/CFT related duties; and

(c) complying with customer due diligence requirements (including ongoing customer due diligence and account monitoring); and

(d) reporting suspicious activities; and

(da) reporting prescribed transactions; and

(e) record keeping; and

(f) setting out what the reporting entity needs to do, or continue to do, to manage and mitigate the risks of money laundering and the financing of terrorism; and

(g) examining, and keeping written findings relating to,—

(i) complex or unusually large transactions; and

(ii) unusual patterns of transactions that have no apparent economic or visible lawful purpose; and

(iii) any other activity that the reporting entity regards as being particularly likely by its nature to be related to money laundering or the financing of terrorism; and

(h) monitoring, examining, and keeping written findings relating to business relationships and transactions from or in countries that do not have or have insufficient anti-money laundering or countering financing of terrorism systems in place and have additional measures for dealing with or restricting dealings with such countries; and

(i) preventing the use, for money laundering or the financing of terrorism, of products (for example, the misuse of technology) and transactions (for example, non-face-to-face business relationships or transactions) that might favour anonymity; and

(j) determining when enhanced customer due diligence is required and when simplified customer due diligence might be permitted; and

(k) providing when a person who is not the reporting entity may, and setting out the procedures for the person to, conduct the relevant customer due diligence on behalf of the reporting entity; and

(l) monitoring and managing compliance with, and the internal communication of and training in, those procedures, policies, and controls.

History

S 57(1) amended by No 35 of 2017, s 28(1) and (2), by (i) inserting ''be in writing and'' after ''programme must''; and (ii) replacing in para (d) ''suspicious transactions'' with ''suspicious activities''; **effective 11 August 2017**.

57(2) [Guidance material] In developing an AML/CFT programme, a reporting entity must have regard to any applicable guidance material produced by AML/CFT supervisors or the Commissioner relating to AML/CFT programmes.

History

S 57(2) inserted by No 35 of 2017, s 28(3), **effective 11 August 2017**.

History

S 57 amended by No 96 of 2015, s 10, by inserting para (da); **effective 1 July 2017**.

SECTION 58 RISK ASSESSMENT

58(1) [Risk assessment prior to programme and due diligence] Before conducting customer due diligence or establishing an AML/CFT programme, a reporting entity must first undertake an assessment of the risk of money laundering and the financing of terrorism (a **risk assessment**) that it may reasonably expect to face in the course of its business.

58(2) [Factors to be assessed] In assessing the risk, the reporting entity must have regard to the following:

(a) the nature, size, and complexity of its business; and

(b) the products and services it offers; and

(c) the methods by which it delivers products and services to its customers; and

(d) the types of customers it deals with; and

(e) the countries it deals with; and

(f) the institutions it deals with; and

(g) any applicable guidance material produced by AML/CFT supervisors or the Commissioner relating to risk assessments; and

(h) any other factors that may be provided for in regulations.

58(3) [Requirements] The risk assessment must be in writing and—

(a) identify the risks faced by the reporting entity in the course of its business; and

(b) describe how the reporting entity will ensure that the assessment remains current; and

(c) enable the reporting entity to determine the level of risk involved in relation to relevant obligations under this Act and regulations.

SECTION 59 REVIEW AND AUDIT OF RISK ASSESSMENT AND AML/CFT PROGRAMMES

59(1) [Goals of review] A reporting entity (other than a high-value dealer) must review its risk assessment and AML/CFT programme to—

(a) ensure that the risk assessment and AML/CFT programme are up to date; and

(b) identify any deficiencies in the effectiveness of the risk assessment and the AML/CFT programme; and

(c) make any changes to the risk assessment or AML/CFT programme identified as being necessary under paragraph (b).

59(2) [Review period] A reporting entity (other than a high-value dealer) must ensure that its risk assessment and AML/CFT programme are audited every 2 years or during a different time period prescribed by regulations, or at any other time at the request of the relevant AML/CFT supervisor.

History

S 59 replaced by No 35 of 2017, s 29, **effective 11 August 2017**. Former s 59 read:

"**SECTION 59 REVIEW AND AUDIT OF RISK ASSESSMENT AND AML/CFT PROGRAMME**

59(1) [Review requirement] A reporting entity must review its risk assessment and AML/CFT programme to—

(a) ensure the risk assessment and AML/CFT programme remain current; and

(b) identify any deficiencies in the effectiveness of the risk assessment and the AML/CFT programme; and

(c) make any changes to the risk assessment or AML/CFT programme identified as being necessary under paragraph (b).

59(2) [Audit two-yearly] A reporting entity must ensure its risk assessment and AML/CFT programme are audited every 2 years or at any other time at the request of the relevant AML/CFT supervisor.

59(3) [Audit by independent person] The audit must be carried out by an independent person appointed by the reporting entity who is appropriately qualified to conduct the audit.

59(4) [Not required to be financial auditor] A person appointed to conduct an audit is not required to be—

(a) a chartered accountant within the meaning of section 19 of the New Zealand Institute of Chartered Accountants Act 1996; or

(b) qualified to undertake financial audits.

[S 59(4)(a) amended by No 74 of 2010, s 10 and sch 1, by substituting "New Zealand Institute of Chartered Accountants Act 1996" for "Institute of Chartered Accountants of New Zealand Act 1996"; **effective 7 July 2010**.]

59(5) [Auditor must not have been involved in programme establishment] A person appointed to conduct an audit must not have been involved in—

(a) the establishment, implementation, or maintenance of the reporting entity's AML/CFT programme:

(b) the undertaking of the reporting entity's risk assessment.

59(6) [Risk assessment audit scope] The audit of the risk assessment is limited to an audit of whether the reporting entity's risk assessment fulfils the requirements in section 58(3).

59(7) [Copy to supervisor] A reporting entity must provide a copy of any audit to its AML/CFT supervisor on request."

SECTION 59A AUDIT OF COMPLIANCE WITH AML/CFT OBLIGATIONS

59A A high-value dealer must ensure that its compliance with its AML/CFT obligations under section 6(4)(d)(ii), and any regulations, is audited when the relevant AML/CFT supervisor requests.

History

S 59A inserted by No 35 of 2017, s 29, **effective 11 August 2017**.

SECTION 59B WHO CARRIES OUT AUDIT

59B(1) [Appointment by entity] An audit under section 59 or 59A must be carried out by an independent person, appointed by the reporting entity, who is appropriately qualified to conduct the audit.

59B(2) [No requirement] A person appointed to conduct an audit is not required to be—

(a) a chartered accountant within the meaning of section 19 of the New Zealand Institute of Chartered Accountants Act 1996; or

(b) qualified to undertake financial audits.

59B(3) [No involvement] A person appointed to conduct an audit must not have been involved in—

(a) the establishment, implementation, or maintenance of the reporting entity's AML/CFT programme (if any); or

(b) the undertaking of the reporting entity's risk assessment (if any).

59B(4) [Scope] The audit of a risk assessment under section 59 is limited to an audit of whether the reporting entity's risk assessment fulfils the requirements in section 58(3).

59B(5) [Copy to supervisor] A reporting entity must provide a copy of any audit to its AML/CFT supervisor on request.

History

S 59B inserted by No 35 of 2017, s 29, **effective 11 August 2017**.

SECTION 60 ANNUAL AML/CFT REPORT

60(1) [Annual report required] The reporting entity must prepare an annual report on its risk assessment and AML/CFT programme.

60(2) [Requirements] An annual report must—

(a) be in the prescribed form; and

(b) take into account the results and implications of the audit required by section 59(2); and

(c) contain any information prescribed by regulations.

60(3) [Annual report to supervisor] The reporting entity must provide the annual report to its AML/CFT supervisor at a time appointed by the AML/CFT supervisor.

60(4) [Supervisor to give notice of requirement for report] The AML/CFT supervisor must give the reporting entity reasonable notice of the requirement to provide the annual report.

SECTION 61 REPORTING ENTITIES TO ENSURE THAT BRANCHES AND SUBSIDIARIES COMPLY WITH AML/CFT REQUIREMENTS

61(1) [Compliance by overseas operations] A reporting entity must ensure that its branches and subsidiaries that are in a foreign country apply, to the extent permitted by the law of that country, measures broadly equivalent to those set out in this Act and regulations with regard to the requirements for customer due diligence (including ongoing customer due diligence), risk assessments, AML/CFT programmes, and record keeping.

61(2) [Requirements if prevented by law of a foreign country] If the law of the foreign country does not permit the application of those equivalent measures by the branch or the subsidiary located in that country, the reporting entity must—

(a) inform its AML/CFT supervisor accordingly; and

(b) take additional measures to effectively handle the risk of a money laundering offence and the financing of terrorism.

61(3) [Communication of policies and procedures to overseas operations] A reporting entity must communicate (where relevant) the policies, procedures, and controls that it establishes, implements, and maintains in accordance with this subpart to its branches and subsidiaries that are outside New Zealand.

Subpart 5 — Codes of practice

SECTION 62 INTERPRETATION

62 In this Part, unless the context otherwise requires,—

code of practice means a code of practice approved by the responsible Minister under section 64, as amended from time to time

proposed code of practice means a document prepared under section 63(1).

SECTION 63 AML/CFT SUPERVISORS TO PREPARE CODES OF PRACTICE FOR RELEVANT SECTORS

63(1) [Direction by Minister] An AML/CFT supervisor must, if directed to do so by the Minister responsible for that AML/CFT supervisor (the **responsible Minister**), prepare—

(a) 1 or more codes of practice for the sector of activity of the reporting entities for which it is the supervisor under section 130 or in respect of different reporting entities specified by the responsible Minister:

(b) an instrument that amends a code of practice or revokes the whole or any provision of a code of practice prepared under paragraph (a).

63(2) [Purpose] The purpose of a code of practice is to provide a statement of practice that assists reporting entities to comply with their obligations under this Act and regulations.

63(3) [Scope of directions] A direction under subsection (1) may (without limitation)—

(a) relate generally to the obligations imposed on the relevant reporting entities by or under this Act or regulations or specify particular aspects of those obligations that are to be covered by the code of practice:

(b) specify the amendments to be made or their intended effect, and specify the extent of the revocation to be made:

(c) indicate the date by which the responsible Minister wishes the code of practice to be provided to him or her:

(d) include details about the recommendation that the AML/CFT supervisor is required to provide under section 64(1)(a).

63(4) [Supervisor compliance] An AML/CFT supervisor must comply with a direction under subsection (1) as soon as practicable.

63(5) [Minister to approve] No code of practice has legal effect until approved by the responsible Minister under section 64(6).

SECTION 64 PROCEDURE FOR APPROVAL AND PUBLICATION OF CODES OF PRACTICE

64(1) The responsible Minister must not approve a code of practice prepared by an AML/CFT supervisor unless—

(a) the AML/CFT supervisor has made a recommendation that the Minister should approve the code of practice; and

(b) the AML/CFT supervisor has consulted the persons and organisations that the Minister thinks appropriate, having regard to the subject matter of the proposed code of practice.

64(2) In consulting under subsection (1)(b), the AML/CFT supervisor must ensure that—

(a) a copy of the proposed code of practice or a summary of its contents, in hard copy or electronic format, is provided to the persons and organisations being consulted; and

(b) the persons and organisations being consulted have at least 20 working days to make submissions or representations about the proposed code of practice.

64(3) The responsible Minister may direct the AML/CFT supervisor to reconsider any aspect of the proposed code of practice and to make any amendments that the Minister considers necessary.

64(4) Despite subsection (3),—

(a) if the AML/CFT supervisor does not amend the proposed code of practice as directed by the Minister or within the time specified by the Minister, the Minister may make those amendments:

(b) the Minister may, after consultation with the AML/CFT supervisor, make any further amendments to the proposed code of practice that he or she considers necessary.

64(5) The responsible Minister must—

(a) approve the proposed code of practice as prepared by the AML/CFT supervisor; or

(b) approve the proposed code of practice as amended by the AML/CFT supervisor; or

(c) approve the proposed code of practice as amended by the Minister after consultation with the AML/CFT supervisor.

64(6) A code of practice is secondary legislation (*see* Part 3 of the Legislation Act 2019 for publication requirements).

History

S 64(6) replaced by No 7 of 2021, s 3 and sch 16, **effective 28 October 2021** (LI 2021/250). Former s 64(6) read:

"64(6) The responsible Minister approves a code of practice by notice in the *Gazette*, and the notice—

(a) must either set out the code of practice or state where copies of the code of practice in hard copy or electronic format may be obtained or viewed:

(b) is a disallowable instrument, but not a legislative instrument, for the purposes of the Legislation Act 2012 and must be presented to the House of Representatives under section 41 of that Act."

S 64(6) amended by No 119 of 2012, s 77(3) and sch, by replacing para (b); **effective 5 August 2013** (SR 2013/242). Former para (b) read:

"(b) is not a regulation for the purposes of the Acts and Regulations Publication Act 1989, but is a regulation for the purposes of the Regulations (Disallowance) Act 1989."

64(7) That Act applies as if—

(a) the Minister were the maker of the code of practice; and

(b) the code of practice were made by the Minister approving it.

History

S 64(7) inserted by No 7 of 2021, s 3 and sch 16, **effective 28 October 2021** (LI 2021/250).

SECTION 65 AMENDMENT AND REVOCATION OF CODES OF PRACTICE

65(1) [Same procedure as for approvals] A code of practice may be amended or revoked in the same manner as that in which it was made.

65(2) [Effect] Sections 63, 64, 66, and 67 apply with the necessary modifications to the amendment or revocation of a code of practice.

SECTION 66 PROOF OF CODES OF PRACTICE

66 Publication under the Legislation Act 2019 of a code of practice is conclusive evidence that the requirements of sections 64(1) to (5) and 65 have been complied with.

History

S 66 inserted by No 7 of 2021, s 3 and sch 16, **effective 28 October 2021** (LI 2021/250). Former s 66 read:

"**SECTION 66 PROOF OF CODES OF PRACTICE**

66 Publication in the *Gazette* of a notice under section 64(6) is conclusive evidence that the requirements of sections 64(1) to (5) and 65 have been complied with in respect of the approval specified in the notice."

SECTION 67 LEGAL EFFECT OF CODES OF PRACTICE

67(1) [Compliance with codes of practice] A reporting entity complies with an obligation imposed on it by or under this Act or regulations by—

(a) complying with those provisions of a code of practice that state a means of satisfying the obligation; or

(b) complying with the obligation by some other equally effective means.

67(2) [No defence to act or omission] However, a reporting entity may not rely on subsection (1)(b) as a defence to an act or omission on its part unless it has, by notice in writing given before the act or omission occurred, advised the AML/CFT supervisor that it has opted out of compliance with the code of practice and intends to satisfy its obligations by some other equally effective means.

67(3) [Court to have regard to code] If a person is charged with an offence in respect of a failure to comply with any provision of this Act, a court must, in determining whether that person has failed to comply with the provision, have regard to any code of practice in force under section 64(6) at the time of the alleged failure relating to matters of the kind to which the provision relates.

67(4) [Court to have regard to code in respect of injunction] If an application for an injunction against a person has been made under this Act, a court must, in determining whether to grant the injunction, have regard to any code of practice in force under section 64(6).

67(5) [Court to have regard to code in respect of penalties] If an application for a pecuniary penalty against a person has been made under this Act, a court must, in determining whether to impose a pecuniary penalty, have regard to any code of practice in force under section 64(6) at the time the person engaged in conduct that constituted the relevant civil liability act.

Subpart 6 — Cross-border transportation of cash

SECTION 68 REPORTS ABOUT MOVEMENT OF CASH INTO OR OUT OF NEW ZEALAND

68(1) [Restriction on movement of cash] A person must not move cash into or out of New Zealand if—

(a) the total amount of the cash is equal to or above the applicable threshold value; and

(b) the person has not given a report in respect of the movement of that cash in accordance with this subpart; and

(c) the movement of that cash is not exempted under this Act or regulations (if any).

History

S 68(1) amended by No 35 of 2017, s 30, by replacing in para (a) "more than" with "equal to or above"; **effective 11 August 2017**.

68(2) [Definition of moving cash into New Zealand] For the purposes of this Act, a person moves cash into New Zealand if the person brings or sends the cash into New Zealand.

68(3) [Definition of moving cash out of New Zealand] For the purposes of this Act, a person moves cash out of New Zealand if the person takes or sends the cash out of New Zealand.

Compare: Anti-Money Laundering and Counter-Terrorism Financing Act 2006 ss 53(3), 57(2), 58 (Aust)

SECTION 69 REPORTS ABOUT RECEIPT OF CASH FROM OUTSIDE NEW ZEALAND

69 A person must not receive cash moved to the person from outside New Zealand if—

(a) the total amount of the cash is equal to or above the applicable threshold value; and

(b) the person has not given a report in respect of the movement of that cash in accordance with this subpart; and

(c) the movement of that cash is not exempted under this Act or regulations (if any).

Compare: Anti-Money Laundering and Counter-Terrorism Financing Act 2006 s 55(3) (Aust)

History

S 69 amended by No 35 of 2017, s 31, by replacing in para (a) "more than" with "equal to or above"; **effective 11 August 2017**.

SECTION 70 REPORTING REQUIREMENTS

70 A report under this subpart must—

(a) be in writing in the appropriate prescribed form; and

(b) contain the prescribed information; and

(c) be completed in accordance with regulations (if any); and

(d) be provided to a Customs officer or any other prescribed person,—

(i) in the case of accompanied cash, at the time prescribed for the purposes of this subparagraph; and

(ii) in the case of unaccompanied cash, at the time prescribed for the purposes of this subparagraph.

Compare: 1996 No 9 s 37; Anti-Money Laundering and Counter-Terrorism Financing Act 2006 s 55(5) (Aust)

History

S 70 amended by No 35 of 2017, s 32(1) and (2), by replacing (i) in para (a) "the prescribed form" with "the appropriate prescribed form"; and (ii) para (d); **effective 11 August 2017**. Former para (d) read:

"(d) be provided to a Customs officer,—

(i) in the case of accompanied cash, at the same time as a departure card is presented in accordance with section 126(2) of the Immigration Act 1987:

(ii) in the case of unaccompanied cash, before the cash leaves New Zealand."

SECTION 71 INFORMATION TO BE FORWARDED TO COMMISSIONER

71(1) [Customs officer to report to Commissioner] If a report is made to a Customs officer under this subpart, that officer must, as soon as practicable, forward the report to the Commissioner.

71(2) [Report on discovery of cash] If, in the course of conducting a search under this Act, a Customs officer discovers any cash in respect of which a report is required to be made under this subpart but has not been made, that officer must, as soon as practicable, report the details of the search, and of the cash, to the Commissioner.

71(3) [Commissioner to determine form of report] Every report made under subsection (2) must be in the form that the Commissioner may determine after consultation with the chief executive of the New Zealand Customs Service.

71(4) [Customs Service record requirement] The chief executive of the New Zealand Customs Service must—

(a) cause a record to be made and kept of—

(i) each occasion on which a cash report is made to a Customs officer; and

(ii) the details of the identity of the person making the cash report; and

(iii) the date on which the cash report is made; and

(b) ensure that the record is retained for a period of not less than 1 year after the date on which the cash report is made.

Compare: 1996 No 9 s 42

PART 3 — ENFORCEMENT

Subpart 1 — General provisions relating to Part

Proceedings for civil penalties

SECTION 72 WHEN AND HOW CIVIL PENALTY PROCEEDINGS BROUGHT

72(1) [Time limit] An application for a civil penalty under this Part may be made no later than 6 years after the conduct giving rise to the liability to pay the civil penalty occurred.

72(2) [Proof and interrogatories] In proceedings for a civil penalty under this Part,—

(a) the standard of proof is the standard of proof that applies in civil proceedings; and

(b) the relevant AML/CFT supervisor may, by order of the court, obtain discovery and administer interrogatories.

Relationship between civil penalty and criminal proceedings

SECTION 73 RELATIONSHIP BETWEEN CONCURRENT CIVIL PENALTY PROCEEDINGS AND CRIMINAL PROCEEDINGS

73(1) [No restriction on criminal proceedings] Criminal proceedings for an offence under this Part may be commenced against a person in relation to particular conduct whether or not proceedings for a civil penalty under this Part have been commenced against the person in relation to the same or substantially the same conduct.

73(2) [Restriction on civil proceedings] Proceedings under this Part for a civil penalty against a person in relation to particular conduct are stayed if criminal proceedings against the person are or have been commenced for an offence under this Part in relation to the same or substantially the same conduct.

73(3) [When civil proceedings may begin] After the criminal proceedings referred to in subsection (2) have been completed or withdrawn, a person may apply to have the stay lifted on the civil penalty proceedings referred to in that subsection.

SECTION 74 ONE PENALTY ONLY RULE

74(1) [A new penalty may not follow an existing one] If civil penalty or criminal proceedings under this Part are brought against a person in relation to particular conduct, a court may not impose a penalty (whether civil or criminal) on the person if a court has already imposed a penalty under this Part in proceedings relating to the same or substantially the same conduct.

74(2) [Limitation of one civil penalty] If a person is or may be liable to more than 1 civil penalty under this Part in respect of the same or substantially the same conduct, civil penalty proceedings may be brought against the person for more than 1 civil penalty, but the person may not be required to pay more than 1 civil penalty in respect of the same or substantially the same conduct.

SECTION 75 RESTRICTION ON USE OF EVIDENCE GIVEN IN CIVIL PENALTY PROCEEDINGS

75(1) [Civil evidence not reusable] Evidence of information given, or evidence of production of documents, by a person is not admissible in criminal proceedings against the person for an offence under this Part or any other enactment if—

(a) the person previously gave the evidence or produced the documents in civil penalty proceedings under this Part against him or her, whether or not a civil penalty was imposed; and

(b) the proceedings for the civil penalty related to conduct that was the same or substantially the same as the conduct constituting the offence.

75(2) [Where subs (1) does not apply] This section does not apply to criminal proceedings in respect of the falsity of the evidence given by the person in the proceedings for the civil penalty.

Immunities

SECTION 76 PROTECTION FOR AML/CFT SUPERVISORS

76 No civil or criminal proceedings may be brought against an AML/CFT supervisor or a person who is or has been an officer, employee, member of, or member of the board of, an AML/CFT supervisor for anything done or omitted to be done in the course of the performance or exercise of the AML/CFT supervisor's functions or powers under this Act or regulations unless it is shown that the AML/CFT supervisor or the person concerned acted in bad faith.

History

S 76 amended by No 35 of 2017, s 33, by inserting ''or regulations'' after ''Act''; **effective 11 August 2017**.

SECTION 77 PROTECTION FOR REPORTING ENTITIES, OFFICERS, ETC, ACTING IN COMPLIANCE WITH THIS ACT

77 No reporting entity, or person who is, or has been, an officer, an employee, or a member of the governing body of the reporting entity, or person appointed under section 56(3) is criminally or civilly liable for any action taken in order to comply with this Act or regulations if the action—

(a) was taken in good faith; and

(b) was reasonable in the circumstances.

Subpart 2 — Civil liability

SECTION 78 MEANING OF CIVIL LIABILITY ACT

78 In this Part, a **civil liability act** occurs when a reporting entity fails to comply with any of the AML/CFT requirements, including, without limitation, when the reporting entity—

(a) fails to conduct customer due diligence as required by subpart 1 of Part 2:

(b) fails to adequately monitor accounts and transactions:

(c) enters into or continues a business relationship with a person who does not produce or provide satisfactory evidence of the person's identity:

(d) enters into or continues a correspondent banking relationship with a shell bank:

(da) fails to report transactions in accordance with subpart 2A of Part 2:

(e) fails to keep records in accordance with the requirements of subpart 3 of Part 2:

(f) fails to establish, implement, or maintain an AML/CFT programme:

(g) fails to ensure that its branches and subsidiaries comply with the relevant AML/CFT requirements.

History

S 78 amended by No 96 of 2015, s 11, by inserting para (da);
effective 1 July 2017.

SECTION 79 POSSIBLE RESPONSES TO CIVIL LIABILITY ACT

79 If a civil liability act is alleged to have occurred, the relevant AML/CFT supervisor may do 1 or more of the following:

(a) issue a formal warning under section 80:

(b) accept an enforceable undertaking under section 81 and seek an order in the court for breach of that undertaking under section 82:

(c) seek an injunction from the High Court under section 85 or 87:

(d) apply to the court for a pecuniary penalty under section 90.

Formal warnings

SECTION 80 FORMAL WARNINGS

80(1) [Multiple warnings may be issued] The relevant AML/CFT supervisor may issue 1 or more formal warnings to a person if the AML/CFT supervisor has reasonable grounds to believe that that person has engaged in conduct that constituted a civil liability act.

80(2) [Form of warning] A formal warning must be—

(a) in the prescribed form; and

(b) issued in the manner specified in regulations (if any).

Enforceable undertakings

SECTION 81 ENFORCEABLE UNDERTAKINGS

81(1) [Acceptance of written undertaking] The relevant AML/CFT supervisor may accept a written undertaking given by a person in connection with compliance with this Act or regulations (if any).

81(2) [Withdrawal of undertaking] The person may withdraw or vary the undertaking at any time, but only with the consent of the relevant AML/CFT supervisor.

SECTION 82 ENFORCEMENT OF UNDERTAKINGS

82(1) [Application to court] If the relevant AML/CFT supervisor considers that a person who gave an undertaking under section 81 has breached 1 or more of its terms, the relevant AML/CFT supervisor may apply to the court for an order under subsection (2).

82(2) [Orders for breach] If the court is satisfied that the person has breached 1 or more of the terms of the undertaking, the court may make any or all of the following orders:

(a) an order directing the person to comply with any of the terms of the undertaking:

(b) an order directing the person to pay to the AML/CFT supervisor an amount up to the amount of any financial benefit that the person has obtained directly or indirectly and that is reasonably attributable to the breach:

(c) any order that the court considers appropriate directing the person to compensate any other person who has suffered loss or damage as a result of the breach.

SECTION 83 ASSESSMENT OF COMPENSATION FOR BREACH OF UNDERTAKINGS

83 For the purposes of section 82(2)(c), in determining whether another person (**person A**) has suffered loss or damage as a result of the breach, and in assessing the amount of compensation payable, the court may have regard to the following:

(a) the extent to which any expenses incurred by person A are attributable to dealing with the breach:

(b) the effect of the breach on person A's ability to carry on business or other activities:

(c) any damage to the reputation of person A's business that is attributable to dealing with the breach:

(d) any loss of business opportunities suffered by person A as a result of dealing with the breach:

(e) any other matters that the court considers relevant.

Injunctions

SECTION 84 POWERS OF HIGH COURT NOT AFFECTED

84 The powers in sections 85 to 89 are in addition to, and do not derogate from, any other powers of the High Court relating to the granting of injunctions.

SECTION 85 PERFORMANCE INJUNCTIONS

85(1) [When court may issue injunction] The High Court may, on the application of the relevant AML/CFT supervisor, grant an injunction requiring a person to do an act or thing if—

(a) that person has refused or failed, or is refusing or failing, or is proposing to refuse or fail, to do that act or thing; and

(b) the refusal or failure was, is, or would be a civil liability act.

85(2) [Court may rescind injunction] The court may rescind or vary an injunction granted under this section.

SECTION 86 WHEN HIGH COURT MAY GRANT PERFORMANCE INJUNCTIONS

86(1) [When court may issue injunction] The High Court may grant an injunction requiring a person to do an act or thing if—

(a) it is satisfied that the person has refused or failed to do that act or thing; or

(b) it appears to the court that, if an injunction is not granted, it is likely that the person will refuse or fail to do that act or thing.

86(2) [When subs (1)(a) applies] Subsection (1)(a) applies whether or not it appears to the court that the person intends to refuse or fail again, or to continue to refuse or fail, to do that act or thing.

86(3) [When subs (1)(b) applies] Subsection (1)(b) applies—

(a) whether or not the person has previously refused or failed to do that act or thing; or

(b) where there is an imminent danger of substantial damage to any other person if that person refuses or fails to do that act or thing.

SECTION 87 RESTRAINING INJUNCTIONS

87(1) [Contravention of Act] The High Court may, on the application of the relevant AML/CFT supervisor, grant an injunction restraining a person from engaging in conduct that constitutes or would constitute a contravention of a provision of this Act.

87(2) [Court may rescind injunction] The court may rescind or vary an injunction granted under this section.

SECTION 88 WHEN HIGH COURT MAY GRANT RESTRAINING INJUNCTIONS AND INTERIM INJUNCTIONS

88(1) [When court may issue restraining injunction] The High Court may grant an injunction restraining a person from engaging in conduct of a particular kind if—

(a) it is satisfied that the person has engaged in conduct of that kind; or

(b) it appears to the court that, if an injunction is not granted, it is likely that the person will engage in conduct of that kind.

88(2) [When court may issue interim injunction] The court may grant an interim injunction restraining a person from engaging in conduct of a particular kind if, in its opinion, it is desirable to do so.

88(3) [When subs (1)(a) and (2) apply] Subsections (1)(a) and (2) apply whether or not it appears to the court that the person intends to engage again, or to continue to engage, in conduct of that kind.

88(4) [When subs (1)(b) and (2) apply] Subsections (1)(b) and (2) apply —

(a) whether or not the person has previously engaged in conduct of that kind; or

(b) where there is an imminent danger of substantial damage to any other person if that person engages in conduct of that kind.

SECTION 89 UNDERTAKING AS TO DAMAGES NOT REQUIRED BY AML/CFT SUPERVISOR

89(1) [No undertaking for damages] If the relevant AML/CFT supervisor applies to the High Court for the grant of an interim injunction under this subpart, the court must not, as a condition of granting an interim injunction, require the AML/CFT supervisor to give an undertaking as to damages.

89(2) [No consideration of undertakings] However, in determining the AML/CFT supervisor's application for the grant of an interim injunction, the court must not take into account that the AML/CFT supervisor is not required to give an undertaking as to damages.

Pecuniary penalties

SECTION 90 PECUNIARY PENALTIES FOR CIVIL LIABILITY ACT

90(1) [Court may issue penalty] On the application of the relevant AML/CFT supervisor, the High Court may order a person to pay a pecuniary penalty to the Crown, or to any other person specified by the court, if the court is satisfied that that person has engaged in conduct that constituted a civil liability act.

90(2) [Maximum penalty for s 78(b), (c), (d) or (g)] For a civil liability act specified in section 78(b), (c), (d), or (g), the maximum amount of a pecuniary penalty under this Act is,—

(a) in the case of an individual, $100,000; and

(b) in the case of a body corporate or partnership, $1 million.

History

S 90(2) amended by No 27 of 2018, s 7(1), by inserting in para (b) ''or partnership'' after ''body corporate''; **effective 8 September 2018**.

90(3) [Maximum penalty for s 78(a), (da), (e), or (f)] For a civil liability act specified in section 78(a), (da), (e), or (f), the maximum amount of a pecuniary penalty under this Act is,—

(a) in the case of an individual, $200,000; and

(b) in the case of a body corporate or partnership, $2 million.

History

S 90(3) amended by No 27 of 2018, s 7(2), by inserting in para (b) ''or partnership'' after ''body corporate''; **effective 8 September 2018**.

S 90(3) amended by No 96 of 2015, s 12, by replacing ''section 78(a), (e), or (f),'' with ''section 78(a), (da), (e), or (f),''; **effective 1 July 2017**.

90(4) [Determination of penalty] In determining an appropriate pecuniary penalty, the court must have regard to all relevant matters, including—

(a) the nature and extent of the civil liability act; and

(b) the likelihood, nature, and extent of any damage to the integrity or reputation of New Zealand's financial system because of the civil liability act; and

(c) the circumstances in which the civil liability act occurred; and

(d) whether the person has previously been found by the court in proceedings under this Act to have engaged in any similar conduct.

Subpart 3 — Offences

Offence and penalties relating to civil liability act

SECTION 91 OFFENCE AND PENALTIES FOR CIVIL LIABILITY ACT

91 A reporting entity that engages in conduct constituting a civil liability act commits an offence if the reporting entity engages in that conduct knowingly or recklessly.

Offences relating to suspicious activity reports and prescribed transaction reports

History

Heading preceding s 92 amended by No 35 of 2017, s 34, by replacing ''transaction'' with ''activity''; **effective 11 August 2017**.

Heading preceding s 92 replaced by No 96 of 2015, s 13, **effective 1 July 2017**. Former preceding heading read: ''Offences relating to suspicious transaction reports''.

SECTION 92 FAILING TO REPORT SUSPICIOUS ACTIVITY

92(1) [Offence] A reporting entity commits an offence if—

(a) an activity is conducted or is sought to be conducted through the reporting entity; and

(b) the reporting entity has reasonable grounds to suspect that the activity or the proposed activity is or may be—

(i) relevant to the investigation or prosecution of any person for a money laundering offence; or

(ii) relevant to the enforcement of the Misuse of Drugs Act 1975; or

(iii) relevant to the enforcement of the Terrorism Suppression Act 2002; or

(iv) relevant to the enforcement of the Proceeds of Crime Act 1991 or the Criminal Proceeds (Recovery) Act 2009; or

(v) relevant to the investigation or prosecution of an offence within the meaning of section 243(1) of the Crimes Act 1961; and

(c) the reporting entity fails to report the activity or the proposed activity to the Commissioner as soon as practicable, but no later than 3 working days, after forming that suspicion.

History

S 92(1) amended by No 35 of 2017, s 35(2)–(4), by replacing (i) in para (a) ''a transaction'' with ''an activity''; (ii) in para (b) ''the transaction or the proposed transaction'' with ''the activity or the proposed activity''; and (iii) in para (c) ''the transaction or the proposed transaction'' with ''the activity or the proposed activity''; **effective 11 August 2017**.

92(2) [Defence] It is a defence to a prosecution under this section if a reporting entity believes on reasonable grounds that the documents or information relating to the activity were privileged communications.

History

S 92(2) inserted by No 35 of 2017, s 35(5), **effective 11 August 2017**.

Compare: 1996 No 9 s 22(1)

History

S 92 heading amended by No 35 of 2017, s 35(1), by replacing "transaction" with "activity"; **effective 11 August 2017**.

S 92 amended by No 96 of 2015, s 14, by replacing in para (b)(v) "a serious offence" with "an offence"; **effective 1 July 2017**.

S 92(b) amended by No 98 of 2012, s 6, by replacing in para (iv) "; and" with "; or"; **effective 12 December 2012**.

SECTION 93 PROVIDING FALSE OR MISLEADING INFORMATION IN CONNECTION WITH SUSPICIOUS ACTIVITY REPORTS OR PRESCRIBED TRANSACTION REPORTS

93 A person commits an offence who, in making a suspicious activity report or a prescribed transaction report, or in supplying information in connection with a suspicious activity report or a prescribed transaction report,—

(a) makes any statement that the person knows is false or misleading in a material particular; or

(b) omits from any statement any matter or thing without which the person knows that the statement is false or misleading in a material particular.

Compare: 1996 No 9 s 22(3)

History

S 93 amended by No 35 of 2017, s 36(1) and (2), by replacing (i) in the heading "suspicious transaction" with "suspicious activity"; and (ii) "suspicious transaction" with "suspicious activity" wherever occurring; **effective 11 August 2017**.

S 93 amended by No 96 of 2015, s 15(1) and (2), by replacing (i) in the heading "suspicious transaction report" with "suspicious transaction reports or prescribed transaction reports"; and (ii) "a suspicious transaction report or in supplying information in connection with that report" with "a suspicious transaction report or a prescribed transaction report, or in supplying information in connection with a suspicious transaction report or a prescribed transaction report"; **effective 1 July 2017**.

SECTION 94 UNLAWFUL DISCLOSURE OF SUSPICIOUS ACTIVITY REPORTS OR PRESCRIBED TRANSACTION REPORTS

94(1) [When offence committed] A person commits an offence who contravenes section 46—

(a) for the purpose of obtaining, directly or indirectly, an advantage or a pecuniary gain for that person or any other person; or

(b) with intent to prejudice any investigation into—

(i) the commission or possible commission of a money laundering offence; or

(ii) the financing of terrorism or the possible financing of terrorism.

94(2) [Who commits an offence] A person commits an offence who—

(a) is an officer or employee or a former officer or employee of a reporting entity, a person appointed as an AML/CFT compliance officer under section 56(3), or an auditor for a reporting entity; and

(b) has become aware, or became aware, in the course of that person's duties as such an officer or employee, that any investigation into any activity or proposed activity that is the subject of a suspicious activity report or a prescribed transaction report is being, or may be, conducted by the Police; and

(c) knows that he or she is not legally authorised to disclose the information; and

(d) discloses that information to any other person—
   (i) for the purpose of obtaining, directly or indirectly, an advantage or a pecuniary gain for that person or any other person; or
   (ii) with intent to prejudice any investigation into—
      (A) the commission or possible commission of a money laundering offence; or
      (B) the financing of terrorism or the possible financing of terrorism.

History

S 94(2) amended by No 35 of 2017, s 37(2), by replacing in para (b) "any transaction or proposed transaction that is the subject of a suspicious transaction report" with "any activity or proposed activity that is the subject of a suspicious activity report"; **effective 11 August 2017**.

S 94(2) amended by No 96 of 2015, s 16(2), by inserting in para (b) "or a prescribed transaction report" after "a suspicious transaction report"; **effective 1 July 2017**.

Compare: 1996 No 9 s 22(4), (5)

History

S 94 heading amended by No 35 of 2017, s 37(1), by replacing "suspicious transaction" with "suspicious activity"; **effective 11 August 2017**.

S 94 heading amended by No 96 of 2015, s 16(1), by replacing "suspicious transaction report" with "suspicious transaction reports or prescribed transaction reports"; **effective 1 July 2017**.

SECTION 95 FAILURE TO KEEP OR RETAIN ADEQUATE RECORDS RELATING TO SUSPICIOUS ACTIVITIES OR PRESCRIBED TRANSACTIONS

95 A reporting entity commits an offence if the reporting entity fails to keep or retain adequate records relating to a suspicious activity or a prescribed transaction.

History

S 95 amended by No 35 of 2017, s 38(1) and (2), by replacing (i) in the heading "suspicious transactions" with "suspicious activities"; and (ii) "suspicious transaction" with "suspicious activity"; **effective 11 August 2017**.

S 95 amended by No 96 of 2015, s 17(1) and (2), by (i) replacing in the heading "suspicious transaction" with "suspicious transactions or prescribed transactions"; and (ii) inserting "or a prescribed transaction" after "suspicious transaction"; **effective 1 July 2017**.

SECTION 96 OBSTRUCTION OF INVESTIGATION RELATING TO SUSPICIOUS ACTIVITY REPORTS OR PRESCRIBED TRANSACTION REPORTS

96(1) [Offence] A person commits an offence if the person obstructs any investigation relating to any suspicious activity report or prescribed transaction report without lawful justification or excuse.

History

S 96(1) amended by No 35 of 2017, s 39(2), by replacing "suspicious transaction" with "suspicious activity"; **effective 11 August 2017**.

96(2) [Defence] It is a defence to a prosecution under this section if the reporting entity believes on reasonable grounds that the documents or information were privileged communications.

History

S 96(2) inserted by No 35 of 2017, s 39(3), **effective 11 August 2017**.

History

S 96 heading amended by No 35 of 2017, s 39(1), by replacing ''suspicious transaction'' with ''suspicious activity''; **effective 11 August 2017**.

S 96 amended by No 96 of 2015, s 18(1) and (2), by (i) replacing in the heading ''suspicious transaction report'' with ''suspicious transaction reports or prescribed transaction reports''; and (ii) inserting ''or prescribed transaction report'' after ''report''; **effective 1 July 2017**.

SECTION 97 CONTRAVENTION OF SECTION 47(1) OR 48A(1)

97 A person commits an offence if the person acts in contravention of section 47(1) or 48A(1) without lawful justification or excuse.

Compare: 1996 No 9 s 22(8)

History

S 97 amended by No 96 of 2015, s 19(1) and (2), by inserting (i) in the heading ''or 48A(1)'' after ''47(1)''; and (ii) ''or 48A(1)'' after ''47(1)''; **effective 1 July 2017**.

SECTION 98 DEFENCE

98(1) [Substance of defence] It is a defence to a charge against a person in relation to a contravention of, or a failure to comply with, Part 2 if the defendant proves that—

(a) the defendant took all reasonable steps to ensure that the defendant complied with that Part; or

(b) in the circumstances of the particular case, the defendant could not reasonably have been expected to ensure that the defendant complied with that Part.

98(2) [Basis of court's decision] In determining, for the purposes of subsection (1)(a), whether or not a defendant took all reasonable steps to comply with Part 2, the court must have regard to—

(a) the nature of the reporting entity and the activities in which it engages; and

(b) the existence and adequacy of any procedures established by the reporting entity to ensure compliance with that Part.

98(3) [Time limit] Except as provided in subsection (4), subsection (1) does not apply unless, within 21 days after the service of the summons, or within such further time as the court may allow, the defendant has delivered to the prosecutor a written notice—

(a) stating that the defendant intends to rely on the defence referred to in subsection (1); and

(b) specifying the reasonable steps that the defendant will claim to have taken.

98(4) [When actions not specified in notice] In any such prosecution, evidence that the defendant took a step not specified in the written notice required by subsection (3) is not, except with the leave of the court, admissible for the purpose of supporting a defence under subsection (1).

Compare: 1996 No 9 s 23

SECTION 99 TIME LIMIT FOR PROSECUTION OF OFFENCES RELATING TO CIVIL LIABILITY ACT AND SUSPICIOUS ACTIVITY REPORTS OR PRESCRIBED TRANSACTION REPORTS

99 Despite anything to the contrary in section 25 of the Criminal Procedure Act 2011, the limitation period in respect of an offence under any of sections 91 to 97 of this Act ends on the date that is 3 years after the date on which the offence was committed.

History

S 99 heading amended by No 35 of 2017, s 40, by replacing "suspicious transaction" with "suspicious activity"; **effective 11 August 2017**.

S 99 heading amended by No 96 of 2015, s 20, by inserting "or prescribed transaction reports" after "reports"; **effective 1 July 2017**.

S 99 replaced by No 81 of 2011, s 413 and sch 3, **effective 1 July 2013** (SR 2013/162). Former s 99 read:

"SECTION 99 TIME LIMIT FOR PROSECUTION OF OFFENCES RELATING TO CIVIL LIABILITY ACT AND SUSPICIOUS TRANSACTION REPORTS

99 Despite anything in section 14 of the Summary Proceedings Act 1957, any information in respect of an offence under any of sections 91 to 97 may be laid at any time within 3 years after the time when the matter of the information arose."

SECTION 100 PENALTIES

100 A reporting entity or person who commits an offence under any of sections 91 to 97 is liable, on conviction, to,—

(a) in the case of an individual, either or both of the following:

(i) a term of imprisonment of not more than 2 years:

(ii) a fine of up to $300,000; and

(b) in the case of a body corporate or partnership, a fine of up to $5 million.

History

S 100 amended by No 27 of 2018, s 8, by inserting in para (b) "or partnership" after "body corporate"; **effective 8 September 2018**.

Other offences relating to non-compliance with AML/CFT requirements

SECTION 101 STRUCTURING TRANSACTION TO AVOID APPLICATION OF AML/CFT REQUIREMENTS

101(1) [Offence] A person commits an offence if the person structures a transaction (other than a transaction that involves the cross-border transportation of cash) to avoid the application of any AML/CFT requirements.

101(2) [Interpretation] For the purposes of this section, **transaction** includes, but is not limited to, a suspicious transaction or a prescribed transaction.

History

S 101(2) inserted by No 96 of 2015, s 21, **effective 1 July 2017**.

SECTION 102 OFFENCE TO OBSTRUCT AML/CFT SUPERVISOR

102 A person commits an offence if the person wilfully obstructs any AML/CFT supervisor in the exercise of any power conferred or the performance of any function imposed on that supervisor by this Act or regulations.

History

S 102 amended by No 35 of 2017, s 41, by inserting "or regulations" after "Act"; **effective 11 August 2017**.

SECTION 103 OFFENCE TO PROVIDE FALSE OR MISLEADING INFORMATION TO AML/CFT SUPERVISOR

103 A person commits an offence if, without reasonable excuse, the person provides information to an AML/CFT supervisor knowing that information to be false or misleading in any material respect.

SECTION 104 TIME LIMIT FOR PROSECUTION OF OFFENCES RELATING TO NON-COMPLIANCE WITH AML/CFT REQUIREMENTS

104 Despite anything to the contrary in section 25 of the Criminal Procedure Act 2011, the limitation period in respect of an offence under any of sections 101 to 103 of this Act ends on the date that is 3 years after the date on which the offence was committed.

History

S 104 replaced by No 81 of 2011, s 413 and sch 3, **effective 1 July 2013** (SR 2013/162). Former s 104 read:

> "**SECTION 104 TIME LIMIT FOR PROSECUTION OF OFFENCES RELATING TO NON-COMPLIANCE WITH AML/CFT REQUIREMENTS**
>
> 104 Despite anything in section 14 of the Summary Proceedings Act 1957, any information in respect of an offence under any of sections 101 to 103 may be laid at any time within 3 years after the time when the matter of the information arose."

S 104 amended by No 98 of 2012, s 7, by replacing "91 to 97" with "101 to 103"; **effective 12 December 2012**.

SECTION 105 PENALTIES

105(1) [Offence under s 101] A person who commits an offence under section 101 is liable, on conviction, to,—

(a) in the case of an individual, either or both of the following:

(i) a term of imprisonment of not more than 2 years:

(ii) a fine of up to $300,000; and

(b) in the case of a body corporate or partnership, a fine of up to $5 million.

History

S 105(1) amended by No 27 of 2018, s 9(1), by inserting in para (b) "or partnership" after "body corporate"; **effective 8 September 2018**.

105(2) [Offence under ss 102 and 103] A person who commits an offence under either of sections 102 and 103 is liable, on conviction, to,—

(a) in the case of an individual, either or both of the following:

(i) a term of imprisonment of not more than 3 months:

(ii) a fine of up to $10,000; and

(b) in the case of a body corporate or partnership, a fine of up to $50,000.

History

S 105(2) amended by No 27 of 2018, s 9(2), by inserting in para (b) "or partnership" after "body corporate"; **effective 8 September 2018**.

Offences relating to cross-border transportation of cash

SECTION 106 FAILURE TO REPORT CASH EQUAL TO OR ABOVE APPLICABLE THRESHOLD VALUE MOVED INTO OR OUT OF NEW ZEALAND

106 A person commits an offence if the person fails, without reasonable excuse, to make or cause to be made a cash report, in accordance with subpart 6 of Part 2, concerning cash equal to or above the applicable threshold value that the person has moved into or out of New Zealand.

History

S 106 amended by No 35 of 2017, s 42(1) and (2), by replacing (i) in the heading "over" with "equal to or above"; and (ii) "over" with "equal to or above"; **effective 11 August 2017**.

SECTION 107 FAILURE TO REPORT CASH EQUAL TO OR ABOVE APPLICABLE THRESHOLD VALUE RECEIVED BY PERSON IN NEW ZEALAND FROM OVERSEAS

107 A person commits an offence if the person fails, without reasonable excuse, to make or cause to be made a cash report, in accordance with subpart 6 of Part 2, concerning cash equal to or above the applicable threshold value that the person has received in New Zealand from overseas.

History

S 107 amended by No 35 of 2017, s 43(1) and (2), by replacing (i) in the heading "over" with "equal to or above"; and (ii) "over" with "equal to or above"; **effective 11 August 2017**.

SECTION 108 STRUCTURING CROSS-BORDER TRANSPORTATION TO AVOID APPLICATION OF AML/CFT REQUIREMENTS

108 A person commits an offence if the person structures a crossborder transportation of cash to avoid the application of any AML/CFT requirements.

SECTION 109 DEFENCE

109 It is a defence to an offence under section 106 or 107 in relation to a failure to make or cause to be made a cash report to a Customs officer under section 70(d) if the defendant proves that—

(a) the failure was due to some emergency or to any other circumstances outside the reasonable control of the defendant; and

(b) the defendant made or caused to be made a report in respect of that cash as soon as practicable after the obligation to make the report arose.

Compare: 1996 No 9 s 40(3)

SECTION 110 PROVIDING FALSE OR MISLEADING INFORMATION IN CONNECTION WITH CASH REPORT

110 A person commits an offence if, without reasonable excuse, the person makes or causes to be made a cash report knowing it is false or misleading in any material respect.

Compare: 1996 No 9 s 40(1)(b)

SECTION 111 OFFENCE TO OBSTRUCT OR NOT TO ANSWER QUESTIONS FROM CUSTOMS OFFICER

111(1) [Obstruction] A person commits an offence if the person wilfully obstructs any Customs officer in the exercise of any power conferred or performance of any duty imposed on that officer by this Act or regulations.

History

S 111(1) amended by No 35 of 2017, s 44, by inserting "or regulations" after "Act"; **effective 11 August 2017**.

111(2) [Failure to answer] A person commits an offence if, without reasonable excuse, the person fails to answer questions from a Customs officer.

Compare: 1996 No 9 s 40(2)

SECTION 112 PENALTIES

112 A person who commits an offence under any of sections 106, 107, 108, 110, and 111 is liable, on conviction, to,—

(a) in the case of an individual, either or both of the following:

(i) a term of imprisonment of not more than 3 months:

(ii) a fine of up to $10,000; and

(b) in the case of a body corporate or partnership, a fine of up to $50,000.

History

S 112 amended by No 27 of 2018, s 10, by inserting in para (b) "or partnership" after "body corporate"; **effective 8 September 2018**.

S 112 amended by No 81 of 2011, s 413 and sch 3, by omitting "summary" after "liable, on"; **effective 1 July 2013** (SR 2013/162).

SECTION 113 CHIEF EXECUTIVE OF NEW ZEALAND CUSTOMS SERVICE MAY DEAL WITH CASH REPORTING OFFENCES

113(1) [Request for summary decision] This section applies if, in any case to which section 106 or 107 applies, a person admits in writing that he or she has committed the offence and requests that the offence be dealt with summarily by the chief executive of the New Zealand Customs Service.

113(2) [Acceptance of prior payment] If this section applies, the chief executive of the New Zealand Customs Service may, at any time before a charging document has been filed in respect of the offence, accept from that person a sum, not exceeding $500, that the chief executive of the New Zealand Customs Service thinks just in the circumstances of the case, in full satisfaction of any fine to which the person would otherwise be liable under section 112.

History

S 113(2) amended by No 81 of 2011, s 413 and sch 3, by replacing "an information has been laid" with "a charging document has been filed"; **effective 1 July 2013** (SR 2013/162).

113(3) [When no prosecution] If the chief executive of the New Zealand Customs Service accepts any sum under this section, the offender is not liable to be prosecuted for the offence in respect of which the payment was made.

Compare: 1996 No 9 s 41

Relationship with Customs and Excise Act 1996
[Effective on a date to be appointed, or 29 March 2019] Relationship with Customs and Excise Act 2018

History

Heading preceding s 114 amended by No 4 of 2018, 443(3) and sch 9, by replacing "Customs and Excise Act 1996" with "Customs and Excise Act 2018"; **effective on a date to be appointed by the Governor-General by Order in Council, or 29 March 2019, whichever is earlier**.

SECTION 114 RELATIONSHIP WITH CUSTOMS AND EXCISE ACT 2018

114(1) [No limitation] Nothing in this Act limits or affects the Customs and Excise Act 2018.

History

S 114(1) amended by No 4 of 2018, s 443(3) and sch 9, by replacing "Customs and Excise Act 1996" with "Customs and Excise Act 2018"; **effective 1 October 2018** (LI 2018/148).

114(2) [Definition of action] The movement of cash in breach of any requirement of this Act or any regulations is, for the purposes of the Customs and Excise Act 2018, the importation or exportation of a prohibited good.

History

S 114(2) amended by No 4 of 2018, s 443(3) and sch 9, by replacing "Customs and Excise Act 1996" with "Customs and Excise Act 2018"; **effective 1 October 2018** (LI 2018/148).

114(3) [Duty of officer] It is the duty of every Customs officer to prevent the movement of cash that is in breach of any requirement of this Act or any regulations.

114(4) [Powers of officer] For the purpose of carrying out the duty in subsection (3), a Customs officer may exercise his or her powers under the following sections of the Customs and Excise Act 2018 in relation to uncustomed or prohibited goods:

(a) section 205 (questioning persons about goods and debt):

(b) section 206 (detention of persons questioned about goods or debt and suspected to be involved in offences):

(c) sections 210, 211, and 214 (which relate to search and seizure):

(d) sections 225 and 226 (which relate to search warrants and use of aids by Customs officers):

(e) sections 227 and 237 (which relate to examination of goods):

(f) section 228 (which relates to search of data in electronic devices):

(g) section 252 (further powers in relation to documents):

(h) section 257 (copying of documents obtained during inspection):

(i) section 258 (retention of documents and goods obtained during inspection):

(j) sections 244 to 249 (which relate to seizure and detention of goods suspected to be tainted property).

History

S 114(4) replaced by No 4 of 2018, s 443(3) and sch 9, **effective 1 October 2018** (LI 2018/148). Former s 114(4) read:

> "114(4) [Powers of officer] For the purpose of carrying out the duty in subsection (3), a Customs officer may exercise his or her powers under the following sections of the Customs and Excise Act 1996 in relation to uncustomed or prohibited goods:
>
> (a) section 145 (questioning persons about goods and debt):
>
> (b) section 148 (detention of persons questioned about goods or debt):
>
> (c) sections 149, 149A, 149B, and 149C(1) (which relate to search and seizure):
>
> (d) sections 151 and 152 (which relate to examination of goods):
>
> (e) section 161 (further powers in relation to documents):
>
> (f) section 165 (copying of documents obtained during search):
>
> (g) section 166 (retention of documents and goods obtained during search):
>
> (h) sections 166A to 166F (which relate to seizure and detention of goods suspected to be tainted property):
>
> (i) sections 167 to 172 (which relate to search warrants and use of aids by Customs officers)."

S 114(4) amended by No 24 of 2012, s 201(2), by replacing in para (c) "149C(1) and (2), and 149D" with "and 149C(1)"; **effective 1 October 2012** (SR 2012/229).

History

S 114 heading amended by No 4 of 2018, 443(3) and sch 9, by replacing "Customs and Excise Act 1996" with "Customs and Excise Act 2018"; **effective 1 October 2018** (LI 2018/148). Former heading read:

> "RELATIONSHIP WITH CUSTOMS AND EXCISE ACT 1996".

Stored value instrument searches by Customs officer

SECTION 115 DUTY TO ASSIST CUSTOMS OFFICER TO ACCESS STORED VALUE INSTRUMENTS

115(1) [Access to information] A Customs officer exercising a search power or an examination power under section 114(4) may require a specified person to provide access information and other information or assistance that is reasonable and necessary to allow the Customs officer to access data held in a stored value instrument.

115(2) [Application] In this case, section 130 of the Search and Surveillance Act 2012 (which requires persons with knowledge of a computer system or other data storage devices or an Internet site to assist access) applies in respect of the stored value instrument with necessary modifications.

115(3) [Interpretation] In this section, **stored value instrument**—

(a) means a portable device (for example, a debit card) that contains monetary value that is not physical currency but that can be reloaded or redeemed for cash; and

(b) includes an instrument that is prescribed as a bearer-negotiable instrument under section 153(b).

History

S 115 and preceding heading replaced by No 4 of 2018, s 443(3) and sch 9, **effective 1 October 2018** (LI 2018/148). Former s 115 and preceding heading read:

"**Computer searches by Customs officer**

SECTION 115 DUTY OF PERSONS WITH KNOWLEDGE OF COMPUTER OR COMPUTER NETWORK OR OTHER DATA STORAGE DEVICES TO ASSIST ACCESS TO CUSTOMS OFFICER

115(1) [Information required] A Customs officer exercising a search or examination power under section 114(4) may require a specified person to provide access information and other information or assistance that is reasonable and necessary to allow the Customs officer to access data held in, or accessible from,—

(a) a computer:

(b) any other data storage device.

115(2) [Definitions] In this section,—

access information includes access codes, passwords, encryption keys, and any related information that enables access to a computer or other data storage device

specified person is a person who—

(a) is the owner or lessee of the computer or other data storage device, or is in possession or control of the computer or other data storage device, is an employee of any of the above, or is a service provider who provides service to the above and holds access information; and

(b) has relevant knowledge of—

(i) the computer or a computer network of which the computer or other data storage device forms a part; or

(ii) measures applied to protect data held in, or accessible from, the computer or other data storage device.

115(3) [No incrimination] A specified person may not be required under subsection (1) to give any information tending to incriminate the person.

115(4) [Information not limited by subs (3)] Subsection (3) does not prevent a Customs officer exercising a search power from requiring a specified person to provide information that—

(a) is reasonable and necessary to allow the person exercising the search power to access data held in, or accessible from, a computer or other storage device that contains or may contain information tending to incriminate the specified person; but

(b) does not itself tend to incriminate the specified person.

115(5) [Assistance not limited by subs (3)] Subsection (3) does not prevent a Customs officer exercising a search power from requiring a specified person to provide assistance that is reasonable and necessary to allow the Customs officer exercising the search power to access data held in, or accessible from, a computer or other storage device that contains, or may contain, information tending to incriminate the specified person.

115(6) [Customs and Excise Act 1996 applies] Subsections (1), (4), and (5) are subject to section 162 of the Customs and Excise Act 1996 (which relates to privilege and confidentiality)."

Subpart 4 — Search and seizure

SECTION 116 DEFINITIONS

116 In this subpart, unless the context otherwise requires,—

document—

(a) means any record of information; and

(b) includes—

(i) anything on which there is writing or any image; and

(ii) anything on which there are marks, figures, symbols, or perforations that have a meaning for persons qualified to interpret them; and

(iii) anything from which sounds, images, or writing can be reproduced, with or without the aid of anything else

dwellinghouse means a building, or an apartment, a flat, or a unit within a building, that is used as a private residence

enforcement officer means the relevant AML/CFT supervisor or the Commissioner (as the case may require) and includes a person appointed under section 141 by an AML/CFT supervisor

evidential material means any thing that there are reasonable grounds for believing is or may be evidence, or may provide or contain evidence, of—

(a) an offence under this Part; or

(b) an attempt to commit an offence under this Part; or

(c) a civil liability act

occupier, in relation to any place, includes—

(a) a person who is present at the place and is in apparent control of it; and

(b) any person acting on behalf of the occupier

place—

(a) means anywhere on, under, or over any land or water; and

(b) includes all or any part of a building, structure, or conveyance

seize includes to secure against interference

thing includes—

(a) any substance, article, document, container, or equipment; and

(b) anything in electronic or magnetic form.

Search warrants

SECTION 117 SEARCH WARRANT

117(1) [Search of a place] An enforcement officer may apply for a search warrant in respect of a place.

117(2) [Form of application] The application must be made by an enforcement officer in the manner provided in subpart 3 of Part 4 of the Search and Surveillance Act 2012.

History

S 117(2) replaced by No 24 of 2012, s 201(3), **effective 30 June 2013** (SR 2012/229). Former s 117(2) read:

> "117(2) [Application in writing] The application must be made in writing, on oath, by an enforcement officer."

117(3) [Who may issue warranty] An issuing officer (within the meaning of section 3 of the Search and Surveillance Act 2012) may issue a search warrant in respect of a place if satisfied that there are reasonable grounds for believing that there is evidential material at that place.

History

S 117(3) amended by No 24 of 2012, s 201(4), by replacing "A District Court Judge, Justice of the Peace, Community Magistrate, or Registrar" with "An issuing officer (within the meaning of section 3 of the Search and Surveillance Act 2012)"; **effective 30 June 2013** (SR 2012/229).

117(4) [Search and Surveillance Act 2012 applies] The provisions of subparts 1, 3, 4, and 9 of Part 4 of the Search and Surveillance Act 2012 apply.

History

S 117(4) amended by No 35 of 2017, s 45, by inserting "4," after "3,"; **effective 11 August 2017**.

S 117(4) replaced by No 24 of 2012, s 201(5), **effective 30 June 2013** (SR 2012/229). Former s 117(4) read:

> "117(4) [Form of application] Every search warrant must be in the form prescribed by regulations and be directed to—
>
> (a) an enforcement officer by name; or
>
> (b) a constable by name; or
>
> (c) every constable."

117(5) *(repealed)*

History

S 117(5) repealed by No 24 of 2012, s 201(5), **effective 30 June 2013** (SR 2012/229). Former s 117(5) read:

> "117(5) [Who may execute warrant] Despite a warrant being directed to another person under subsection (4), it may be executed by any constable."

117(6) *(repealed)*

History

S 117(6) repealed by No 24 of 2012, s 201(5), **effective 30 June 2013** (SR 2012/229). Former s 117(6) read:

> "117(6) [Conditions on execution of warrant] The Judge, Justice of the Peace, Community Magistrate, or Registrar issuing the warrant may impose reasonable conditions on its execution."

SECTION 118 POWERS UNDER SEARCH WARRANT

118(1) [Actions allowed] A search warrant issued under section 117 authorises the enforcement officer or constable who is executing it, and any person called on by that officer or constable to assist, to do any of the following:

(a) *(repealed)*

(b) *(repealed)*

(c) search for any evidential material at the place:

(d) inspect and copy any document; and for that purpose also do any of the following:

(i) require any person at the place to produce a particular document:

(ii) require any person at the place who has control or knowledge of a document to reproduce, or assist in reproducing, the document in usable form:

(iii) operate any equipment at the place:

(iv) remove a document temporarily to another place in order to copy it:

(e) (*repealed*)

(f) require the occupier of the place to answer any questions put by the enforcement officer or constable.

History

S 118(1) amended by No 24 of 2012, s 201(7), by omitting in para (c) ''and seize''; **effective 30 June 2013** (SR 2012/229).

S 118(1) amended by No 24 of 2012, s 201(6), by repealing para (a), (b) and (e); **effective 30 June 2013** (SR 2012/229). Former para (a) and (b) read:

''(a) enter and search the place at any reasonable time, on 1 occasion within 14 days after the date of the warrant being issued:

(b) use reasonable force to—

(i) make entry (for example, by breaking open a door); and

(ii) open any thing at the place that it is reasonable in the circumstances to open:''.

Former para (e) read:

''(e) take into or onto the place whatever equipment and materials the enforcement officer or constable requires for the search:''.

118(2) [What officer may require] An enforcement officer or constable may require the occupier of the place to do the following:

(a) hold any thing at the place in an unaltered state for a specified period of up to 5 working days:

(b) provide a copy of particular documents within a specified period (which must be a period that is reasonable in the circumstances).

118(3) [Search and Surveillance Act 2012 applies] The provisions of Part 4 of the Search and Surveillance Act 2012 (except subpart 3 and sections 118, 119, and 130) apply.

History

S 118(3) replaced by No 24 of 2012, s 201(8), **effective 30 June 2013** (SR 2012/229). Former s 118(3) read:

''118(3) [Privilege against self-incrimination] Nothing in this section limits or affects the privilege against self-incrimination.''

Conduct of entry, search, and seizure

SECTION 119 ASSISTANCE WITH SEARCHES (*repealed*)

History

S 119 repealed by No 24 of 2012, s 201(9), **effective 30 June 2013** (SR 2012/229). Former s 119 read:

''SECTION 119 ASSISTANCE WITH SEARCHES

119(1) [Officer may request assistance] An enforcement officer or constable may ask any person to assist the enforcement officer or constable with a search under this subpart.

119(2) [Supervision of assistant] A person who assists an enforcement officer or constable must be under the supervision of an enforcement officer or constable.''

SECTION 120 ENFORCEMENT OFFICERS TO SHOW IDENTITY CARD ON REQUEST (*repealed*)

History

S 120 repealed by No 24 of 2012, s 201(9), **effective 30 June 2013** (SR 2012/229). Former s 120 read:

"**SECTION 120 ENFORCEMENT OFFICERS TO SHOW IDENTITY CARD ON REQUEST**

120(1) [When identity card required] An enforcement officer must produce his or her identity card (as issued under section 141(2)) for inspection—

(a) on entering a place under this subpart; and

(b) at any later time, on request, during a search under this subpart.

120(2) [Failure to comply with subs (1)] An enforcement officer who fails to comply with subsection (1) ceases to be authorised to enter the place or to exercise any power under this Act or any regulations with respect to the search."

SECTION 121 ANNOUNCEMENT BEFORE ENTRY (*repealed*)

History

S 121 repealed by No 24 of 2012, s 201(9), **effective 30 June 2013** (SR 2012/229). Former s 121 read:

"**SECTION 121 ANNOUNCEMENT BEFORE ENTRY**

121(1) [When this section applies] This section applies whenever an enforcement officer or constable enters a place under this subpart, unless the entry is made by consent.

121(2) [Requirement before entry] Before entering the place, the enforcement officer or constable must—

(a) announce that he or she is authorised to enter the place; and

(b) give any person at the place an opportunity to consent to the entry.

121(3) [When subs (2) does not apply] However, subsection (2) does not apply if the enforcement officer or constable believes on reasonable grounds that—

(a) announcing entry would frustrate the purpose of the entry; or

(b) immediate entry to the place is required to ensure the safety of any person."

SECTION 122 DETAILS OF WARRANT TO BE GIVEN TO OCCUPIER (*repealed*)

History

S 122 repealed by No 24 of 2012, s 201(9), **effective 30 June 2013** (SR 2012/229). Former s 122 read:

"**SECTION 122 DETAILS OF WARRANT TO BE GIVEN TO OCCUPIER**

122 If a place is being searched under a warrant, the enforcement officer or constable must give a copy of the warrant to the occupier or, if no person is present at the time, must leave a copy of the warrant in a prominent situation, marked for the attention of the occupier."

SECTION 123 OCCUPIER ENTITLED TO BE PRESENT DURING SEARCH

123(1) [Occupier may observe] The occupier of a place that is subject to a search under this subpart, and who is present at any time during the search, is entitled to observe the search as it is being carried out.

123(2) [No right to impede] The right to observe the search ceases if the person observing impedes the search.

123(3) [Places of search not limited] This section does not prevent 2 or more parts of the place being searched at the same time.

SECTION 124 USE OF ELECTRONIC EQUIPMENT

124(1) [No damage or corruption] If an enforcement officer, a constable, or a person assisting a search operates electronic equipment found at a place during a search, the officer, constable, or person must take all reasonable care not to damage the equipment or corrupt information stored on it.

124(2) [Liability for damages] If, as a result of a failure to take the care required by subsection (1), the owner of the equipment or information, or the occupier of the place that was searched, suffers damage, the owner or occupier may seek damages from the relevant AML/CFT supervisor or the Police (as the case may require) in respect of that damage.

SECTION 125 COPIES OF DOCUMENTS SEIZED TO BE PROVIDED (*repealed*)

History

S 125 repealed by No 24 of 2012, s 201(9), **effective 30 June 2013** (SR 2012/229). Former s 125 read:

"**SECTION 125 COPIES OF DOCUMENTS SEIZED TO BE PROVIDED**

125(1) [Document copies to be left at site] When a document that is capable of being copied is seized from a place, it must (if practicable) be copied before the original is removed, and the copy must be left at the place.

125(2) [Prompt delivery of copy] If it is not practicable to copy the document before removing it, it must be copied as soon as practicable after it is removed, and (if practicable) the copy must be promptly delivered to the occupier of the place.

125(3) [When subs (1) does not apply] Subsection (1) does not apply—

(a) to documents obtained as a result of operating electronic equipment found at the place if the equipment is not seized and the documents remain stored on it; or

(b) if an order under subsection (4) has been made.

125(4) [Waiver for cost] A District Court Judge, Community Magistrate, or Justice of the Peace may make an order waiving the application of subsections (1) and (2) if satisfied that the volume of material to be copied is such that copying it will involve substantial cost and that the cost is not justified.

125(5) [Conditions on subs (4)] An order under subsection (4) may be subject to whatever conditions the person making the order thinks are necessary to protect the interests of the person from whom the documents have been seized."

SECTION 126 RECEIPTS FOR THINGS SEIZED (*repealed*)

History

S 126 repealed by No 24 of 2012, s 201(9), **effective 30 June 2013** (SR 2012/229). Former s 126 read:

"**SECTION 126 RECEIPTS FOR THINGS SEIZED**

126(1) [Receipt required] A person who seizes any thing during a search under this subpart must provide the occupier with a receipt for the thing seized.

126(2) [Single receipt sufficient] A single receipt may be given for more than 1 thing."

SECTION 127 APPLICATION OF SECTIONS 198A AND 198B OF SUMMARY PROCEEDINGS ACT 1957 (*repealed*)

History

S 127 repealed by No 24 of 2012, s 201(9), **effective 30 June 2013** (SR 2012/229). Former s 127 read:

"**SECTION 127 APPLICATION OF SECTIONS 198A AND 198B OF SUMMARY PROCEEDINGS ACT 1957**

127(1) [Seizure of documents] Section 198A of the Summary Proceedings Act 1957, so far as applicable and with all necessary modifications, applies in respect of the seizure of any documents under any search warrant as if the search warrant had been issued under section 198 of that Act.

127(2) [Accessing documents] Section 198B of the Summary Proceedings Act 1957, so far as applicable and with all necessary modifications, applies in respect of accessing any documents under any search warrant as if the search warrant had been issued under section 198 of that Act.

Compare: 1996 No 9 s 50"

Return and retention of things seized (*repealed*)

History

Heading repealed pursuant to No 24 of 2012, s 201(9), **effective 30 June 2013**.

SECTION 128 RETURN AND RETENTION OF THINGS SEIZED (*repealed*)

History

S 128 repealed by No 24 of 2012, s 201(9), **effective 30 June 2013** (SR 2012/229). Former s 128 read:

"**SECTION 128 RETURN AND RETENTION OF THINGS SEIZED**

128(1) [When no reason to retain item] An enforcement officer or constable must (subject to any order of a court) immediately return any thing seized under this subpart to the person from whom it was seized if the reason for the thing's seizure no longer exists or it is decided that the thing is not to be used in evidence.

128(2) [Time limit] If a thing has not been returned under subsection (1) within 90 days of its seizure, the enforcement officer or constable must return the thing unless—

(a) proceedings in respect of which the thing may afford evidence were instituted within 90 days of its seizure, and those proceedings (including any appeal) have not been completed, or the time within which an appeal may be lodged in those proceedings has not expired; or

(b) there is an order in force under section 129 in respect of the thing; or

(c) the enforcement officer or constable is otherwise authorised to retain, destroy, or dispose of the thing other than by returning it to the person from whom it was seized; or

(d) the person to whom it is to be returned cannot be found or does not wish to take back the thing.

128(3) [Conditional return] A thing may be returned conditionally or under such terms and conditions as the relevant AML/CFT supervisor or the Commissioner (as the case may require) thinks fit.

128(4) [Forfeiture to Crown] A thing may not be returned if it is, or is liable to be, forfeited to the Crown."

SECTION 129 ORDER TO RETAIN THINGS SEIZED (*repealed*)

History

S 129 repealed by No 24 of 2012, s 201(9), **effective 30 June 2013** (SR 2012/229). Former s 129 read:

"**SECTION 129 ORDER TO RETAIN THINGS SEIZED**

129(1) [Extension of time] If an enforcement officer or constable wishes to retain any thing seized under this subpart for more than 90 days, he or she may apply to a District Court for an order under this section.

129(2) [Who may make order] A District Court Judge, Community Magistrate, or Justice of the Peace may make an order under this section if he or she is satisfied that retention of the thing is necessary—

(a) for the purpose of investigating an alleged offence or a civil liability act under this Part; or

(b) as evidence of an alleged offence or a civil liability act under this Part; or

(c) to secure evidence of an alleged offence or a civil liability act under this Part.

129(3) [Maximum period] An order made under this section may be made for any period of up to 4 years.

129(4) [Option for renewal] If made for a shorter period, the order may be renewed at any interval, but the total period of the order, with any renewals, may not exceed 4 years.

129(5) [Interested parties] Before making an application, the enforcement officer or constable must—

(a) take reasonable steps to discover who has an interest in the thing; and

(b) if practicable, notify each person who the enforcement officer or constable believes has such an interest in the proposed application and any application for a renewal. "

PART 4 — INSTITUTIONAL ARRANGEMENTS AND MISCELLANEOUS PROVISIONS

Subpart 1 — Institutional arrangements

AML/CFT supervisors

SECTION 130 AML/CFT SUPERVISORS

130(1) The AML/CFT supervisors are as follows:

(a) for registered banks, life insurers, and non-bank deposit takers, the Reserve Bank of New Zealand (**Reserve Bank**) is the relevant AML/CFT supervisor:

(b) for persons referred to in subsection (1A) (other than banks, life insurers, and non-bank deposit takers), the Financial Markets Authority is the relevant AML/CFT supervisor:

(c) for designated non-financial businesses or professions and high-value dealers, the Department of Internal Affairs, or another AML/CFT supervisor prescribed for the purpose, is the relevant AML/CFT supervisor:

(d) for TAB NZ, casinos, non-deposit-taking lenders, money changers, and other reporting entities that are not covered by paragraphs (a) to (c), the Department of Internal Affairs is the relevant AML/CFT supervisor.

History

S 130(1) amended by No 28 of 2020, s 129 and sch 5, by replacing in para (d) "the Racing Industry Transition Agency" with "TAB NZ"; **effective 1 August 2020**.

S 130(1) amended by No 32 of 2019, s 25(2) and sch 3, by replacing in para (d) "New Zealand Racing Board" with "Racing Industry Transition Agency"; **effective 1 July 2019**.

S 130(1) amended by No 35 of 2017, s 46, by replacing para (c) with para (c) and (d); **effective 11 August 2017**. Former para (c) read:

> "(c) for casinos, non-deposit-taking lenders, money changers, and other reporting entities that are not covered by paragraph (a) or (b), the Department of Internal Affairs is the relevant AML/CFT supervisor."

S 130(1) amended by No 106 of 2013, s 9, by inserting in para (a) "registered"; **effective 5 December 2013**.

S 130(1) amended by No 70 of 2013, s 150 and sch, by replacing para (b); **effective 1 December 2014** (LI 2014/325). Former para (b) read:

> "(b) for issuers of securities, trustee companies, futures dealers, collective investment schemes, brokers, and financial advisers, the Financial Markets Authority is the relevant AML/CFT supervisor:"

S 130(1) amended by No 5 of 2011, s 82 and sch 3, by substituting in para (b) "Financial Markets Authority" for "Securities Commission"; **effective 1 May 2011**.

130(1A) For the purposes of subsection (1)(b), the persons are any of the following:

(a) persons registered, or required to be registered, under the Financial Service Providers (Registration and Dispute Resolution) Act 2008 by virtue of providing any of the services referred to in—

(i) section 5(1)(a), (ab), (d), (i) to (id), and (ma) of that Act; or

(ii) section 5(1)(k) of that Act (but only to the extent that it relates to the service of trading in financial products on behalf of other persons):

(b) statutory supervisors within the meaning of section 5 of the Retirement Villages Act 2003.

History

S 130(1A) amended by No 8 of 2019, s 98 and sch 4, by replacing para (a)(i); **effective 15 March 2021** (LI 2020/131). Former para (a)(i) read:

> "(i) section 5(1)(a), (ab), (d), or (i) to (id) of that Act; or".

S 130(1A) inserted by No 70 of 2013, s 150 and sch, **effective 1 December 2014** (LI 2014/325).

130(2) If the products or services provided by a particular reporting entity are covered by more than 1 AML/CFT supervisor,—

(a) the AML/CFT supervisors concerned may agree on the relevant AML/CFT supervisor that will be the reporting entity's AML/CFT supervisor for the purposes of this Act; and

(b) the relevant AML/CFT supervisor will notify the reporting entity accordingly.

130(3) If a reporting entity is a member of a designated business group and the products and services provided by members of that designated business group are covered by more than 1 AML/CFT supervisor,—

(a) the AML/CFT supervisors concerned may agree on 1 AML/CFT supervisor that will be the AML/CFT supervisor for all the reporting entities that are members of the designated business group for the purposes of this Act; and

(b) that AML/CFT supervisor will notify the reporting entities accordingly.

130(4) If the AML/CFT supervisors cannot agree on which AML/CFT supervisor is to be a reporting entity's supervisor under subsection (2) or (3), then the AML/CFT co-ordination committee must appoint the AML/CFT supervisor for that entity.

130(5) A reporting entity may have only 1 AML/CFT supervisor.

SECTION 131 FUNCTIONS

131 The functions of an AML/CFT supervisor are to—

(a) monitor and assess the level of risk of money laundering and the financing of terrorism across all of the reporting entities that it supervises:

(b) monitor the reporting entities that it supervises for compliance with this Act and regulations, and for this purpose to develop and implement a supervisory programme:

(c) provide guidance to the reporting entities it supervises in order to assist those entities to comply with this Act and regulations:

(d) investigate the reporting entities it supervises and enforce compliance with this Act and regulations:

(e) co-operate through the AML/CFT co-ordination committee (or any other mechanism that may be appropriate) with domestic and international counterparts to ensure the consistent, effective, and efficient implementation of this Act.

SECTION 132 POWERS

132(1) [Necessary powers granted] An AML/CFT supervisor has all the powers necessary to carry out its functions under this Act or regulations.

History

S 132(1) amended by No 35 of 2017, s 47(1), by inserting "or regulations" after "Act"; **effective 11 August 2017**.

132(2) [Options available] Without limiting the power conferred by subsection (1), an AML/CFT supervisor may,—

(a) on notice, require production of, or access to, all records, documents, or information relevant to its supervision and monitoring of reporting entities for compliance with this Act; and

(b) conduct on-site inspections in accordance with section 133; and

(c) provide guidance to the reporting entities it supervises by—

   (i) producing guidelines; and

   (ii) preparing codes of practice in accordance with section 63; and

(iii) providing feedback on reporting entities' compliance with obligations under this Act and regulations; and

(iv) undertaking any other activities necessary for assisting reporting entities to understand their obligations under this Act and regulations, including how best to achieve compliance with those obligations; and

(d) co-operate and share information in accordance with sections 46, 48, and 137 to 140 by communicating or making arrangements to communicate information obtained by the AML/CFT supervisor in the performance of its functions and the exercise of its powers under this Act; and

(e) in accordance with this Act and any other enactment, initiate and act on requests from any overseas counterparts; and

(f) approve the formation of, and addition of members to, designated business groups.

132(3) [Limited to purposes of Act] An AML/CFT supervisor may only use the powers conferred on it under this Act and regulations for the purposes of this Act.

132(4) [Privileged communication] Nothing in this section requires any person to disclose any privileged communication.

History

S 132(4) inserted by No 35 of 2017, s 47(2), **effective 11 August 2017**.

SECTION 133 MATTERS RELATING TO CONDUCT OF ON-SITE INSPECTIONS

133(1) [Entry to site] An AML/CFT supervisor may, at any reasonable time, enter and remain at any place (other than a dwellinghouse or a marae) for the purpose of conducting an on-site inspection of a reporting entity.

133(2) [Provision of information] During an inspection, an AML/CFT supervisor may require any employee, officer, or agent of the reporting entity to answer questions relating to its records and documents and to provide any other information that the AML/CFT supervisor may reasonably require for the purpose of the inspection.

133(3) [No self-incrimination] A person is not required to answer a question asked by an AML/CFT supervisor under this section if the answer would or could incriminate the person.

133(4) [Informing of rights] Before an AML/CFT supervisor requires a person to answer a question, the person must be informed of the right specified in subsection (3).

133(5) [Privileged communication protected] Nothing in this section requires any person to disclose any privileged communication (as defined in section 42).

History

S 133(5) amended by No 35 of 2017, s 48, by replacing "lawyer" with "person"; **effective 11 August 2017**.

SECTION 134 DELEGATION OF SUPERVISORY FUNCTION AND POWERS

134(1) [Delegation of functions] An AML/CFT supervisor may delegate the following function and powers to a person who, by reason of his or her training or experience, is suitably qualified to perform that function and exercise those powers:

(a) its function under section 131(d) of investigating the reporting entities it supervises:

(b) its powers under section 132(2)(a) and (b), for the purpose only of performing the function of investigation under section 131(d).

History

S 134(1) amended by No 106 of 2013, s 10, by replacing in para (b) "section 131(b)" with "section 131(d)"; **effective 5 December 2013**.

134(2) [Who may make delegation] A delegation under subsection (1)—

(a) must be made by the chief executive of the AML/CFT supervisor in writing; and

(b) may be made subject to any restrictions and conditions that the AML/CFT supervisor thinks fit; and

(c) may be revoked at any time by written notice to the delegate.

134(3) [Requirements on delegate] A person to whom a function or power of the AML/CFT supervisor is delegated under this section—

(a) may, unless the delegation provides otherwise, perform the function or exercise the power in the same manner, and with the same effect, as if the delegate were the AML/CFT supervisor; and

(b) must disclose to the AML/CFT supervisor and manage appropriately any conflict of interest that might arise in relation to the performance of the function or exercise of the power; and

(c) must not disclose any information obtained under subsection (1) other than to the AML/CFT supervisor.

SECTION 135 AUTHORITY TO ACT AS DELEGATE

135(1) [Written authorisation] The chief executive of the AML/CFT supervisor must issue a written authorisation to every person to whom a delegation is made under section 134 stating—

(a) the name of the authorised person; and

(b) the function that he or she is authorised to perform; and

(c) the powers that he or she may exercise.

135(2) [Delegate must carry authorisation] The delegate, when acting in the capacity of a delegate of the AML/CFT supervisor,—

(a) must carry on him or her—

(i) the written authorisation provided under subsection (1); and

(ii) evidence of his or her identity; and

(b) must produce the written authorisation and evidence referred to in paragraph (a), if requested to do so by a reporting entity that is subject to the delegated function or powers being performed or exercised by the delegate.

135(3) [Return of authorisation] The delegate must return the written authorisation to the AML/CFT supervisor as soon as his or her delegation is revoked.

SECTION 136 EFFECT OF DELEGATION

136(1) [Functions and responsibilities not affected] No delegation under section 134—

(a) affects or prevents the performance of any function or the exercise of any power by the AML/CFT supervisor; or

(b) affects the responsibility of the AML/CFT supervisor for the performance of its functions and the exercise of its powers.

136(2) [Immunities] Every person to whom a function or power is delegated under section 134 has the same immunities in relation to the performance of that function or the exercise of that power as the AML/CFT supervisor that made the delegation.

Use and disclosure of information

SECTION 137 POWER TO USE INFORMATION OBTAINED AS AML/CFT SUPERVISOR IN OTHER CAPACITY AND VICE VERSA

137(1) This section applies to information other than personal information.

[Effective on a date to be appointed, or 1 October 2022]

137(2) The Reserve Bank may use any information obtained or held by it in the exercise of its powers or the performance of its functions and duties under the Reserve Bank of New Zealand Act 2021, the Banking (Prudential Supervision) Act 1989, the Insurance (Prudential Supervision) Act 2010, the Financial Market Infrastructures Act 2021, and the Non-bank Deposit Takers Act 2013 for the purpose of exercising its powers or performing its functions and duties under this Act as an AML/CFT supervisor.

History

S 137(2) amended by No 31 of 2021, s 300(1) and sch 4, by replacing "Reserve Bank of New Zealand Act 1989" with "Reserve Bank of New Zealand Act 2021, the Banking (Prudential Supervision) Act 1989"; **effective on a date to be appointed by the Governor-General by Order in Council, or 1 October 2022, whichever is earlier**.

137(2) The Reserve Bank may use any information obtained or held by it in the exercise of its powers or the performance of its functions and duties under the Reserve Bank of New Zealand Act 1989, the Insurance (Prudential Supervision) Act 2010, the Financial Market Infrastructures Act 2021, and the Non-bank Deposit Takers Act 2013 for the purpose of exercising its powers or performing its functions and duties under this Act as an AML/CFT supervisor.

History

S 137(2) amended by No 13 of 2021, s 162 and sch 2, by inserting "the Financial Market Infrastructures Act 2021," after "Act 2010,"; **effective 11 May 2021**.

S 137(2) amended by No 35 of 2017, s 49(1), by inserting ", the Insurance (Prudential Supervision) Act 2010, and the Non-bank Deposit Takers Act 2013" after "Reserve Bank of New Zealand Act 1989"; **effective 11 August 2017**.

[Effective on a date to be appointed, or 1 October 2022]

137(3) The Reserve Bank may use any information obtained or held by it in the exercise of its powers or the performance of its functions and duties under this Act as an AML/CFT supervisor for the purpose of exercising its powers or performing its functions and duties under the Reserve Bank of New Zealand Act 2021, the Banking (Prudential

Supervision) Act 1989, the Insurance (Prudential Supervision) Act 2010, the Financial Market Infrastructures Act 2021, and the Non-bank Deposit Takers Act 2013.

History

S 137(3) amended by No 31 of 2021, s 300(1) and sch 4, by replacing "Reserve Bank of New Zealand Act 1989" with "Reserve Bank of New Zealand Act 2021, the Banking (Prudential Supervision) Act 1989"; **effective on a date to be appointed by the Governor-General by Order in Council, or 1 October 2022, whichever is earlier**.

137(3) The Reserve Bank may use any information obtained or held by it in the exercise of its powers or the performance of its functions and duties under this Act as an AML/CFT supervisor for the purpose of exercising its powers or performing its functions and duties under the Reserve Bank of New Zealand Act 1989, the Insurance (Prudential Supervision) Act 2010, the Financial Market Infrastructures Act 2021, and the Non-bank Deposit Takers Act 2013.

History

S 137(3) amended by No 13 of 2021, s 162 and sch 2, by inserting "the Financial Market Infrastructures Act 2021," after "Act 2010,"; **effective 11 May 2021**.

S 137(3) amended by No 35 of 2017, s 49(2), by inserting ", the Insurance (Prudential Supervision) Act 2010, and the Non-bank Deposit Takers Act 2013" after "Reserve Bank of New Zealand Act 1989"; **effective 11 August 2017**.

137(4) The Financial Markets Authority may use any information obtained or held by it in the exercise of its powers or the performance of its functions and duties under the Financial Markets Authority Act 2011, the Financial Market Infrastructures Act 2021, and the Financial Markets Conduct Act 2013 for the purpose of exercising its powers or performing its functions and duties under this Act as an AML/CFT supervisor.

History

S 137(4) amended by No 13 of 2021, s 162 and sch 2, by inserting ", the Financial Market Infrastructures Act 2021," after "Act 2011"; **effective 11 May 2021**.

S 137(4) amended by No 8 of 2019, s 98 and sch 4, by replacing ", the Financial Markets Conduct Act 2013, and the Financial Advisers Act 2008" with "and the Financial Markets Conduct Act 2013"; **effective 15 March 2021** (LI 2020/131).

S 137(4) amended by No 70 of 2013, s 150 and sch, by replacing "Securities Act 1978, the Securities Markets Act 1988" with "Financial Markets Conduct Act 2013"; **effective 1 December 2014** (LI 2014/325).

S 137(4) substituted by No 5 of 2011, s 82 and sch 3, **effective 1 May 2011**. Former s 137(4) read:

> "137(4) The Securities Commission may use any information obtained or held by it in the exercise of its powers or the performance of its functions and duties under the Securities Act 1978, the Securities Markets Act 1988, and the Financial Advisers Act 2008 for the purpose of exercising its powers or performing its functions and duties under this Act as an AML/CFT supervisor."

137(5) The Financial Markets Authority may use any information obtained or held by it in the exercise of its powers or the performance of its functions and duties under this Act as an AML/CFT supervisor for the purpose of exercising its powers or performing its functions and duties under the Financial Markets Authority Act 2011, the Financial Market Infrastructures Act 2021, and the Financial Markets Conduct Act 2013.

History

S 137(5) amended by No 13 of 2021, s 162 and sch 2, by inserting ", the Financial Market Infrastructures Act 2021," after "Act 2011"; **effective 11 May 2021**.

S 137(5) amended by No 8 of 2019, s 98 and sch 4, by replacing ", the Financial Markets Conduct Act 2013, and the Financial Advisers Act 2008" with "and the Financial Markets Conduct Act 2013"; **effective 15 March 2021** (LI 2020/131).

S 137(5) amended by No 70 of 2013, s 150 and sch, by replacing "Securities Act 1978, the Securities Markets Act 1988" with "Financial Markets Conduct Act 2013"; **effective 1 December 2014** (LI 2014/325).

S 137(5) substituted by No 5 of 2011, s 82 and sch 3, **effective 1 May 2011**. Former s 137(5) read:

"137(5) The Securities Commission may use any information obtained or held by it in the exercise of its powers or the performance of its functions and duties under this Act as an AML/CFT supervisor for the purpose of exercising its powers or performing its functions and duties under the Securities Act 1978, the Securities Markets Act 1988, and the Financial Advisers Act 2008."

137(6) The Department of Internal Affairs may use any information obtained or held by it in the exercise of its powers or the performance of its functions and duties under the Gambling Act 2003, the Racing Industry Act 2020, and the Charities Act 2005 for the purpose of exercising its powers or performing its functions and duties under this Act as an AML/CFT supervisor.

History

S 137(6) amended by No 28 of 2020, s 129 and sch 5, by replacing "Racing Act 2003" with "Racing Industry Act 2020"; **effective 1 August 2020**.

S 137(6) amended by No 35 of 2017, s 49(3), by inserting ", the Racing Act 2003, and the Charities Act 2005" after "the Gambling Act 2003"; **effective 11 August 2017**.

137(7) The Department of Internal Affairs may use any information obtained or held by it in the exercise of its powers or the performance of its functions and duties under this Act as an AML/CFT supervisor for the purpose of exercising its powers or performing its functions and duties under the Gambling Act 2003, the Racing Industry Act 2020, and the Charities Act 2005.

History

S 137(7) amended by No 28 of 2020, s 129 and sch 5, by replacing "Racing Act 2003" with "Racing Industry Act 2020"; **effective 1 August 2020**.

S 137(7) amended by No 35 of 2017, s 49(4), by inserting ", the Racing Act 2003, and the Charities Act 2005" after "the Gambling Act 2003"; **effective 11 August 2017**.

SECTION 138 RESTRICTION ON POWER TO USE INFORMATION UNDER SECTION 137

138 An AML/CFT supervisor may only use information obtained under section 137 if the person providing the information was advised of the purpose or purposes for which the information was obtained at the time he or she provided that information.

SECTION 139 POWER TO DISCLOSE INFORMATION

139(1) The Commissioner, the New Zealand Customs Service, or an AML/CFT supervisor may disclose any information (that is not personal information) supplied or obtained by it in the exercise of its powers or the performance of its functions and duties under this Act to any government agency or any regulator for law enforcement purposes if it is satisfied that the agency or regulator has a proper interest in receiving such information.

History

S 139(1) amended by No 35 of 2017, s 50(2)(a) and (b), by inserting (i) "or any regulator" after "government agency"; and (ii) "or regulator" after "the agency"; **effective 11 August 2017**.

139(2) If not authorised under any other provision of this Act, disclosure of any information between a government agency, a regulator, the Commissioner, the New Zealand Customs Service, an AML/CFT supervisor, or reporting entities, or to or from any of those parties, may be made for law enforcement purposes in accordance with regulations made under section 139A.

History

S 139(2) inserted by No 35 of 2017, s 50(3), **effective 11 August 2017**.

139(3) Nothing in this section limits the Privacy Act 2020 (which permits certain disclosures in addition to those authorised under this section).

History

S 139(3) amended by No 31 of 2020, s 217 and sch 9, by replacing "Privacy Act 1993" with "Privacy Act 2020"; **effective 1 December 2020**.

S 139(3) inserted by No 35 of 2017, s 50(3), **effective 11 August 2017**.

History

S 139 heading amended by No 35 of 2017, s 50(1), by deleting "supplied or obtained as AML/CFT supervisor" after "disclose information"; **effective 11 August 2017**.

SECTION 139A REGULATIONS RELATING TO INFORMATION SHARING

139A(1) The Governor-General may, by Order in Council made on the recommendation of the Minister, make regulations for the purpose of section 139(2)—

(a) specifying the type of information that may or may not be disclosed:

(b) prescribing the conditions under which the information may be disclosed and the conditions applying to the use of that information (for example, conditions relating to storage, copying, access, and the return of information).

139A(2) Before recommending the making of regulations under this section, the Minister must consult—

(a) the agencies and regulators that may be affected by the proposed regulations; and

(b) the Privacy Commissioner; and

(c) any other person or body that the Minister considers may be affected by the proposed regulations.

139A(3) Regulations under this section are secondary legislation (*see* Part 3 of the Legislation Act 2019 for publication requirements).

History

S 139A(3) inserted by No 7 of 2021, s 3 and sch 16, **effective 28 October 2021** (LI 2021/250).

History

S 139A inserted by No 35 of 2017, s 51, **effective 11 August 2017**.

SECTION 140 POWER TO USE AND DISCLOSE INFORMATION SUPPLIED OR OBTAINED UNDER OTHER ENACTMENTS FOR AML/CFT PURPOSES

140(1) A government agency or an AML/CFT supervisor may disclose to any other AML/CFT supervisor or government agency any information supplied or obtained under an enactment listed in subsection (2) if the disclosing entity has reasonable grounds to believe that the disclosure of that information is necessary or desirable for the purpose of ensuring compliance with this Act and regulations.

History

S 140(1) amended by No 35 of 2017, s 52(1), by inserting "the disclosing entity has reasonable grounds to believe that" after "subsection (2) if"; **effective 11 August 2017**.

140(2) The enactments referred to in subsection (1) are—

(a) the Charities Act 2005:

(b) the Companies Act 1993:

(c) the Customs and Excise Act 2018:

(d) the Customs and Excise Act 1996:

(e) (*repealed*)

(f) the Financial Markets Authority Act 2011:

(g) the Financial Markets Conduct Act 2013:

(h) Parts 1 to 7 of the Intelligence and Security Act 2017:

(ha) the Financial Service Providers (Registration and Dispute Resolution) Act 2008:

(i) the Financial Transactions Reporting Act 1996:

(j) the Gambling Act 2003:

(k) the Goods and Services Tax Act 1985:

(l) the Income Tax Act 2007:

(m) the Insurance (Prudential Supervision) Act 2010:

(n) the Lawyers and Conveyancers Act 2006:

(o) the New Zealand Institute of Chartered Accountants Act 1996:

(p) the Non-bank Deposit Takers Act 2013:

(pa) the Overseas Investment Act 2005:

(q) the Proceeds of Crime Act 1991:

(r) the Racing Industry Act 2020:

(s) the Real Estate Agents Act 2008:

[Effective on a date to be appointed, or 1 October 2022]

(t) the Banking (Prudential Supervision) Act 1989:

(t) the Reserve Bank of New Zealand Act 1989:

(u) the Secondhand Dealers and Pawnbrokers Act 2004:

(v) the Tax Administration Act 1994:

(w) the Terrorism Suppression Act 2002:

(x) any other Act prescribed by regulations.

History

S 140(2) amended by No 31 of 2021, s 300(1) and sch 4, by replacing in para (t) "Reserve Bank of New Zealand Act 1989" with "Banking (Prudential Supervision) Act 1989"; **effective on a date to be appointed by the Governor-General by Order in Council, or 1 October 2022, whichever is earlier**.

S 140(2) amended by No 28 of 2020, s 129 and sch 5, by replacing in para (r) "Racing Act 2003" with "Racing Industry Act 2020"; **effective 1 August 2020**.

S 140(2) amended by No 56 of 2019, s 5, by inserting para (ha); **effective 24 October 2019**.

S 140(2) amended by No 8 of 2019, s 98 and sch 4, by repealing para (e); **effective 15 March 2021** (LI 2020/131). Former para (e) read:

"(e) the Financial Advisers Act 2008:".

S 140(2) amended by No 4 of 2018, s 443(3) and sch 9, by replacing para (b); **effective 1 October 2018** (LI 2018/148).

S 140(2) amended by No 10 of 2017, s 335 and sch 4, by replacing para (h); **effective 28 September 2017**. Former para (h) read:

"(h) the Financial Service Providers (Registration and Dispute Resolution) Act 2008:".

S 140(2) replaced by No 35 of 2017, s 52(2), **effective 11 August 2017**. Former s 140(2) read:

"140(2) [Relevant Acts] The enactments referred to in subsection (1) are—

(a) the Companies Act 1993:

(b) the Criminal Proceeds (Recovery) Act 2009:

(c) the Customs and Excise Act 2018:

(d) the Financial Advisers Act 2008:

(da) the Financial Markets Authority Act 2011:

(e) the Financial Service Providers (Registration and Dispute Resolution) Act 2008:

(f) the Financial Transactions Reporting Act 1996:

(g) the Gambling Act 2003:

(h) the Financial Service Providers (Registration and Dispute Resolution) Act 2008:

(i) the Proceeds of Crime Act 1991:

(j) the Reserve Bank of New Zealand Act 1989:

(k) the Financial Markets Conduct Act 2013:

(l) (*repealed*)

(m) the Terrorism Suppression Act 2002."

S 140(2) amended by No 21 of 2020, s 58, by inserting para (pa); **effective 16 June 2020**.

S 140(2) amended by No 4 of 2018, s 443 and sch 9, by replacing in para (c) "Customs and Excise Act 1996" with "Customs and Excise Act 2018"; **effective 1 October 2018** (LI 2018/148).

S 140(2) amended by No 70 of 2013, s 150 and sch, by replacing para (k) and (l) with para (k); **effective 1 December 2014** (LI 2014/325). Former para (k) and (l) read:

"(k) the Securities Act 1978:

(l) the Securities Markets Act 1988:"

S 140(2) amended by No 5 of 2011, s 82 and sch 3, by inserting para (da); **effective 1 May 2011**.

SECTION 141 ENFORCEMENT OFFICERS

141(1) [Appointment of employee] For the purposes of this Act, an AML/CFT supervisor may appoint any employee as an enforcement officer, on a permanent or temporary basis, to exercise the powers conferred on the AML/CFT supervisor by this Act.

141(2) [Issuing of identity card] An AML/CFT supervisor must issue its enforcement officers with an identity card.

141(3) [Office must carry card] An enforcement officer must—

(a) carry his or her identity card at all times when acting as an enforcement officer under this Act or regulations; and

(b) return his or her identity card to the relevant AML/CFT supervisor immediately upon ceasing to be an enforcement officer.

Financial intelligence functions of Commissioner

SECTION 142 FINANCIAL INTELLIGENCE FUNCTIONS OF COMMISSIONER

142 The financial intelligence functions of the Commissioner are to—

(a) receive suspicious activity reports:

(b) produce guidance material, including—

(i) typologies of money laundering and financing of terrorism transactions:

(ii) information for reporting entities on their obligations to report suspicious activities and prescribed transactions, and how to meet those obligations:

(c) provide feedback to reporting entities on the quality and timeliness of their suspicious activity reporting:

(d) enforce requirements to provide suspicious activity reports:

(e) analyse suspicious activity reports to assess whether any should be referred to investigative branches of the New Zealand Police and to other law enforcement agencies for criminal investigation:

(f) access, directly or indirectly, on a timely basis the financial, administrative, and law enforcement information that the Commissioner requires to properly undertake his or her financial intelligence functions, including the analysis of suspicious activity reports and prescribed transaction reports:

(g) refer to investigative branches of the New Zealand Police and to other law enforcement agencies any suspicious activity reports and prescribed transaction reports that, in the view of the Commissioner, indicate grounds for criminal investigation:

(h) refer suspicious activity reports and prescribed transaction reports and feedback provided to reporting entities on any suspicious activity reports and prescribed transaction reports to AML/CFT supervisors:

(i) receive, analyse, and (if appropriate) refer to law enforcement agencies any cash reports:

(j) receive, analyse, and (if appropriate) refer to law enforcement agencies any suspicious property reports:

(ja) receive, analyse, and (if appropriate) refer to investigative branches of the New Zealand Police and to other law enforcement agencies, any prescribed transaction reports:

(k) produce risk assessments relating to money laundering offences and the financing of terrorism to be used by the Ministry, the Ministry of Justice, AML/CFT supervisors, and the New Zealand Customs Service:

(ka) receive and analyse financial intelligence relating to law enforcement purposes from international authorities authorised to perform functions broadly equivalent to the Commissioner's financial intelligence functions:

(l) co-operate with the Ministry, the Ministry of Justice, AML/CFT supervisors, the New Zealand Customs Service, regulators, and any other relevant agencies to help ensure the effective implementation of the requirements under this Act and regulations.

History

S 142 amended by No 35 of 2017, s 53(1)–(10), by (i) replacing in para (a) ''suspicious transaction'' with ''suspicious activity''; (ii) replacing para (b)(ii); (iii) replacing in para (c)–(g) ''suspicious transaction'' with ''suspicious activity''; (iv) replacing in para (h) ''suspicious transaction'' with ''suspicious activity'' wherever occurring; (v) inserting para (ka); and (vi) inserting in para (l) ''regulators,'' after ''New Zealand Customs Service,''; **effective 11 August 2017**. Former para (b)(ii) read:

''(ii) information for reporting entities on their obligations to report suspicious transactions and how to meet those obligations:''.

S 142 amended by No 96 of 2015, s 22(1)–(4), by inserting (i) para (ja); (ii) in para (f) ''and prescribed transaction reports'' after ''reports''; (iii) in para (g) ''and prescribed transaction reports'' after ''reports''; and (iv) in para (h) ''and prescribed transaction reports'' after ''reports'' wherever occurring; **effective 1 July 2017**.

SECTION 143 POWERS RELATING TO FINANCIAL INTELLIGENCE FUNCTIONS OF COMMISSIONER

143(1) [Information disclosure] The Commissioner may—

(a) order production of or access to all records, documents, or information from any reporting entity that is relevant to analysing information received by the Commissioner under this Act, with or without a court order; and

(b) share suspicious activity reports, prescribed transaction reports, cash reports, suspicious property reports, and other financial information and intelligence with regulators and domestic and international authorities for the purposes of this Act and regulations.

History

S 143(1) amended by No 35 of 2017, s 54(1)–(3), by (i) replacing in para (a) ''a suspicious transaction report or a prescribed transaction report received by the Commissioner'' with ''information received by the Commissioner under this Act''; (ii) replacing in para (b) ''suspicious transaction reports'' with ''suspicious activity reports''; and (iii) inserting in para (b) ''regulators and'' after ''with''; **effective 11 August 2017**.

143(2) [Privileged communication] Nothing in this section requires any person to disclose any privileged communication.

History

S 143(2) inserted by No 35 of 2017, s 54(4), **effective 11 August 2017**.

History

S 143 amended by No 96 of 2015, s 23(1) and (2), by inserting (i) in para (a) ''or a prescribed transaction report'' after ''report''; and (ii) in para (b) ''prescribed transaction reports,'' after ''suspicious transaction reports,''; **effective 1 July 2017**.

SECTION 144 DELEGATION OF POWERS OF COMMISSIONER

144(1) [Delegation to constable] The Commissioner may from time to time in writing, either generally or particularly, delegate to a constable of a level of position not less than inspector or an equally senior or more senior Police employee the Commissioner's powers under section 143(a).

History

S 144(1) amended by No 35 of 2017, s 55, by inserting ''or an equally senior or more senior Police employee'' after ''inspector''; **effective 11 August 2017**.

144(2) [Written report] Where any constable exercises any power conferred under subsection (1), that constable must, within 5 days after the day on which the constable exercises the power, give the Commissioner a written report on the exercise of that power and the circumstances in which it was exercised.

144(3) [Proof of powers] A constable who purports to perform a power under a delegation—

(a) is, in the absence of proof to the contrary, presumed to do so in accordance with the terms of that delegation; and

(b) must produce evidence of his or her authority to do so, if reasonably requested to do so.

144(4) [Delegation revocable] Every delegation under this section is revocable at will and does not prevent the exercise of any power by the Commissioner.

SECTION 145 GUIDELINES RELATING TO REPORTING OF SUSPICIOUS ACTIVITIES

145(1) [Guidelines for suspicion] Subject to section 146, the Commissioner must issue, in respect of each kind of reporting entity to which this Act applies, guidelines—

(a) setting out any features of a transaction or other activity that may give rise to a suspicion that the transaction or other activity is or may be—

(i) relevant to the investigation or prosecution of any person for a money laundering offence; or

(ii) relevant to the enforcement of the Misuse of Drugs Act 1975; or

(iii) relevant to the enforcement of the Terrorism Suppression Act 2002; or

(iv) relevant to the enforcement of the Proceeds of Crime Act 1991 or the Criminal Proceeds (Recovery) Act 2009; or

(v) relevant to the investigation or prosecution of an offence within the meaning of section 243(1) of the Crimes Act 1961; and

(b) setting out any circumstances in which a suspicious activity report relating to such an activity may be made orally in accordance with section 41(2), and the procedures for making such an oral report.

History

S 145(1) amended by No 35 of 2017, s 56(2) and (3), by (i) inserting in para (a) ''or other activity'' after ''a transaction'' and ''or other activity'' after ''the transaction''; and (ii) replacing in para (b) ''suspicious transaction report relating to such a transaction'' with ''suspicious activity report relating to such an activity''; **effective 11 August 2017**.

S 145(1) amended by No 96 of 2015, s 24, by replacing in para (a)(v) ''a serious offence'' with ''an offence''; **effective 1 July 2017**.

145(2) [Commissioner's requirements] Suspicious transaction or other activity guidelines must be issued in such manner as the Commissioner from time to time determines.

History

S 145(2) amended by No 35 of 2017, s 56(4), by inserting ''or other activity'' after ''transaction''; **effective 11 August 2017**.

145(3) [Commissioner may amend guidelines] The Commissioner may issue an amendment or revocation of any suspicious transaction or other activity guidelines.

History

S 145(3) amended by No 35 of 2017, s 56(5), by inserting ''or other activity'' after ''transaction''; **effective 11 August 2017**.

145(4) [Provisions for differing entities] Without limiting subsection (1), suspicious transaction or other activity guidelines issued under this section may relate to 1 or more kinds of reporting entities, and such guidelines may make different provision for different kinds of reporting entities and different kinds of transactions or other activities.

History

S 145(4) amended by No 35 of 2017, s 56(6)(a) and (b), by inserting (i) ''or other activity'' after ''transaction''; and (ii) ''or other activities'' after ''transactions''; **effective 11 August 2017**.

Compare: 1996 No 9 s 24

History

S 145 heading amended by No 35 of 2017, s 56(1), by replacing ''transactions'' with ''activities''; **effective 11 August 2017**.

SECTION 146 CONSULTATION ON PROPOSED GUIDELINES

146(1) The Commissioner must, before issuing any suspicious transaction or other activity guidelines,—

(a) consult with, and invite representations from, the Privacy Commissioner under the Privacy Act 2020, and must have regard to any such representations; and

(b) give public notice of the Commissioner's intention to issue the guidelines, which notice must contain a statement—

(i) indicating the Commissioner's intention to issue the guidelines; and

(ii) inviting reporting entities that are likely to be affected by the proposed guidelines, and industry organisations that are representative of those reporting entities, to express to the Commissioner, within any reasonable period that is specified in the notice, their interest in being consulted in the course of the development of the guidelines; and

(c) consult with, and invite representations from, those reporting entities and industry organisations who express such an interest, and must have regard to any such representations.

History

S 146(1) amended by No 31 of 2020, s 217 and sch 9, by replacing in para (a) ''Privacy Act 1993'' with ''Privacy Act 2020''; **effective 1 December 2020**.

S 146(1) amended by No 35 of 2017, s 57(1), by inserting ''or other activity'' after ''transaction''; **effective 11 August 2017**.

146(2) Nothing in subsection (1) prevents the Commissioner from adopting any additional means of publicising the proposal to issue any suspicious transaction or other activity guidelines or of consulting with interested parties in relation to such a proposal.

History

S 146(2) amended by No 35 of 2017, s 57(2), by inserting ''or other activity'' after ''transaction''; **effective 11 August 2017**.

146(3) This section applies to any amendment or revocation of any suspicious transaction or other activity guidelines.

History

S 146(3) amended by No 35 of 2017, s 57(3), by inserting ''or other activity'' after ''transaction''; **effective 11 August 2017**.

Compare: 1996 No 9 s 25

SECTION 147 AVAILABILITY OF GUIDELINES

147 On a request by any reporting entity in respect of which any suspicious transaction or other activity guidelines are for the time being in force, or by any industry organisation that represents the reporting entity, the Commissioner must, without charge,—

(a) make those guidelines, and all amendments to those guidelines, available for inspection by that reporting entity or, as the case requires, that industry organisation at Police National Headquarters; and

(b) provide copies of those guidelines, and all amendments to those guidelines, to that reporting entity or, as the case requires, that industry organisation.

Compare: 1996 No 9 s 26

History

S 147 amended by No 35 of 2017, s 58, by inserting "or other activity" after "transaction"; **effective 11 August 2017**.

SECTION 148 REVIEW OF GUIDELINES

148(1) [Commissioner must review guidelines] The Commissioner must review from time to time any suspicious transaction or other activity guidelines for the time being in force.

History

S 148(1) amended by No 35 of 2017, s 59(1), by inserting "or other activity" after "transaction"; **effective 11 August 2017**.

148(2) [Review treated as proposal] Sections 145 and 146 apply, with all necessary modifications, in relation to any such review as if the review were a proposal to issue suspicious transaction or other activity guidelines.

History

S 148(2) amended by No 35 of 2017, s 59(2), by inserting "or other activity" after "transaction"; **effective 11 August 2017**.

Compare: 1996 No 9 s 27

Co-ordination

SECTION 149 ROLE OF MINISTRY

149 The Ministry, in consultation with other agencies with AML/CFT roles and functions, is responsible for advising on the overall effectiveness and efficiency of the AML/CFT regulatory system, including—

(a) advising the Minister on outcomes and objectives for AML/CFT regulation and how best to achieve these (including links to other Government initiatives relevant to the purposes of this Act); and

(b) monitoring, evaluating, and advising the Minister on the performance of the AML/CFT regulatory system in achieving the Government's outcomes and objectives for it; and

(c) advising the Minister on any changes necessary to the AML/CFT regulatory system to improve its effectiveness; and

(d) administering the relevant AML/CFT legislation.

SECTION 150 AML/CFT CO-ORDINATION COMMITTEE

150(1) [Committee members] The chief executive must establish an AML/CFT co-ordination committee consisting of—

(a) a representative from the Ministry; and

(b) a representative from the New Zealand Customs Service; and

(c) every AML/CFT supervisor; and

(d) a representative of the Commissioner; and

(e) such other persons as are invited from time to time by the chief executive in accordance with subsection (2).

150(2) [Employee of government agency] Any person invited under subsection (1)(e) must be employed in a government agency.

150(3) [Chief executive is chair] The chair of the AML/CFT co-ordination committee is the chief executive.

SECTION 151 ROLE OF AML/CFT CO-ORDINATION COMMITTEE

151 The role of the AML/CFT co-ordination committee is to ensure that the necessary connections between the AML/CFT supervisors, the Commissioner, and other agencies are made in order to ensure the consistent, effective, and efficient operation of the AML/CFT regulatory system.

SECTION 152 FUNCTIONS

152 The functions of the AML/CFT co-ordination committee are to—

(a) facilitate necessary information flows between the AML/CFT supervisors, the Commissioner, and other agencies involved in the operation of the AML/CFT regulatory system:

(b) facilitate the production and dissemination of information on the risks of money-laundering offences and the financing of terrorism in order to give advice and make decisions on AML/CFT requirements and the risk-based implementation of those requirements:

(c) facilitate co-operation amongst AML/CFT supervisors and consultation with other agencies in the development of AML/CFT policies and legislation:

(d) facilitate consistent and co-ordinated approaches to the development and dissemination of AML/CFT guidance materials and training initiatives by AML/CFT supervisors and the Commissioner:

(e) facilitate good practice and consistent approaches to AML/CFT supervision between the AML/CFT supervisors and the Commissioner:

(f) provide a forum for examining any operational or policy issues that have implications for the effectiveness or efficiency of the AML/CFT regulatory system.

Subpart 2 — Miscellaneous provisions

Regulations

SECTION 153 REGULATIONS

153(1) The Governor-General may, by Order in Council, make regulations for all or any of the following purposes:

(a) prescribing requirements (generic and sector-specific) for standard, simplified, enhanced, and ongoing customer due diligence and any other AML/CFT requirements, including, but not limited to, the following:

(i) information to be provided or obtained for the purposes of identification and verification:

(ii) the circumstances in which a particular type of customer due diligence must be conducted:

(iii) specifying entities or classes of entities, or products, services, or transactions for which a reporting entity may conduct simplified customer due diligence:

(iv) the conditions in which third parties may be relied on to conduct customer due diligence:

(v) the conditions on which a member of a designated business group may adopt an AML/CFT programme of another member of the group and share and use the policies, controls, and procedures of that programme:

(vi) the circumstances in which corporations are deemed to be affiliated:

(vii) the factors that a reporting entity must have regard to when assessing risk:

(b) prescribing instruments to be bearer-negotiable instruments for the purposes of this Act:

(c) prescribing the forms of, and the information to be included in, applications, warrants, reports, and other documents required under this Act:

(d) prescribing amounts or thresholds that are required to be prescribed for the purposes of this Act or regulations (and 1 or more amounts or thresholds may be prescribed for the purposes of different provisions of this Act or regulations):

(e) prescribing the information to be included in records and the manner in which records are to be kept by reporting entities, or any specified class or classes of reporting entities:

(f) prescribing other identifying information that allows a transaction to be traced back to the originator for the purposes of section 27(1):

(g) prescribing the manner in which any notice, report, or other document required by this Act is to be given or served:

(h) prescribing for the form of a formal warning and the manner in which it must be issued:

(i) specifying Acts for which disclosure of personal information may be made by an AML/CFT supervisor for the purposes of the detection, investigation, and prosecution of offences under the specified Act:

(j) providing for any other matters contemplated by this Act or necessary for its administration or necessary for giving it full effect.

History

S 153(1) amended by No 35 of 2017, s 60, by replacing para (d); **effective 11 August 2017**. Former para (d) read:

> "(d) prescribing amounts or thresholds that are required to be prescribed for the purposes of this Act:".

153(2) Regulations under this section are secondary legislation (*see* Part 3 of the Legislation Act 2019 for publication requirements).

History

S 153(2) inserted by No 7 of 2021, s 3 and sch 16, **effective 28 October 2021** (LI 2021/250).

Compare: 1996 No 9 s 56

SECTION 154 REGULATIONS RELATING TO APPLICATION OF ACT

154(1) The Governor-General may, by Order in Council on the recommendation of the Minister, make regulations for the following purposes:

(a) exempting or providing for the exemption of any transaction, product, or service or class of transactions, products, or services from all or any of the provisions of this Act:

(ab) exempting or providing for the exemption of any financial activity or class of financial activities described in the definition of financial institution in section 5 from all or any of the provisions of this Act:

(ac) declaring an entity or a class of entities to be an approved entity or approved class of entities for the purposes of section 33(3A):

(b) excluding certain relationships or banking services from the application of section 29 (which relates to correspondent banking relationships):

(c) exempting a reporting entity from its obligation to obtain some or all of the information set out in section 27(1) in relation to a specified transfer or transaction:

(ca) exempting a reporting entity or a class of reporting entity from the obligation to report under section 48A in relation to international wire transfers:

(d) exempting certain movements of cash from the application of subpart 6 of Part 2:

(e) prescribing threshold values for the purposes of sections 68 and 69 and the person or class of persons, transaction or class of transactions, financial activity or class of financial activities to which that threshold value applies:

(f) declaring an account or arrangement to be, or not to be, a facility and the circumstances and conditions in which an account or arrangement is to be, or not to be, a facility for the purposes of this Act:

(g) declaring a person or class of persons to be, or not to be, a reporting entity and the circumstances and conditions in which a person or class of persons is to be, or not to be, a reporting entity for the purposes of this Act:

(ga) declaring an activity or a class of activities to be, or not to be, an occasional activity and the circumstances and conditions in which an activity or a class of activities is to be, or not to be, an occasional activity for the purposes of the Act.

(h) declaring a transaction or class of transactions to be, or not to be, an occasional transaction and the circumstances and conditions in which a transaction or class of transactions is to be, or not to be, an occasional transaction for the purposes of this Act:

(ha) declaring an activity or a class of activities to be, or not to be, an occasional activity for the purposes of this Act:

(i) declaring a transfer or transaction or a class of transfers or transactions not to be a wire transfer and the circumstances and conditions in which a transfer or transaction or class of transfers or transactions is not a wire transfer for the purposes of this Act:

(j) declaring a person or class of persons to be, or not to be, a customer and the circumstances and conditions in which a person or class of persons is to be, or not to be, a customer for the purposes of this Act:

(k) declaring an entity or class of entities (whether domestic or overseas) to be eligible for inclusion in a designated business group:

(l) declaring a person or class of persons to be, or not to be, a financial institution for the purposes of this Act.

History

S 154(1) amended by No 35 of 2017, s 61(1), (2), 68 and sch 2, by inserting para (ab), (ac), (ha) and (ga); **effective 11 August 2017**.

S 154(1) amended by No 96 of 2015, s 25, by inserting para (ca); **effective 1 July 2017**.

S 154(1) amended by No 98 of 2012, s 8, by replacing in para (k) "a member of a specified" with "eligible for inclusion in a"; **effective 12 December 2012**.

154(2) The Minister must, before making any recommendation, have regard to—

(a) the purposes of this Act; and

(b) the risk of money laundering and the financing of terrorism; and

(c) the impact on the prevention, detection, investigation, and prosecution of offences; and

(d) the level of regulatory burden on a reporting entity; and

(e) whether the making of the regulation would create an unfair advantage for a reporting entity or would disadvantage other reporting entities; and

(f) the overall impact that making the regulation would have on the integrity of, and compliance with, the AML/CFT regulatory regime.

History

S 154(2) amended by No 35 of 2017, s 61(3), by deleting in para (a) "and the Financial Transactions Reporting Act 1996" after "this Act"; **effective 11 August 2017**.

154(3) The Minister must also, before making any recommendation,—

(a) do everything reasonably possible on the Minister's part to advise all persons who in the Minister's opinion will be affected by any regulations made in accordance with the recommendation, or representatives of those persons, of the proposed terms of the recommendation and of the reasons for it; and

(b) give such persons or their representatives a reasonable opportunity to consider the recommendation and to make submissions on it to the Minister, and the Minister must consider those submissions; and

(c) (*repealed*)

(d) make copies of the recommendation available for inspection by any person who so requests before any regulations are made in accordance with the recommendation.

History

S 154(3) amended by No 35 of 2017, s 61(4), by repealing para (c); **effective 11 August 2017**. Former para (c) read:

"(c) give notice in the *Gazette*, not less than 28 days before making the recommendation, of the Minister's intention to make the recommendation and state in the notice the matters to which the recommendation relates; and".

154(4) Failure to comply with subsection (3) does not affect the validity of any regulations made under this section.

154(5) Regulations under this section are secondary legislation (*see* Part 3 of the Legislation Act 2019 for publication requirements).

History

S 154(5) inserted by No 7 of 2021, s 3 and sch 16, **effective 28 October 2021** (LI 2021/250).

154(5) (*repealed*)

History

S 154(5) repealed by No 35 of 2017, s 61(4), **effective 11 August 2017**. Former s 154(5) read:

"154(5) [Time limit] Any regulations made under this section expire on the day that is 5 years after the date on which regulations come into force."

SECTION 155 REGULATIONS RELATING TO COUNTERMEASURES

155(1) The Governor-General may, by Order in Council made on the recommendation of the Minister, make regulations for, or in relation to, prohibiting or regulating the entering into of transactions or business relationships between a reporting entity and any other person.

155(2) Regulations made for the purposes of subsection (1)—

(a) may be of general application; or

(b) may be limited by reference to any or all of the following:

(i) a specified transaction:

(ii) a specified party:

(iii) a specified overseas country.

155(3) The Governor-General may, by Order in Council, declare a country outside New Zealand to be a prescribed overseas country for the purposes of this section.

155(4) Any regulations made under subsection (1) expire on the day that is 5 years after the date on which regulations come into force.

155(5) The following are secondary legislation (*see* Part 3 of the Legislation Act 2019 for publication requirements):

History

S 155(5) inserted by No 7 of 2021, s 3 and sch 16, **effective 28 October 2021** (LI 2021/250).

Compare: Anti-Money Laundering and Counter-Terrorism Financing Act 2006 s 102 (Aust)

SECTION 156 CONSULTATION NOT REQUIRED FOR CONSOLIDATION OF CERTAIN REGULATIONS AND MINOR AMENDMENTS

156 The Minister is not required to comply with section 154(3) in respect of the making of any regulations to the extent that regulations—

(a) revoke any regulations made under section 154 and, at the same time, consolidate the revoked regulations, so that they have the same effect as those revoked regulations; or

(b) make minor amendments to regulations.

Compare: 1996 No 9 s 56A

Review provision

SECTION 156A REVIEW OF OPERATION OF ACT

156A(1) [Matters for consideration] The Minister of Justice must, not later than 1 July 2021, refer to the Ministry of Justice for consideration the following matters:

(a) the operation of the provisions of this Act since the commencement of this section; and

(b) whether any amendments to this Act are necessary or desirable.

156A(2) [Report to Minister] The Ministry must report on those matters to the Minister of Justice within 1 year of the date on which the reference occurs.

156A(3) [Report to House] The Minister of Justice must present a copy of the report provided under this section to the House of Representatives as soon as practicable after receiving it.

History

S 156A and preceding heading inserted by No 35 of 2017, s 62, **effective 11 August 2017**.

Ministerial exemptions

SECTION 157 MINISTER MAY GRANT EXEMPTIONS

157(1) The Minister may exempt either or both of the following from the requirements of all or any of the provisions of this Act:

(a) a reporting entity or class of reporting entities:

(b) a transaction or class of transactions.

History

S 157(1) amended by No 35 of 2017, s 63(1) and (2), by replacing (i) ", in the prescribed form, exempt any" with "exempt either or both"; and (ii) in para (a) "entities; or" with "entities:"; **effective 11 August 2017**.

157(1A) The Minister may grant an exemption—

(a) to an individual reporting entity on application by that entity in a manner and form approved by the chief executive (if any):

(b) to a class of reporting entities on the Minister's own motion or on application by 1 or more reporting entities made in a manner or form approved by the chief executive (if any).

History

S 157(1A) inserted by No 35 of 2017, s 63(3), **effective 11 August 2017**.

157(2) The Minister may grant the exemption—

(a) unconditionally; or

(b) subject to any conditions the Minister thinks fit.

157(3) Before deciding to grant an exemption and whether to attach any conditions to the exemption, the Minister must have regard to the following:

(a) (*repealed*)

(b) the intent and purpose of this Act and any regulations:

(c) the risk of money laundering and the financing of terrorism associated with the reporting entity, including, where appropriate, the products and services offered by the reporting entity and the circumstances in which the products and services are provided:

(d) the impacts on prevention, detection, investigation, and prosecution of offences:

(e) the level of regulatory burden to which the reporting entity would be subjected in the absence of an exemption:

(f) whether the exemption would create an unfair advantage for the reporting entity or disadvantage third party reporting entities:

(g) the overall impact that the exemption would have on the integrity of, and compliance with, the AML/CFT regulatory regime.

History

S 157(3) amended by No 35 of 2017, s 63(4), by repealing para (a); **effective 11 August 2017**. Former para (a) read:

> "(a) the intent and purposes of the Financial Transactions Reporting Act 1996:".

157(4) An exemption under this section is secondary legislation (*see* Part 3 of the Legislation Act 2019 for publication requirements).

History

S 157(4) replaced by No 7 of 2021, s 3 and sch 16, **effective 28 October 2021** (LI 2021/250). Former s 157(4) read:

> "157(4) An exemption under this section is a disallowable instrument but not a legislative instrument for the purposes of the Legislation Act 2012 and must be presented to the House of Representatives under section 41 of that Act."

S 157(4) amended by No 35 of 2017, s 63(5), by inserting "but not a legislative instrument" after "disallowable instrument"; **effective 11 August 2017**.

S 157(4) substituted by No 119 of 2012, s 77(3) and sch, **effective 5 August 2013** (SR 2013/242). Former s 157(4) read:

> "157(4) [Deemed regulation] Every exemption made under this section is deemed to be a regulation for the purposes of the Regulations (Disallowance) Act 1989."

157(5) (*repealed*)

History

S 157(5) repealed by No 7 of 2021, s 3 and sch 16, **effective 28 October 2021** (LI 2021/250). Former s 157(5) read:

> "157(5) A class exemption under this section is a legislative instrument and must be published under section 6 of the Legislation Act 2012 and, for this purpose, **class exemption**—
>
> (a) means an exemption of general application that applies to a class of reporting entities or transactions; but
>
> (b) does not include an exemption granted in relation to a particular reporting entity or transaction."

S 157(5) amended by No 35 of 2017, s 63(6), by inserting "is a legislative instrument and" after "this section"; **effective 11 August 2017**.

S 157(5) inserted by No 119 of 2012, s 77(3) and sch, **effective 5 August 2013** (SR 2013/242).

157(6) *(repealed)*

History

S 157(6) repealed by No 7 of 2021, s 3 and sch 16, **effective 28 October 2021** (LI 2021/250). Former s 157(6) read:

"157(6) An exemption under this section that is not a class exemption under subsection (5) must, as soon as practicable after being granted, be—

(a) published on an Internet site maintained by or on behalf of the chief executive; and

(b) notified in the *Gazette*; and

(c) made available in printed form for purchase on request by members of the public."

S 157(6) inserted by No 119 of 2012, s 77(3) and sch, **effective 5 August 2013** (SR 2013/242).

157(7) A notification in the *Gazette* for the purpose of subsection (6)(b) does not have to incorporate the exemption.

History

S 157(7) inserted by No 119 of 2012, s 77(3) and sch, **effective 5 August 2013** (SR 2013/242).

SECTION 158 MINISTER MUST CONSULT BEFORE GRANTING EXEMPTION

158 Before granting an exemption under section 157, the Minister must consult with—

(a) the Ministers responsible for the AML/CFT supervisors; and

(b) any other persons the Minister considers appropriate having regard to those matters listed in section 157(3).

SECTION 159 REQUIREMENTS RELATING TO EXEMPTIONS

159(1) [Explanation required] The exemption must include an explanation of the reason for granting the exemption.

159(2) [Time limit] The exemption—

(a) must be granted for a period specified by the Minister but that period must not be more than 5 years; and

(b) may, at any time, be varied or revoked by the Minister.

159(3) *(repealed)*

History

S 159(3) repealed by No 119 of 2012, s 77(3) and sch, **effective 5 August 2013** (SR 2013/242). Former s 159(3) read:

"159(3) [Notification in *Gazette*] The exemption must be notified in the *Gazette*."

Resolution of disputes about privilege

SECTION 159A PROCEDURE FOR TESTING ASSERTIONS THAT DOCUMENT PRIVILEGED

159A(1) [Application to court] If any person refuses to disclose any information or document on the grounds that it is a privileged communication and that section 132(4), 133(5), or 143(3) applies, the Commissioner, an AML/CFT supervisor, or that person may apply to a District Court Judge for an order determining whether or not the claim of privilege is valid.

159A(2) [Disclosure of information] For the purposes of determining that application, the District Court Judge may require the information or document to be produced to the District Court Judge.

History

S 159A and preceding heading inserted by No 35 of 2017, s 64, **effective 11 August 2017**.

Transitional and savings provisions (*repealed*)

SECTION 160 TRANSITIONAL AND SAVINGS PROVISIONS (*repealed*)

History

S 160 and preceding heading repealed by No 35 of 2017, s 65, **effective 11 August 2017**. Former s 160 and preceding heading read:

"**Transitional and savings provisions**

SECTION 160 TRANSITIONAL AND SAVINGS PROVISIONS

160 Transitional and savings provisions relating to the coming into force of this Act are set out in Schedule 1."

Consequential amendments, repeals, and revocation

SECTION 161 AMENDMENTS TO OTHER ENACTMENTS

161(1) [Cross-border transportation of cash] The enactment specified in Part 1 of Schedule 2 is amended in the manner indicated in that part of that schedule (being consequential amendments relating to the bringing into force of provisions relating to cross-border transportation of cash).

161(2) [Consequential amendments] The enactments specified in Part 2 of Schedule 2 are amended in the manner indicated in that schedule (being consequential amendments to other enactments).

161(3) [Revocations] The regulations specified in Part 3 of Schedule 2 are revoked.

SECTION 162 AMENDMENT TO FINANCIAL TRANSACTIONS REPORTING ACT 1996 CONSEQUENTIAL ON BRINGING INTO FORCE OF PART 2 (*repealed*)

History

S 162 repealed by No 35 of 2017, s 66, **effective 11 August 2017**. Former s 162 read:

"**SECTION 162 AMENDMENT TO FINANCIAL TRANSACTIONS REPORTING ACT 1996 CONSEQUENTIAL ON BRINGING INTO FORCE OF PART 2**

162 The Financial Transactions Reporting Act 1996 is amended by repealing paragraphs (a) to (f), (h), (i), and (k) of the definition of **financial institution** in section 3(1)."

SECTION 163 AMENDMENT TO FINANCIAL TRANSACTIONS REPORTING ACT 1996 RELATING TO CROSS-BORDER TRANSPORTATION OF CASH (*repealed*)

History

S 163 repealed by No 35 of 2017, s 66, **effective 11 August 2017**. Former s 163 read:

"**SECTION 163 AMENDMENT TO FINANCIAL TRANSACTIONS REPORTING ACT 1996 RELATING TO CROSS-BORDER TRANSPORTATION OF CASH**

163 The Financial Transactions Reporting Act 1996 is amended by repealing Part 5."

SCHEDULES
SCHEDULE 1
Transitional savings, and related provisions

s 7A

Part 1 — Transitional, savings, and related provisions relating to Financial Transactions Reporting Act 1996

History

Sch 1, pt 1 heading, inserted by No 35 of 2017, s 67(3), **effective 11 August 2017**.

CLAUSE 1 OFFENCES AND BREACHES OF FINANCIAL TRANSACTIONS REPORTING ACT 1996

1(1) This clause applies to an offence under, or a breach of, the Financial Transactions Reporting Act 1996 that was committed before the commencement of this Act.

1(2) If this clause applies, then for the purpose of doing the things specified in subclause (3), the Financial Transactions Reporting Act 1996 continues to have effect as if this Act had not been enacted.

1(3) The things referred to in subclause (2) are as follows:

(a) investigating the offence or breach:

(b) commencing, continuing, or completing proceedings for the offence or breach:

(c) imposing a penalty for the offence or breach (which, for the avoidance of doubt, must be the same as the penalty that applied to the offence or the breach before this Act was enacted).

CLAUSE 2 BARRED PROCEEDINGS

2 Nothing in this Act enables any proceedings to be brought that were barred before the commencement of this Act.

CLAUSE 3 PENDING PROCEEDINGS

3 Any proceedings that have been commenced under the Financial Transactions Reporting Act 1996 before the commencement of this Act may be continued and completed after that commencement as if this Act had not been enacted, and the Financial Transactions Reporting Act 1996 applies accordingly.

Part 2 — Transitional provisions relating to Anti-Money Laundering and Countering Financing of Terrorism Amendment Act 2017

History

Sch 1, pt 2, inserted by No 35 of 2017, s 67(4) and sch 1, **effective 11 August 2017**.

CLAUSE 4 APPLICATION FOR EXEMPTION

4 Any application for an exemption under section 157 that has been lodged but not determined by the Minister, immediately before the commencement of this clause, must be determined by the

Minister under section 157 (as amended by section 63 of the Anti-Money Laundering and Countering Financing of Terrorism Amendment Act 2017 (the 2017 Act)).

History

Sch 1, pt 2, cl 4, inserted by No 35 of 2017, s 67(4) and sch 1, **effective 11 August 2017**.

Suspicious transaction reports continue until 1 July 2018 or earlier date appointed by Order in Council

CLAUSE 5 REPORTING ENTITY MUST CONTINUE TO REPORT SUSPICIOUS TRANSACTIONS

5(1) Despite section 25 of the 2017 Act, in the period between the commencement of this clause and 1 July 2018 or an earlier date appointed by the Governor-General by Order in Council,—

(a) a reporting entity must comply with sections 40, 41, and 43 to 48 (as they read before the commencement of section 25 of the 2017 Act) (which relate to suspicious transaction reports); and

(b) a reporting entity and any other person may rely on section 42 of the principal Act (as inserted by section 25 of the 2017 Act); and

(c) a reporting entity must not comply with sections 39A, 41, and 43 to 48 (as inserted by section 25 of the 2017 Act); and

(d) for the purposes of giving effect to paragraphs (a) and (c), section 42 (as inserted by section 25 of the 2017 Act) and sections 139, 140, 140A, 142, 143, 144, 145, 146, 147, 148, 153, 154, and 154A (as amended or inserted by sections 50 to 49A of the 2017 Act) apply with any necessary modifications; and

(e) subject to paragraphs (b) and (d), for the purposes of, and to the extent necessary for, giving effect to paragraphs (a) and (c), this Act (as it read before the enactment of the 2017 Act) continues in force.

5(2) An order under this clause is secondary legislation (*see* Part 3 of the Legislation Act 2019 for publication requirements).

History

Sch 1, pt 2, cl 5(2), inserted by No 7 of 2021, s 3 and sch 16, **effective 28 October 2021** (LI 2021/250).

History

Sch 1, pt 2, cl 5 and preceding heading, inserted by No 35 of 2017, s 67(4) and sch 1, **effective 11 August 2017**.

CLAUSE 6 TREATMENT OF EXISTING SUSPICIOUS TRANSACTION REPORTS

6 If, on the commencement of section 25, the Commissioner of Police holds 1 or more suspicious transaction reports given to the Commissioner before the commencement of section 50, the provisions of this Act (as amended by the 2017 Act) apply to those reports as if they were suspicious activity reports.

History

Sch 1, pt 2, cl 6, inserted by No 35 of 2017, s 67(4) and sch 1, **effective 11 August 2017**.

Sch 1

CLAUSE 7 EXEMPTION POWERS APPLY IMMEDIATELY TO NEW REPORTING ENTITIES

7 Any reporting entity or class of reporting entity to which, under section 6(3), this Act does not yet apply but will apply at a future date may, on or after the commencement of this clause, apply for an exemption under section 157, and the powers and duties conferred by sections 157 to 159 in relation to applications for exemptions apply immediately.

History

Sch 1, pt 2, cl 7, inserted by No 35 of 2017, s 67(4) and sch 1, **effective 11 August 2017**.

History

Sch 1 heading amended by No 35 of 2017, s 67(1) and (2), by replacing (i) "s 160" with "s 7A"; and (ii) "and savings provisions" with "savings, and related provisions"; **effective 11 August 2017**.

SCHEDULE 2
Consequential amendments

s 161

Part 1 — Amendments to Financial Transactions Reporting Act 1996 relating to cross-border transportation of cash

Section 2(1)

Definitions of **cash report** and **Customs officer**: repeal.

Definition of **cash**: omit "except in Part 5 of this Act,".

Part 2 — Amendments to other enactments

Crimes Act 1961 (1961 No 43)

Section 244: insert after paragraph (b):

"(ba) the enforcement or intended enforcement of the Anti-Money Laundering and Countering Financing of Terrorism Act 2009; or".

Criminal Proceeds (Recovery) Act 2009 (2009 No 8)

Definition of **financial institution** in section 5(1): repeal and substitute:

"**financial institution** means either a person within the meaning of financial institution as defined in section 3 of the Financial Transactions Reporting Act 1996 or as defined in section 5 of the Anti-Money Laundering and Countering Financing of Terrorism Act 2009".

Customs and Excise Act 1996 (1996 No 27)

Section 166A(b)(ii): repeal and substitute:

"(ii) subpart 6 of Part 2 and sections 114 and 115 of the Anti-Money Laundering and Countering Financing of Terrorism Act 2009; and".

Section 166C(4): insert after paragraph (b):

"(ba) Anti-Money Laundering and Countering Financing of Terrorism Act 2009:".

Financial Transactions Reporting Act 1996 (1996 No 9)

Long Title: insert "**the Terrorism Suppression Act 2002 and**" after "**enforcement of**".

Paragraph (b) of the Long Title: repeal.

Section 15(1)(b): insert after subparagraph (i):

> ''(ia) that the transaction or proposed transaction is or may be relevant to the enforcement of the Terrorism Suppression Act 2002; or''.

Section 16: insert after paragraph (a):

> ''(ab) that the transaction or proposed transaction is or may be relevant to the enforcement of the Terrorism Suppression Act 2002; or''.

Section 21(2): insert after paragraph (a):

> ''(ab) the enforcement of the Terrorism Suppression Act 2002:''.

Section 22(1)(b): insert after subparagraph (i):

> ''(ia) that the transaction or proposed transaction is or may be relevant to the enforcement of the Terrorism Suppression Act 2002; or''.

Section 24(1)(a): insert after subparagraph (i):

> ''(ia) that the transaction or proposed transaction is or may be relevant to the enforcement of the Terrorism Suppression Act 2002; or''.

Section 28: insert after paragraph (d):

> ''(da) the enforcement of the Terrorism Suppression Act 2002:''.

Section 56(1)(b): omit ''Parts 2 and 5 of this Act'' and substitute ''Part 2''.

Misuse of Drugs Act 1975 (1975 No 116)

Section 12B(6): insert after paragraph (b):

> ''(ba) the enforcement or intended enforcement of the Anti-Money Laundering and Countering Financing of Terrorism Act 2009; or''.

Mutual Assistance in Criminal Matters Act 1992 (1992 No 86)

Definition of **financial institution** in section 2(1): repeal and substitute:

> **financial institution** means either a person within the meaning of financial institution as defined in section 3 of the Financial Transactions Reporting Act 1996 or as defined in section 5 of the Anti-Money Laundering and Countering Financing of Terrorism Act 2009''.

Reserve Bank of New Zealand Act 1989 (1989 No 157)

Section 41(1): add ''and the Anti-Money Laundering and Countering Financing of Terrorism Act 2009''.

Section 41(2): insert '', or the Anti-Money Laundering and Countering Financing of Terrorism Act 2009,'' after ''by this Act''.

Section 51(5): insert ''or under the Anti-Money Laundering and Countering Financing of Terrorism Act 2009,'' after ''by this Act''.

Section 51: add:

> **''(9)** To avoid doubt, the Governor's functions and powers include his or her functions and powers under the Anti-Money Laundering and Countering Financing of Terrorism Act 2009.''

Terrorism Suppression Act 2002 (2002 No 34)

Section 44(1)(b): insert ''or by a reporting entity'' after ''by a financial institution''.

Section 44(1)(b): insert ''or the reporting entity'' after ''the financial institution''.

Section 44(1)(d)(ii): insert ''or reporting entity, as the case may be,'' after ''that Commissioner and the financial institution''.

Section 44(2): insert ''or the reporting entity'' after ''the financial institution''.

Section 44(4): insert ''or reporting entity'' after ''financial institution'' in each place where it appears.

Section 44(5): repeal and substitute:

''(5) In this section, section 47, and Schedule 5,—

''(a) in the case of a financial institution to which the Financial Transactions Reporting Act 1996 applies, **facility, financial institution, suspicious transaction report**, and **transaction** have the meanings given to them in section 2(1) of that Act; and

''(b) in the case of a reporting entity to which the Anti-Money Laundering and Countering Financing of Terrorism Act 2009 applies, **facility, reporting entity, suspicious transaction report**, and **transaction** have the meanings given to them in section 5 of that Act.''

Section 47(1)(b)(i): insert ''or reporting entity'' after ''financial institution''.

Section 47A(1)(a): insert after subparagraph (i):

''(ia) subpart 6 of Part 2 and sections 114 and 115 of the Anti-Money Laundering and Countering Financing of Terrorism Act 2009; or''.

Section 47C(5): insert after paragraph (a):

''(ab) Anti-Money Laundering and Countering Financing of Terrorism Act 2009:''.

Schedule 5: insert ''or reporting entity'' after ''financial institution'' in each place where it appears.

Part 3 — Regulations revoked

Financial Transactions Reporting (Interpretation) Regulations 1997 (SR 1997/48)